LAW IN THEORY AND HISTORY

This collection of original essays brings together leading legal historians and theorists to explore the oft-neglected but important relationship between these two disciplines. Legal historians have often been sceptical of theory. The methodology which informs their own work is often said to be an empirical one, of gathering information from the archives and presenting it in a narrative form. The narrative produced by history is often said to be provisional, insofar as further research in the archives might falsify present understandings and demand revisions. On the other side, legal theorists are often dismissive of historical works. History itself seems to many theorists not to offer any jurisprudential insights of use for their projects: at best, history is a repository of data and examples, which may be drawn on by the theorist for her own purposes. The aim of this collection is to invite participants from both sides to ask what lessons legal history can bring to legal theory, and what legal theory can bring to history. What is the theorist to do with the empirical data generated by archival research? What theories should drive the historical enterprise, and what wider lessons can be learned from it? This collection brings together a number of major theorists and legal historians to debate these ideas.

Law in Theory and History

New Essays on a Neglected Dialogue

Edited by
Maksymilian Del Mar and Michael Lobban

• HART •
OXFORD • LONDON • NEW YORK • NEW DELHI • SYDNEY

HART PUBLISHING
Bloomsbury Publishing Plc
Kemp House, Chawley Park, Cumnor Hill, Oxford, OX2 9PH, UK

HART PUBLISHING, the Hart/Stag logo, BLOOMSBURY and the Diana logo
are trademarks of Bloomsbury Publishing Plc

First published 2016
Paperback edition, 2019

A catalogue record for this book is available from the British Library.

Library of Congress Cataloging-in-Publication Data
Names: Del Mar, Maksymilian, 1979– editor. | Lobban, Michael, editor.
Title: Law in theory and history : new essays on a neglected dialogue / edited by
Maksymilian del Mar and Michael Lobban.
Description: Oxford [UK] ; Portland, Oregon : Hart Publishing, 2016. | Includes bibliographical
references and index.
Identifiers: LCCN 2016034343 (print) | LCCN 2016034951 (ebook) | ISBN 9781849467995
(hardback) | ISBN 9781509903870 (Epub)
Subjects: LCSH: Law—Philosophy. | Law—History.
Classifica tion: LCC K235 .L385 2016 (print) | LCC K235 (ebook) | DDC 340/.1—dc23
LC record available at https://lccn.loc.gov/2016034343

ISBN: HBK: 978-1-84946-799-5
PB: 978-1-50992-797-5
ePDF: 978-1-50990-386-3
ePub: 978-1-50990-387-0

Typeset by Compuscript Ltd, Shannon

PREFACE

MAKS DEL MAR AND MICHAEL LOBBAN

In April 2013, the Department of Law at Queen Mary University of London hosted the annual conference of the UK IVR—the UK Branch of the International Association for Legal and Social Philosophy. The theme was: 'Legal Theory and Legal History: A Neglected Dialogue?'. This collection is, in large part, the result of that conference, although it has been supplemented by a number of specially commissioned contributions.

When we proposed the theme back in 2013, it stood out as a relatively isolated attempt to bring legal theorists and legal historians together—in particular, to talk about potential methodological obstacles to, and prospects for, collaboration between the two disciplines and traditions. Even so, we were surprised at the level of interest shown—we received around 100 abstracts, and had to make painful but necessary decisions to select the numbers we could accommodate. Since then, however, there have been a number of similar events, which have also produced important publications. Two prominent examples are: 1) Charles Barzun and Dan Priel organised a symposium in Virginia on 'Jurisprudence and (Its) History' in September 2014, and this resulted in a special issue of the *Virginia Law Review* (see Volume 101, June 2015);[1] and 2) the *Critical Analysis of Law* open-access online journal based at the University of Toronto published a special issue, edited by Markus Dubber, on 'New Historical Jurisprudence & Historical Analysis of Law' (Volume 2(1) of 2015).[2] Both collections contain a wonderful range of papers by both philosophers and historians, all of whom argue, in various ways, that not only can legal theory and legal history collaborate, but that they ought to, offering many illustrations of the potential fruits of such collaboration.[3]

In terms of the 'neglect' of such dialogue, then, we are in a better position in 2016 than we were in 2013. But both the dialogue between, and the interdisciplinary space of, legal theory and legal history are still very young—at least in terms of contemporary legal scholarship, which is slowly re-discovering (as Brian Tamanaha has articulated in his writings) the third pillar (in addition to positivism

[1] See www.virginialawreview.org/volumes/symposia/content/jurisprudence-and-its-history.

[2] See http://cal.library.utoronto.ca/index.php/cal/issue/view/1420.

[3] In another collaboration, we have sought to identify the most important papers contributing to this dialogue, or offering examples of inter- and cross-disciplinary research in the history and theory of law, in M Del Mar and M Lobban (eds), *Legal Theory and Legal History* (Ashgate, 2014).

and natural law) of theorising about law, namely historical jurisprudence.[4] We hope that the essays in this collection will help to contribute to developing this new-found enthusiasm for this dialogue and collaboration, and that they offer some fresh perspectives on the benefits to be gleaned from it.

The collection is divided into four parts, together with an afterword. The afterword—by ***Brian Tamanaha***—was commissioned after the first drafts of all the chapters (save for those in Part I) had been completed. In it, Tamanaha offers both a commentary on those chapters, and a statement as to whether jurisprudence must be historical (his answer is no) and whether it ought to be (here, his answer is an emphatic yes). This afterword may be profitably read in conjunction with the introductory chapters in Part I, in which we, the editors, set the scene for the entire collection and frame it by reference to its primary question: can, and if so how ought, legal theory and legal history collaborate? In these opening chapters, we seek to push the proposition that legal theory will be all the poorer (and, in some cases, misleading) if it is not historically sensitive, and that legal history can and does generate theoretical insights and can be enhanced by being theoretically sensitive. Our two chapters are responded to with brief comments by ***Fernanda Pirie*** and ***Sionaidh Douglas-Scott***.

The second part of the collection continues the focus of Part I on methodology and historiography. Working within what might be called the new 'material' turn in history, ***Christopher Tomlins*** offers a critique of 'historicism'—which he defines as a method seeking to show legal ideas to be contingent products of particular contexts, which can be reconstructed and understood—and seeks to offer an alternative methodology for legal historians, drawing on the thought of Walter Benjamin. For Tomlins, the claim that one can truly know the past is a false one: rather, one should accept that meaning can only arise from the 'critical interpretive gaze that apprehends the work'. Instead of seeking to put law in context, the legal historian should strive to' determine how the law *emerges* in material practices that construct its categorical differentiation' and 'to enquire critically into the fabricated condition of law's differentiation'. In his chapter, ***Jonathan Gorman*** picks apart and deconstructs the very idea (and possibility) of theory being uninformed by history. In many ways, Gorman also offers a response to Tomlins' critique of context—articulating how one might temporalise the idea of context, and thus study the variation of meaning over time. For Gorman, this means adopting what he calls 'a temporal stance, in that what one is thinking about as a historian is essentially mentally "observable" as enduring, continuing, changing or becoming, perhaps with temporally distinct parts'. This same interest in the descriptive and explanatory potential of temporalising is what interests ***Maksymilian Del Mar*** in his chapter. Del Mar suggests that it is time for legal theory to take a 'diachronic turn', and thus to look at the variety of ways in which we can model law temporally.

[4] See, eg B Tamanaha 'The Third Pillar of Jurisprudence: Social Legal Theory' (2015) 56 *William & Mary Law Review* 2235.

This is best done if we acknowledge, but also play with, the varieties of the temporal, for example identifying the different pace at and duration during which things change, or whether those changes occur progressively / regressively or cyclically. Del Mar also offers some examples of the kinds of insights one might generate on the back of such variability in the diachronic modelling of law, including in theories of legal reasoning. The final chapter in this part—by ***John Bell***—adds an important interlocutor to this dialogue between legal theory and legal history, namely: comparative law. There has been a flowering in the academy in the last decade of comparative legal history—signalled, for instance, by the emergence of a new journal, *Comparative Legal History*.[5] Like legal history, comparative law challenges legal theory, for instance by confronting its general claims with counter-examples in particular contexts of practice. However, as Bell illustrates, and again like legal history, comparative law also offers resources that can improve the practice of legal theory (both descriptively and normatively).

One of the themes of this collection (as also in the special issue of the *Virginia Law Review* mentioned above) are the benefits to historicising the very practice of legal theory. This is the precise focus of the second part of this collection. ***Roger Cotterrell*** argues that although it is in general possible for theorists to glean insights from past theories that travel across historical contexts, we can learn a great deal about which of those ideas might travel better than others by historically contextualising a theory. Further, carefully placing of a theorist's work in context can generate new insights about it—sometimes to the point of rescuing theorists who have been grossly misunderstood and underestimated. Cotterrell offers an incisive illustration of such benefits of historical contextualisation in a re-reading of the work of Vilhelm Lundstedt. Also arguing for the benefits of historicising theory are ***Dan Priel*** and ***Charles Barzun***, who offer creative new interpretations of two American legal realists, Karl Llewellyn and Jerome Frank. In both cases, though in slightly different ways, Llewellyn and Frank can—they argue—be profitably examined under the rubric of the natural law tradition. In performing this re-interpretation, Priel and Barzun offer new resources for understanding not only legal realism but also natural law. Further, their chapter provides compelling arguments for more anti-canonistic and revisionary histories of theorising about law. Also placing theory in historical context—specifically in the early modern common law—is the chapter by ***Ian Williams***. His focus is on the role of legal maxims, comparing the use of these maxims in both theory and practice along a range of issues (ie their identification, their incontrovertibility, and their content and scope, and their relation to equity). As Williams shows, maxims often played a much more prominent role in theory than they did in practice. Williams' chapter, then, offers an example of how history can help illuminate the relationship between

[5] The general editor is Sean Donlan, who has also been an important contributor to this dialogue, both as an author and as an editor—for the latter, see eg S Donlan and L Heckendorn Urscheler (eds), *Concepts of Law: Comparative, Jurisprudence and Social Science Perspectives* (Ashgate, 2014).

theorising law and practising it. A similar theme—as to the relationship between theory and practice of law in history—is the concern of ***Michael Lobban's*** chapter. Part of the point here is that we can understand more about a theory of law when we see how it is used—or not used—in the practice of law. But also important is that this historical contextualisation of theory in its relation to practice reveals the necessary explanatory limits of any one theory. Put another way, the very fact that no one theory has a monopoly of usefulness should give us cause to accept that 'no single theory has the monopoly of truth'. Lobban illustrates this by examining the uses to which theories of positivism, natural law and conjectural history were put in seventeenth- and eighteenth-century English legal thought.

The fourth and final part of the collection continues one of the thematic strands of Part III—namely, the uses, including the limitations, of theory in explaining and describing law (including in the practice of history). ***Pierre Brunet*** and ***Jean-Louis Halpérin***, for instance, consider which theoretical resources may be most useful in a history of the state. Their chapter is a dialogue in very real terms, with Brunet identifying as a philosopher of law, and Halpérin as a legal historian. Their chapter is also significant for how they swim against the tide of the historiography of the state, which tends to adopt Max Weber's definition of law. They argue, instead, that much is to be gained historiographically if one adopts a legal definition of the state (in particular, by drawing on Hans Kelsen). In his chapter, ***Joshua Getzler*** shows how contemporary jurists might profit from revisiting and rethinking past moral and legal debates. Arguing that the voluntarist model which dominates contemporary theoretical accounts of the law of obligations 'departs radically from lived experience', he seeks to show the relevance and coherence of an equitable model based on a notion of conscience, which has strong affinities to the theory of the impartial spectator developed by Adam Smith. At the same time, Getzler explores the possible genealogy of an emerging eighteenth-century notion of conscience as a presumption of honesty, in tracing how English lawyers may have developed Smith's ideas in a way Smith himself did not. Stephen Waddams and Steve Hedley, by contrast, show the importance of history and context in calling in question theoretical constructs which fail to take into account the contexts in which law develops. ***Steve Hedley*** questions the claims of corrective justice theorists to have uncovered a timeless theory, which is uniquely capable of coherently explaining private law. In his view, while the theory may usefully explain an aspect of tort law, there are large swathes of the law—the intrusion of public law, the evolution of new collective mechanisms (such as corporations and insurance)—which it cannot account for. For Hedley, the theoretical categories used by jurists exist primarily to make pedagogic sense of a vastly complicated legal universe; but it cannot theorise the complexities away. ***Stephen Waddams's*** chapter also points out that law 'is not only a set of conceptual constructs; it also constitutes a practice, and has been strongly influenced by its anticipated practical effects'. Legal doctrine, Waddams shows, is often fluid, developing as judges speculate about the possible impact of their decisions, and make decisions based on their own presumptions about past and future conduct.

Finally, we would like to thank the Law Department at Queen Mary, University of London, which hosted the 2013 conference, and has subsequently provided all manner of administrative and logistical support. We also thank the *Modern Law Review* for their sponsorship of the event. Many kind thanks are also due to Judith Skillen for her assistance with copy-editing.

CONTENTS

BIOGRAPHIES

Charles Barzun is Professor of Law at the University of Virginia School of Law.

John Bell is Professor of Law and Director of the Centre for Public Law at the University of Cambridge.

Pierre Brunet is Professor of Public Law at the Ecole de droit de la Sorbonne (Sorbonne Law School) of Université Paris 1 (Panthéon-Sorbonne) and a member of the UMR 8103, Institut des Sciences Juridiques et Philosophiques de la Sorbonne.

Roger Cotterrell is Anniversary Professor of Legal Theory at the Department of Law, Queen Mary University of London.

Maksymilian Del Mar is Reader in Legal Theory and Co-Director of the Centre for Law and Society in a Global Context at the Department of Law, Queen Mary University of London.

Sionaidh Douglas-Scott is Anniversary Professor of Law and Co-Director of the Centre for Law and Society in a Global Context at the Department of Law, Queen Mary University of London, and Honorary Fellow at Lady Margaret Hall, University of Oxford.

Joshua Getzler is Professor of Law and Legal History, University of Oxford; Fellow and Tutor in Law, St Hugh's College, Oxford; and Conjoint Professor of Law, University of New South Wales.

Jonathan Gorman is Emeritus Professor of Moral Philosophy at Queen's University Belfast.

Jean-Louis Halpérin is Professor of Legal History at the Ecole Normale Supérieure and now the Director of the UMR 7074 CNRS, Centre de Théorie et d'Analyse du Droit.

Steve Hedley is Professor of Law at the Faculty of Law, University College Cork.

Michael Lobban is Professor of Legal History at the London School of Economics.

Fernanda Pirie is Associate Professor in Socio-Legal Studies at the University of Oxford.

Dan Priel is Associate Professor of Law at Osgoode Hall Law School, York University.

Brian Z Tamanaha is William Gardiner Hammond Professor of Law at Washington University Law School.

Christopher Tomlins is Professor of Law at the University of California, Berkeley.

Stephen Waddams is University Professor and the holder of the Goodman/Schipper chair at the Faculty of Law, University of Toronto.

Ian Williams is a Lecturer at the Faculty of Laws, University College London.

Part I

Introducing the Dialogue Between Legal Theory and Legal History

1

Legal Theory and Legal History: Prospects for Dialogue

MICHAEL LOBBAN*

There are very many theoretical questions which may be asked of law. Law can be studied as an instrument of power, as a vehicle of economic opportunity, or as a tool of oppression. It can be studied as a means of setting rules to guide conduct, or as a method of resolving disputes. It can be studied as a structure of empowerment, or as a coercive mechanism of social discipline. Given these multiple ways in which we may think of law, it seems odd at first glance to suggest that one might study law theoretically without drawing on history, or to hold that theory and history have been ships passing each other in the night, with barely a light to signal each other's presence. Is it not self-evident that anyone interested in sociological questions about law, or economic questions, or questions about the interaction of law and society in general, cannot do it in ignorance of history, even if their main concerns are with the present? Is it not obvious that the theorist who wishes to understand how any particular law or legal system came about, how it operates, what effect it has, will need to look empirically, and so will need to engage with history? At the same time, is it not clear that what distinguishes historians from antiquarians is that they seek explanations, and patterns of change, which requires them to think theoretically? The very discipline of legal history has been shaped by much theoretical reflection on the methodology of the subject, and by theoretical influences from other disciplines.[1] Does this not prove that history and theory are in a constant dialogue?

If one focuses on theorists who are interested in what law *does*, then it does seem evident that history and theory have long been bedfellows. By contrast, if one turns to theorists interested in what law *is*, there has been rather less dialogue. The attitude which prevails among many legal philosophers is that perhaps most

* I have benefited enormously from many conversations with Maks Del Mar on the interactions of history and theory, and am grateful for his many insights.

[1] See, for instance, the essays in A Lewis and M Lobban (eds), *Law and History* (Oxford University Press, 2004); A Musson and C Stebbings (eds), *Making Legal History: Approaches and Methodologies* (Cambridge University Press, 2012); M Lobban, 'The Varieties of Legal History' *clio@themis* 5 (www.cliothemis.com/The–Varieties–of–Legal–History).

clearly expressed by Hans Kelsen. In his view, the 'jurist, as the theoretical exponent of the law' and the sociologist or historian (who consider 'the causes of the coming into existence of the law in general or of a particular legal order') deal with 'completely different problems'. For such thinkers, the juristic enterprise is also an essential preliminary: as Kelsen put it, '[t]he sociology of law cannot draw a line between its subject—law—and the other social phenomena; it cannot define its special object as distinct from the object of general sociology—society—without in so doing presupposing the concept of law as defined by normative jurisprudence.'[2] According to this view, the jurist is engaged in the philosophical task of clarifying concepts abstracted from all context which the sociologist, comparatist, anthropologist or historian can then use in their distinct work.

If we focus on jurisprudence as the theoretical study of the nature of law—what law *is*—then this view of the subject does pose a major challenge for those interested in a dialogue. Insofar as much of jurisprudence, as taught in university law schools, omits historical perspectives, it is a challenge worth taking up, and it is one taken up by the chapters collected in this volume. In what follows in this introduction, we will therefore concentrate on those theories that discuss what law is, rather than what law does, and ask how far there can be a fruitful dialogue between this arena of legal theory and legal history.

I

Legal philosophers who confine themselves to the analytical discussion of legal concepts are sometimes criticised for defining the 'province of jurisprudence' too narrowly, making it entirely analytical by excluding questions of moral, political and social theory, as if they had nothing to do with the object in hand. Furthermore, it is sometimes argued that this very move is a modern turn, taken by jurists like John Austin, who departed from the more holistic philosophies of Thomas Hobbes and Jeremy Bentham.[3] By narrowing the province of jurisprudence—and by implication suggesting that it is only formal, analytical questions about the nature of law, rights, duties and so on, which should be of interest to the lawyer—they have been accused of confining the field much too narrowly.[4] In answering this criticism, analytical jurists can say perfectly convincingly that they are not seeking to say everything that can theoretically be said about law: they are simply trying to clear the ground for further study by helping us understand what we mean by certain key concepts, whose meaning we need to be clear on before we

[2] H Kelsen, 'The Pure Theory of Law and Analytical Jurisprudence' (1941) 55 *Harvard Law Review* 44, 52–53. For Kelsen 'a normative theory of the law', which analyses law as a system of norms, is a 'specifically "juristic" view of the law'.

[3] See MJ Horwitz, 'Why is Anglo-American Jurisprudence Unhistorical?' (1997) 17 *OJLS* 551; GJ Postema, 'Jurisprudence, the Sociable Science' (2015) 101 *Virginia Law Review* 869.

[4] See in general R Cotterrell, 'Why Jurisprudence is not Legal Philosophy' (2014) 5 *Jurisprudence* 41.

can go on to ask other kinds of theoretical questions. Thus, one cannot properly understand the question of the impact of law on society unless we first have an idea of what we mean by 'law';[5] we cannot understand the relationship between law and morality unless we have some kind of idea of what distinguishes them as concepts. Analytical jurists can therefore finesse the criticism that they are jurisprudential imperialists by the modest retort that they have no gripe about others asking their own theoretical questions. As Kelsen put it, '[l]ike any science, the science of law must first of all define its object by differentiating it from other similar objects, in answering the question: what is the law as object of a particular science'.[6]

Analytical jurisprudence therefore seeks (in Kelsen's words) 'to discover the nature of law itself, to determine its structure and its typical forms, independent of the changing content which it exhibits at different times and among different peoples'.[7] By elucidating the meaning of 'law' and other legal concepts, analytical jurisprudence aims to provide the conceptual tools for making sense of the data of experience. According to its defenders, one needs to have categories and classifications into which to place data in order to make sense of it. What makes this a *philosophical* question is that it is not dependent on empirical observation or context. One cannot simply use the categories and classifications made by the people under study. To begin with, the people who are being studied may not articulate concepts which explain their behaviour: they may be speaking 'law' (as we understand it) without knowing it. Furthermore, even if they do articulate concepts in their own language, these will need to be translated into a conceptual language which the observer can understand. All this suggests that without a clear toolbox of concepts to begin with, the scholar cannot know what she is looking for, and cannot understand what she finds. To make sense of experience, it is argued, we need concepts or categories which are not dependent on experience.

Philosophical reflection has certainly generated useful insights, as one philosopher engaging with the ideas of another has refined definitions. Bentham and Austin's insistence against the natural lawyers that the positive law enforced by a sovereign ruler (law 'as it is') is a distinct system from the rules of morality (law as it 'ought to be'), and that the province of the expositor is not the same as that of the censor helped clarify the thinking of nineteenth century jurists. Equally, the criticisms made by Kelsen and Hart of Austin's notion of law as the command of a sovereign habitually obeyed by the bulk of the people were seen to reveal flaws in the theory, by showing that a conception of law as command explained neither the (continuing) normativity of a law nor the existence of power-conferring rules: the theory needed to be modified to account for factors unexplained by its

[5] As John Gardner has put it, 'one must already know what counts as law before one can make either empirical or evaluative observations about it *qua* law': *Law as a Leap of Faith, and other essays on Law in General* (Oxford University Press, 2012) 273–74.

[6] H Kelsen, 'Law, State and Justice in the Pure Theory of Law' (1947–48) 57 *Yale Law Journal* 377.

[7] Kelsen (n 2) 55.

original formulation. As philosophers reflect on the flaws in preceding definitions of law, they elaborate a more nuanced view, which is intended better to capture what is understood by the concept of 'law'. Nor can it be denied that the theories elaborated by modern analytical jurists—Kelsen's and Hart's views of law as a system of norms or rules, united in a hierarchy validated by a *Grundnorm* or a rule of recognition—are conceptually useful in helping us to identify what law is. As Jean–Louis Halpérin and Pierre Brunet argue in their contribution to this volume, a theory such as Kelsen's can usefully provide 'neutral (or formal) criteria for identifying legal systems and for distinguishing these systems from other forms of normativity'. They find particular utility in Kelsen's definition of the state as a legal order, as a tool to help the historian track the evolution of the modern state.

At the same time, there are limits to the analytical empire. As Halpérin and Brunet observe, Kelsen's legal definition is not (as he thought) 'a pre–condition of all research about the state, but is one of the possible tools for studying and understanding the state, a tool that legal historians and legal theorists can use with profit'.[8] We might add that analytical philosophy itself has not given a definitive answer to the core question of what is law: there is a multiplicity of positions. For Kelsen, the notion of coercion is central to the existence of law. For Hart, it is the presence of a set of officials: in his view, 'law' is always to be associated with the pronouncements of a special cadre, which has authority in any given society to pronounce it. Where such a cadre exists, one has 'law'; if there is no such cadre, there is no 'law', though there might be other forms of normative conduct. Analytical jurisprudence therefore offers not one but a number of different conceptual tools for the historian to choose from. If she is looking for the history of 'law', should she search for Hartian institutions or Kelsenian norms?

Questions may also be asked about the 'purity' of these philosophical concepts. Neither Kelsen nor Hart were defining concepts which were entirely abstract, that is, concepts which might have a timeless meaning. Kelsen himself spoke of determining the nature of law itself '[f]rom a comparison of all the phenomena which go under the name of law.'[9] Elsewhere, he explained why coercion was such a central element to his theory:

> If the Pure Theory of Law assumes that coercion is an essential element of law, it does so because a careful examination of the social orders termed 'law' in the history of mankind shows that these social orders in spite of their great differences present one common element, an element of great importance in social life: they all prescribe coercive acts as sanctions.[10]

Thus far, Kelsen was conceding that his theory was not abstract Kantian philosophy, but premised on being an accurate reflection of historical experience. Hart's philosophy was one which even more explicitly aimed to explain human practices

[8] Chapter 13 of this volume, p 238.
[9] Kelsen (n 2) 44.
[10] Kelsen (n 6) 378.

and understandings,[11] which suggested that even the most abstract of legal theory would need some empirical foundation. Hence his notorious remark that his work was not simply one of 'analytical jurisprudence' but also of 'descriptive sociology'. His theory was consequently premised on the existence of a certain structure of society, with certain patterns of behaviour, and certain internal attitudes to law. In his view, law only came into being at a particular stage of development—when the system was institutionalised, with the emergence of secondary rules and a set of officials. A customary system without such a set of secondary rules and institutions was for Hart 'pre-legal': while this may have been a normative order, it was distinct in kind.

Kelsen's and Hart's theories might therefore be regarded as stipulative, rather than descriptive. For Hart, we should only describe as 'legal' those systems in which there is some form of officials, for Kelsen, we need a system of coercion. We should use a different name for normative orders which do not have this form. As stipulative definitions, they may be of great use to the historian, in identifying and classifying what is found, to be able to compare and contrast different examples of the same thing. They allow us to identify a particular class of human activity to study. However, these theories only give the most general and provisional of indications even of that activity, and are therefore only a start. They invite us to look at this object of study, and then reflect further on it, in a way which may test and refine their theories. For instance, Hart did not explain in any detail what 'officials' were, beyond making it clear that the only necessary officials were those who articulated (or 'applied') the rules, rather than those who enforced them.[12] It was clear that he did not think these officials had to be part of a state, for his theory also sought to explain non-state systems of law.[13] Nor did he explain how it came to pass that they had obtained their authority.[14] All one needed for a legal system to exist (in Hart's theory) was for officials to have their own customary system *in foro*. Rather than telling us all we need to know theoretically about law, a theory such as Hart's only invites us to go further; and since the theory was at least in part based on assumptions about empirical behaviour, it invites the theorist to look more at empirical—including historical—evidence.

Furthermore, if we see Hart's definition of law as one stipulated for a particular (institutional) understanding of law, rather than being a universally accurate one, then it can consequently be tested by asking how it explains other ideas or behaviours which would commonly be described as law. As Maksymilian Del Mar

[11] cf Peter Winch, The Idea of a Social Science and its Relation to Philosophy (Routledge and Kegan Paul, 1958).

[12] Gardner (n 5) 286.

[13] Hart noted that not all legal systems have states: *The Concept of Law* 3rd edn (Oxford University Press, 2012) 221–23.

[14] In his view, their authority came from themselves: the rule of recognition which stood at the heart of the system was itself a customary rule, rooted in the practices of the officials themselves. cf Gardner (n 5) 283: 'The relevant officials each follow what they take to be the rule that the others are following. Thereby they contribute to making it the rule, and to making themselves the officials under the rule'.

points out, analytical jurists tend to focus on an unhistoricised single definition (or 'central case') of law or a legal system, and thereby fail to see that there may be a multiplicity of ways to conceptualise law, which may undermine the status of their insights as offering a universal truth. As he puts it, '[t]o think diachronically is … to increase (if not maximise) the amount of variables one indexes to what one claims we can know about law in general'. Many past (and present) societies think of law in customary terms, where the 'law' in question is identified not by its source, or its articulation by particular officials, but from the fact that communities act in accordance with the customary norms, and feel that they are obligatory (rather than being merely habitual). Equally, a system of law may be intellectual, being neither coercively enforced or authoritatively articulated by particular individuals, nor observed by communities: one example would be Roman law, as rediscovered and reformulated in the Middle Ages.

This raises the question of how definitive the 'central case' is. Are these various other kinds of 'law' only to be described (as John Austin put it) as law 'improperly so called', or so called by analogy—that is, as something superficially similar but conceptually distinct? Or are they all species of a single *genus* which we need to redefine? In fact, we have a choice. The historian seeking to identify and explain custom as a form of law may find the Kelsenian model better than Hart's, which might lead her to seek an underlying customary *Grundnorm*.[15] On the other hand, the historian following Hart's distinction between primary and secondary rules might agree that a purely customary system only becomes a system of *law* once there are *jurisperiti* in place to indicate what the custom requires. Custom, it may be argued, only becomes problematic once there are disagreements over what it means, and once you establish officials to determine what should be done, you are moving from custom to law.[16] Turning to the intellectual system, if we regard medieval Roman law as a system of law properly so called, we might need to rethink our theory of law, to stress the notion of law as an identifiable set of norms within a system based on a set of original texts viewed as authoritative—whose *Grundnorm* might be that the *Digest* of Justinian contains all legal truth—rather than as the rules produced by authoritative officials. If it is true that a wholly intellectual system of law is not quite the same as a working, effective, enforced system—and so may not contain *everything* we know of law—it is also true that it does contain *something* of it. Looking at it this way, we may see that there is no definitive answer, but there is plenty of room for dialogue.

[15] Kelsen spoke of the constitution as a 'complex of norms which … includes also the norm by which custom is recognised as a creator of law. To be included within this complex, a norm need not be found in a written constitution—it may be a part of the unwritten constitution created by custom'. Kelsen (n 2) 62.

[16] If this seems a neat resolution of the problem—and a useful guide for historians—it does not wholly resolve the problem of whether pure custom can be law. After all, Hart's very rule of recognition is a customary rule: and if a conventional rule can be made by the officials through their conduct, why can not other such rules exist in society?

History can test how well the theory explains the subject under study. For instance, while Hart's theory may usefully guide us to the persons who have the authority to speak the law—so that we can see a system of law once there is a specialist cadre pronouncing it—he does not tell us much about how they saw the law. One common criticism made of Hart's theory is that it describes law as a system of rules, whereas for much of its history the common law has been a system of reasoning, by 12 judges seeking to resolve problems put to them through forensic discussion, but without articulating real rules. Critics like Brian Simpson have pointed out that the 12 judges of the common law did not see themselves as making rules, but as working out a customary system they assumed was as coherent as the famed Roman law.[17] If we ask not what is the *source* of law, or where we can find the borderline of what is legal and what is not, but ask what jurists thought the law was, we may then find that custom and knowledge plays a significant part: the real locus of law might be the customary and the intellectual, and not the institutional. Penetrating into the world of pre-modern officials might therefore take us into a world of what the positivist might regard as law by analogy or law improperly so called, or—with Jeremy Bentham—as law by a kind of pernicious fiction. Moreover, insofar as contemporary common law practice shares features with contemporary judging, it might raise questions about how well the theory explains present practice.

As many of the chapters in this collection suggest, analytical jurisprudence can give us theoretical tools in understanding the concept of law, but they are only tools for further work, and are only useful insofar as they help us make sense of our data. As Del Mar suggests, one lesson to draw from this is that rather than seeking final answers, one might rather seek the 'middle ground' of the

> modest generalist: someone who realises their theoretical tools are only ever instantiated in particular descriptions, but one who also realises that it is useful (even if ultimately somewhat fictional) to think that theoretical tools can potentially travel from any one description to another (at least until they prove to no longer be useful).[18]

II

If the concept of law itself is sufficiently fluid and contestable to allow for a fruitful dialogue between theory and history, what of other legal concepts and categories? Sociologists and anthropologists have long recognised that legal concepts can have a life of their own: they shape and constrain the language in which claims can be made or power asserted, they can be constitutive of social relations (as through

[17] AWB Simpson, 'The Common Law and Legal Theory', in his *Legal Theory and Legal History: Essays on the Common Law* (Hambledon Press, 1987) 376.
[18] Chapter 7 of this volume, p 113.

property or marriage), and they can even assume powerful symbolic significance. Just as there is something clearly distinctive about 'law', so there is something distinctive about legal ideas and concepts. In what ways can theory, or history, or a dialogue of the two, help reveal what is distinctive about these concepts and their operation?

There is a long analytical tradition which regards legal concepts as 'pure' classifications. For Austin, concepts such as right, duty, contract, tort and intention were 'necessary principles, notions, and distinctions',[19] found in all (advanced) legal systems. Similarly, Hohfeld argued that the jurist needed 'at the very threshold' of his study of any doctrine to analyse and discriminate 'the various fundamental conceptions that are involved in practically every legal problem'.[20] The idea that the structure of legal relations can be correctly identified and mapped has also been defended in recent years by a number of private law scholars, most notably Peter Birks, who felt that the scholar could better understand the legal issues being dealt with by setting out the correct classifications.[21] Implicit in this view is the notion that legal doctrine is developed by jurists, uncovering timeless truths and facilitating their application to modern problems. It is to argue that legal relations can be classified according to observable differences between them, just as animals and plants can be classified according to observable differences. It might suggest that contract law, tort and unjust enrichment began to be coherent only when jurists at different times began to figure out their underlying concepts.[22] If (following Holmes) we define jurisprudence as 'simply law in its most generalized part', which aims at identifying the 'most fundamental conceptions', then it can promise to elucidate the meaning of legal concepts, by categorising and classifying legal relations at the most general level. This can in turn be serviceable to the jurist when faced with complex combinations of facts.[23] A better understanding of the concepts will lead to a better, more logical, and even more *accurate* development of legal doctrine.

[19] J Austin, *Lectures on Jurisprudence, or the Philosophy of Positive Law*, 4th edn (John Murray, 1873) 1108.

[20] WN Hohfeld, 'Some Fundamental Legal Conceptions as applied in Judicial Reasoning' (1913) 23 *Yale Law Journal 19.*

[21] Building on the civilian model of Gaius, Birks argued that legal rights (which can be vindicated in court) always arise from manifestations of consent (such as contracts or wills) or events which operate independently of consent (such as wrongs or unjust enrichments): Peter Birks, *Unjust Enrichment* (Oxford University Press, 2005) 21.

[22] David Ibbetson has written, 'The Natural lawyers of the seventeenth century played a crucial part in the history of the tort of negligence by articulating a framework within which it could develop in the eighteenth and nineteenth centuries; by providing a skeletal structure that appeared to be both rational and self-consistent, Pothier's version of the Will Theory, itself with roots in the Natural lawyers' writings, played a crucial part in the emergent contract law of the nineteenth century; so too the writings of Birks and others will prove to have been crucial in moulding the law of unjust enrichment in the twentieth and twenty-first centuries': *Historical Introduction to the Law of Obligations* (Oxford University Press, 1999) 291–92.

[23] OW Holmes, 'The Path of the Law' (1897)10 *Harvard Law Review* 474–75.

Such a view has many attractions for those seeking to make sense of a mass of legal materials, for it helps to assume that there is an underlying order into which different material can be sorted. However, we must be cautious of a view which implies that pure analysis can tease out timeless legal categories. For while it may be true that there are some core ideas, generalised and abstracted from actual systems, which can provide a theoretical guide to scholars seeking to make sense of experience, these ideas—like Hart's more general concept of law—are only generalisations, whose specific working out may be contingent and variable over time. As Sir Henry Maine taught us a century and a half ago, concepts do not exist in a social or chronological vacuum, but are developed at particular times and places for particular purposes.[24]

This is true even of the area of doctrine which has perhaps attracted more theoretical attention than any other: the law of contract. At first glance, the same questions seem to have occupied the minds of Ulpian, Accursius, Lessius, Pufendorf and Savigny. A philosophically-minded contract jurist might therefore assume that she can engage in debate with Ulpian, and agree with him that a contract is 'the agreement and consent of two or more persons about the same thing'.[25] She may assume that it is a timeless truth that contractual obligations proceed from consent, determined by the mutual exercise of two (or more) free wills imposing obligations on themselves, unvitiated by mistake or fraud. She may point out that jurists who have articulated such a theory have done so by abstract reflection on the nature of contractual relations, rather than by looking at social practice. However, a little historical investigation soon reveals that past thinkers did not necessarily share the same concept of contract that she is using.

It is well known, for instance, that Roman jurists did not have this general conception of contract, which only emerged in the later middle ages as scholars reformulated the material rediscovered in Justinian's *Digest*.[26] Nor was the later elaboration of contract doctrine merely the discovery of underlying principles which had somehow escaped the notice of medieval jurists. Those who sought in later ages to contribute to the elaboration of contract were not simply engaged in an abstract philosophical exercise: they were also seeking to contribute to particular theological and political debates, and shaped their concepts in particular ways to serve those often polemical purposes. Thus, the sixteenth-century Catholic jurists who developed the theory of freedom of contract were interested

[24] Maine however hedged his bets by acknowledging the importance of Austinian analysis for developed systems, and by hinting that the 'progress of Roman ideas from a gross to a refined conception' may have exemplified 'the necessary progress of human thought'. H Maine, *Ancient Law* 17th edn (John Murray, 1901) 339. He also observed 'how it is that the human mind has never grappled with any subject of thought, unless it has been provided beforehand with a proper store of language and with an apparatus of appropriate logical methods'.

[25] D. 2.14.1.

[26] See R Zimmermann, The Law of Obligations: Roman Foundations of the Civilian Tradition (Oxford University Press, 1990) ch 18; J Gordley, The Philosophical Origins of Modern Contract Doctrine (Oxford University Press, 1993) ch 3.

in developing their theories as part of a dialogue with a hostile, anti-legalistic Protestant theology.[27] The seventeenth century Protestant jurists who developed their natural law theories also had an eye outside the classroom: Grotius and Hobbes were not interested simply in elaborating contract doctrine, but to establish a juristic basis in the one case for an international order and in the other for domestic harmony. The theories of contracting which these writers developed were not necessary ones, the simple working out of scientific truths. The nature of the theories they developed was shaped by the purposes they had in mind, which purposes can only be fully understood by bearing in mind the wider intellectual contexts in which they wrote.[28] Theories are never self-defining: as I suggest in my chapter, there are various ways in which theorists can look at the world, and their different presuppositions of the problem to be solved may impact significantly on the way they order their conceptual views.

A diachronic approach can also show the rise and fall of different concepts. New legal conceptions may emerge at particular times and in particular contexts. One example might be the concept of 'genocide', articulated by Raphael Lemkin in 1944 to mean 'the destruction of a nation or of an ethnic group'.[29] Although Lemkin used the concept to identify historical examples of genocide, the idea itself was the product of the attempted extermination of the Jews in the Holocaust. The second half of the twentieth century has also seen the development of a new legal notion of discrimination, which has not only developed a large body of case law but also theoretical discussions.[30] Such concepts are not timeless abstractions but arise in particular historical contexts, in which new ideas emerge to deal with newly perceived problems. Furthermore, as John Bell shows in his contribution, concepts may change their meaning not only over time, but in different places. Comparative studies can reveal that what may look like superficially similar conceptual apparatuses may be used in entirely different ways by jurists working in different contexts. Different societies expect law to do different things, and have different institutional structures in which the concepts are deployed. Contextual understandings may complicate our understanding of what might otherwise appear as

[27] See W Decock, *Theologians and Contract Law: The Moral Transformation of the Ius Commune, (ca 1500–1650)* (Martinus Nijhoff, 2013).

[28] For the context of Pufendorf's natural law theory, see I Hunter, *Rival Enlightenments: Civil and Metaphysical Philosophy in Early Modern Germany* (Cambridge University Press, 2001).

[29] R Lemkin, *Axis Rule in Occupied Europe: Laws of Occupation—Analysis of Government—Proposals for Redress* (Carnegie Endowment for International Peace, 1944) 79.

[30] See D Hellman and S Moreau (eds) *Philosophical Foundations of Discrimination Law* (Oxford University Press, 2013). Reviewing this work, Andrew Alman notes the importance of examining this concept in its historical context: 'The concept of discrimination does not refer to a natural kind and has no ahistorical essence. It is a construction addressing certain social, political and ethical problems that, though rooted in forms of group disadvantage characterising most of human history, became especially salient with the advent of modern ideas of citizenship and popular sovereignty. Even if not every philosophical discussion of discrimination must explicitly adopt a socio–historical orientation, it seems to me that the power of theorising to illuminate the concept is substantially weakened if the relevant history is set aside': 'Discrimination Debated' (2015) 6 *Jurisprudence* 157.

timeless; but at the same time, it might enrich our understanding of the uses of the concept. Equally, as Joshua Getzler's chapter shows, we can enrich our own conceptual vocabulary by re-examining the use of conceptual formulations made in earlier times.

Concepts can be used, moulded and combined in a variety of ways and for a variety of purposes. As Ian Williams's contribution shows, not all legal concepts are developed by lawyers to be used for the practical purpose of solving legal problems. He argues that early modern lawyers who set out maxims sought to demonstrate that the common law was a science, and aimed to provide a method for learning and understanding the law. They also sought thereby to bolster the status of the common law.

History can also test the accuracy of theoretical formulations, exposing flaws in the theory. For instance, a number of theorists have in recent years sought to explain the concept of tort by explaining tort law as a system of corrective justice. They have done this in particular by analysing the structure of litigation—in which a plaintiff who has been harmed seeks redress from the defendant whose actions have harmed her[31]—and by seeking to construct the best moral theory to justify why redress is due. These theories are both analytical—seeking to explain the underlying logical structure of the system—and normative, for they see tort law as 'a repository of moral reasoning about responsibility for harm.'[32] A historian might not be in a position to dispute that the best way to conceive of a correlative system of tort law would be through a theory of responsibility, and might not be able to challenge the notion that a certain normative practice was 'immanent' in the system. But—as the contributions of Steve Hedley and Stephen Waddams show in this volume—she could question whether the description of the practice of tort law ever was what corrective justice theorists claim, for instance by showing that the structure and practice of tort law in the past (or present) operated in ways not considered by corrective justice theorists, or was undergirded by different—and consciously articulated—presumptions. Insofar as the normative theory of corrective justice seeking 'oughts' which are 'internal to the law'[33] rests on a factual understanding of that law and its past, it might be open to historical challenge, which might call for a reformulation of the theory. Secondly, an historical critique might challenge not only the theorists' interpretation of the doctrine, but their wider claims that this doctrine represents the proper understanding of tort law in general. Thus, a historical critic might argue that the corrective justice theory might claim better to describe the early nineteenth century system of tort law (before the age of regulation, insurance and public law accountability) than

[31] Corrective justice theorists have long criticised their rival Law & Economics theorists by pointing out that the latter theory is unable to account for the particular structure of tort law.

[32] EJ Weinrib, 'Correlativity, Personality and the Emerging Consensus on Corrective Justice' (2001) 2 *Theoretical Inquiries in Law* 3.

[33] A Beever and C Rickett, 'Interpretive Legal Theory and the Academic Lawyer' (2005) 68 *MLR* 322n.

the contemporary one. It might therefore be anachronistic for the present to seek to use this theory as exclusively able to account for tort law, since it cannot explain the current world. As Hedley argues, corrective justice theories cannot provide 'an "explanation" of the whole' of tort law, though they can offer useful insights if 'seen as a significant strand within modern thinking about obligations'.[34] This is to suggest that we need to have multiple theoretical perspectives to make full sense of the law: one needs not only to explain the correlativity of tort litigation, but also how tort law relates to public law and to modern collectivism.

A historical sensitivity to how legal concepts have evolved can therefore be of considerable use to the theorist. The theorist may learn from listening to the historian. But the dialogue is not just one–way. Just as the history of the uses of legal concepts can help the jurist better to understand the contingency of the concepts she is using, so the abstractions made by the theorist may help the historian to find things she might otherwise miss. Past conduct may be explained in terms of concepts which were not articulated by the actors whose conduct is the object of study. For instance, corrective justice theory might be very useful in explaining what an early nineteenth century jurist thought he was doing in an era when jurists and judges were seeking to create a clear unified notion of tort law. Equally, we may find past societies expressing similar ideas to those articulated by modern theory, but in distinct ways or in different contexts. This point may be illustrated (for instance) by considering the history of the notion of criminal responsibility. It is often said that English criminal law knew little of such concepts until the nineteenth century, when jurists began to develop the 'general part' of criminal law.[35] In the middle ages, determining guilt or innocence was simply a matter for the jury; and there was little room for modern ideas of criminal responsibility to evolve until the legal mechanisms for identifying them had emerged[36]—such as lawyer participation in criminal trials, rules of evidence, and means with which to challenge erroneous decisions. This (it is argued) did not occur in England until the dismantling of the blunt but discretionary system of the Bloody Code, when jurists began to elaborate concepts of criminal responsibility for a particular purpose—to allow for the transformation of penal policy. An examination of criminal doctrine alone would suggest that the medieval mind knew nothing of the concept of intent and the guilty mind. However, if we use our models of responsibility and intention and look for parallels elsewhere, we may find insights to help us rethink out presuppositions. Thus, if we look at the writings of medieval philosophers and theologians—Peter Abelard is a notable example—we will find extensive discussion of conscience and intention. Question of intention also loomed large in the penitential literature, which expanded significantly in the

[34] Chapter 16 of this volume, p 318.

[35] See N Lacey, 'Jurisprudence, History and the Institutional Quality of Law' (2015) 101 *Virginia Law Review* 919.

[36] SFC Milsom, *Historical Foundations of the Common Law* 2nd edn (Butterworths 1981) 8.

twelfth century Gregorian reforms.[37] Although such works had a very wide range of concerns, there was much material of relevance to crime. Thus, Raymond of Peñafort, who wrote both a confessor's manual and a collection of canon laws, spent much time in his *Summa de casibus poenitentiae* discussing such questions as what excused homicide: those who killed from necessity, or in self–defence or by accident did not share the same degree of guilt as those who killed intentionally. If not elaborated in doctrine, such ideas were not unknown to the participants in the English legal system. Raymond's work was drawn on by the author of *Bracton*, who distinguished (for instance) between homicides done 'out of malice or from pleasure', and killing by unavoidable necessity where it was done 'without premeditated hatred'.[38] These distinctions may not have entered the criminal law directly, but they were used to determine whether a pardon should be given for homicide,[39] and such distinctions may have been in the minds of jurors who acquitted felons, in an apparent nullification of the rules of law.[40] The fact that concepts of criminal responsibility were only articulated in legal rules at a later period—and for particular purposes—is significant for our understanding of the contingency of these concepts as tools of formal *law*; but at the same time, the model provided by these concepts may help us make sense of past practices, including the practices of juries.

While much valuable work has been done in recent years in theorising many areas of law, there is much still to be done. Legal theorists have yet to decode an immanent set of structures and principles, whether in tort law, public law, criminal law or even contract law. Concepts remain contested, and contingent. The theorist can therefore benefit from a dialogue with history, both in exploring how past thinkers have developed their concepts, and in testing their theory against past experience. At the same time, it is clear that legal ideas and constructs do shape behaviour and help constitute social relations. There is something distinct about legal concepts, just as there is something distinct about law. Legal concepts also develop and become sharper and more sophisticated as they are elaborated over time. They provide useful tools for the historian visiting the past. The historian will find past concepts and conduct to be different; but he will get a sharper understanding of the past by adapting the concepts developed by theorists. Historians who are engaged in the task of attempting to reconstruct the world view of past lawyers—who may not themselves have overtly articulated that world view—may

[37] Penitential manuals provided a guide to what penance was suitable: and the nature of the penance was linked to the degree of moral guilt. JF Benton. 'Consciousness of self and perceptions of individuality' in RL Benson and G Constable (eds) *Renaissance and Renewal in the Twelfth Century* (University of Toronto Press 1991) 272–3.

[38] SE Thorne and G Woodbine (eds), *Bracton On the Laws and Customs of England* (Harvard University Press, 1968–77) 2: 340.

[39] Those who killed by accident, out of necessity or in self-defence were pardoned, with judges by the early thirteenth century questioning the jury closely on matters of intent. ND Hurnard, *The King's Pardon for Homicide before AD 1307* (Oxford University Press, 1969) ch 3.

[40] TA Green, *Verdict According to Conscience: Perspectives on the English Criminal Trial Jury, 1200–1800* (University of Chicago Press, 1985) 62–63.

usefully draw on the interpretations and explanations made by current theorists to see if they—or variants of them—help make sense of the practices of past lawyers. We need to bear in mind that the language used by past lawyers was not always the same as that used in later times, but that their actions might be more comprehensible if we examine them through modern conceptual models. For instance, by asking questions of past practices generated by modern theories of unjust enrichment, we might find patterns of thought and behaviour we had not previously found, even if they are different from the modern ones.

III

If theory can provide tools for historians to use, what positive things can history offer to theory? As has been seen, history can provide a repository of examples against which to test current theory: insofar as a theory aims to offer a timeless, universal explanation of legal phenomena, history poses a challenge, to see whether the data it provides can be explained by the model. History may also offer the theorist examples of how other philosophers have treated similar questions in the past. As Jonathan Gorman notes in his contribution, the theories of contemporary jurists and philosophers are generally informed by the history of political thought, insofar as they seek to engage with the articulation of philosophical positions made by past thinkers. Legal and moral philosophy does not exist in a timeless vacuum: thinkers are part of a tradition, contributing to and seeking to advance debates which have a history and a genealogy.[41] Intellectual historians have long stressed the point that there are no essential, timeless ideas—such as liberty, democracy or the state—but that the meaning of these notions must be explored in context.[42] They have shown that in seeking fully to understand the thought of any historical philosopher, one cannot assume that he has understood the concepts under investigation in exactly the same way as the contemporary investigator. Moreover, as Roger Cotterrell's contribution to this collection shows, by re-examining a past thinker in light of the historical context in which he worked, one can obtain new insights about that thinker's work, by revealing features which have been overlooked by scholars looking only for contributions to a timeless debate. In revisiting the contexts in which Karl Llewellyn and Jerome Frank wrote their works, Dan Priel and Charles Barzun also rethink their legacy. Insofar as contemporary philosophy engages with a 'canon', it is useful to revisit and rethink the canon. As these essays show, such reconstructions can be fertile

[41] A number of modern legal philosophers, including HLA Hart and John Finnis, have indeed written books about thinkers in the history of philosophy. HLA Hart, *Essays on Bentham: Jurisprudence and Political Philosophy* (Oxford University Press, 1982); J Finnis *Aquinas: Moral, Political and Legal Theory* (Oxford University Press, 1998).

[42] The classic exposition of this view is Quentin Skinner, 'Meaning and Understanding in the History of Ideas' in his *Visions of Politics I: Regarding Method* (Cambridge University Press, 2002) 57–89.

for the contemporary theorist, in revealing lost insights and ideas which may have contemporary relevance.

At the same time, as Gorman also points out, philosophers do not have to be historians: in developing a theory for the present, they may find it more profitable to generate ideal versions of the thoughts of past thinkers, sketching out a tenable philosophical position with which to engage through their best interpretation of those ideas, rather than seeking to reconstruct the ideas of past thinkers (which when interpreted in a historical way may prove less useful). Nevertheless, even here historical explanations of past thinkers may be of assistance. For instance, they may show that a past thinker could not have held the views attributable to him in this ideal type (perhaps because it would be inconsistent with that thinker's wider thought), or that his views were richer than has been realised. Such a challenge might at the same time open up new theoretical possibilities by revealing hitherto unnoticed theoretical nuances which contemporary theory might wish to take into account. Thus, the work done in recent years by the Bentham Project in editing the unpublished manuscripts of Jeremy Bentham has led some scholars to call into question HLA Hart's interpretation of Bentham's ideas, an interpretation which served as a springboard for much of his own jurisprudential thought. The historiographical task of reconstructing Bentham's ideas may therefore contribute to generating fresh perspectives on modern debates on legal positivism.[43]

Just as history can offer new interpretations of past thinkers' ideas, which may be serviceable to contemporary jurists, so history can provide data on which theorists can draw, insofar as their theory is premised on factual bases. In this way, history can be of use to normative theorists, as well as analytical ones. A theorist seeking to explain why a current state of affairs is unjust, and to construct an alternative, may commence with her own intuitions or personal experience. However, a fuller understanding of the problem to be solved may entail looking historically and comparatively at other experiences in other times. For instance, much recent Feminist and Critical Race theory has been premised on the notion that women and minority groups have suffered disadvantage as a result of discrimination against them on the basis of their gender and race. It is not because the theorist alone has felt and experienced discrimination, but because she perceives a generalised experience of oppression among all women or minority groups in her society, that she seeks to develop a theory, both to explain the oppression, and to describe an alternative. An historical and comparative study can enrich her understanding of the nature of this experience, and its generality, and so inform her as to the problem to be addressed. Indeed, for theorists of gender and race discrimination, history is an essential part of the story: insofar as Feminist theorists and Critical Race theorists explain discrimination as structural, and embedded in society, it must be explained in historical terms. However, if history can help

[43] See P Schofield, 'Jeremy Bentham, the Principle of Utility and Legal Positivism' (2004) 56 *Current Legal Problems* 1; P Schofield, 'Jeremy Bentham and HLA Hart's Utilitarian Tradition in Jurisprudence' (2010) 1 *Jurisprudence* 147.

explain the problem, it cannot provide a solution: the historian cannot determine whether a Liberal Feminist vision is better than a Radical Feminist or a Cultural Feminist vision. History cannot guide the Feminist in deliberating over whether women and men should be treated exactly the same, since they are equal humans, or whether treating them equally requires the law to take into account differences between men and women; though as John Bell points out, a comparative study (and a fortiori a historical one) may provide examples of where particular social arrangements have operated well or badly.

The above mentioned uses of history are all examples of history as the servant of theory, offering information and insights when required, but taking a backseat when it comes to constructing a positive theory. But can history offer more? In answering this question, it is worth bearing in mind the ways in which history differs from philosophy. Whereas (some) philosophers begin with the assumption that people have the same core ideas, thoughts and motivations, historians (as well as comparatists and anthropologists) look at the environments in which people find themselves. They assume that different environments generate different behaviours, as the impulses to which humans respond will vary. Peoples with different cultures in distinct environments will not see things in the same way. Instead of seeking a universal view, the historian tries to rediscover how past people saw the world, and how they acted on that understanding. At the same time, history also seeks to explain change over time: how one mode of thought influenced or gave way to another. It seeks not only to describe change, but to explain it. These two features are linked: for history does not only show that past societies were in certain respects different from ours, but shows also how they moved from one state of affairs to another.

While much legal philosophy deals with law in a static state, we need to remember that law exists in time, and that time is not static. This insight is useful in helping explain both short term and longer term developments in ways which may generate larger insights about the nature of law. Analytical jurists are often uninterested in explaining how the content of law is developed: the law simply consists of the rules or norms made by those with power in the system to make them. Insofar as analytical jurisprudence seeks to set out a structure of accurate concepts, the presumption may be (as it may have been for John Austin) that judges simply figure out the best logical answer to any problem. However, a number of contributors to this volume argue that we need to pay more attention to how law is made. As Stephen Waddams argues, if one looks at empirical practice, one finds that legal development is not shaped by conceptual reasoning, but by practical considerations, including the judges' own predictions of the impact of their decisions on social behaviour. Judges seek to resolve problems which come before them in the best way for society, in a way often driven by policy considerations. As Waddams explains, law is in a constant state of flux, which is to be better understood if we look at judges' pragmatic reasoning. Priel and Barzun's examination of the work of Llewellyn and Frank shows that these jurists also argued that the judges should develop the law in the way best suited to the community: Karl Llewellyn, they point out, sought in this process to connect 'three ideas—historical jurisprudence, the common law, and democracy—to the people.'[44] Such visions link law in some sense to the community, and may remind us that the common law, as a system of reasoning, is premised on the notion that judges interpret a body of norms developed over time, resolving disputes generated within the community: to that degree, at least, there is a communitarian basis of law, suggesting that we can never fully understand law floating free of its community. However, as Llewellyn himself noted—in distinguishing the different 'period-styles' in judging, and as Del Mar points out in speaking of the different speed of change—the nature and pace of change is contingent.

Just as history may offer us useful insights into how the content of a legal system changes, and changes in response to the perceived needs of a community, so it can help show that the very way in which law is perceived and acts changes over time, and is in constant motion. A study of medieval Europe, for example, can show us that a number of different conceptions of law—as customary, as 'learned', or as a set of 'rules'—may coexist at the same time, and may interact with each other, with the dialectic between them influencing and motoring change. Thus, in England before the Angevin reforms, a multiplicity of courts existed in which judgment was pronounced by 'suitors' who settled disputes on the basis of customary norms. When Henry II created a new set of remedies, which gave royal justices the role of pronouncing judgment, the new courts enforced existing customary norms (notably of inheritance to land) rather than creating new ones: for his intention was not to create a new system of law, but to ensure that existing custom was properly observed. In fact, the courts continued to apply the 'custom of the realm' in cases where there was 'no firm evidence of any contrary custom'.[45] Northern France also had a multiplicity of customary systems, which were redacted in the twelfth and thirteenth centuries into written custumals which sought to formalise them. On an international level, there was a customary *ius maritimum*, which was also set down in a number of written texts in the later middle ages, including the *Llibre del Consolat de mar*. In each of these areas, we can conclude that there were customary usages which were regarded as being normatively binding and which shaped behaviour. The rules of conduct in question were not created by lawyers or by legislation, but by customary practices which were regarded as binding by those communities as any form of law. At the same time, a new breed of professional jurists was emerging, in response to the recovery of the *Digest* of Justinian by Irnerius and his followers in Bologna. Though Roman law was nowhere in force, the most sophisticated legal learning developed in medieval universities, as generations of jurists sought to tease general principles and clear rules from the fragmentary material of Roman law. If Roman civil law had no courts, and no 'officials' to apply it, it was clearly regarded as a system of law—whose borders

[44] Chapter 10 of this volume, p 175.
[45] P Brand (ed), *The Earliest English Law Reports* vol ii (Selden Society, 1996) 216.

were determined by the original primary source being glossed and interpreted—which was interpreted with some degree of authority by the university doctors of the civil law. Moreover, their intellectual apparatuses influenced the shape of the redactions of customs which followed.

A historical study can show how medieval law was transformed, as customary norms came to be enforced in 'official' courts by a cadre of lawyers, whose professionalism derived from their specialised technical knowledge. That is, historical study can show how one form of law can be transformed by interaction with another. Thus, the customary systems of England and northern France were transformed by being 'officialised'. If Henry II's aim in creating the returnable writ of right and the possessory assizes was simply to offer new remedies for failure of local justice, the remedies he created soon generated their own complex learning and specialised forms. The rise of the common law writs was soon followed by the rise of professional lawyers, and the custom of the community—the general custom of the common law—became the custom of the courts, where rules of inheritance or property ownership depended not on simple custom but on increasingly complex rules. The rise of these technical forms allowed for the emergence of abstract legal categories, which might be seen as transforming a 'customary' system into a 'legal' one, in which the relevant discourse was no longer that of the community but of lawyers. Similarly, the redaction of French custumals into written texts may be seen as a way of both deracinating and judicialising them.

At the same time, medieval law was also transformed by being rethought. In medieval Italy, the local law—the *ius proprium*—which was applied by local officials, was transformed as jurists in Bologna and elsewhere began to reconstruct and rethink the newly rediscovered *Digest* of Justinian, developing new ways of thinking previously unimagined. New juristic techniques generated new distinctions and new questions, which served to complicate the issues before the court. As in England, law became much more complex; but it was not the result of custom entering the judicial forum for the first time; but the result of sophisticated jurisprudential concepts invading. Unless you had your Azo, the saying went, you should keep clear of the *palazzo*, the courtroom.[46] The new legal learning coming out of Bologna also had an impact on the writers of the treatise known as *Bracton* and the redactors of the French custumals.

However, we need to be wary of being too quick to assume a move from 'pre-legal' to a 'legal' world, as custom was judicialised and rethought. For there remained areas where custom continued to be vibrant: where the 'legal' and the 'customary' continued to interact, without the customary basis of the norms being suppressed. This can be seen, for instance, with the evolving custom of merchants of the later middle ages, which was enforced in legal tribunals—and often using procedures modelled on the *ius commune*—but where the substantive rules enforced were distinctly mercantile ones, produced by the custom of the community. If in one sphere we can see a gradual transmutation of 'customary' to 'official'

[46] M Bellomo, *The Common Legal Past of Europe* (The Catholic University of America Press, 1995) 168.

law, in another we can see the two as acting in a complementary way, complicating our idea of what counts as law.

By looking at the three different conceptions of law—as custom, as idea and as institution—and how they interacted at particular moments in history, we may get a richer understanding not only of the nature of law, but also of how it develops, changes and mutates. It suggests that ideas of law are not static: they can both change, and be the agents of change. The kind of study suggested here shows that the very concept of law is not static, but dynamic, and needs to be studied in the context of its change. Moreover, the kind of study outlined here—an 'internal' or hermeneutic study of the concept of law—is only one aspect of the theoretical possibilities offered by history. It needs to be reiterated that legal theory and legal history are more than the internal study of legal concepts and their ideas—legal change needs to be understood in a much wider social, political and economic set of contexts. To theorise is to simplify, to generalise, to pick out particular aspects to focus on. But the empirical shows that life is always more complex, and that factors omitted from the theory might be more important than one first thought.

2

Beyond Universality and Particularity, Necessity and Contingency: On Collaboration Between Legal Theory and Legal History

MAKS DEL MAR*

I. Introduction

If looked at frankly, it would be hard to disagree with the proposition that a good deal of scholarship is about fighting for, but also expressing anxiety about, the status of one's discipline. How else, after all, to read the claims of (some) philosophers to have discovered universal truths, or the claims of (some) historians to have captured the particularity of a time and place? The alternative certainly sounds less impressive: to build models of modest and revisable generality, with inevitably limited utility, and shot through with the accidents that influence its construction. Less impressive though it sounds, it is the methodological stance I will advocate for here—all in the name of enabling dialogue and facilitating collaboration between legal theory and legal history. Venturing beyond, or finding a middle path between, universality and particularity—and, as we shall see, also necessity and contingency—could prepare the ground for a cross-disciplinary project that models the variability of law across time and space.

I proceed in three steps (corresponding to three sections): I turn first to canvassing the various ways in which one might go about enabling dialogue between legal theory and legal history, thereby also locating the strategy I take here. Second, I take on the task of de-universalising the claims of legal theory (by having history look critically at theory), before doing the same in the other direction (in section three), namely de-particularising the claims of legal history (by having theory look critically at history).

* The ideas expressed here could not have been formulated without the many discussions I have had on this theme with Michael Lobban. I owe him more than I can say.

II. Strategies for Enabling Dialogue

One of the aims for this collection—and the conference from which it originated[1]—was to challenge what is an all too common attitude amongst legal theorists to legal history (or history more generally): that it is, at best, an optional extra—a charming source of illustrations, perhaps—but nothing more than a gloss, the froth; useful potentially (though only in the drawing room of legal theory, after all the 'real' conceptual work has been done), but not vital. We wanted, by contrast, to explore the intuition we had that there was something awry, misleading, about a theory of law that was uninformed by history.

There are, however, at least three ways one could unpack this basic intuition. The first strategy would be to say that legal theory is always, necessarily, informed by history, just that it is so unconsciously and un-rigorously (and vice-versa, but let us stick with this direction for now). For example, one could say that even those theories that firmly focus on the municipal legal system must have some sense of how municipal law is different from non-municipal law—that they must draw at least implicitly on certain contrasts and comparisons. And, in fact, one could go on, theories of municipal legal systems have done so, much more often than their authors realise, for example Herbert Hart's (in)famous use of 'primitive communities', and the defects they allegedly suffer from without secondary rules, is used as a device to describe the nature of municipal legal systems.[2] To be fair, Hart was in fact careful about this, and hedged his claims with various qualifications (which appear more in his footnotes; I return to this later)—just as he hedged them with respect to his contrast between municipal law and international law.[3] But it remains the case that he used a comparison with distant times and places, which drew on a very limited range of historical and anthropological studies. He might have been more systematic and rigorous about his sources; instead, his attitude to those studies was to use them as snapshots to help illuminate the system with which he was most familiar, the municipal legal system of England.

The second possible strategy for enabling dialogue between legal theory and legal history is to say: no, theory is not inevitably historical, but when it is uninformed by history, its insights about law are much weaker—much less insightful—than they might be if it was informed by history. One can make this criticism more or less strongly: a strong version would be to say that one will simply miss so much (too much) of what is important to understanding law without being informed historically, that is say, without examining how it has changed over

[1] UK IVR 2013 Annual Conference: 'Legal Theory and Legal History: a Neglected Dialogue?', which I co-organised with Michael Lobban at the Department of Law, Queen Mary University of London.

[2] See chapter 5 of H Hart, *The Concept of Law* (Clarendon Press, 1961).

[3] See chapter 10 of Hart, ibid. Here, Hart is often misread—he did not say that international law was not law because it was unlike municipal law. He said instead that there were limitations of the analogy between municipal law and international law. In this respect, his treatment of international law was more generous than that of 'primitive communities'.

time in a way that is linked to various variables (eg indexed to changes in economic structures, or gender politics, or the size and make-up of the population, or the level of literacy, etc). Or, less strongly, one can say that one's insights about law—for example, about how it can differ from morality or politics, will—without being informed by history—not pick up on the variety of ways in which law relates with (without collapsing into) morality and politics.

This second strategy shades somewhat into the third, namely: to say that the methodologies of legal theory and legal history are very different, and their respective virtues and vices (benefits and limits) are distinctive—and, then, to argue that much is to be gained by combining their differences. There is great danger in this strategy—in particular, in not recognising the diversity of methods (not to mention styles, temperaments) drawn on in theory and history, and thus in offering but caricatures of each. But, despite this, there may be something to be gained for enabling dialogue by thinking about the (alleged) differences between doing legal theory and doing legal history.

There are various ways in which one can attempt to articulate such differences—and, of course, many different ways in which they have been articulated in the past. For instance, Thomas Kuhn, in *The Essential Tension*,[4] argues that philosophy and history (in his case, in the context of science) have different goals and techniques. Whereas historians aim to produce a narrative, a story, about the particulars of the past, philosophers aim principally at explicit generalisations with a universal scope.[5] Further, the training for becoming a historian and philosopher are very different (their 'learning experiences' are different), and, as a result, historians and philosophers acquire different 'mental sets',[6] or different techniques for asking questions and resolving problems. For Louis O Mink, in turn, history and philosophy are two irreducible ways of knowing—they offer two different 'modes of comprehension'.[7] Modes of comprehension in general are ways of seeing-things-together, and of integrating various elements into a larger whole. History does that via the 'configurational mode', which is essentially narratological, treating objects as elements in a single complex of concrete relationships. Philosophy does it via the 'theoretical mode', which posits universal types and then asks us to understand individual entities as instances of them.

There is a certain sense in which seeing such differences must ring true to some extent—after all, even if there are individuals who cross between disciplines, on the whole there do exist communities of scholars, with their own literatures and training, and it would be a surprise if they did not develop their own ways of asking questions and solving them, or perhaps even their own 'modes of comprehension'.[8]

[4] T Kuhn, The Essential Tension: Selected Studies in Scientific Tradition and Change (University of Chicago Press, 1977).

[5] ibid, 5.

[6] ibid.

[7] L Mink, 'History and Fiction as Modes of Comprehension' (1970) 1(3) *New Literary History* 541.

[8] There is a lot to be gained here, surely, from material histories of disciplines as crafts—and doing so comparatively, mindful of how techniques travel amongst scholarly communities.

One clue to that (but this surely must not be a decisive one) is to see how historians and philosophers talk about their own work, and what they hold up as exemplars within their respective disciplines (and for what reasons). Thus, in history, one will often find historians praising other historians for capturing something of the contingency of some phenomenon, of its peculiarity (its being an anomaly), or of its evanescence or fragility (so much so it escaped the attention of previous historians). One will hear historians saying that what they are interested in is context, discontinuity, unintended consequences, the unpredictable, and the many lost or neglected figures, traditions and discourses. As for philosophers, one will typically hear praise based on clarity, systematicity and universalisability. In terms of their interests, philosophers will often say that they are interested in classifying, distinguishing, analysing, and in revealing the nature of something, its essence, or its underlying structure.

Another way of getting at the differences might be to study the emotions at play in the different disciplines: what do historians / philosophers get excited about, what disappoints them, what frustrates them? Yet another would be to try to map their aesthetics—do historians (more than philosophers) tend to be drawn to concepts that are highly ambiguous and carry many associations, for this helps them point to more relations between various phenomena? By contrast, philosophers might be said to work with lots of little concepts, splitting them (again and again) in their hunt for 'fundamental' distinctions. One could also ask philosophers and historians about what they take to be the ethics of philosophical or historical work: in history, for instance, one might argue a hermeneutic ethic applies, that is a highly developed reflexivity about introducing and imposing one's own views (familiarities, values) onto others (for this would be anachronistic). In history, then, one might say there is an awareness of the ethics of trying to understand others and their distant worlds. In philosophy, the ethics lies (one might say) elsewhere: in clarity, for instance, partly out of respect for communicating one's ideas to others.

Having identified certain general virtues of either history or philosophy, one can then argue as to why one should draw on the insights of the other. For instance, one could say that historians develop and work with a rich imaginary of time—with many different kinds of temporality—and that this allows them to bring certain things into view that would otherwise be occluded. An example of that might be called 'thinking in possibilities', that is going back to a moment in time when what later became a reality was but a possibility. For instance, one could go back to the negotiating table before genocide became an international crime, when it was just one of the possibilities, and ask: how and why did it win over other alternatives? The other advantage of thinking in possibilities might be that it will help disentangle the many associations that may build up with a concept over time—so genocide has come to be used in many different ways since it emerged, and it may be difficult to see those different ways until one strips back to its first uses.[9]

[9] One can imagine this working better with other concepts, eg sovereignty.

In addition to asserting that history can see in ways that theory cannot, one could also argue that history allows theory to avoid certain dogmas that tend to attach to theory (this might be arguable vice versa too). In other words, taking it for granted that to be a theorist is to be schooled into a particular set of techniques and literatures, one might claim that this disposes one to certain kinds of thoughtless assumptions—history then comes in (as presumably other disciplines could) to unearth and de-naturalise these assumptions. For example, one could say that being committed to understanding how law changes over time makes it less likely that one will think that one can 'freeze' a legal system at a certain point time and read off its content. This is because the very changeability of the law implies its non-freezability, eg it needs the resourcefulness of incompleteness, internal tension / contradiction and gaps in order to change. And, one might be able to think of other candidates for 'dogmas of theory', eg the autonomy of law, or law being self-contained in one jurisdiction, or tying law to the practice of officials (explaining law in a top-down way), and so on.

All these various versions of the third strategy to enable dialogue—again, to point to differences between history and theory, and to argue that they can and ought to be informed by each other—can be useful. However, I remain somewhat sceptical about them, in large part because this strategy risks essentialising what it is to theorise or historicise the law. My strategy of preference, then, is largely the first one: to show how inevitably entangled theory is with history, and, equally, history with theory. We are always drawing on history in some way when theorising, and we are always theorising law when doing historical work—but we could be considerably more rigorous about doing so. In order to be more rigorous, however, we need to give up—or so I shall argue now—on claims to universality (on the theory side) and particularity (on the history side). Let me, then, turn to this task in the next two sections.

III. History in Theory

In his last publication before he died, Hart reviewed Raymond Cocks' book on Sir Henry Maine.[10] Expressing admiration not only for the book, but also for Maine's work, Hart said—with apparent approval—that Maine did not have a theory of law. He continued:

> Cocks finds much to admire in Maine's work; he believes, as did another historical jurist, Vinogradoff, that insufficient attention has been paid to his ideas [ie Maine's] by English jurists, and that general theories of law (including this reviewer's) often need qualification and supplementation in light of the variety of legal phenomena disclosed by historical studies of the kind that Maine favoured.[11]

[10] R Cocks, Sir Henry Maine: A Study in Victorian Jurisprudence (Cambridge University Press, 1988).
[11] HLA Hart, 'Review' (1990) 105(416) *The English Historical Review* 700, 701.

Nicola Lacey's biography of Hart[12] revealed many of his anxieties about his own work—but more with other philosophical interlocutors (especially Ronald Dworkin) than with historians. It is, then, interesting to see Hart, in this the very twilight of his career, signalling awareness of the lack of historical sensibility displayed in his own work and that of other general theories of law. It is also interesting to note that he approves of Cocks' assertion that Maine did not have a theory of law—as if having a theory would have got in the way of seeing and describing the variety of legal phenomena. It appears, from Hart's reading, that there are only two options: one, to produce a general theory of law, but then miss much of the diversity and variability of law; or two, produce a history of law, but then without any claim to having delivered a theory of law. Must this be so?

There is an argument to be made that Hart's 'descriptive sociology' was actually an attempt at anthropology[13]—an argument strengthened by the references in the footnotes of *The Concept of Law* to anthropological works of the time,[14] as well as by the very foundation of the entire theory, namely the internal point of view. For instance, there is the same sense of reflexivity about the capacity for intrusion by the theorist (especially at the level of values) into describing faithfully the practices of a community—and here, no doubt, Hart was influenced by Peter Winch's reading of Wittgenstein's critique of Frazer.[15] However, if this were to be thought of as an anthropology, it was most certainly an anthropology of the municipal legal system—the one most familiar to Hart (also as a practitioner). It was so very consciously, for example at various points in *The Concept of Law*, Hart suggests that what illuminates the municipal may not illuminate other kinds of law or legal tradition in the past, for example that for the purposes of understanding Roman Law, one would need to draw distinctions between other kinds of rules, not just primary and secondary ones.[16]

It may be correct, then, to view Hart as someone with a pragmatic attitude to the status of his own theoretical instruments (eg to the distinctions he drew between different kinds of rules). On this reading, Hart defended these instruments insofar as he thought that they illuminated some important feature of the municipal legal system. Outside of that context, those same theoretical instruments might not be so useful—they were, then, of necessarily limited value. In the case of the distinction between primary and secondary rules, this helped solve a problem in making sense of the municipal legal order, in particular marking out the limits of explaining or describing all laws of that system as coercive, backed up by sanctions. In a sense, this is an anthropological insight, that is it displaces a theorist's assumptions (Bentham and Austin's idea that laws were commands backed up by

[12] N Lacey, *HLA Hart: The Nightmare and the Noble Dream* (Oxford University Press, 2004).

[13] I am indebted to a working paper by Coel Kirkby for this observation.

[14] Hart (n 2), and see the footnotes to ch 5, citing Evans-Pritchard, Gluckman, Malinowski, Diamond, and Llewellyn and Hoebel.

[15] P Winch, *The Idea of a Social Science* (Routledge & Kegan Paul, 1958).

[16] In his notes to ch 3 of *The Concept of Law*, Hart cites David Daube's *Forms of Roman Legislation* (Clarendon Press, 1958).

sanctions) by prioritising the way persons in the practice experienced them (as enabling, as power-conferring). However, one would not claim any more for the distinction than that—it was a partially useful illumination of law in a particular context (the municipal).

Put generally, then, the attitude one could ascribe to Hart holds that theoretical instruments are of necessarily limited utility in illuminating features in particular contexts, which help solve certain problems of explanation or description. Theory on this view would be present both in any anthropology of the contemporary (eg of the municipal legal system) as it would be in any historical anthropology—but the theoretical instruments useful in one context would not necessarily be useful in another. This (reconstructed) attitude is attractive, but it still has the drawback that it makes it seem as if one could do without history (ie that one could theorise about law in the form of an anthropology of the contemporary). That is an issue I will come back to in a moment.

Needless to say, Hart's influence on twentieth century legal theory cannot be underestimated. And yet, many of those who see themselves as Hart successors, or as inspired by Hart, appear to adopt very different attitudes to their own theories—to the status of their theoretical instruments. Some of these claims are well-known, and it is always dangerous to quote them out of context. In citing some examples here, then, I am not ascribing them to the views of these theorists—just illustrating what these claims have looked like or may look like. Here is Joseph Raz:

> It is easy to explain in what sense legal philosophy is universal. Its theses, if true, apply universally, that is they speak of all law, of all legal systems; of those that exist, or that will exist, and even of those that can exist though they never will. Moreover, its theses are advanced as necessarily universal.[17]

It is difficult to think of a more ambitious claim for the status of one's theory—and, to boot, one allegedly 'easy to explain'. A little more explanation is offered by Raz here:

> Legal theory contributes … to an improved understanding of society. But it would be wrong to conclude … that one judges the success of an analysis of the concept of law by its theoretical sociological fruitfulness. To do so is to miss the point that, unlike concepts like 'mass' or 'electron', 'the law' is a concept used by people to understand themselves. We are not free to pick on any fruitful concepts. It is a major task of legal theory to advance our understanding of society by helping us understand how people understand themselves.[18]

There is, in this second quote, a qualification that Raz uses to defend the universal claim made in the first quote. The idea is that legal theory can claim universality, but only for 'our' concept of law. This is the concept that people, within 'our' society, use to understand themselves—and what the legal theorist is doing is helping

[17] J Raz, *Between Authority and Interpretation* (Oxford University Press, 2009) 91.
[18] J Raz, *Ethics in the Public Domain* (Clarendon Press, 1995) 237.

us to see how we understand ourselves. On this view, once again, theory need not be historical or even perhaps historically informed: we are back to Hart's stark choice between either theory or history.

I will not dare say it is 'easy' to point out what is wrong with this view—for it is not easy. But it is puzzling. Putting aside issues about 'us' and 'our', and the implication that society has a homogenous rather than heterogeneous and intensively contested understanding of law and its own identity, there is the problem of moving from trying to understand how we understand ourselves to claiming that the features identified 'apply universally'. The two principal problems I see with this are as follows: 1) it suggests that 'our' concept of law does not have its own histories, as if it were unconnected with the past; and 2) it neglects the difficulties and virtues of attempting to understand what law (which may, to someone sensitive historically, not always be the best term)[19] meant for whom and why in different times and places.

To say more about the first point: we ought to recognise, surely, that not only do 'our' concepts have histories, but so do 'our' problems. Thus, the very project of differentiating law from other phenomena (eg morality, politics) is an ambition that makes sense (only, mainly) in a particular society at a particular time (eg arguably, with modernity). But looking at this historically will also help us see the heterogeneity and contestedness of the use of a concept such as law—this being a concept that is not (only) used by 'people to understand themselves', but also one used to advocate for a certain normative change (to legalise, say, or de-legalise) or to justify political violence (eg by classifying who counts as an insider, and who as an outsider). By thinking historically, we come to see more clearly the varying uses of the concept by different individuals and / or groups, especially as those uses conflict and result in tensions that are never quite resolved. Surely, awareness of such multiplicity and contestability of uses helps us understand ourselves better than smoothing out the terrain with the mystical 'we'?

The second point relates back to the hermeneutic ethic of anthropology. There is something odd, and disappointing, about a theorist confining the project of legal theory to how 'we' understand ourselves, and thus a theorist not interested in confronting the difficulties of how others, in distant times and places, understood themselves. A possible rebuke to this is to say that it is the more modest project—that it is sheer chutzpah to think one could even get close to how others—in the distant past—understood themselves. I think this is false modesty, and also misses out (although this is not what counts the most) on the lessons we can glean for ourselves following the struggle of trying to understand distant others. Of course, it would be arrogant beyond belief to think that at any point one has come to understand how distant others understood themselves—but, as long as

[19] In various publications on the methodology of comparative legal history, Sean Donlan suggests we work with normativity rather than law, eg see S Donlan and L Heckendorn Urscheler, 'Concepts of Law: An Introduction', in their edited volume, *Concepts of Law: Comparative, Jurisprudential and Social Science Perspectives* (Ashgate, 2014).

one is armed with the knowledge one cannot succeed, the task of endeavouring to understand those distant others is an important one to undertake, not only for the benefits it might bring to understanding ourselves, but for its own sake. All this suggests that legal theory has been asking the wrong question—the 'what is law' question. The question, instead, could (and I want to say should) be: 'what has law been, for whom, and when, and why?'. Formulated in this way, the task of legal theory would be to offer necessarily incomplete, contingent and partial models of the variability of law across time and place.

There is one very simple and yet robust reply to the above suggestion. It is one that appears in much of the writings of analytical jurisprudence, John Gardner being a good example:

> … one must already know what counts as law before one can make either empirical or evaluative observations about qua law. Naturally one may still make empirical or evaluative observations about a particular example of law under various other headings; eg as an example of a form of social control, or as an example of a structure of governance. But as we noted, this is not making observations about it qua law unless by its nature law is a form of social control or a structure of governance. And whether that is what law is, is neither an empirical nor an evaluative question. It is a question of a third type, a classificatory (sometimes also known as 'conceptual') question.[20]

Gardner combines this with the view that there are 'true and interesting things to be said about law in general and some of these bear on the very nature of law.'[21] That is, for Gardner, there is something we can call the nature of law such that if anything is to qualify as law, then it must count as an instance of it. This is a common way of understanding what philosophy does—recall Mink's idea, mentioned above, that philosophy's mode of comprehension is the 'theoretical mode', which posits universal types and then asks us to understand individual entities as instances of them. But Mink's point also helps make another one: that this is but one *form* of comprehension—one way of presenting, expressing or communicating one's insights. It is a rather tempting one—and also a generative one (a point I will come back to), for, as Gardner points out, there is a sense in which it enables further observation and description (it allows one to go forth and find instances of that 'universal'). However, the question remains: if it is but one form of expression or communication, why would one claim that it has universal status, that it identifies something in the nature of law? Why not just say that it is a potentially useful (but necessarily limited) classificatory scheme? As a scheme, surely, it allows us to see, but it also occludes much from view: we see that which we take to be an instance of the universal, but we do not see that which does not fit the frame (ie that is neither classifiable as an instance or not an instance).

In order to avoid being too abstract, let us take an example from Gardner. According to Gardner, one thing that differentiates law from (almost) anything

[20] J Gardner, 'Law in General', in his *Law as a Leap of Faith: Essays on Law in General* (Oxford University Press, 2012) 275–76.

[21] ibid 270.

else is that it is jurisdiction-specific. He asks: 'How can law be such that something that is true of it at Phuntsholing is not true of it at Jaigaon', and he continues: 'Do "morality, religion, force, [and] terror" cleave to any analogous boundaries?' Gardner also confidently answers the question: 'it seems to me that they do not'.[22] Presumably, then, Gardner thinks that this jurisdiction-specificity is part of law's nature. Armed with this insight, we can venture forth and observe and describe—classify phenomena as either instances or not of jurisdiction-specificity.

If we did that, however, we would soon come up against some rather tough questions. For a start, it is not easy to run an argument that there is a matter of fact about whether a law applies within a certain boundary or not—instead, it is more like a claim that is likely to be contested and uncertain. If one looks, for instance, at the Investiture disputes in the eleventh and twelfth centuries, we can see great and protracted battles over whether and where, and to what extent, the Popes in Rome had the authority to speak the law. Whether we look then, or at Europe in the sixteenth to the nineteenth century,[23] or at the histories of colonial and imperial law,[24] we will come across, again and again, battles about precisely whether, and to what extent, some particular law is jurisdiction-specific. Jurisdictional-specificity is not something that can be taken for granted—it is something claimed and fought over.

One can go further: one could argue that, when looked at over time, the norm has been for communities to be marked by what historians and comparativists have called 'jurisdictional complexity' or 'jurisdictional hybridity'.[25] An attempted riposte by a theorist to that might be that the positing of jurisdictional complexity or hybridity—the very ability to characterise it as such, and observe and describe it—is dependent on the idea of laws being jurisdiction-specific, that is one needs to have that concept before one can posit jurisdictional complexity / hybridity. The reply is not convincing: the problem is that the notion of law as jurisdiction-specific gets in the way of understanding the character of that complexity and hybridity, the sheer scale and speed of mutual borrowing and adaptation, and generally the ease and fluidity with which legal resources travelled across space and time.

It is also worth asking: what sort of a claim exactly is it to say that law's jurisdiction-specificity is part of the nature of law? Gardner presumably would say it is a 'classificatory' claim—something that allows us to classify some things as law and others as non-law. But can such a claim immunise itself entirely from being empirically responsible? Must it not resonate, at least to an extent, with our observations? And if so, what ought to be the standard of empirical responsibility that such a claim ought to meet? It seems disingenuous to say that a classification

[22] ibid 271.

[23] See S Donlan and D Heirbaut (eds), *The Laws' Many Bodies* (Duncker & Humblot, 2015).

[24] For example, L Benton, *Law and Colonial Cultures* (Cambridge University Press, 2002); and L Benton and R Ross (eds), *Legal Pluralism and Empires, 1500–1850* (New York University Press, 2013).

[25] Again, see the chs in Donlan and Heirbaut (n 23).

enables empirical inquiry, but at the same time to insist that it is immune from being embarrassed by empirical investigation. However, if one allows it to be so embarrassed—to be revisable—then what is to be gained by presenting it, at the outset, as revealing (part of) the nature of law? Is this not a form of exaggeration that makes it harder—not easier—to be more careful, more reflexive, more circumspect in our empirical investigations? Why not just say: I am interested in exploring law insofar as we think of it as jurisdiction-specific—let us see where such a way of understanding law gets us, let us explore its hermeneutic/explanatory limits?

I promised to return to the claim that setting things up in this philosophical way—as universals that enable us to count instances—is generative of empirical work, or even the condition of its possibility. Gardner reiterates this point again and again in 'Law in General':

> The first problem of the nature of law is the problem of how law is capable of all this variety. How can law be such that so much variety is nevertheless all of it the variety of law? … That sociologists also need to classify some things as law and others as non-law in order to explore law's variety. Is this classification, for them, wholly arbitrary, without rhyme or reason?[26]

Sociologists, and others who do empirical work, would be—it seems—lost without the prior assistance of philosophers. 'If there is nothing to be said about law in general', asserts Gardner, 'then there is also nothing to be said about particular instances of law qua law'.[27] A world without the classificatory work of legal philosophy 'would put paid to all scholarly work on law.'[28] These are strong claims, to say the least. The imagery also does not help—Gardner refers to empirical researchers as 'clipboard bearers', following the maps drawn for them by philosophers:

> The question of what it takes to qualify [as law], Hart's main question, is a classificatory one. Thus Hart did not go, clipboard in hand, to Nunavut or to Badakshan or to the Ogaden, to see whether there were practices or attitudes or institutions there meeting the specifications set out in his book. He left such work to others with training in fieldwork. He merely advised on the practices and attitudes and institutions that the clipboard-bearers should look for, if perchance they were looking for law. If there were no such practices or attitudes or institutions to be found, that would no skin off Hart's nose. For him it would only go to show that in some places and at sometimes life goes on without law (for better or worse or quite possibly both).[29]

It is difficult to read this in a way that does not trivialise empirical work and its methods. To be sure, the context here is that Gardner is trying to find the distinct virtues of legal theory. He says, for instance, that: 'What we can hope to offer as philosophers is perspicuity (ie elucidation of more complex ideas by their relationship with less complex ones), although, sometimes, inevitably, the puzzles get

[26] Gardner (n 20) 279.
[27] ibid.
[28] ibid.
[29] ibid 277.

worse before they get better'.[30] There is virtue in this exercise, certainly—though clearly it is one that sociologists, anthropologists and historians do engage in, ceaselessly. They too, like philosophers, often juxtapose law 'with nearby things that are not law, and to isolate the various axes or dimensions in which it differs from its many neighbours.'[31] They do this as part of their investigations, in the course of which they consider various possible ways to differentiate, and thus also relate, law to other social phenomena. There is a sense—there has to be—in which Gardner agrees that, no matter what our discipline, we can all be engaged in such inquiries, for example he talks about 'the shared project' of 'sociologists like Weber and philosophers like Hart.'[32] But the way he characterises their aims betrays a philosophical sensibility, namely that that project is one of 'getting the classification right.'[33] Here, we must ask again—why? Why this need to say there is so much at stake in our construction of theoretical instruments?

The idea that classifications can be right or wrong also seems difficult to square with understanding the practice of philosophy—or any form of classification or distinction-making—as necessarily situated, working within the confines of the language one is communicating with (its vocabulary, the forms of its grammar), with a particular inherited tradition of what counts as a problem and as a satisfactory solution. One can be more or less supple, hold more or less variables, in one's classificatory schemes; and one can be better or worse at making distinctions that resonate with what we observe and describe. But this is a matter of skill—which is also always evaluated within the frames of knowledge (and these too, of course, are highly contested). We can, thus, speak of virtues and skills of making classifications and distinctions—but what does it mean to say that the classifications or distinctions themselves are right or wrong?

Put more generally, the point here is that there is space between the alleged universality of the philosopher and the 'arbitrariness' (as Gardner put it) of the non-philosophically-guided sociologist or anthropologist. To try to carve out this space a little more, let me turn now—though also considerably more briefly—to how theory might look at history.

IV. Theory in History

Just as many historians experience exasperation reading theory, so theorists will often report frustration with the work of historians. Why is that so? Theorists often complain that historians are sloppy with their terms, that they are not sharp enough in their distinctions, and that they make unjustified leaps or draw unwarranted

[30] ibid 277, fn 15.
[31] ibid 298.
[32] ibid 279.
[33] ibid.

conclusions from their observations and descriptions. In addition, just like theorists sometimes make exaggerated claims about the status of their work and what their insights reveal, so do historians. Whereas theorists will sometimes claim to have revealed the universal nature of something, historians will sometimes claim to have captured the particularity of some phenomenon (whether it be an intellectual or political movement, or the experience of living in a city at a certain time, or any other historical object). Like theory, then, the practice of history might be said to carry its own disciplinary dangers, its own disciplinary vanities. And, there is good reason to think that in confronting those, history can learn a great deal from theory.

One thing that theorists can make historians much more sensitive to is that every observation and description made by a historian raises 'classificatory' (to use Gardner's term) questions. In his paper arguing against metaphysical quietism, Charles Barzun makes something like that claim.[34] Barzun examines four different historical accounts of the 'origins of the concept of negligence'. The details of these need not detain us. What is of interest is that having set them out, he then suggests that over and above various forms of empirical testing of the claims made, one can also ask 'questions of a different sort'.[35] For example, when a historian uses the term 'social interest' in explaining the use to which the concept of 'negligence' was put in the nineteenth century, we can ask: 'What exactly is a "social interest" anyway?'.[36] He continues:

> This question asks not merely whether that concept is used in a consistent and non-tautological way in the explanation itself, but rather about what, if anything, in the world it purports to describe. Is it merely an expression of an attitude of approval of a certain event or state of affairs, or does it describe a set of real features of the world?[37]

What strikes me as useful about these questions is that, by scrutinising terms used by historians in their explanations (perhaps, sometimes, without much forethought), they generate new possibilities for further observation and description. Thus (and this is now my view rather than Barzun's), we do not have to buy into any correspondence theory of truth, or there being any metaphysical answer to the question of what 'social interest' 'really is', to see the value in introducing critical reflexivity—especially about terms that typically do a lot of the explanatory heavy-lifting. Just as historians have highly developed sensitivities to the multiple uses to which concepts are subjected to in the time and place they are studying, so they could be more attuned to the multiple uses of the concepts they use in their own explanations.

A related role for theory, insofar as it is looking at history, is identified by Gardner. Towards the end of 'Law in General', Gardner suggests that what philosophy

[34] C Barzun, 'Metaphysical Quietism and Functional Explanation in the Law' (2015) 34 *Law and Philosophy* 89.

[35] ibid 101.

[36] ibid.

[37] ibid.

can do is to show us why something that we had been treating as necessary is not necessarily so. Philosophers, then, can scrutinise the leaps that historians (though this applies also to philosophers) tend to make, often unthinkingly, between observations and conclusions—for example assuming or asserting that it follows from the idea that 'one cannot be a rule-user unless one has the concept of a rule' to the idea that 'one cannot be a law-user until one has the concept of law'.[38] That 'doesn't follow', says Gardner, and gives some reasons why.[39] Putting aside the merits of his argument, what is useful here is the critical scrutiny of inferences. This can result in seeing more, and observing and describing more carefully—being sensitive precisely to the contingency (in this case) of the relations between being law-users and possessing concepts of law. Of course, this would not be an exclusive task for philosophers—but it would be a task that those trained in philosophy might find themselves more drawn to, and devote more time to, than those who spend more time in the field. In any event, whoever is exercising it, it would surely help make historical investigations suppler.

The idea that philosophy ought to be as interested, or more interested, or perhaps even only interested, in contingency (in distinction from necessity) has a long history (it is sufficient to mention WVO Quine), but it is one that is gaining some traction at the moment within analytical legal theory. One key voice in this respect is Michael Giudice who, in a recent book,[40] argues 'for the recognition of the importance of contingent features and relations.'[41] Giudice suggests—and this seems persuasive—that focusing on contingent, rather than necessary, features of law can create 'new points of meaningful intersection between analytical jurisprudence and moral, political, and social scientific theories'.[42] An example of such a feature is 'law's relation to practical reason', which has (says Giudice) been traditionally understood as a necessary relation in analytical jurisprudence, eg with Raz claiming that 'where law exists, it necessarily claims to provide reasons for action for its subjects in the form of directives claiming authority'.[43] According to Giudice, law's relation to practical reason is not necessary but contingent, that is, 'it might not always be the case that law operates by making claims of practical reason on subjects'.[44] It may, for instance, impose itself on subjects in a way that does not treat them as reason-responsive agents.[45]

The interest expressed here in contingency is a laudatory one—but it is telling that someone as original and adventurous methodologically and substantively

[38] Gardner (n 20) 300.
[39] ibid.
[40] M Giudice, Understanding the Nature of Law: A Case for Constructive Conceptual Explanation (Edward Elgar, 2015).
[41] ibid 7.
[42] ibid.
[43] ibid 6.
[44] ibid.
[45] ibid. No doubt this claim would, in turn, be contested by other legal theorists—consider Lon Fuller's idea of legality as requiring respect for agency (though for Fuller this may come in degrees—so perhaps there is a half-way house between Fuller and Giudice).

as Giudice, still insists on the importance of necessary features. He qualifies that importance in various ways—downplaying it, and suggesting that such necessary features 'may be relatively few and in any event encourage a kind of single-mindedness and ignorance of complementary investigations.'[46] Giudice also adds that 'a conceptual account of law which identifies contingent features and relations' will be richer (than one focused only on necessary features).[47] And yet, despite the virtues of contingency, and the vices of necessity, Giudice seeks to retain necessary features. A full-scale discussion of Giudice's new book will need to await another occasion, but it is worth mentioning perhaps the most plausible reason he gives for hanging on to the idea of necessary features:

> [T]he kind of necessity I think Hart and others are committed to is a kind of pragmatic necessity, in which theses about law are held to be true if they successfully illuminate some aspect of the social reality of law. The precise reason why we hold onto them (though not, come what may) is to resist the temptation to give them up too quickly in the face of purported counter-examples.[48]

Put another way, the idea here is that there is pragmatic value in 'provisional fixing',[49] or as I see it, the treating of something feature as if it were necessary. For example, recall Hart's idea that all rules have an open texture. What attitude one takes to the status of this feature will have repercussions for how one confronts and responds to what one observes:

> [I]f one really supposed to have found a legal rule which did not have any open texture, it would be important to ask whether the specific really was a legal rule at all, or something else. The very fact of claiming necessity serves, then, to ensure that this issue and possibility will always be considered, whatever the answer or resolution.[50]

Perhaps somewhat paradoxically, treating something as necessary, then, might allow one to be more, rather than less, flexible in how one observes and describes. The proviso, of course, to this—which Giudice does not make enough of—is the need for recognition of provisionality, or the as-if element to this attitude. In order for the pragmatic value of necessity to emerge one has to treat it *as if* it were necessary, not simply as necessary. This might seem like an insignificant change in attitude—but it has enormous effects. For treating something as necessary (rather than as if it were necessary) would mean that one would immediately dismiss a potential rule without open texture as not a rule at all. What one needs, then, is a more complex attitude, with provisional necessity at the forefront, taking the lead, but with contingency always in the background.

At bottom, it seems to me, Giudice is a pragmatist, not a metaphysician—but it is a mark of the social pressure of disciplinary cultures (in this case, within

[46] Giudice (n 40) 8.
[47] ibid.
[48] ibid 108.
[49] ibid.
[50] ibid.

analytical philosophy) that he dresses part of this argument up with talk of necessity. Putting that aside, for the moment, there is perhaps a larger lesson here. And it is this: that we might be better off (certainly for the purposes of enhancing dialogue between history and theory) without the dichotomy of the necessary and the contingent. Let me, in closing this section, elaborate on this briefly.

Giudice's idea that there is some pragmatic value in 'provisional fixing' might suggest we are better off thinking about the status of concepts in terms of attitudes of varying commitment to the relative robustness of variables. We know, for instance, from many observations—in comparative legal history, in legal historical anthropology—that there is often some relation between the emergence of (some degree of) professional personnel ('officials', say) and the emergence of law. One is reminded, for instance, of Aldo Schiavone's *The Invention of Law in the West*,[51] where he traces how a growing body of trained jurists transformed variegated customs into a network of related concepts. One might propose, then, on the back of such and many other studies, that the presence of (more or less) professional personnel is a factor that one can treat as having (take the attitude that it has) a high degree of robustness in understanding law. Notice, though, that the factor remains a variable one: it thinks of professionalisation in terms of degree, and it takes seriously the idea that the character of law may change depending on the scale and extent of professionalisation.

As robust as such a variable factor may be, one may think that there are yet more robust variable factors: for example the presence of writing and literacy (and related practices, such as archiving),[52] or the very idea of rules that are not identical to though still related variably to practice (which forms the core of the wonderful *Legalism* project in Oxford).[53] Other factors one might treat as being considerably less robust, for instance, the idea that law is used to resolve disputes, which can be and has been challenged by examples of codes that were never so applied, but that served instead to symbolise a community's values or a ruler's alleged wisdom (see, in this respect, the important work of Fernanda Pirie).[54] As many have pointed out, virtually any 'function' attributed to law has to be treated with caution, ie in the terms being explored here, with an attitude ascribing relatively low robustness to that factor.

What one is doing here, then, is identifying factors (which themselves come in degrees), and to which one adopts attitudes ascribing to those factors varying

[51] A Schiavone, *The Invention of Law in the West* (Harvard University Press, 2012).

[52] But see R Sacco, 'Mute Law' (1995) 43 *American Journal of Comparative Law* 455. On the importance of archives, suggesting that what theorists tend to think of as such an integral part of common law reasoning (use of precedent) is dependent on the materialities and administration of archives, see P Halliday, 'Authority in the Archives' (2014) 1(1) *Critical Analysis of Law* 110, available here: http://cal.library.utoronto.ca/index.php/cal/article/view/21057.

[53] See the three volumes that have appeared so far: P Dresch and H Skoda (eds), *Legalism: Anthropology and History* (Oxford University Press, 2012); F Pirie and J Scheele (eds), *Legalism: Community and Justice* (Oxford University Press, 2014); and P Dresch and J Scheele (eds), *Legalism: Rules and Categories* (Oxford University Press, 2015).

[54] See F Pirie, 'Law before Government: Ideology and Aspiration' (2010) 30 *Oxford Journal of Legal Studies* 207; and F Pirie, *The Anthropology of Law* (Clarendon Press, 2013).

levels of robustness. This would need, of course, to be responsive to practices of observation, and equally a high level of critical reflexivity about the terms one uses in description and explanation, as well as, more generally, the forms via which one expresses and communicates one's insights. Thus, part of the task would be to identify what forms of expression and communication might be obstacles to thinking in variabilities and degrees. One example of that—already noted above—is the tendency in philosophy to think in terms of objects that have properties, or universals that have instantiations. As I see them, such forms of expression or communication are not conducive to being sensitive to variability and multiplicity. They are more like exaggerations of insights that are better framed more pragmatically than metaphysically. An important aspect, then, of any such collaborative enterprise would be identifying obstacles to what we might call 'ground-level variability'. Such an object of inquiry—namely, the ground-level variability of law across time and space—strikes me as more promising than one still working under the burden of necessary and contingent features.

V. Conclusion

Here, then, is the proposal for dialogue—perhaps more than that, genuine collaboration—between legal theory and legal history. The project is one that avoids the dichotomy of universality and particularity—though also, relatedly, that of necessity and contingency. It aims and claims nothing more than modest, revisable, necessarily limited generality. Its object is the modelling of the variability of law across time and place—in full recognition that any one such model may vary in its utility for different research purposes. As I see it, this is a research agenda that confronts the ethics and aesthetics of attempting to understand how distant others understood themselves (and is thus not focused only on elucidating 'our' concept of law). It is also one that exercises a high degree of reflexivity as to the terms it uses (including 'law' itself) in its descriptions and explanations; adopts a variety of different attitudes as to the factors it puts forward as helping identify law and its relations with other phenomena; and treats those factors as being internally variable—coming in degrees rather than strict thresholds. Such a project seems to me to be a potential meeting place for both legal theory and legal history, which, as I have been suggesting, are already entangled in each other.

3

Legal Theory and Legal History: A View from Anthropology

FERNANDA PIRIE

There is a compelling view among legal theorists that their work is logically prior to that of legal historians. Gardner argues that 'one must already know what counts as law before one can make either empirical or evaluative observations about it *qua* law'.[1] As Lobban comments, in his introduction to this volume, legal theorists generally regard their task as that of clarifying concepts, abstracted from all context. Their theories, he says, are often presented as 'stipulative', implying that only systems that have certain features and meet certain criteria should be described as 'legal'. They present the object of legal theory as making generalisations with universal scope, positing a universal type and identifying its essence or underlying structure, as Del Mar also points out, in this volume. Both editors are cautious about the implications of these views, and both put forward other possibilities for dialogue between legal theorist and historian. Lobban suggests that the historian might take the theorist's stipulative definition and test or refine it on the basis of empirical examples. The theory then becomes a 'tool for further work'. Del Mar is more critical of the claims to universality and necessity made by legal theorists, and suggests that work can be done in the space between the alleged universality of the philosopher and the 'arbitrariness' of the non-philosophically guided sociologist (or historian).

Whilst agreeing with these comments, I would go further, and suggest that it would be a mistake for the historian to take any stipulative theoretical definition as a starting point. This is particularly so when he is considering the legal realms of very different times and places. No theory can be completely abstracted from its social and historical context and those who take an analytic philosophical approach build, test, refine and problematise theories about law on the basis of a historically and culturally specific vision of their subject matter. Even the most abstract philosophy must start somewhere, with words and their meanings. These emerge, and make sense, in social and historical contexts. We use the word 'law' in ordinary language, where it refers to phenomena as they are perceived to exist

[1] J Gardner, *Law as a Leap of Faith* (Oxford University Press, 2012) 273–74.

in the world around us, or which are familiar from historical and other accounts. The legal theorists' ideas are ultimately rooted in the meanings developed in ordinary language use, in this way. Some legal scholars, indeed, acknowledge this: Hart builds a theory of the 'municipal legal system',[2] Raz talks of 'common conceptions of law' and 'intuitively clear instances of municipal legal systems'.[3] It is necessary to start with certain images or ideas about what law is, in order for intuitions to come into play. Our theorists are analysing a concept of law rooted in a time, place and tradition of scholarship.[4] Gardner's 'law in general' is an abstraction from the forms of law familiar to the reflective English-speaker, refined in debate amongst legal scholars educated in the academic traditions of the contemporary world.

There is, of course, nothing wrong with this. Philosophy, like all scholarship, has to start somewhere. But recognising this contextualises the resulting theories. Jurisprudence often seems wholly abstract—particularly when the scholar is subjecting existing debates and theories to further scrutiny—but any theory must ultimately be rooted in a context. Contemporary understandings of law are based, among other things, on what we know of, and refer to as, the laws of different times and places. But this does not mean that all people, at all times, have shared the same concept of law. Lobban is quite right to criticise the philosopher's assumption that people everywhere have the same core ideas, thoughts and motivations. The value of historical examples is that they serve to contextualise and throw into perspective the empirical basis of these theoretical accounts. The many historical examples that Lobban cites, particularly those from the medieval West, illustrate very well the strikingly different forms that law has taken in different contexts, and the different concepts of law that people have held. This last point is crucial. As he shows, in medieval Europe people thought of law as customary, as 'learned', or as sets of rules. There was not a single or unified set of ideas. One might add the sense of law as statute, found in England at least from Magna Carta.[5] To these historical examples one could add a myriad of anthropological case studies, which indicate that ideas about law, or what is close enough to be described as—or by analogy with—law, are nevertheless different in striking and important ways.

What are the consequences of this? The historian cannot accept the theorists' claims that analytic legal theory can and should be used as a starting point for the empirical study of law. Working with a stipulative theory, one that defines what

[2] HLA Hart, *The Concept of Law* (Oxford University Press, 2012) 17, 79.

[3] J Raz, *The Concept of a Legal System* (Clarendon Press, 1970) 3; J Raz, *The Authority of Law: Essays on Law and Morality* (Oxford University Press, 1979) 104, 116.

[4] This is not to repeat Farrell's criticism that analytic legal philosophy is the product of a socially narrow set of Oxford dons: 'HLA Hart and the Methodology of Jurisprudence' (2005) 84 *Texas Law Review* 983–1011, 1009–10. The social background of the scholars is irrelevant, although the scholarly tradition in which they work is not.

[5] Such examples can be multiplied when looking at particular types of law, as Lobban does in the second section of his chapter. It is, however, important to bear in mind that legal doctrines generally emerge from, or are refined in, legalistic contexts, where the goal is specificity and precision. The concept of law, itself, is part of general language, where such precision is not to be expected.

counts as law, or not, risks imposing a set of ideas rooted in a particular time and place on those to which it does not apply.[6] At the very least, it would tend to obscure the insights that can be gained from empirical examples, which might suggest different ways of understanding what law is, and has been, to different people. As Lobban's examples indicate, empirical cases must be understood on their own terms, and the theorist must be open to a sense of surprise about what he finds law to be and to mean. This does not, on the other hand, mean that legal theory, even of the more extreme, 'universalising' character, is not relevant to legal history, or vice versa. But I would suggest that the historian can do more than test or refine abstract theories. In what follows I sketch out some of the ways in which legal theorists can benefit from the work of legal historians, and then what historians can draw from legal theory.

Simply by describing empirical examples, historians can, in many cases, offer philosophical insights into the nature of law. This is because, as scholars, historians need to use a particular language and set of concepts to describe what they observe in other times and places. They must explain the concepts that others use—or formerly used—and which are not quite like those of contemporary scholarship, by reference to, or analogy with, the latter. Anthropological material is replete with examples of phenomena that are like, but not quite the same as, such things as religion, family, money or witchcraft, but which are often explained by analogy, or sometimes direct contrast, with phenomena of the familiar Western world. In legal history, as Lobban shows, we do not have to go too far back in time to find ideas that were conceptualised in different terms: *lex*, *ius*, *ley*, *consuetudines*. Yet, as generations of legal historians have demonstrated, even if ideas and practices were not quite law, they can still be understood and analysed by reference to modern legal concepts and ideas. Difference can be noted and analogy employed.

It may, of course, turn out that what the legal historian is examining in medieval France is not really an example of law. Cheyette's description of the emergence of legalistic practices in the twelfth century is exemplary in this regard.[7] This is a common experience on the part of the anthropologist: what might have seemed like a legal code turns out to contain examples of good behaviour, rather than legalistic rules; and practices of conflict resolution may be found not to involve rules or precedents.[8] But if ideas or practices fall outside the ambit of what we can properly describe as 'law', that may make them all the more interesting for the legal scholar. Juxtaposing them with common examples of law may, in turn, shed light

[6] Colonial history is replete with examples of scholars and lawyers, often well-meaning, who have discovered 'traditional' or 'customary' law among informal and customary practices that are very different in nature. The trend continues today among many who advocate for recognition of 'indigenous law': M Chanock, '"Culture" and Human Rights: Orientalizing, Occidentalizing and Authenticity' in M Mamdani (ed), *Beyond Rights-Talk and Culture-Talk* (David Philip Publishers, 2000).

[7] F Cheyette, 'Suum Cuiuque Tribuere' (1970) 6 *French Historical Studies* 287–99.

[8] F Pirie, Peace and Conflict in Ladakh (Brill, 2007).

on our own concept of law and the phenomena to which it applies. The same goes for other legal concepts—'justice', 'responsibility', 'contract', 'compensation', and so on. Some turn out to be more cross-culturally applicable than others, but most can be used by analogy, if not direct application, in other contexts. In the process the historian (or anthropologist) may illuminate both what is being studied and the concepts used for description and analysis.

In many cases, then, such examples can be used to test the boundaries of our own legal concepts. Even if they show that ideas about 'law' have changed over the centuries; even if the term is used to refer to a multiplicity of phenomena, which do not share necessary or universal features; and even if there are borderline cases; there are still right and wrong ways of using the concept of law. It may be 'vague', as Raz acknowledges, such that 'a correct account of the nature of law will be more or less vague in the same way as the concept of law is vague'.[9] But the native speaker can still make mistakes about concepts. We still need to analyse them.[10] I would, therefore, urge caution with the idea put forward by both editors that the concept of law is 'fluid and contestable'. 'Law' is an ordinary language concept, one that refers to a broad class of phenomena, not all of which share any particular features. In Wittgenstein's terms, it is a 'family resemblance' concept. To ground both empirical and philosophical work we must rely on common linguistic usage, or on the institutions commonly designated as legal.[11] However, conceptual analysis can still unveil common properties and underlying relationships, identifying those phenomena to which the concept properly applies, so that sense can be made of it. This analysis, as Farrell explains, must survive the method of 'possible cases'.[12] What the historian can offer is a multiplicity of possible cases. It may be that in some particular instance the historian will decide that it is more appropriate to use a different term to describe the phenomena at hand, one that is more straightforward or precise, like 'rule', or 'charter', or 'custom'. But in doing so, he may also provide, for the legal theorist, a useful example with which to explore the concept of law, its boundaries and limitations.

For the legal theorist, then, recognising the extensive and varied set of empirical legal phenomena and ideas about law, as they have emerged in different times and places, opens up a world of possibilities. As the work of historically-minded legal theorists, such as Brian Simpson and Gerald Postema, has shown, examination of the history of the common law highlights the importance of law as a system of reasoning, as much as a system of rules. Rather than contradicting or undermining Hart's theory of law as rules, these scholars add nuance and depth to our

[9] J Raz, 'Two Views of the Nature of the Theory of Law: A Partial Comparison' (1998) 4 *Legal Theory* 249–82, 272.

[10] J Raz, *Between Authority and Interpretation* (Oxford University Press, 2009) 24.

[11] F Schauer, 'Necessity, Importance, and the Nature of Law' in J Ferrer Beltrán, J Moreso, and D Papayannis (eds), *Neutrality and Theory of Law* (Springer, 2013) 17–31, 25, 30.

[12] Farrell (n 3) 996–98; and see also Gardner (n 1) 296.

understanding of what law is and may be. Lacey's work on the history of criminal responsibility similarly indicates the institutional and other conditions in which the relevant concepts have emerged.[13] Historians, like other empirical legal scholars, offer a rich source of material for theoretical analysis. At the very least, they put in context the more abstract theories of the legal philosophers.

The importance of legal theory for legal historians and other empirical legal scholars is oddly more difficult to specify. If the theorists' stipulative definitions cannot provide a starting point, then what? I would suggest that their work is important in two ways, methodological and substantive. Methodologically, Del Mar is right to chide those historians (and other empirical scholars) who do not acknowledge the philosophical aspects of their work. Even if they are setting out to understand empirical examples on their own terms, to describe what is contingent and historically or culturally specific, their choice of language has a philosophical element. This is true even when the analysis employs metaphor or analogy; these also need to be used with philosophical sensitivity to language and meaning. As Raz emphasises, we can make mistakes about our own concepts, which are the tools we must use for even the most straightforward description. Del Mar highlights the need to scrutinize the terms we use, to be sensitive to the multiple uses of concepts, and to take particular care with inferences. As he points out, legal theorists offer much important guidance and caution in this regard.

Maybe more contentiously, I would also suggest that legal theories can highlight aspects of the complex set of phenomena commonly referred to by our ordinary language concept of law, and that these can be useful to empirical scholars as models, or even Weberian 'ideal-types'. Referring to the theorists' stipulative definitions, Lobban talks of the 'conceptual tools' they offer. I would suggest that the theories of Hart, Kelsen and others are most useful if they are regarded as analyses of modern law, or as ideal types, built from examples familiar from the contemporary world.[14] As such, they may be referred to in other contexts. Hart's account of municipal law, for example, and his distinction between primary and secondary rules, can be used by the historian or anthropologist to make sense of phenomena observed in very different settings. Dresch, analysing the historic laws of Yemeni tribes, for example, finds it illuminating to refer to Hart's distinction between primary and secondary rules.[15] It does not matter that other aspects of Hart's account, such as the role of officials, are not applicable here. Raz's insight that law 'claims to provide reasons for action for its subjects' (mentioned by Del Mar), has

[13] N Lacey, 'Institutionalizing Responsibility: Implications for Jurisprudence' (2013) 4 *Jurisprudence* 1–19.

[14] D Galligan takes this approach to Hart's *The Concept of Law*, in 'Concepts: The Currency of Social Understanding of Law' (2015) 35 *Oxford Journal of Legal Studies* 373–401.

[15] P Dresch, 'Written Law as Words to Live By' in P Dresch and J Scheele (eds), *Legalism: Rules and Categories* (Oxford University Press, 2015) 63–64.

been inspirational in the analysis of legalism in anthropology and history.[16] Del Mar goes so far as to suggest that Hart's *The Concept of Law* might be regarded as an anthropology of a municipal legal system. I would agree. Recognising that the theories of academic lawyers are rooted in a time and place, opens up the possibility that they might be drawn upon as philosophically sophisticated accounts of a modern concept of law, one that has developed in a particular social, political and intellectual tradition. Theories about law as a system of rules (Hart), as a style of reasoning (Postema), a system of reasons (Raz), or a modal type (Gardner), can all be drawn upon by the historian or anthropologist concerned with very different eras or parts of the world. They deserve to be taken seriously far beyond the circles of jurisprudential debate.

[16] See, for example, F Pirie and J Scheele (eds), *Legalism: Community and Justice* (Oxford University Press, 2014).

4

Legal Theory and Legal History: *Which* Legal Theory?

SIONAIDH DOUGLAS-SCOTT

I agree with Michael Lobban's first sentence: 'There are very many theoretical questions which may be asked of law.' I also agree with his subsequent comment that 'it seems odd at first glance to suggest that one might study law theoretically without drawing on history, or to hold that theory and history have been ships passing each other in the night.' In fact, neither Del Mar nor Lobban believe that legal theory or legal history (should) operate independently of each other. But both writers do identify an approach in legal theory that is problematic for the formation of constructive dialogue.

This approach is, as Lobban expresses it, the view that 'the jurist is engaged in the philosophical task of clarifying concepts abstracted from all context which the sociologist, comparatist, anthropologist or historian can then use in their distinct work.' Similarly, in the words of John Gardner (with whom Del Mar engages): 'one must already know what counts as law before one can make either empirical or evaluative observations about it qua law.'[1] So, according to this approach, one should first know what one's target is, before one takes aim.

It is this view—that the task of the legal theorist is to clarify, classify and to abstract from context various legal concepts—which Del Mar and Lobban identify as often inimical to the work of other disciplines, such as that of the historian, for whom the particular, the contextual, the exact nuance or subtlety or distinction, is everything. If we take this view of legal theory—as grounded in an abstract universalising philosophical methodology—then a constructive dialogue with legal history is indeed problematic.

With so much I agree. I am also generally sympathetic to Del Mar's suggestion that, 'venturing beyond and finding a middle path between, universality and particularity—and, as we shall see, also necessity and contingency—could prepare the ground for a cross-disciplinary project that models the variability of law across time and space.'

[1] J Gardner, 'Law in General', in his *Law as a Leap of Faith: Essays on Law in General* (Oxford University Press, 2012) 275–76.

However, I am interested in the fact that much of these introductory chapters is given over to a discussion of this particular type of legal theory, so typical of analytical jurisprudence. For much of Lobban's chapter, Kelsen and Hart are his main interlocutors, as far as legal theory is concerned. Del Mar spends much time engaging with Raz and Gardner. Of course, to an extent this is understandable. Analytical jurisprudence is a dominant school of legal philosophy in the Anglo-American academy. For some it may be the only game in town. But only for some. And we miss much about the contribution legal theory can make to legal history, and vice versa, if we over focus on analytical jurisprudence, and ignore other varieties of jurisprudence. I shall try to take this point further in the rest of this response. However, first, I wish to take issue with a preliminary, classificatory point that Lobban makes at the outset of his introductory chapter.

I. 'What Law Is' and 'What Law Does': A Meaningful Distinction?

To start with, Lobban draws a distinction between those jurists who are interested in 'what law is' and those who focus on 'what law does'. It is, in particular, those theorists who are concerned with 'what law is' whom he sees as problematic for an engagement with legal history. Lobban seems to suggest that this distinction is salient to the nature of jurisprudence: 'jurisprudence as the theoretical study of the nature of law—what law *is*.' But I am not sure I really understand this distinction. For some jurists, *law is what it does*. For Karl Llewellyn, what law was, was inevitably connected with what it does, as law performed various 'law-jobs',[2] even if Llewellyn was not strictly committed to the view that 'What officials do about disputes is, to my mind, the law itself.'[3] Karl Marx, (to whom I will return shortly) undoubtedly a theorist, if not strictly speaking a legal theorist, provides an account of law that is also deeply interwoven with what law does, namely, in Marx's interpretation, the imposition of an ideology—the mechanics, tools and mind-set of capitalism. Indeed, even with Dworkin, a central figure for much Anglo-American jurisprudence, it is difficult to separate what law is from what law does. Dworkin's theory of law as integrity presents a vision for judges which states that, as far as possible, judges should identify legal rights and duties on the assumption that they were all created by the community as a holistic body, and express the community's conception of justice and fairness. This is as much about what law does as what

[2] K Llewellyn, 'The Normative, the Legal and the Law-Jobs: The Job of Juristic Method' (1940) 40 *Yale Law Journal* 1355.

[3] K Llewellyn, *The Bramble Bush* (Oceana, 1951) 12. See, for a commentary on whether this could ever be described as Llewellyn's 'philosophy of law', W Twining, 'Two Works of Karl Llewellyn-II' (1968) 31 *Modern Law Review* 165, 176.

it is. We might also add that a distinction between what law is and what it does leaves out the whole natural law school of legal theory, for which the very nature of law cannot be determined independently of its capacity to function morally. So I find this distinction between what law is and what law does problematic—indeed, accepting this distinction seems to allow too much to the legal positivist's vision of legal theory—that the is and the ought must be kept separate.

My point, therefore, is that we concede too much to the terrain of analytical jurisprudence if we accept the distinction. Indeed, in thus addressing Lobban's distinction, I am also embarking on the main work of my response. For there are other theoretical approaches to be had. And if we exclude these, we miss out on the opportunity for a more fruitful dialogue between legal theory and legal history. Legal theory can be richer than a narrow focus on analytical jurisprudence allows.

II. Rejecting the Notion of 'The Central Case'

Both Del Mar and Lobban rightly insist that legal concepts do not exist in a social vacuum. Lobban considers just how definitive may be the notion of 'the central case', a device beloved of analytical jurists to highlight what they undoubtedly take to be law. Are custom, or intellectual systems of law (such as Roman law in the Middle Ages) 'only to be described (as John Austin might) as law "improperly so called"?' Lobban suggests that in fact we have a choice, that there may in fact be 'no definitive answer, but there is plenty of room for dialogue.' Yet Lobban still applies Kelsen and Hart as the standards against which to assess other types of 'law' and to refine our categories where history tells us that the central case of twentieth century jurisprudence may be too crude. But why stifle legal theory in this way? Why accept the category of 'central case' or 'law properly so called' at all? Or why not look at other points of view outside of those taken within a certain canon of analytical jurisprudence?

Theorising about any subject requires some value judgements that are selective, along with a focus on those aspects of a practice considered by theorists to be the most important. Given that all types of theorising appear to involve evaluation to some extent, in this way all legal philosophy is at the very least what Julie Dickson describes as 'indirectly evaluative'.[4]

However, given that some sort of evaluation is inevitably involved in legal theory, why do we focus on some theories rather than others? Why do we see those theories as somehow objective and authoritative? For example, John Finnis acknowledges the evaluative element involved in theorising about law but claims his own evaluation is objective because it is based on 'sound judgement' and 'authentic practical

[4] J Dickson, *Evaluation and Legal Theory* (Hart Publishing, 2001) chs 2 and 3.

reason'.[5] Yet Finnis' evaluation still reflects his world view. Why should we accept his view over another? In modern times, there has been a focus on what lawyers and policy-makers designate as law, to see a practical point of view, that is one with a view to decision and action, as important, and this results in a concomitant overemphasis on disputes and adjudication—on what is in fact the pathology of social life. However, why should we acknowledge Hart's 'internal point of view', or Kelsen's viewpoint of the 'man of legal science', as the key to understanding the mystery of law and legal systems? In contrast, over 100 years ago, Oliver Wendell Homes focused on the point of view of the 'Bad Man', who only cares about the material consequences of the law on him personally.[6] If the 'Bad Man' viewpoint is considered relevant, why not also that of a feminist or anarchist or legal 'primitive' for that matter? I would make a plea for acknowledging that *legal theory itself* is capable of offering many different viewpoints for historians to work with, and the more viewpoints we consider, the more profound the dialogue with legal history may become.

Indeed, Roger Cotterrell seems to recognise as much when in *The Politics of Jurisprudence*, he urges:

> Rather than close off law analytically, legal theory should interpret it in ever widening perspectives. As the attempt to understand law as a social phenomenon, legal theory *should* require that the limited views of law held by different kinds of participants in legal processes … be confronted with wider theoretical perspectives that can incorporate and transcend these partial views and thereby broaden understanding of the nature of law.[7]

The conclusion is surely not to limit the scope of legal theory to the one 'correct' point of view, always inevitably a singular, limited perspective, nor to seek a universal jurisprudence, inevitably so general as to be commonplace, but to recognise the existence and significance of broader theoretical perspectives within legal theory. In this respect, it is not then a matter of history enlarging on the perspective of theory by revealing the contingency and accident of what theory had taken to be a central case. Theory can do some of that work all by itself, enabling a different starting point for its dialogue with history.

III. The Entanglement of Legal Theory and History

At this point it is useful to engage with Marx. Why do I do so here, when Marx was neither a (conventional) legal theorist nor a legal historian? Marx's work is salient in this context because he undoubtedly employed both history and theory in his

[5] See J Finnis, *Natural Law and Natural Rights* (Clarendon, 1980).
[6] O Wendell Holmes, 'The Path of the Law' (1897) 10 *Harvard Law Review* 457.
[7] R Cotterrell, *The Politics of Jurisprudence* (Butterworths, 2003) 15.

writing, and the results are enlightening for the Legal Theory and Legal History project. Marx's *Capital* is a study of a society dominated by the compulsion of economic forces.[8] But Marx recognised that law was developing in a certain way that drew heavily on its relationship with capitalism. His analysis of law was historical and *Capital* could not have been written without Marx's deep knowledge of history. Indeed everything Marx writes about law is richly historical, drawing on comparisons with the classical era, feudalism and Marx's own time. Only with this historical background could Marx present his own thesis: that a self-contained, systematic legal order was perceived as a clear aid to the growing commercial community that needed predictable and calculable rules to govern its transactions. So law had to be developed in this way. Therefore in Marxist visions, law became an ideological tool for the furtherance of economic interests. In this way, law and capitalism were perceived to be essentially linked, but with oppressive effects. Even the supposedly neutral Rule of Law, along with individual rights and the Separation of Powers, could appear to further this purpose where disproportionate economic power lurked behind the apparently neutral mask of law.[9] Not only are theory and practice intermingled in Marx's work, but also, importantly for our purposes, theory and history.

In contrast to Marx, Max Weber, with his positivist theory of legal rational authority, which linked law's perceived authority to its *legality*, rather than asserting any moral foundations for law, seemed less willing to give up on an abstract definition of law, independent and autonomous from other societal elements. Weber's methodology at first sight seems to have more in common with analytical jurisprudence. For Weber, valid law is a bureaucratic, formally rational structure, with an emphasis on posited legal rules.[10] Yet Weber's account of law is a deeply historical one, and whatever theory of law Weber developed emerged from that historical investigation. Weber, unlike Marx, did not see the relationship between law and capitalism as one in which law was causally determined by the economy, but nonetheless the relationship between the two was a continually pressing issue for Weber and required a historical investigation. In seeking to determine why capitalism had only arisen in certain societies, Weber pondered whether law had an essential impact, questioning whether a particular type of law was necessary for capitalism to arise. However, rather than positing a causal relationship between law and capitalism, Weber believed them to be rooted in the same beliefs and attitudes and thus sharing an exegesis. Yet Weber did believe that formal legal rationality, with its systematic rule-governed procedures, had been significant, especially modern contract law—writing that, 'the most essential feature of modern substantive law … is the greatly increased significance of legal

[8] Karl Marx, *Capital*, vol 1 (London, Penguin 1976).

[9] See Marx, 'On the Jewish Question', in *Marx: Early Writings* (Penguin, 1992).

[10] M Weber, 'The Sociology of Law' in *Max Weber on Economy and Society*, M Rheinstein (ed and trans) (Harvard University Press, 1954) 274–78.

transactions, particularly contracts, as a source of claims guaranteed by legal coercion.'[11] Indeed, Weber designated modern society as 'contractual', devoting a huge part of the *Rechtssoziologie* to contracts.

Therefore, Weber seems to have perceived modern contract law at least as contributing to the growth of capitalism, increasing societal wealth and personal freedom, in comparison with former societies which had consisted of feudal practices. However Weber's approach to law, and its relationship with capitalism, was ambivalent. Weber was not, unlike Marx, fiercely critical of the effects of capitalism, but nor was he ingenuous about it, realising that freedom of contract could aggravate inequalities, with economic power producing a special kind of coercive situation, which might in its turn rebound on law. For all his emphasis on 'formal rationality', Weber's account of law is deeply historical—law is embedded in certain historical contexts and, if not fully dependent on them, in a symbiotic relationship with society.

The lesson I think can be drawn from this exegesis into the work of Marx and Weber is that history and theory can be entangled, and interconnected, even mutually dependent. Not all legal theory is isolationist, nor premised on legal autonomy, indeed some theory even embraces an historical element.

IV. Legal Pluralism

Marx and Weber illustrate an interdependence of theoretical and historical method. However, other writers have sought to distinguish history from philosophy in terms of their methodology. Del Mar cites Kuhn in this context, and there certainly is no lack of authors who wish to keep the methodology separate. Reporting on this perceived distinction in method, Lobban writes, 'Whereas (some) philosophers begin with the assumption that people have the same core ideas, thoughts and motivations, historians … assume that different environments generate different behaviours, as the impulses to which humans respond will vary.' But it is important to remember that not all philosophers accept this view. Take, for example, the views of Sir Isaiah Berlin, who wrote:

> I came to the conclusion that there is a plurality of ideals, as there is a plurality of cultures and of temperaments … It may be of interest to remark, incidentally, that there are certain values that we in our world accept which were probably created by early Romanticism and did not exist before: for example, the idea that variety is a good thing, that a society in which many opinions are held, and those holding different opinions are tolerant of each other, is better than a monolithic in which one opinion is binding on

[11] ibid.

everyone. Nobody before the eighteenth century could have accepted that: the truth was one and the idea of variety was inimical to it.[12]

Berlin is but one example from a variety of schools of philosophy that do not stipulate an acceptance of universal values. A further example lies in Wittgenstein's account of language-games which holds that there exists no overarching, single, fundamental ontology, but only a patchwork of overlapping interconnected ontologies ineluctably leading from one to another—there are many interconnected meanings that transition one to another.[13]

There may not exist a smooth, seamless transition from moral or ontological pluralism to legal pluralism, but it is a transition which I shall make, nonetheless, in order to conclude this response. Is legal pluralism not also a school of legal theory? For surely we cannot dismiss it as 'only' sociological or anthropological jurisprudence. Legal pluralism exists when there is a state of affairs, within any social field, in which behaviour pursuant to more than one legal order occurs, sometimes in a contradictory way, in which each may have equally plausible claims to authority. In this way, pluralism introduces incommensurability as a feature of legal life to be reckoned with, and, rather than a centralised unity of law, legal relationships are characterised by heterarchical interactions of different levels and sources of law. Many pluralists also include the further and distinct claim that not all law-like phenomena have their source in institutionalised law—in contrast to views of positivists such Hart, for whom law took the form of institutionalised enforcement of norms.

Pluralism, of whatever sort, is, to be sure, not a new concept—it has been valued and theorised for millennia, in, for example, the works of Ancient Greek philosophers such as Empedocles, and in the Tao of Lao Tzu. More recently, a strong recommendation of it is to be found in William James' pragmatist works. Nor is *legal* pluralism a new phenomenon—Roman law, for example, was pluralist in employing the concepts of *ius gentium* and *ius civile,* and in medieval England there existed the customary law of the realm and divergent manorial, ecclesiastical and mercantile legal regimes.[14] However, the more recent roots of legal pluralism lie in anthropology, sociology and colonial experience.[15] Earlier pluralists such as Ehrlich or Malinowski located law in many places, identifying a coalescence of law with religion, custom, morality, decorum, fashion and etiquette. Legal anthropologists such as Sally Falk Moore characterised law as 'semi-autonomous' from,

[12] I Berlin, 'My Intellectual Path' in his *The Power of Ideas* 2nd edn (Princeton University Press, 2013) 15–16.

[13] See eg L Wittgenstein, *Philosophical Investigations* 4th edn (Blackwell, 2009) §68.

[14] See eg B Nicholas, *Introduction to Roman Law* (Oxford University Press, 1962); JH Baker, *Introduction to English Legal History* 4th edn (Butterworths, 2002).

[15] See eg E Ehrlich, *Fundamental Principles of the Sociology of Law* (W Moll trans, Russell and Russell, 1936).

and dynamically interrelated with, other fields.[16] Legal pluralism has long since moved beyond its earlier locus in the anthropology of law—as Sally Engle Merry expresses it: 'the intellectual odyssey of the concept of legal pluralism moves from the discovery of indigenous forms of law among remote African villages and New Guinea tribesmen to debates concerning the pluralistic qualities of law under advanced capitalism.'[17] The American legal theorist, Lon Fuller, challenged the positivist tendency to equate law with state authority, instead insisting that law resulted from human interaction, and that activities could be 'more or less' legal, a matter of degree—and he thereby also located law in universities, clubs and associations, proclaiming these to be 'miniature legal systems'.[18] Sousa Santos has also embraced the theme of legal pluralism: he describes a cluster of 'interpenetrating legalities', whereby law moves from the old and familiar to the new and innovative, becoming in the process tangled, fluid and difficult to pin down.[19]

These days pluralism has burgeoned and attracted so many adherents that it has been described by some as 'the new orthodoxy,' or possibly 'uninteresting' when so prevalent.[20] This is important because it presents evidence of a legal theory that most certainly does *not* assume 'that people have the same core ideas, thoughts and motivations', and yet it is a legal theory that has become viewed as orthodox and mainstream. Notably, one crucial strand in contemporary legal pluralism is situated at transnational or global level, where a varied and often competing proliferation of rules and norms are to be found. Whereas the state once defined the geographical boundaries of law, there now exists a multitude of laws and legal orders at supranational and international levels. Indeed, William Twining suggests that the Westphalian state legal order should be viewed as the exception—existing for a mere two centuries or so in the North, an anomaly in a broader historical mass of legal experience of coexisting multiple legal orders.[21]

What has been the point of this excursus into legal pluralism? At its most basic, my aim has been another illustration of the wide range of resources that legal theory possesses. To be sure, I am in agreement with a great deal of what Del Mar and Lobban write, but I hope that my response does not seem to be merely on the level of a quibble. For it goes to the heart of what jurisprudence is. Why choose analytical jurisprudence as a benchmark, even if it is a benchmark that is recognised as undesirable and inappropriate in the context of an attempted dialogue between legal theory and legal history? Some types of legal theory do present a problem for a fruitful dialogue with legal history. Yet my response is that we should not

[16] S Falk Moore, 'Law and Social Change: The Semi-Autonomous Social Field as an Appropriate Subject for Study' (1972/73) 7 *Law and Society Review* 719.

[17] See S Engle Merry, 'Legal Pluralism' (1988) 29 *Law and Society Review* 869 at 872.

[18] L Fuller, *The Morality of Law* (Yale University Press, 1965).

[19] S Santos, *Towards a New Legal Common Sense* 2nd edn (Butterworths, 2002).

[20] See N Barber, 'Legal Pluralism and the European Union' (2006) 12 *European Law Journal* 306.

[21] W Twining, 'Normative and Legal Pluralism: A Global Perspective' (2010) 20 *Duke Journal of Comparative and International Law* 47.

let those types of theory occupy too much of the legal terrain. In order to cut off the King's head we must first acknowledge that he is King. But maybe there is no Kingdom at all?

So, in conclusion, while I endorse the argument made by both Del Mar and Lobban that a certain type of 'stipulative' jurisprudence renders problematic a dialogue between legal theory and legal history, I would urge less of a focus on that type of jurisprudence. Consider the richness of legal theory—of legal pluralism, of legal realism, the insights of Marx and Weber, and let us find fertile and worthwhile connections there. In this way, I believe that Del Mar's 'middle path' will not be as modest as might at first be thought.

Part II

Methodology and Historiography

5

Historicism and Materiality in Legal Theory

CHRISTOPHER TOMLINS

In this work I mean to wrest from primal history [*Urgeschichte*] a portion of the nineteenth century.[1]

In 1996, Robert W Gordon wrote of a 'remarkable revival of interest … in history' underway 'among lawyers and legal scholars', a revival particularly marked in the United States, but observable 'worldwide'.[2] Now of course, history as such has never been exactly a stranger in law's precincts, so much of Gordon's commentary was devoted to an exposition of 'standard modes' of lawyerly resort to history: past texts and practices endlessly recycled to serve as authority for present (usually quite distinct) purposes; imagined continuities and traditions created to contain current hopes within established ruts, or alternatively to conjure up heartening narratives of evolution, amelioration, even radical change. Largely, Gordon argued, lawyers had used history as a genre of apology, 'to endow currently dominant claims of entitlements and distributions of legal advantage and modes of legitimating property and power with the authority of the past'.[3] But the 'standard modes' could also be found lending themselves to 'critical and destabilizing' functions that challenged ruling assumptions and the received wisdoms that sustained them.[4]

What had especially caught Gordon's eye, however, was something else. The revival—ongoing at that point for a good 20 years—had extended well beyond the standard modes of engagement between law and history to the point where something distinct, 'historicism', had become its defining characteristic. By historicism, Gordon meant the practice of demonstrating that 'a social practice or a document

[1] W Benjamin, *The Arcades Project* (Harvard University Press, 1999) 393.

[2] RW Gordon, 'The Past as Authority and as Social Critic: Stabilizing and Destabilizing Functions of History in Legal Argument' in TJ McDonald (ed), *The Historic Turn in the Human Sciences* (University of Michigan Press, 1996) 339.

[3] ibid 344.

[4] ibid 345.

is a product of the preoccupations of its own time and place'.[5] As applied to law, historicism showed 'legal ideas, rules, institutions, and procedures [to be] contingent products of time and circumstances: contested in their content, multiple in their forms, variable across time, place, and social group in the ways they are put to practical use'.[6] Writ small, historicism meant no more than 'rescuing the past from the distortions of the present-minded and of emphasizing the embeddedness of legal forms in the particularities of context';[7] in other words it meant the disciplining of the standard modes of lawyerly resort to history by a corrective dose of professional historical method. Writ large, however, as a genre of critique, historicism turned in a very different direction. By showing 'how past forms were made and unmade, and how present forms in their turn came to be put together, we can make the present seem more plastic, more amenable to present re-imagination and change'.[8] Gordon was recalling and updating for his audience FW Maitland's powerful observation a century earlier that the utility of legal history lay in its lesson 'that each generation has an enormous power of shaping its own law', that it had 'free hands'.[9] Within a few months, in another commentary, Gordon was hailing 'the arrival of critical historicism' as perhaps 'the most exciting work currently being done on law'.[10]

Precisely because of its emergence at the centre of legal history's remarkable later-twentieth century revival, the historicist perspective supplies the default setting for encounters between legal history and other genres of legal study, such as legal theory. Historicism marks law as a phenomenon characterised by ceaseless change over time, and holds that it should be studied as such; it recommends that theorists of law interrogate their subject from a standpoint acutely sensitive to the multitude of historical contexts in which it is embedded and from which it is produced; and it proposes no limit to the historical contexts relevant to that interrogation. From the point of view of the legal theorist, that is, the formative contexts relevant to inquiry should not be restricted to the immediate institutional and intellectual exchanges that comprise lawmaking, or to the somewhat wider range of intellectual and disciplinary exchanges that occur among theorists of law in the course of their observation of lawmaking. They should extend to the broad range of historical circumstances—political and economic, social and cultural—in which not only law but also legal theory (and legal theorist) are immersed.[11]

[5] RW Gordon, '"Critical Legal Histories Revisited": A Response' (2012) 37 *Law & Social Inquiry* 200.

[6] Gordon (n 2) 359.

[7] ibid 359.

[8] ibid 359.

[9] FW Maitland to AV Dicey (c July 1896) in CHS Fifoot and PNR Zutshi (eds), *The Letters of Frederick William Maitland* (Selden Society, 1995) II, 116.

[10] RW Gordon, 'The Arrival of Critical Historicism' (1997) 49 *Stanford Law Review* 1023, 1029.

[11] Critical historicism means, for law, 'any approach to the past that produces disturbances in the [legal] field—that inverts or scrambles familiar narratives of stasis, recovery or progress; anything that advances rival perspectives (such as those of the losers rather than the winners) for surveying developments, or that posits alternative trajectories that might have produced a very different present—in short any approach that unsettles the familiar strategies that we use to tame the past in order to normalize the present'; ibid 1024.

But although the ascendancy of historicism in contemporary legal history probably makes it inevitable that in fact historicism will furnish the point of departure for historically-minded revisionism in legal theory, there are good reasons, both practical and philosophical, to consider other ways historically-minded legal theorists might proceed. First, then, I will offer a critique of historicism—an account of why it might *not* be the best way forward for legal theory. Second I will consider a rival to historicism, which for want of a better descriptor I will call 'materiality', that I think has as much or more to offer. A less developed, more eclectic, standpoint than historicism, materiality stresses the formative intersection between law and legal thought and technologies, artifacts and material practices; it considers how law might be expressed as technology and artifact, how law as a differentiated category of action is fabricated.[12]

Materiality's potential for legal history, and hence for a revisionist legal theory attentive to history, is on display (in rather different ways) in work as varied as Cornelia Vismann's *Files: Law and Media Technology* and Bruno Latour's *The Making of Law.*[13] My main emphasis, however, will be on the potential of materiality for legal history and legal theory as articulated in the species of historical materialism developed in the work of Walter Benjamin.[14] Here one finds both an intense stress on the materiality of an object of attention—not simply on the material conditions of its existence, but on its existence as a material condition—coupled to an understanding of historical perspective to mean much more than the derivation of the object's meaning from its circumstances. Benjamin articulates the past at the moment of its recognisability, which is the here-and-now. If we understand history to promise to enliven our understanding of an object (such as law, or legal thought) that we contemplate, we must recognise that the contemplated object is not enlivened by the relationalities within which it allegedly belongs, the relationalities of *its* time, but by the fold of time that creates it in constellation with the present, the moment of its recognition.

I. Historicism and Structuralism

The legal theorist encountering historicism is encountering not simply a perspective, but a method and, most important, a philosophy of history. The method

[12] See generally A Faulkner, B Lange and C Lawless, 'Introduction: Material Worlds: Intersections of Law, Science, Technology, and Society' (2012) 39 *Journal of Law and Society* 1.

[13] C Vismann, *Files: Law and Media Technology* (G Winthrop-Young trans, Stanford University Press, 2008); B Latour, *The Making of Law: An Ethnography of the Conseil d'État* (M Brilman and A Pottage trans, Polity Press, 2010).

[14] Both in its critique of historicism and in its invocation of Benjamin, this essay returns to and attempts to utilise and to build upon previous work. See in particular C Tomlins, 'Toward a Materialist Jurisprudence' in A Brophy and D Hamilton (eds), *Transformations in American Legal History: Law,*

historicism implies is essentially that of contemporary professional history, to which 'context' (notably social context) has become all-important. Professional history 'historicises' its subjects by placing them in context, which means in practice by placing subjects in relation to one another at appropriate points in the medium of historical time. It will immediately be apparent that the universe of potential spatio-temporal subject relationalities is infinite, governed only by the historian's judgement of what is appropriate. Unsurprisingly, professional judgement of what is appropriate varies constantly as new schools or methods of interpretation come into being and old ones pass away. Hence, the universe of subject positions and relations is unstable, its tendency always expansive, filling historical time with ever greater complexity in relations among historically situated subjects. The lesson professional history has drawn from its examinations of what it does (historiography) is that what it examines—the past—is irreducibly contingent.[15]

As a philosophy of history, historicism's roots lie in post-Enlightenment, particularly German, scholarly discourse, in the proposition that all social and cultural phenomena, as well as the categories to which they belonged, the truths they were understood to convey, and the values that might be generalised from them, are comprehensible only by an examination of the historical context in which they occurred, an examination rigorously detached from any evaluative criteria belonging to the historian's present that might distort comprehension.[16] As such, historicism could be made a source of teleological statements about the historical determination of the course of human development, or metaphysical statements, as in Hegelian philosophy in which historicism stands for the ideal unity of reason, being and time. Contemporary historicism, however, is neither teleological nor metaphysical. Rather, it is an expression of what one might call, following Dorothy Ross, modernist antimetaphysical contingency.[17] Historicism in this vein is an antifoundational philosophy of history. By pinning phenomena in time and place we render their meaning entirely consequential upon circumstance, so much so that a practice or text 'reenacted or reread at a later time ... will acquire a new set

Ideology, and Methods—Essays in Honor of Morton J Horwitz, Volume II (Harvard University Press, 2010); C Tomlins, 'After Critical Legal History: Scope, Scale, Structure' (2012) 8 *Annual Review of Law and Social Science* 31.

[15] Among historians in the last 30-odd years, the proverbial first line of LP Harley's novel *The Go-Between* (Hamish Hamilton, 1953)—'The past is a foreign country: they do things differently there'—has become a (by now clichéd) form of acknowledging that history has become, very largely, a contextualising discipline, a discipline that fetishises thick description, contingency, and complexity. For an early (and critical) examination of the trope, see D Lowenthal, *The Past is a Foreign Country* (Cambridge University Press, 1985).

[16] See generally P Novick, *That Noble Dream: The 'Objectivity Question' and the American Historical Profession* (Cambridge University Press, 1988) 7; D Ross, *The Origins of American Social Science* (Cambridge University Press, 1991) 3–9, 19–21; C Fasolt, *The Limits of History* (University of Chicago Press, 2004) 30–31.

[17] Ross (n 11) 474–76; D Ross, 'Modernism Reconsidered' and 'Modernist Social Science in the Land of the New/Old' in D Ross (ed), *Modernist Impulses in the Human Sciences, 1870–1930* (The Johns Hopkins University Press, 1994).

of meanings from its new context'.[18] Effectively, the new context, which supplies a new meaning, creates a new phenomenon.

As Kunal Parker has recently pointed out—and as Gordon's channeling of Maitland concedes—there is actually nothing wildly novel in the contemporary emergence of historicism, save only, perhaps, the completeness of its hegemony. In legal history it returns us to the end of the nineteenth century when Oliver Wendell Holmes, Jr, among others, invoked history 'to tear down the suprahistorical foundations'—logic, morality and so forth—of law. In the very act 'of sweeping away such foundations', Parker continues, Holmes' history reveals itself as antimetaphysical modernism.[19] To expose the spatio-temporal location of legal phenomena—their 'felt necessities'—is to dismantle the foundations of legitimacy upon which they rest: the logic that allegedly underlies them, or the accumulated weight of the past that authorises their repetition in the future. But this historicist corrosion of existing foundations reveals no substitute underlying order. Modernist history 'possesses no necessary or coherent direction or meaning. It simply sweeps away foundations, clears ground, and invites self-reflection'.[20]

The (re)emergence of such an antifoundational philosophy of history at the centre of Gordon's 'remarkable revival' is no accident, because the revival itself owes much of its impetus and character to the determinedly antifoundational movement in late twentieth century legal education and legal thought known as critical legal studies (CLS). Though relatively brief in duration (circa 1975–1995), in its best-known US incarnation the CLS 'moment' coincides with the acceleration of the legal history revival into self-sustained growth, largely due to the active interest leading exponents of critical legal studies—Gordon himself, Morton Horwitz, Duncan Kennedy, John Henry Schlegel, Mark Tushnet and others—took in developing and sustaining a historical understanding, and critique, of American law and legal thought.[21]

Before CLS history could become 'historicist', however, it first had to resolve something of an internal confrontation between a structuralist tendency associated principally with Duncan Kennedy, which was (and remains) decidedly non-historicist, and the post-structural historicism evident in the work of other critical legal historians, notably Gordon.[22]

Kennedy's object of attention is not the history of law per se but the history of legal thought, and in particular of legal consciousness; that is, the 'structure

[18] Gordon (n 2) 200.

[19] KM Parker, Common Law, History, and Democracy in America: Legal Thought Before Modernism (Cambridge University Press, 2011) 5.

[20] ibid 7.

[21] Here I am concentrating on CLS in its US form. On the role of history in the formation of critical legal studies in Europe see C Douzinas 'A Short History of the British Critical Legal Conference or, the Responsibility of the Critic' (2014) 25 *Law and Critique* 187.

[22] On legal structuralism in general and Duncan Kennedy's structuralism in particular, see J Desautels-Stein, 'Structuralist Legal Histories' (2014) 77 *Law & Contemporary Problems* 37, and 'What is Contemporary Legal Thought?' (currently unpublished, copy on file with author). RW Gordon's historicism can be dated to his 'Historicism in Legal Scholarship' (1981) 90 *Yale Law Journal* 1017.

of categories, concepts, conventionally understood procedures, and conventionally given typical legal arguments' *within* which thinking about law occurs, supplemented by structures of subjective experience.[23] The 'structure of categories' constitutes a mode of thought, or *langue*, that is sufficiently stable to be capable of production, transmission and reproduction, but not so constraining as to predicate specific outcomes. Outcomes—the 'specific, positively-enacted rules' that express the mode of thought in action in different fields of law—are *parole*, practices capable of indefinite variation within the boundaries of the mode of thought, according to subjective circumstance, locality, and so forth.[24] As this indicates, Kennedy's method is derived from Saussurean semiotics.[25] In the 1970s it was on full display in his famous essays on 'The Structure of Blackstone's Commentaries', and 'The Rise and Fall of Classical Legal Thought'.[26]

The tension between Kennedy's structuralist quest for system underlying variation in an account of legal thought with historicist description of law as 'plural, contested, constructed'[27]—in other words as nothing but *parole*—is clear in Gordon's description of Kennedy's trajectory in his well-known essay, 'Critical Legal Histories':

> I love the work that the Critical doctrinal historians have been doing. I think it's among the most exciting intellectual work being done anywhere and that it has revolutionized our vision of our legal past. But I also think that, just as the Critical narrative mode of intellectual history has misled readers into supposing that the Critics have bought into the idealism of the old Formalists who thought that legal ideas just 'evolved' according to some mysterious inner dynamic, its focus on mandarin materials has led readers to suppose Critics to be trapped in the old Formalist belief that only specialized-law-stuff-separate-from-politics *is* law.[28]

To ram the critique home, Gordon appended a long quotation on the insufficiencies of structuralist analysis of law from *The Poverty of Theory*, EP Thompson's lengthy and self-indulgent assault on Louis Althusser, the 'structuralist philosopher' who

[23] http://duncankennedy.net/legal_history/index.html#LC.

[24] There is some tension in Kennedy's account between the emphasis upon *parole* variation and the contention (in the US case) that 'development in different fields of law over the last century followed a single pattern'. D Kennedy, 'Three Globalizations of Law and Legal Thought: 1850–2000' in D Trubek and A Santos (eds), *The New Law and Economic Development: A Critical Appraisal* (Cambridge University Press, 2006) 25.

[25] See J Desautels-Stein, 'Experimental Pragmatism in the Third Globalization' (2012) 9 *Contemporary Pragmatism* 181.

[26] D Kennedy, 'The Structure of Blackstone's Commentaries' (1979) 28 *Buffalo Law Review* 205; 'The Rise and Fall of Classical Legal Thought' (1975) unpublished manuscript, (1998) published in limited edition, (2006) published with an author's preface, 'Thirty Years Later' (Beard Books), ch 1 excerpted as 'Toward an Historical Understanding of Legal Consciousness: The Case of Classical Legal Thought in America, 1850–1940' (1980) 3 *Research in Law & Sociology* 3.

[27] Gordon (n 1) 358.

[28] RW Gordon, 'Critical Legal Histories' (1984) 36 *Stanford Law Review* 57, 122–23.

had first attracted Thompson's ire in *Whigs and Hunters*.[29] Gordon's argument was that 'field-level' research into vernacular legal consciousness showed that *parole* was all there was. '[T]he forms that go into the constitution of legal relations ... are manufactured, reproduced, and modified for special purposes by everyone, at every level, all the time. *Critics are not going to get this insight across if they don't switch their focus*'.[30] By 1996, the joust (in Gordon's eyes, at least) was won. Critical doctrinal history had been assimilated to the post-structural multiplicity—'indeterminacy located in contradiction'—he had recommended 12 years earlier.[31] Kennedy's essay on Blackstone's *Commentaries* was brilliant, but 'so gnomic as to have remained almost unread'.[32] By 2012, critical doctrinal history had quite 'petered out', overwhelmed by the huge wave of historicist inquiry into 'the study of law at the vernacular level' that marked the climax of legal history's remarkable revival.[33]

Perhaps the best representation of what legal history looks like at its historicist apogee appears in a recent review of current work in the history of civil rights:

> It uses the sources and analytics of both legal and social history. It takes law seriously on its own terms but defines 'law' capaciously. It attempts to capture what happens before, behind, after, in front of, and with little relationship to [courts]. It is thus less linear, more multiple. It highlights complexity and contingency. In doing so, it addresses the people, institutions, and legal and nonlegal arenas where actors and arguments meet. It identifies intermediaries, liaisons, ambassadors. It explains how ideas, movements, and legal doctrines cross the boundaries of space, class, race, and time. It explores the relationship between the many lay and professional actors involved in changing legal conceptions and

[29] ibid 123. See EP Thompson, *The Poverty of Theory and Other Essays* (Merlin Press, 1978) 96; EP Thompson, *Whigs and Hunters: The Origin of the Black Act* (Penguin Books, 1977) 262. The quotation in question speaks to Thompson's rejection of Althusser's contention that (in Thompson's version of Althusser) law kept to a superstructural level. Thompson replied 'I found that law did not keep politely to a "level", but was at *every* bloody level; it was imbricated within the mode of production and productive relations themselves (as property-rights, definitions of agrarian practice) and it was simultaneously present in the philosophy of Locke; it intruded brusquely within alien categories, reappearing bewigged and gowned in the guise of ideology; it danced a cotillion with religion, moralizing over the theater of Tyburn; it was an arm of politics and politics was one of its arms; it was an academic discipline, subjected to the rigor of its own autonomous logic; it contributed to the definition of the self-identity both of rulers and of ruled; above all, it afforded an arena for class struggle, within which alternative notions of law were fought out'.

[30] Gordon (n 22) 123 (emphasis added).

[31] Gordon (n 1) 361–62. Meanwhile, the version of 'indeterminacy located in contradiction' Gordon recommended had itself evolved quite significantly. Compare (a) '[The Critics] don't mean [by indeterminacy] ... that there are never any predictable causal relations between legal forms and anything else ... [T]here are plenty of short- and medium-run stable regularities in social life, including regularities in the interpretation and application, in given contexts, of legal rules ... The Critical claim of indeterminacy is simply that none of these regularities are necessary consequences of the adoption of a given regime of rules' (Gordon (n 22) 125) with (b) 'The critical historians' main point about ... legal arrangements is that the basic principles behind them are so indeterminate, and their historical interpretations so variable and multiform, that one cannot plausibly speak of a single "capitalist" [legal] order at all' (Gordon (n 1) 362).

[32] Gordon (n 1) 361. It is curious to describe an essay as 'almost unread' and simultaneously as the foundational document for an entire school of critical doctrinal history.

[33] Gordon (n 22) 209.

> in [social] struggle more generally … [It] is interested in possibilities as well as eventualities … in understanding not only what was but also what might have been.[34]

Not much structuralism to be found here.[35]

II. Difference

One of the beauties of Kunal Parker's work on legal thought *before* modernism is its careful recovery of how deeply imbued that thought was with conceptions of history that were knowing rather than naïve, but also explanatory in that they were not contingent but directional: the immemoriality and insensibility of early modern common law; the ontologies of consent attending the epoch of democratic revolutions; the idea of time itself not as modernity's relentlessly sequential chronology, but as a succession of discontinuous ages each imbued by its particular 'spirit'; the idea of underlying laws of development; the idea of law itself as a temporal relationship between custom and instantiation in which custom lay simultaneously ahead of law as its guiding light and behind it as its point of origin.[36] Twentieth century historical practice contains remnants and remainders of all these—one never entirely eliminates the trace of previous ideas. The point is, however, to recognise that our own now-dominant affection for complexity and contingency is simply the latest in a series of styles of doing history, a style that has been given extra staying power by academic professionalisation and self-reproduction, with all its attendant scleroses, but a style nevertheless.[37] It is a style whose fetishisation of contextual contingency and complexity substitutes Geertzian thick description for both structural and causal explanation, or as Clifford Geertz himself argued in his 1981 Storrs Lectures at Yale Law School, 'meaning [for] machinery'.[38] Thinking about law had been too functionalist, Geertz claimed, too interested in law 'as a clever device to keep people from tearing one another limb from limb, advance the interests of the dominant classes, defend the rights of the weak against the predations of the strong, or render social life a bit more predictable at its fuzzy edges'. It wasn't that Geertz denied law could in fact be any or indeed all of these. It was just that he preferred 'hermeneutic thinking' about law—'as a mode of giving particular sense to particular things in particular places (things that happen, things that fail to, things that might)'.[39]

[34] R Goluboff, 'Lawyers, Law, and the New Civil Rights History: Representing the Race: the Creation of the Civil Rights Lawyer, by KW Mack' (2013) 126 *Harvard Law Review* 2312.

[35] Nevertheless, structuralist legal history never died, and indeed is making a comeback. See Kennedy (n 18); J Desautels-Stein, 'Back in Style' (2014) 25 *Law and Critique* 141.

[36] Parker (n 14) 25–278.

[37] Desautels-Stein (n 29) 149–58; KM Parker, 'Historicising *Blackstone's Commentaries on the Laws of England*: Difference and Sameness in Historical Time' in A Fernandez and MD Dubber (eds), *Law Books in Action: Essays on the Anglo-American Legal Treatise* (Hart Publishing, 2012).

[38] C Geertz, Local Knowledge: Further Essays in Interpretive Anthropology (Basic Books, 1983) 232

[39] ibid 232.

Geertz is describing a post-structural, certainly a non-functionalist, style of history—an antifoundational historicism. In two important respects, however, a style that prefers meaning to machinery still runs aground on difficult philosophical problematics first posed as an element of post-structuralism's critique of 'machinery' but endemic, I think, in historicist inquiry too. The first problematic is that of intelligibility, usually formulated as 'the metaphysics of presence', referring to the denial of time implicit in structuralism's quest for an ontology of general and absolute concepts. 'The past and the future are always determined as past presents or future presents', Derrida writes. Being is 'already determined as being-present'.[40] The quest for universality necessarily renders all modes of being as timeless modes of presence, restating all modes of temporality as facets of a single primordial present.[41] Derrida's deconstructive response is *différance*—a non-metaphysical past, irreducibly in time and endlessly deferred, a past that has never been and could never be present.[42] And one can see in contemporary historicism, with its basic proposition that (to repeat) 'a social practice or a document is a product of the preoccupations of its own time and place, and that if it survives to be reenacted or reread at a later time, it will acquire a new set of meanings from its new context', an attempt to replicate the irreducible temporal particularity of *différance* by stressing the temporal particularity of context.[43] How, though, in that case, is the observer-historian, who is not in the particular time or place of the object of inquiry, to know its meaning? The historicist must argue that although meaning is a creature of context, the observer can nevertheless tap that meaning—can access some trace of intelligibility inherent in the object or in the formative preoccupations of the object's time and place. But in that case we have simply returned to the shared presence that post-structuralism denies, for the presumption of the object's intelligibility to the observer-historian is a presumption of their shared presence. In other words, the style of historicist contextualisation repeats the error of the style of universalisation, and unlike universality (which at least offers us hypothetical generalisation) has nothing to show for it. True historicism—absolute *différance*—would have to deny the possibility that its object of attention is intelligible, rendering it a species of antiquarianism: the past for its own sake, impossible to understand, entirely enigmatic; phenomena to preserve as best one can, in a state of reverence.[44]

Without some attempt to resolve the problematic of presence, history arguably offers nothing to legal theory other than decoration. Historicism's context—thick

[40] J Derrida, '*Ousia* and *Grammé*: Note on a Note from *Being and Time*' in *Margins of Philosophy*, A Bass (trans) (University of Chicago Press, 1982) 34, 47, quoted in F Söderbäck, 'Being in the Present: Derrida and Irigaray on the Metaphysics of Presence' (2013) 27 *Journal of Speculative Philosophy* 253.

[41] ibid 254.

[42] ibid.

[43] Gordon (n 2) 200.

[44] For recognition of antiquarianism as a mode of history, see F Nietzsche, 'On the Uses and Disadvantages of History for Life' in F Nietzsche, *Untimely Meditations* (Cambridge University Press, 1983) 72–75.

description—is an illusory route to meaning. We must allow that meaning arises not from what is observed or its relationship with its context but from the image formed by the relationship in the observer's present between the observer and what is observed. Here and here only lies a philosophically-defensible form of intelligibility.[45]

Historicism poses a second and related problem, that of differentiation. Or rather, as Pierre Schlag puts it, dedifferentiation.[46] It is now commonplace in post-structural socio-legal studies to argue that law and society are 'mutually constitutive'. What formerly were theoretical debates over the nature and extent of legal autonomy (formalism, instrumentalism, the constitutive role of law, the several distinct varieties of relative autonomy), have become debates over mutuality (law and society simultaneously constitute each other). Where the autonomy paradigm parsed relationships between the social and the legal as discrete objects, the mutuality paradigm attends to the ways in which the social and the legal blur—penetrate and form each other.[47] 'Identities previously thought separate and distinct', Schlag writes, 'turn out to be inextricably intertwined. Each is already inextricably the other—in ways that cannot be disentangled through any definition, specification, stipulation, or theorization'.[48] Laconically, he adds '[t]his is rather bad news for the ways in which we have traditionally conceived theories of law—indeed any theory which gets off the ground by distinguishing law from a discrete something else (which on first glance would seem to include all legal theory)'.[49] Once the thread is pulled, in fact, *all* hypotheses founded on the in-principle assumption of distinct identities majestically unravel ('epidemic dedifferentiation').[50]

Schlag traverses two pairs of responses to the differentiation problem. The first pair is rejectionist: (1a) practical rejection—dedifferentiation may have intellectual heft, but legal theory is a practical exercise in normative and political thought, so it can proceed much as it has; (1b) dogmatic rejection—identities are analytically essential to theory and dedifferentiation is simply a boundary problem. Schlag does not have much time for either rejectionist position. The second pair is accepting: (2a) passive acceptance—retreat from the ambition to construct theory into descriptive particularity; (2b) active acceptance—take the purposeful construction of difference (intellectual, cultural, disciplinary) out of sameness to be itself the object of study and build theory around that as a new point of

[45] 'What distinguishes images from the "essences" of phenomenology is their historical index. (Heidegger seeks in vain to rescue history for phenomenology abstractly through "historicity.") … For the historical index of the images not only says that they belong to a particular time; it says, above all, that they attain to legibility only at a particular time': Benjamin (n 1) 462.

[46] P Schlag, 'The Dedifferentiation Problem' (2009) 42 *Continental Philosophy Review* 35.

[47] C Tomlins, 'Bucking the Party Line: Calavita's Invitation to Law and Society' (2014) 39 *Law & Social Inquiry* 226, 229–30.

[48] Schlag (n 39) 37.

[49] ibid 35.

[50] ibid 53–54.

departure.[51] Schlag favours active acceptance: the construction of differentiation is an aesthetic enterprise founded on disciplinarity and can be studied as such.[52] It is worth noting, however, that he fingers legal history as the principal example of passive acceptance. Schlag puts this down to historians' 'professional commitment to particularism'—to the concrete, the local, the factual, rather than to theory-building.[53] As we have seen, however, it is less legal history's genetic predisposition to concrete factuality that explains its 'untroubled' acceptance of dedifferentiation than the hegemony of historicism—a radically dedifferentiating perspective—in legal history. Historicist law *is* plural, contested, socially constructed, vernacular. Its meanings *are* produced from, created by, the circumstances (contexts) that it simultaneously moulds, to such an extent that, if context changes, meaning changes with it. Critical historicism in other words has played an active part in constructing Schlag's dedifferentiation problem by undermining legal differentiation. That is why historians seem blasé about the problem's existence.

Schlag's argument, and that of critical historicism, depends upon the collapse of difference that occurs once one recognises that the conventional markers of law's differentiation—particular authoritative texts, an identifiable professional corps, a distinctive expertise, determinate legal institutions, recognisable rituals and ritual sites, each element possessed of historical pedigree—are all artificial reifications. 'Each of the[se] demarcations … reduces law to a thing-like manifestation of law'.[54] So reduced, 'much of what we consider law to be' is left out.[55] Schlag surveys each mode of demarcation and shows how in each case the boundary it has constructed is essentially arbitrary. Law is too protean to be demarcated; the markers themselves are too discrete to contain it. The result is categorical collapse. Schlag recognises that 'differentiation between law and the social remain[s] to some degree ideationally perspicuous as well as socially real and effective'.[56] It is the use of the markers as 'unproblematic referents', as assumed theoretical categories, that is his concern.[57] Still, Schlag's argument proceeds as though his markers *are* routinely so used, hence that categorical collapse has indeed been completely effected.

It is worth asking whether differentiation is under quite as much epistemological pressure as Schlag believes. Individually none of his markers can represent law, nor should we expect (or want) it to do so. Collectively, however, their effectuation of differentiation is descriptively powerful and non-arbitrary: authoritative texts *marshalled by* an identifiable professional corps *wielding* a distinctive expertise *within the precincts of* determinate legal institutions *engaged in* recognisable ritual

[51] ibid 57–60.
[52] ibid 60.
[53] ibid 58.
[54] ibid 49.
[55] ibid 49.
[56] ibid 51.
[57] ibid 51.

practices and *possessed of a recoverable* historical pedigree furnishes a reasonable and testable working definition of law. It does not pretend to exclusivity—much law or law-like behaviour remains outside the definition—but it is not wrong on its face, and it has the potential to capture a significant realm of action.[58]

A distinct response, however, would be to join Schlag in studying the fabrication of difference.[59] This response is not incompatible with that which defends the effectivity of differentiating, for Schlag's own list of demarcations actually supplies a rather useful point of departure in studying the fabrication of law's difference. It is quite instructive, and not at all reductive, to think of law as reified, materialised as things. Two recent studies are of assistance in pursuing the matter, albeit in markedly different ways: Cornelia Vismann's *Files: Law and Media Technology*, and Bruno Latour's *The Making of Law*.[60]

III. Fabricating Difference

Files, Cornelia Vismann says, are law's point of origin, the locus at which law splits off from administrative actuality, and the messy business of execution, into authoritative legal form.[61] Her *Files* is a history of files and their capacity to instantiate the legal subject, truth, and the state. The outcome is an astonishingly beautiful meditation on law's materiality. *Files* is at once a history of records, their locales, of the file as the signifier of the state, of the authorisation of law in techniques of administrative recurrence (fil*ing*) and the media in which they are materialised; and simultaneously it is a history of law's recurrence as *detritus*, cancelled originals and floods of discarded files left in the wake of the state's movement through time.[62] Vismann conveys a sense of how the trace of the state continues to reside in

[58] It is important to avoid mistaking the attempt to assemble components of a working definition for an attempt at complete definition. The goal is the creation of a basis for the testing of hypotheses that will themselves necessarily be no more than provisional in scope. But provisionality is no argument against engaging in the exercise. Approximations that capture, say, 60% of a phenomenon are not automatically invalid because they cannot capture 100%. A 60% approximation is usually preferable to forgoing the attempt altogether because the phenomenon under observation is presumptively too 'complex' to be captured fully. The point is to establish how much of a phenomenon one can explain, and how much is not amenable to (that) explanation, and requires an approach that is methodologically distinct. See generally M Bevir, 'How to be an Intentionalist' (2002) 41 *History and Theory* 209. For my own attempts to assemble the components of a history of national legal practices in the US case, see C Tomlins, 'Law and History in the US Case: Toward a Structural History of National Legal Practices' (2005) unpublished manuscript drawing on C Tomlins, 'Law's Disciplinary Encounters: A Historical Narrative' (2000) 34 *Law & Society Review* 911 and C Tomlins, 'History in the Juridical Field: Narrative, Justification and Explanation in the American Case' (2004) 16 *Yale Journal of Law and the Humanities* 323.

[59] Tomlins, 'Law and History' (ibid) proposed just that.

[60] Latour (n 8), Vismann (n 8).

[61] Vismann (n 8), xii, 13, 39.

[62] ibid xi–xiii.

its *detritus*. That is, in the very chaos of files she invokes throughout there resides as important a representation of power as in its shiniest and most recent act. In all these respects *Files* is an *Arcades Project* of law—an object lesson in how to write of law fetishised as things, and in how also to write of the specific ways in which law is produced out of technologies of administration, decision and execution, of things fetishised as law.

Vismann's actual history of files, of law's physical texture, is a reminder of how the language of *social* construction almost invariably elides materiality. Law is scrivened text,[63] stitched together,[64] cut and pasted.[65] We forget that the history of law is a history of the book as much as it is of the ideas in the book.[66] Vismann's is a history of the generation of documents and their physical characteristics, the establishment of registers, the keeping of records. Frederick II (1194–1250), Holy Roman Emperor, carried his files with him wherever he journeyed throughout his Sicilian home kingdom—a train of packhorses carrying 'the transportable thesaurus of the state', a very material public display of authority.[67] And authority resides not merely in what is recorded but how—the replacement of scroll file by codex in second century Rome meant a major alteration in the manipulability of records.[68] *Files* renders the history of law as the history of successive techniques of recording.

As her attention to Frederick's *scrinia* suggests, Vismann dwells on the file as the signifier of the state.[69] Because *Files* gives particular attention to cameralist administrative practice (*polizei*), one can put her account down alongside Foucault's *Security, Territory, Population*, for example, and gain a very clear sense of the materiality of governmentality.[70] Thus the file becomes a tangible instantiation of the particularities of the state. It is also, I think, the tangible instantiation of the state's being in time, a reproductive technology of the state. But there is a question here, of course, of priority, of purpose. Of this Vismann writes, 'because historians search for the essence of the state behind profane administrative techniques, they do not dwell for very long on the files themselves'.[71] The question that is posed here, obviously, is whether the state generates files or files generate the state.

[63] ibid 29–38 (commentary on 'Bartleby the Scrivener').

[64] ST Bindoff, 'The Making of the Statute of Artificers' in ST Bindoff, J Hurstfield and CH Williams (eds), *Elizabethan Government and Society: Essays Presented to Sir John Neale* (Athlone Press, 1961) 56–94.

[65] Y Berda, 'The Peculiar Persistence of Colonial Emergency Laws: Why New Nations Reproduce Legal Practices Against Which Their Founders Struggled' (currently unpublished, available at http://papers.ssrn.com/sol3/papers.cfm?abstract_id=2297278).

[66] See, generally, Fernandez and Dubber (n 31).

[67] Vismann (n 8) 84.

[68] ibid 41–43.

[69] 'Scrinia' are the 'leather-covered woven chests, cases and coffers' in which Frederick's files were packed; ibid 84.

[70] ibid 91–160. M Foucault, Security, Territory, Population: Lectures at the Collège de France (Palgrave Macmillan, 2007).

[71] Vismann (n 8) 122.

Files, finally, is a history of time, and of the origin of historical time. A definite ordering of time is embodied in the media and disciplines of recording and filing:

> On the basis of their material, the [Roman] media technologies scroll and codex determine differing concepts of time and law. Papyrus scrolls are linked to the purely actual, coextensive law of an imperial administration. In contrast, the organization of files as loose-leaf collections in connection with their independence from the act of writing predestines codices for the retroactive compilation of legal texts.[72]

With the invention of registers comes the ordering of documents issued by chronology.[73] Naturally one asks whether chronologised history has its origins in practices for registering documents. Just as potent is the identity of record with history and the distinct sense of time that recording produces. Time is homogenised by the ever-presence of recording: it becomes the homogenous empty time that historicism fills with relations among recorded events.[74] Given that it is record that produces both time and event rather than the reverse, and that changes in recording media changes conceptions of both time and law, *Files* renders historicism's emphasis on deriving the meaning of events—documents and practices—from spatio-temporal context suspect.[75]

The Making of Law appears, at first sight, to replicate *Files*' insistent emphasis on law's materiality. Bruno Latour's ethnography of the Conseil d'État (Council of State) opens and closes with material, visible, instantiations of the juridical: the first is the symbol by which the Council represents itself on its second centenary in 1999, a disembodied section of Doric column attached to the cornice of a classical building, which Latour describes as a 'fragment of power suspended in midair'; the second is 'the humble signature ... deformed, twisted, wobbling' that, once appended, connects statement to enunciator, completes the circuit of 'archives, texts and files', people and things, 'assignment and imputation' that is law.[76] In the space between column and signature, among 'texts, people, architecture, concepts, and everyday office objects', all carefully illustrated, all invoked 'to restore to [the Council] its materiality, its colours, its textures and its opulence', law is constantly visible.[77] It is patently visible as material object—the file (once more), which progressively becomes an artifact of legality in the process of its composition, journeying from office to office according to protocols of management, recruiting to

[72] ibid 43.

[73] ibid 79–83.

[74] ibid 82; W Benjamin, '*Trauerspiel* and Tragedy' in H Eiland (ed), *Walter Benjamin: Early Writings, 1910–1917* (Harvard University Press, 2011) 241–42; W Benjamin, 'On the Concept of History' in H Eiland and MW Jennings (eds), *Walter Benjamin: Selected Writings, Volume 4, 1938–1940* (Harvard University Press, 2006) 394–95.

[75] Vismann (n 8) 82. *Files* also poses something of a retort to Derrida's insistence on the irreducibility of temporality (see above, text at nn 33–35), although the retort is nicely camouflaged as a defence of Lévi-Strauss. See Vismann (n 8) 1–13.

[76] Latour (n 8) 3, 276–77.

[77] ibid 5; R Levi and M Valverde, 'Studying Law by Association: Bruno Latour goes to the Conseil d'État' (2008) 33 *Law & Social Inquiry* 805, 813.

itself an accumulation of texts for inspection and reconciliation, establishing the essence of law as 'a practice, a situated material practice that ties a whole range of heterogeneous phenomena in a certain specific way'.[78] It is also visible, quite distinctly, as the 'shimmer' that in the discourse of the counsellors identifies moments of law for examination and hesitation—moments for adjustment amongst the file's texts that acknowledge resistances and presage conclusion.[79]

Historicism might attempt to recruit Latour's ethnography as an instance of the social construction of law. Latour would no doubt demur. Describing 'the demise of society as a source of explanation', Latour writes

> the existence of society is part of the problem and not of the solution. 'Society' has to be composed, made up, constructed, established, maintained, and assembled. It is no longer to be taken as the hidden source of causality which could be mobilized so as to account for the existence and stability of some other action or behaviour.[80]

Society is to be explained in terms of its constituting networks, not explain them. In other words it cannot be context for 'socially-constructed' law. Historicism might simply amend social construction to mutual constitution, for Latour holds that 'law itself secretes an original form of contextual networking of people, acts and texts, so that it would be very difficult to define the notion of social context without resorting to legal concepts'.[81] Legality, then, is 'a way in which the world is assembled, an attribute … attached to events, people, documents'.[82] As Latour's description ('people, acts and texts') indicates, actor-network theory represents 'law' not as doctrine or decisional rule created by the designated law-makers (courts, legislatures and so forth) with whom we are familiar but in precisely the same way as 'society', as materially 'made up, constructed, established' by networks (threads) of 'actants', that is, people and things (files and their contents), their movements, translations and enrolments. Actants weave texts together. Law is 'delicately knitted lace', a 'spider's web', gaps held together by a fragile network of threads that 'stitch[] together the social'.[83]

If legality is a way in which the world is assembled, we might conclude (with Vismann) that legality is *material* agency. But as Alain Pottage points out, in Latour's ethnography law's materialities are wholly discursive. Law is 'a communicative or enunciative artefact', constituted through self-description, that 'precipitates from the material worlds of actor-network sociality by translating, reconstructing, or

[78] Latour (n 8) x, 76–77, and generally 70–106.
[79] ibid 159.
[80] B Latour, 'When Things Strike Back: a Possible Contribution of "Science Studies" to the Social Sciences' (2000) 51 *British Journal of Sociology* 107, 113.
[81] Latour (n 8) 260.
[82] Levi and Valverde (n 68) 806.
[83] ibid 813; Latour (n 8) 264, 277. Latour is so enamoured of his 'lace' metaphor that he fails to notice he has completely contradicted himself within 20 pages. At 243 it is 'the fabric of science' that 'extends everywhere but leaves a lot of voids, rather like a lace cloth', whereas 'the fabric of law has to cover everything completely and seamlessly. Two entirely different ways to cover the whole world'.

re-engineering the sociality of actor-networks into the dynamics of communicative or enunciative action'.[84] It is, moreover, pre-given. Latour asks us to recognise 'that law is … a mode of exploration of being, a particular mode of existence, and that it has its own ontology, that it engenders humans without being made by them'.[85] It is of interest to realise that by the end of *The Making of Law*, 'we', as EP Thompson put it in *Whigs and Hunters*, some 30 years before Latour and in inauspiciously similar circumstances, have fetched up 'back, once again, with *that* law', that 'rule of law', that 'unqualified human good', that 'cultural achievement' that we shared with others[86]—others to whom, Latour concludes, we can 'present ourselves with some self-respect' because we came up with this rule of law, 'a treasure to be cherished'.[87] And how does this law make itself apparent to us? As aura, as *nothing but* aura—'its reality is indeed to *precede* any enunciator, any speaking human'.[88] It is the counsellors' shimmer, '*quelque chose qui miroite*'.[89]

Pottage argues that this way of thinking—of law as that which stands anterior to, and connects, enunciations—is entirely too accepting of 'the lawyer's sense of law'.[90] It is symptomatic of an entire and diverse tradition of twentieth century inquiry into 'law' as a phenomenon, in that the existence of the phenomenon to be explained is taken to be 'too evident to require justification'.[91] And so he recommends that, rather than resort to theorisations of materiality simply to give substance to 'law' as a pre-given (presumptively differentiated) category, we attempt instead to imagine material worlds 'not always already configured into law, science, politics, and so on'.[92] Let us, that is, reverse direction, 'and instead of presuming "law", and asking how materiality should be configured to make good on that presumption' let us 'begin with the extensive potentialities of "materiality" and ask what becomes of "law" if we try to hold those potentialities open'.[93] This is to adopt the same point of departure that Schlag recommends, to ask how the 'difference' that constitutes law as a category of action is fabricated. His recommended course is Foucauldian:

> [I]nstead of presuming 'law', one would begin with a set of raw elements: texts, institutions, statements, gestures, architectural and material forms, formalized roles and competences, and self-descriptions (people often characterize themselves as practitioners or

[84] A Pottage, 'The Materiality of What?' (2012) 39 *Journal of Law and Society* 167, 173.
[85] Latour (n 8) 276.
[86] Thompson (n 23) 261, 266, 267.
[87] Latour (n 8) 277.
[88] Latour (n 8) 277. 'Aura' is a term in Benjamin's lexicon of literary criticism denoting the claim that a work makes to 'unique status based less on quality, use value or worth per se than on its figurative distance from the beholder … position within a tradition … inclusion in a time-tested canon'. See M Jennings, *Dialectical Images: Walter Benjamin's Theory of Literary Criticism* (Cornell University Press, 1987) 168–69.
[89] Latour (n 8) 157.
[90] Pottage (n 75) 170.
[91] ibid 179.
[92] ibid 178.
[93] ibid 180.

participants in 'law'). And, instead of abstracting to a field, medium, code or rationality in which these elements cohere into 'law', one would explore the ways in which elements are assembled into *dispositifs*.[94]

Pottage does not insist that Foucault is the only way forward. He emphasises the promise of the *dispositif* because it offers an 'intensive treatment of law that does not presuppose "law" as a basic social category'.[95]

IV. A Historical Materialism

Our substantive objective is now (at last) defined. It is to facilitate the intersection of legal history and legal theory by addressing Pierre Schlag's differentiation problematic through attention to the material fabrication of the category 'law'; that is, the fabrication of law's differentiation. This objective has been conceived in a departure from historicism, a radically dedifferentiating philosophy of history. Where historicism dedifferentiates law by deriving its meaning from its context (collapsing law into context), the objective here is to determine how law *emerges* in material practices that construct its categorical differentiation (which is as a practical matter observable). We can think of all this as a turn away from post-structural historicism, back toward a structuralist account of law.[96]

We must proceed, however, in a manner that also addresses the other problematic revealed in the course of our examination of historicism but endemic to historical inquiry in general, the problematic of intelligibility (presence). As already explained, history (like other empirical social sciences, and for that matter physical sciences too) assumes that its objects of inquiry are intelligible, hence in some essential sense present to the enquirer. Post-structural critique rejects the denial of temporality implicit in the assumption of intelligibility that renders being as primordial presence.[97] Contemporary historicism attempts to participate in the critique by emphasising the temporal particularity of context from which meanings arise, but cannot overcome the necessity that, to know meaning, both object and context must necessarily be intelligible to the observer. Historicism, hence, is no escape from the problematic of primordial presence. The proper solution

[94] ibid 181. *Dispositif* is Foucault's term for 'an apparatus, assemblage, arrangement, network, or device' that is 'an essentially heterogeneous ensemble, composed of discourses, institutions, architectural formations, regulatory decisions, laws, administrative measures, scientific statements, philosophical, moral, and philanthropic arguments … linked by something like a game, with changes of position or modifications of functions that can themselves be very different', which has 'in a particular historical moment been given the important function of addressing some kind of some urgent situation'. A *dispositif* 'has a predominantly strategic function, [which involves] a rational and concerted intervention in relations of force, either so as to develop them in a particular direction or so as to block them, stabilize them, or exploit them'.

[95] ibid 182.

[96] See above (nn 49–50) and accompanying text.

[97] See above, text at (n 33).

is to accept that in historical inquiry meaning arises not from context at all but from the image formed by the relationship in the observer's present between the observer and what is observed.

Walter Benjamin's historical materialism is a particularly potent response to both the substantive and the philosophical aspects of our inquiry, as I have now defined it. First, substantively, Benjamin's historical practice was uniquely sensitive to the materialisation of forms and relations in things—hence uniquely appropriate to studying the material fabrication of law's differentiation. Thus in his *Arcades Project*, 'I pursue the origins of the forms and mutations of the Paris arcades … and I locate this origin in the economic facts'.[98] Benjamin's prospectus for the book described an attempt to displace one materialised history with another. The *Arcades Project* was to be an assault on the nineteenth century's illusory conception of history, which represented the course of the world as 'an endless series of facts congealed in the form of things', from which it produced 'the "History of Civilization" … an inventory, point by point, of humanity's life forms and creations … identified for all time', a fixed and complete order, 'what has been'.[99] Benjamin would instead tell the history of the nineteenth century from a quite distinct array of things collected from his voluminous research on the arcades—'the rags, the refuse'.[100] His method was montage, the assembly of large-scale constructions 'out of the smallest and most precisely cut components'.[101] Montage began with 'the things of the world' and with the condition in which they actually existed—dispersed, confused, scattered. The historian as collector struggled against confusion, 'bringing together what belongs together; by keeping in mind their affinities and their succession in time, he can eventually furnish information about his objects'.[102] But the historian must also be allegorist, for the collector's collection could never be complete, and as long as it was incomplete it would remain merely 'a patchwork'.[103] The nineteenth century's conception of history was illusory precisely because it was a patchwork masquerading as completion. For the allegorist, history had always been a patchwork, always incomplete. Hence, the historian as allegorist ceased attempting to harvest information about things from their properties and relations, the alleged affinities existing among the elements of an allegedly complete collection. Instead he 'dislodges things from their context and … relies on his profundity to illuminate their meaning'.[104] His method was

[98] Benjamin (n 38) 462. By 'economic facts' Benjamin means specific manifestations of the economy which 'in their own individual development … give rise to the whole series of the arcades' concrete historical forms, just as the leaf unfolds from itself all the riches of the empirical world of plants'. Hence 'it is not the economic origins of culture that will be presented, but the expression of the economy in *its* culture': ibid 460.

[99] ibid 14, 883.

[100] ibid 460.

[101] ibid 461.

[102] ibid 211. Collecting was, Benjamin argued, 'a form of practical memory', a means of working free of the dream world of 'what has been'; ibid 883–84.

[103] ibid 211.

[104] ibid 211.

'physiognomic' or 'expressive'—he 'proceeds from the tangible object' and 'infers the interior from the exterior'.[105] For the allegorist, objects represented 'keywords in a secret dictionary, which will make known their meanings to the initiated'.[106]

The absence of any necessary relationship between the meaning of the object/event and its context or moment of occurrence does not render it meaningless or, therefore, indeterminate; as Benjamin's materialist physiognomics indicates, the object contains its own meanings. In his own words, 'The historical materialist approaches a historical object only where it confronts him as a monad'.[107] Here Benjamin invokes Leibniz's conception of the monad as the fundamental unit of existence, containing within itself all the predicates, both past and future, of which it is the subject.[108] Applied, for example, to a document or text, this idea gives rise to a form of history that considers the text as containing all its meanings within itself and therefore approaches texts not 'in the context of their age' but instead in a manner that represented 'the age that perceives them—our age—in the age during which they arose', thus rendering the text itself 'an organon of history'.[109] As Michael Jennings has observed, the contention is easy to misunderstand. It does not mean 'that we bring a previous age to representation in our own', but the reverse—that 'we bring the salient ... features of our own age to consciousness' by recognising their representation in the text to which we give our attention.[110]

The process of recognition is not straightforward. Because a monad contains *all* its predicates, the role of the critic/historian becomes essential, in that criticism (profundity) must complete the text's meaning retrospectively by revealing its pre-history and its post-history, which is to say its role in the pre-history of what follows. That is, criticism loosens from the text the meanings contained within it. It does so by 'mortifying' the text, not by evaluating or interpreting it as a thing in itself but by corroding it—rendering it a rubble of fragments such that its fragment of truth may be extracted from amid the material content in which that truth is imprisoned and by which it is obscured.[111] It will be apparent that one

105 R Tiedeman, 'Dialectics at a Standstill: Approaches to the *Passagen-Werk*', in Benjamin (n 38) 940. Or as Benjamin put it himself, the physiognomist became the 'interpreter[] of fate'. He 'seems to look through [the items in his showcase] into their distance'; ibid 858. He seeks 'the expressive character' of material products, 'of the earliest industrial products, the earliest industrial architecture, the earliest machines, but also the earliest department stores, advertisements, and so on'; ibid 460.

106 ibid 211.

107 Benjamin, 'Concept of History' (n 65) 396.

108 Tomlins, 'Materialist Jurisprudence' (n 9) 202.

109 W Benjamin, 'Literary History and the Study of Literature', in MW Jennings, H Eiland, and G Smith (eds), *Walter Benjamin: Selected Writings, Volume 2, Part 2, 1931–1934* (Harvard University Press 2005) 464. (By 'organon' Benjamin means 'an instrument of thought or knowledge; a means of reasoning, discovery ... a system of rules or principles of demonstration or investigation'.)

110 Jennings (n 78) 40. I attempt something along these lines in C Tomlins 'Constellations of Class in North America and the Atlantic World', in S Middleton and BG Smith (eds) *Class Matters: Early North America and the Atlantic World* (University of Pennsylvania Press 2008), 213-33, 305-13. For a more extensive attempt, see I Baucom, *Specters of the Atlantic: Finance Capital, Slavery, and the Philosophy of History* (Duke University Press 2005).

111 Jennings (n 78) 164–211.

sees here a repetition of the idea that context must be dissolved if what is sought is to be exposed. The critic/historian 'blasts[s] a specific era out of the homogenous course of history ... [H]e blasts a specific life out of the era, a specific work out of the life work'.[112] Out of the fragments of meaning amassed from the subjection of past phenomena to the critical process, the critic/historian constructs constellations—'large-scale constructions'[113]—new historical objects or dialectical images that join together what may be quite distinct phenomena, whose significance can emerge only posthumously or retrospectively, in a relationship with the now that has apprehended their significance. '[I]mage is that wherein what has been comes together in a flash with the now to form a constellation'.[114] One of Benjamin's most famous allegorical images, his angel of history, expresses this relationship. The angel's face is turned toward the past, which he sees not as a chain of events but as a single catastrophe 'which keeps piling wreckage upon wreckage and hurls it at his feet'.[115] Facing the past, the angel is driven irresistibly into the future by a storm blowing from Paradise. In this image the past is primordial—a *single* catastrophe expressed as an immense and constantly growing pile of debris; of, as it were, facts. The angel departs from that past while fixedly gazing at it, the lines of perspective on the pile of debris changing constantly as the pile grows and as the angel is blown backwards into the future by the storm.[116]

Theodor Adorno sternly reproached Benjamin for indulging a vulgar facticity that suggested an 'unmediated or even causal relationship' between the material and the ideational. Adorno saw nothing in his work but the assembly of a profusion of facts. Benjamin omitted 'the crucial theoretical answers' by 'blockading the ideas behind impenetrable walls of material'.[117] Only theory supplied answers. Benjamin's answer was simple and direct. 'The appearance of self-contained facticity ... is dispelled according to the degree to which the object is constructed in historical perspective. The lines of perspective in this construction, receding to the vanishing point, *converge in our own historical experience*'.[118]

The primary objective of history in this mode is not, obviously enough, to satisfy an imagined desire for an improved understanding of the past. It is, by

[112] Benjamin, 'Concept of History' (n 65) 396.

[113] Benjamin (n 38) 461.

[114] ibid 463.

[115] Benjamin, 'Concept of History' (n 65) 392.

[116] ibid 392. Note that Benjamin's image expresses an extraordinary tension between stasis and movement—the angel is 'about to move away ... would like to stay' but is driven 'irresistibly into the future'. This tension expresses the 'now' of apprehension, which is quite distinct from 'the present' or 'the future'. Every moment of the angel's gaze as it is blown backwards through time is such a moment of tension between stasis and movement, of 'dialectics at a standstill', of perspective at a moment of 'now'.

[117] T Adorno to W Benjamin (November 10, 1938), in 'Exchange with Theodor W. Adorno on "The Paris of the Second Empire in Baudelaire"', in Eiland and Jennings (n 65) 100, and see 101-03.

[118] W Benjamin to T Adorno (December 9, 1938), in Eiland and Jennings (n 65) 108 (emphasis added).

conjoining moments, building constellations, to create an explosively heightened awareness of the nature of the present. Again, in Benjamin's own words:

> It is said that the dialectical method consists in doing justice each time to the concrete historical situation of its object. But that is not enough. For it is just as much a matter of doing justice to the concrete historical situation of the *interest* taken in the object. And *this* situation is always so constituted that the interest is itself preformed in that object and, above all, feels this object concretized in itself and upraised from its former being into the higher concretion of now-being [*Jetztsein*].[119]

The resemblance between Foucault's *dispositifs* and Benjamin's large-scale constructions is striking. So, too, is the critical process—mortification—by which the meaning of the object of attention is produced. As Justin Desautels-Stein has argued, using 'political economy' (rather than 'law') as the object of attention:

> Foucault's goal was to describe the *structure* of something called 'political economy.' Foucault explained that in taking it on, he would assume at the start that there really is such a thing as political economy, a discipline with this name. But in going on to describe it, he would take nothing for granted. None of the historical landmarks, none of the divisions, none of the heroes were available: 'I shall accept the groupings that history suggests only to subject them at once to interrogation; *to break them up* and to see whether they can be legitimately reformed; or whether other groupings should be made; to replace them in a more general space which, while dissipating their apparent familiarity, makes it possible to construct a theory of them.' *Like his friend and structuralist Roland Barthes, Foucault wanted to 'demolish' the object in order to erect a composition of it.*[120]

Just as striking is Benjamin's image of the allegorist's secret dictionary of keywords, for this recalls nothing so much as Foucault's archaeology—the grubbing out of the rules of discursive formations, which in their turn recall structuralism's *langue*, the grammar underlying *parole* that historicism rejects in favour of nothing but *parole*.[121] Benjamin was certainly familiar with Saussure; his philosophy

[119] Benjamin (n 38) 391–2. Jennings comments: 'On the one hand, the theory of the dialectical image, with its redemption of certain moments of the past, does claim a certain veracity. In such images, the relationship of the previous moment to the present moment is *objective*; the earlier moment is a constituent part of the prehistory of the later one, the later one an element in the posthistory of its forerunner ... On the other hand, it cannot be denied that Benjamin attempts to reintroduce an explicit and conscious ethical element in history writing. The truth claims of historicism give way not merely to the different claims of the dialectical image but to the materialist historian's impulse to rewrite history in such a way that a purgative and redemptive political action ensues'. Jennings (n 78) 51.

[120] Desautels-Stein, 'Contemporary Legal Thought' (n 16) (emphasis added). In *The Arcades Project* (n 38) 470, Benjamin writes: 'It is important for the materialist historian, in the most rigorous way possible, to differentiate the construction of a historical state of affairs from what one customarily calls its "reconstruction." The "reconstruction" in empathy is one-dimensional. "Construction" presupposes "destruction."'

[121] Benjamin's commentary on Marxism's base/superstructure relationship (ibid 392) is particularly interesting in this connection: 'If the infrastructure in a certain way (in the materials of thought and experience) determines the superstructure, but if such determination is not reducible to simple reflection, how is it then—entirely apart from any question about the originating cause—to be characterized? As its expression. The superstructure is the expression of the infrastructure. The economic

of language obstinately (as was Benjamin's wont) rejected the arbitrariness of the sign in favour of a distinctly non-arbitrary, theologically-inflected theory of prelapsarian *name*. But name was the key to 'language as such', the meta-language that encompassed all of creation, uniting all material existence, animate and inanimate, with God, in one great flow of communication, from which Benjamin's own theory of language distinguished the postlapsarian languages of man ('prattle') in terms that distinctly resemble Saussurean *langue/parole* semiotics:

> After the Fall, which, in making language mediate, laid the foundation for its multiplicity, linguistic confusion could be only a step away. Once men had injured the purity of name, the turning away from that contemplation of things in which their language passes into man needed only to be completed in order to deprive men of the common foundation of an already shaken spirit of language. *Signs* must become confused where things are entangled. The enslavement of language in prattle is joined by the enslavement of things in folly almost as its inevitable consequence.[122]

Benjamin's historical materialism resolves both our post-structural problematics. It resolves the problematic of differentiation, in that it is a differentiating rather than a dedifferentiating philosophy of history, one that examines the fabrication of difference through techniques of demolition and recomposition of its objects of attention. It also resolves the problematic of presence: it does not pretend that meaning arises from spatio-temporal contexts in which the observer is not present but to which, somehow, the observer has access.[123] It proceeds dialectically, constructing the object of contemplation at the point of 'our own historical experience', where it 'comes alive'.[124] The two resolutions are conjoined in Benjamin's 'dialectical image'—a montage of fragments uprooted from their given surroundings and established anew as a constellation by the now that recognises the image thus formed. Nor is this constellation located in a primordial present that is indifferent to time. In Benjamin's historical materialism it is the past that is primordial, petrified—a *single* catastrophe. Dialectics springs objects of attention loose from the primordial past, turning them into images that can be read in the now of their recognisability. This is what Benjamin means by history:

> It is not that what is past casts its light on what is present, or what is present its light on what is past; rather, image is that wherein what has been comes together in a flash with the now to form a constellation … Only dialectical images are genuinely historical—that is, not archaic—images. The image that is read—which is to say the image in the now

conditions under which society exists are expressed in the superstructure'. In Benjamin's physiognomic materialism, the infrastructure as such was knowable only through rigorous inquiry into its particular manifestations. See also Tomlins (n 96) 216–19.

[122] W Benjamin, 'On Language as Such and on the Language of Man', in M Bullock and MW Jennings (eds), *Walter Benjamin: Selected Writings, Volume 1, 1913–1926* (Harvard University Press 2004) 72. In a somewhat similar vein (at 62) Benjamin speculates about the existence of 'a language of justice that has nothing directly to do with those in which German or English legal judgments are couched'.

[123] 'In Benjamin's theory, the context, conceived as a totality, dissolves, exposing the historical event as a radically unique fragment of time'. Jennings (n 78) 47.

[124] Benjamin (n 103) 108.

of its recognizability—bears to the highest degree the imprint of the perilous critical moment on which all reading is founded.[125]

The dialectical image unites Benjamin's historical materialism with his earlier literary criticism. Both depend upon the same conception, that meaning—of historical data, of a work of art—is not contextualist, but retrospective. As Jennings puts it, 'originary images from a previous time which are contained in the work of art become originary only retrospectively as they are integrated into a new critical constellation and finally read'.[126] In Benjamin's own words, 'the historical index of the images not only says that they belong to a particular time; it says above all that they attain to legibility only at a particular time'.[127] To attempt to determine a work's meaning by situating it in its times ('the social structure of its age') was therefore deeply flawed, for 'the appearance of this structure' and hence the work's meaning 'changes according to the various epochs that direct their gaze back upon it'.[128] The comment should not be confused with the historicist contention that the meaning of a work is always the product of temporal context and hence that meaning will change as the work's context changes. It is rather to contend that meanings can never be read from context because perception of context is historically variable.[129] Meaning can only result from the critical interpretive gaze that apprehends the work and, in separating its truth content from its material content, completes it. As with the mortification of the text, which allows the truth content of the work of art to appear, so with Benjamin's historical materialism: The 'critical momentum of materialist historiography is registered in that blasting [apart] of historical continuity with which the historical object first constitutes itself'.[130]

V. Legal Theory and Historical Materialism

At the end of the first volume of Marx and Engels' incomplete work, *The German Ideology*, appear fragmentary notes (on 'forms of social consciousness') for the

125 Benjamin (n 38) 463.

126 Jennings (n 78) 205.

127 Benjamin (n 38) 462.

128 Benjamin to Gisele Freund, in Jennings (n 78) 205.

129 'The events surrounding the historian, and in which he himself takes part, will underlie his presentation in the form of a text written in invisible ink. The history which he lays before the reader comprises, as it were, the citations occurring in this text, and it is only these citations that occur in a manner legible to all. To write history thus means to *cite* history. It belongs to the concept of citation, however, that the historical object in each case is torn from its context'. Benjamin (n 38) 476.

130 ibid 475. This passage continues: 'In fact, an object of history cannot be targeted at all within the continuous elapse of history. And so, from time immemorial historical narration has simply picked out an object from this continuous succession. But it has done so without foundation, as an expedient; and its first thought was then always to reinsert the object into the continuum, which it would create anew through empathy. Materialist historiography does not choose its objects arbitrarily. It does not fasten on them but rather springs them loose from the order of succession. Its provisions are more extensive, its occurrences more essential'.

intended remainder, among which one finds the following: 'There is no history of politics, law, science, etc, of art, religion, etc'.[131] This was a materialist conclusion, not an expression of frustration at the absence of source. As the authors had written in the first chapter's exposition of the materialist conception of history:

> In direct contrast to German philosophy, which descends from heaven to earth, here it is a matter of ascending from earth to heaven. That is, not of setting out from what men say, imagine, conceive, nor from men as narrated, thought of, imagined, conceived, in order to arrive at men in the flesh; but setting out from real, active men, and on the basis of their real life-process demonstrating the development of the ideological reflexes and echoes of this life-process. The phantoms formed in the brains of men are also, necessarily, sublimates of their material life-process, which is empirically verifiable and bound to material premises. Morality, religion, metaphysics, and all the rest of ideology as well as the forms of consciousness corresponding to these, thus no longer retain the semblance of independence. They have no history, no development.[132]

Benjamin noted the fragment. Typically, his own conceptualisation of historical materialism twisted its valence. In his essay on Eduard Fuchs, Benjamin notes Engels' reiteration of the deceptive 'semblance of an independent history of state constitutions, of legal systems, and of ideological conceptions in each specialized field of study', each as if containing within itself its own conditions of existence and growth.[133] Engels, he says, is first criticising the representation in each field of each new development as an extension of, reaction to, or overcoming of an earlier situation within that field. Second ('implicitly') Engels is criticising the representation of change as if detached from human beings and their processes of spiritual and economic production. Engels thus places 'the closed unity of the disciplines and their products in question'.[134] But does the exposure of closed unity's spurious heterogeneity herald its replacement by a materialist homogeneity as *The German Ideology* appeared to propose? Not in Benjamin's discourse.[135] Homogeneity was part of the illusion created by the nineteenth century's brand of history: 'the eternal image of the past' unalterable and always the same ('*wie es eigentlich gewesen ist*') was in fact the foundation upon which the closed unity of the disciplines sat. The challenge of the dialectical historian was precisely to that unity, aroused not

[131] K Marx with F Engels, *The German Ideology* (Prometheus Books 1998) 101–2.

[132] ibid 42. See also 61.

[133] F Engels, letter of July 14, 1893, quoted in W Benjamin, 'Eduard Fuchs, Collector and Historian', in H Eiland and MW Jennings (eds) *Walter Benjamin: Selected Writings, Volume 3, 1935–1938* (Harvard University Press 2002) 261.

[134] Benjamin (n 133), 'Eduard Fuchs, Collector and Historian', in H Eiland and MW Jennings (eds) *Walter Benjamin: Selected Writings, Volume 3, 1935–1938* (Harvard University Press 2002) 261.

[135] 'Historical materialism aspires to neither a homogenous nor a continuous exposition of history. From the fact that the superstructure reacts upon the base, it follows that a homogenous history, say, of economics exists as little as a homogenous history of literature or of jurisprudence. On the other hand, since the different epochs of the past are not all touched in the same degree by the present day of the historian … continuity in the presentation of history is unattainable'. Benjamin (n 38) 470.

to establish in its place a supervening and dogmatic *materialist* unity but rather to prise open the fissures that the materialist conception of history had begun to tear:

> So far as art is concerned, this thought challenges the unity of art itself as well as that of those works which purportedly come under the rubric of art. For the dialectical historian concerned with works of art, these works integrate their fore-history as well as their after-history; and it is by virtue of their after-history that their fore-history is recognizable as involved in a continuous process of change. Works of art teach him how their function outlives their creator and how the artist's intentions are left behind. They demonstrate how the reception of a work by its contemporaries is part of the effect that the work of art has on us today … [T]his effect depends on an encounter not only with the work of art alone but with the history which has allowed the work to come down to our own age.[136]

The dialectical historian dealt in history not as time experiencing its consummation but as a crowd of specificities—'the specific epoch, the specific life, the specific work' and so on.[137] By blasting each object out of the historicist's continuum—'the epoch out of its reified "historical continuity" … the life out of the epoch … the work out of the lifework'—each became instead 'a given experience with the past',[138] unique, unrepeatable, that destroyed the eternal image. Simultaneously, the dialectic construction of the historical process meant the sublation (*Aufhebung*) of each—'the lifework *in* the work … the epoch *in* the lifework … the course of history *in* the epoch'.[139] Specificities blasted out of spurious continuity did not fall to earth, as it were, but into new historical conjunctures. This historical materialism was materialist in conception, one might say, and dialectical in execution. Its materialism was expressed not in determining economic processes but in its attention to specificities (the things of the world that the collector collected); its dialectic lay in the allegorists's construction of the conjunctures into which those specificities fell once 'liberated' from the embrace of bourgeois history's '"Once upon a time"', the dialectical images 'in which precisely this fragment of the past finds itself with precisely this present'.[140]

Benjamin was not unaware of the demands of this conception of history:

> One must admit without reservation that only in isolated instances has it been possible to grasp the historical content of a work of art in such a way that it becomes more transparent as a work of art. All more intimate engagements with a work of art must remain a vain endeavor, so long as the work's sober historical content is untouched by dialectical knowledge.[141]

Yet his method created no 'tangle of mere facticities' to be mediated by theory (as Adorno had alleged) but an object fashioned historically 'out of the numbered

[136] Benjamin (n 118) 261, 262.
[137] ibid 262.
[138] ibid 262.
[139] ibid 262.
[140] ibid 262.
[141] ibid 263.

group of threads [of expression] representing the woof of a past fed into the warp of the present'.[142] The thread was in no sense an expression of a *causal* connection. Rather 'it is thoroughly dialectical. For centuries threads can become lost, only to be picked up again by the present course of history'.[143] Its dialectical character underlined, finally and crucially, that the exercise was definitively *not* one of reduction to material sameness. Thus, in arguing that it was the task of the literary historian 'not to portray literary works in the context of their age, but to represent the age that perceives them—our age—in the age during which they arose', Benjamin pointed out that the objective was to make literature 'an organon of history' not reduce it 'to the material of history'.[144]

Just as on these terms there could clearly be a materialist literary history, or a materialist art history, so too there could be a materialist history of law. The key in each case is the same—the nature of the entire encounter between history and the subject of history lies in the conception of what was being encountered and its presentation. For this we already have Benjamin's answer: 'a historical materialist approaches a historical subject only where he encounters it as a monad'.[145] The subject's monadological structure expresses itself in the confrontation of fore-history and after-history that makes up its interior.[146] Benjamin elaborated:

> The fore- and after-history of a historical phenomenon shows up in the phenomenon itself in the strength of its dialectical presentation. What is more, every dialectically-presented historical circumstance polarizes itself and becomes a force-field in which the confrontation between its fore-history and after-history is played out. It becomes such a field insofar as the present instant interpenetrates it. And thus the historical evidence polarizes into fore- and after-history always anew, never in the same way. And it does so at a distance from its own existence, in the present instance itself.[147]

Appearing at a moment of extreme tension between dialectical opposites caused by the interpenetration of the present, and occurring in the present instance itself, 'the object constructed in the materialist presentation of history is itself the dialectical image … identical with the historical object'.[148] The appearance of the image

[142] ibid 269.
[143] ibid 269.
[144] Benjamin (n 95) 464.
[145] Benjamin, 'Concept of History' (n 65) 396. See above (nn 93–95) and accompanying text.
[146] 'If the object of history is to be blasted out of the continuum of historical succession, that is because its monadological structure demands it. This structure first comes to light in the extracted object itself. And it does so in the form of the historical confrontation that makes up the interior (and, as it were, the bowels) of the historical object, and into which all the forces and interests of history enter on a reduced scale. It is owing to this monadological structure that the historical object finds represented in its interior its own fore-history and after-history. (Thus, for example, the fore-history of Baudelaire, as educed by current scholarship, lies in allegory; his after-history, in Jugendstil [Art Nouveau])'. Benjamin (n 38) 475.
[147] ibid 470.
[148] ibid 475.

was the moment of cessation ('caesura') in the movement of thought—dialectics at a standstill.[149]

The proto-structuralist valence of 'dialectics at a standstill' is as clear as its capacity to express how the object of attention has been fabricated, how it has been differentiated from context—'wrest[ed] from primal history', from 'the material of history'.[150] The concept gives profound point to the actual look of things in a frame frozen for inspection, and simultaneously makes that frame the point of access to the total event, the object at the moment of its recognition, forced to a halt. The historicism that was the target of Benjamin's historical materialism was the historicism of empathy, the historicism that wished 'to relive an era'.[151] But his historical materialism reaches out to controvert contemporary historicism, with its spurious location of meaning in the object's own time and place, as well. If legal theory is to turn to legal history it must do so with an awareness that the effect of contemporary historicism is to dedifferentiate the law that is legal theory's object of attention, and that the proper response is not to participate in the collapse of law into context, but to enquire critically into the fabricated conditions of law's differentiation. Materiality, and in particular Benjamin's historical materialism, provide means to engage in that inquiry.

[149] 'To thinking belongs the movement as well as the arrest of thoughts. Where thinking comes to a standstill in a constellation saturated with tensions—there the dialectical image appears. It is the caesura in the movement of thought. Its position is naturally not an arbitrary one. It is to be found, in a word, where the tension between dialectical opposites is greatest. Hence the object constructed in the materialist presentation of history is itself the dialectical image. The latter is identical with the historical object; it justifies its violent expulsion from the continuum of historical process'; ibid 475. 'Image is dialectics at a standstill'; ibid 462.

[150] ibid 393.

[151] Benjamin, 'Concept of History' (n 65) 391.

6

Legal Consciousness: A Metahistory

JONATHAN GORMAN

I. Analysing the Issue

I propose in this chapter to offer a characterisation of a historical approach in legal theorising, and will begin by addressing the assertion that some contemporary legal theories are informed by history and some are not.[1] This—seemingly straightforward—assertion involving the classification of legal theories is commonly presupposed by those who think that some legal theories are not informed by history when they ought to be, and is also commonly presupposed by those who think that some legal theories are informed by history when they ought not to be. The issue is not, at least not directly, whether this assertion is true, for that suggests that a 'true' or 'false' answer is in principle readily understandable even if not easily available.

Given the apparent weakness of the assertion that some contemporary theories are informed by history and some are not (for, as it stands, the assertion does not even tell us which is which and leaves open to multiple interpretations what 'informed by history' might mean), legal theorists' ordinary familiarity with contemporary legal theories might well suggest that a 'true' answer is obvious: highly probable and also uninteresting, its lack of interest matching the permissive weakness of the assertion. Taking the weak assertion for granted, legal theorists might well think that the 'real' issue should rather be whether legal theorising 'ought' to be informed, or ought not to be informed, by history. It would then seem natural that we ought to start by observing which theories fall into which camp and why. However, this is too quick a move: neither 'true' nor 'false' answers are readily available if the presupposed distinction between being informed by history, and being not so informed, cannot be clearly, even properly, drawn. Our first concern then must rather be with the *analysis* of the issue. We can engage with this analysis

[1] As made to stimulate contributions to the 2013 UK International Association for the Philosophy of Law and Social Philosophy (IVR) Annual Conference on 'Legal Theory and Legal History: A Neglected Dialogue?'

by examining how one would set about determining whether the assertion were true.

Ignoring issues of epistemological doubt, in everyday cases we ordinarily attend, first, to an assertion's *content*, usually something readily recognised by competent readers or hearers, and this helps us to choose what approach to take in determining whether an assertion is true. Second, we determine an assertion's truth in the light of that choice. For an assertion about the presently and immediately experienced world we normally recognise this content for what it is at once and can then turn without further reflection to our own present and immediate experience in order to determine its truth. In other cases we may need help: for example, while the least mathematically able of us can often recognise when an assertion has mathematical content, such a person, when there is a need to determine the truth of what is recognised as a mathematical assertion, nevertheless knows at least in vague terms where to look or what other kind of person to approach: an 'expert' in mathematics.

A similar situation arises in determining the truth of an assertion with scientific content, often recognised as such even by those without scientific knowledge or understanding: an expert on science is required. Yet in matters that might concern law it is not always clear to ordinarily competent readers or hearers whether the content of an assertion is a legal one, and they are uncertain whether to approach an expert on law at all. It is not enough merely to approach a legal expert anyway on the ground that a good lawyer is bound to know where to look for the limits of what is legal, for the problem is multi-faceted and more deep seated. For one illustration, 'you ought not to do that' might be moral rather than legal, and one might (like some politicians, lawyers and even legal theorists) be thoroughly confused about the connections and differences between morality and legality. In public debate, for example, there is rarely a clear recognition that it may not always be right to exercise a right. The nature of the content of this thought is uncertain for many and hence the kind of expertise required to assess its truth is also not readily apparent.

Moreover, it is not enough only to decide between 'moral' and 'legal', assuming for a moment that one can properly do that. Even if some expression's content can be clearly determined to be, say, moral, deciding its truth is still in various ways problematic. 'Truth' may not be appropriate for morality at all: perhaps 'assertion' is not what is involved with respect to the expression in question.[2] Indeed, it may not be appropriate for law, or even for legal theorising. But even if 'truth' were appropriate for morality, to which expert should we turn? Closure for our moral puzzlements or disagreements is not easily achieved when there is a plurality—maybe necessarily a plurality—of moral theories and metatheories and of people propounding them. There may not be a moral 'expert',[3] and it may well be success

[2] For example, following the meta-ethical position known as 'expressivism'.
[3] Despite Aristotle's view of 'phronesis', *Nicomachean Ethics*, Book VI.

rather than failure in understanding morality to recognise the plurality involved. Again, analogical—or identical—issues may be raised for law, without necessarily asserting or denying a moral/legal distinction; such issues might nevertheless impact any such distinction.

Alert to a range of such possible difficulties, and before we can assess its truth (let alone address the merits of the opposed views about whether history 'should' inform legal theories), we should therefore ask what kind of content is involved in the assertion that some contemporary legal theories are informed by history and some are not. The content of the assertion seems on the face of it to be factual: if true, it characterises some contemporary contingent state of affairs; if false, it is made so by contemporary contingent states of affairs.

'Factual' for us here involves a contrast with 'theoretical' in a sense that needs to be understood. One supposed fact/theory contrast should be denied, for it is not as if 'fact' should be conceived as 'pure experience' of the external world to be contrasted with the mere 'theorising' of our mental imaginings. Rather, we must allow that a sound understanding of 'factual' may very well require—in a neo-Kantian way—recognition of a priori elements of classification or conceptualisation as necessarily involved in any and every factual assertion about the world as we experience it. There are, some philosophers plausibly hold, no unconceptualised experiences.[4] Following them, we should not be taken to be asserting here a fact/theory distinction conceived as a denial of such a neo-Kantian approach.

The contrast between 'factual' and 'theoretical' to be used at this point is different: the factual content of the assertion about contemporary legal theories involves and is supported by an *observation* of those theories, and however 'theoretical' or 'theory-loaded' that observation may well have to be given a neo-Kantian understanding of its content, the assertion is nevertheless 'untheoretical' in the sense that it is not based on and does not require any *engagement* with the legal theories themselves. Here we understand 'engagement' as an investigation into the *merits* of the theories. In other words, engagement with the question whether any of those legal theories are sound is not required in order to observe the alleged fact that some contemporary legal theories are informed by history and some are not.

Given that the assertion that some contemporary legal theories are informed by history and some are not is factual in the relevant sense, the 'expert' we would then be looking for is not a legal theorist, assuming for a moment that a legal theorist is someone whose primary interest is in the merits of legal theories rather than with the mere observation of them; we need rather someone with the expertise to determine the answer to our factual question, and that is a *historian* of

[4] There is a long tradition of analytical discussion. Important works apart from Kant's include: W Sellars, 'Empiricism and the Philosophy of Mind' in H Feigl and M Scriven (eds), *Minnesota Studies in the Philosophy of Science I* (University of Minnesota Press, 1956) 253–329; WVO Quine, 'Two Dogmas of Empiricism' reprinted in his *From a Logical Point of View: Logico-Philosophical Essays* (Harper and Row, 1963) 20–46; J McDowell, *Mind and World* (Harvard University Press, 1994); RB Brandom, *Making It Explicit* (Harvard University Press, 1994).

contemporary legal theories. Here a historian is characterised in terms of appropriate expertise; we do not need to, and we should not, identify historians by, to give a proposal long discarded by theorists of history, their having only 'the past' as their subject matter. This hoary suggestion about the characterisation of 'history' should be rejected. Here the subject matter is contemporary.

Moreover, identifying a 'historian' as the required expert gives us at least one route into identifying what 'history' might be when we reflect on legal theories being informed by 'history'. Supposing, then, that the assertion is a factual one appropriate for a historian of contemporary theory, the expertise required to determine its truth may well seem to require those factors usual for such a historian: *historical accuracy* and *reference to historical sources*, conceiving these as involving a historian's characteristic skills in the use of evidence and those professionally trained abilities in analysis and interpretation which are appropriate to the contemporary sources involved.

Analysing the truth of the assertion that some contemporary legal theories are informed by history and some are not then suggests that we need to engage with a factual issue using the relevant skills of historical accuracy and reference to historical sources. Using those skills, we would be able to check its truth, and only when that was determined would we be in a position to address what was suggested earlier as perhaps the 'real' question, the merits or otherwise of legal theories being informed, or uninformed, by history. Would the same abilities or skills be needed to determine these merits as were needed to investigate the fact of the matter? At first sight, not necessarily; factual issues may well be separate in this regard from evaluative issues.

On the other hand, while we have identified historians as having the appropriate expertise to address the factual issue, it would be jumping the gun to conclude that a legal theorist is required to address the evaluative issue *using expertise different from a historian's*; the evaluative issue has not been analysed and any contrast that might have with a factual issue appropriate for historians remains to be seen. Just because, as we have seen, factual observation of theories does not require investigation into the merits of those theories does not imply anything about the nature of the expertise required to assess those merits.

In any event, we first must check the truth of the assertion that some contemporary legal theories are informed by history and some are not. This now seems plausibly to require, next, our finding appropriate examples of contemporary legal theory. That looks easy: most of us recognise a 'legal theory' when we see one. However, academic accuracy may seem to demand that we make explicit our criterion of exactly what is to count as a 'legal theory', for perhaps we cannot take that for granted as understood. In addition, we need, having found our examples, to distinguish the historically informed theories from the historically uninformed theories. Again, academic accuracy may seem to require that we also make explicit our criterion of exactly what is to count as one or the other. That, too, we cannot take for granted as understood, for it is precisely the nature of 'history' or 'historically informed' that makes the distinction unclear, even perhaps unsound.

As earlier asserted, a distinction between what are recognised as the historically informed theories and the historically uninformed theories is not essentially to be made in terms of whether they have 'the past' as their subject matter. Yet we now have a second suggested ground for distinguishing between legal theories: the historically informed theories are, and the historically uninformed theories are not, informed by the very criteria that we seem to be obliged to adopt in assessing the truth of the assertion, namely, informed (or not) by *historical accuracy* and *reference to historical sources*. Understanding 'history' in this way, we would in some way search for legal theories that were (or were not) 'informed' by historical accuracy and reference to historical sources, and only then could we evaluate the merits of their being so, whatever that involves.

However, this second interpretation of 'history' also needs to be resisted. While we might well need—whatever else we need—historical accuracy and reference to historical sources to determine the fact of the matter, it does not follow that a theory's being informed or uninformed by history must involve 'history' understood merely—if at all—as characterised by 'historical accuracy and reference to historical sources'. Theorists of history—who face their own problems about the relationship between the theory of history and the history of historiography—know that there is much more to 'history' than 'historical accuracy' and 'reference to historical sources'.[5] What else might 'informed by history' mean? What else *ought it to be understood* to mean, particularly in the context of legal theorising? There is a choice of answers and the alternatives need to be evaluated.

In any event, it is a mistake to think that all we have to do here is make explicit criteria that are presently implicit. Such moves offer only the spurious clarity involved in initially defining ones' terms, as if staking out the ground first were inherently unproblematic. The content of any such criteria is not, at least not at all obviously, itself to be *recovered* from the contemporary history of legal theory without risking some kind of circularity, while a priori justifications of the criteria which ignore the practice of contemporary history of legal theory seem merely speculative, quite apart from probably begging the question and perhaps being ad hoc or even ad personam. As WVO Quine put it, 'definition' has 'a dangerously reassuring sound'.[6] The quest for criteria has been said to be a 'Wittgensteinian obsession'.[7] At best any such criteria would be the outcome of an investigation; they are not the place to start it. Are the difficulties themselves theoretical or historical? Is there such a contrast? We need not decide here. There are prior difficulties to be overcome, whatever their disciplinary status.

[5] I address this matter in J Gorman, *Historical Judgement: The Limits of Historiographical Choice* (Acumen, 2007).

[6] Quine (n 4) 20.

[7] 'Isaiah used to think that the quest for criteria is a Wittgensteinian obsession': A Margalit, discussion contribution, 'Nationalism and Israel' in R Dworkin, M Lilla and RB Silvers (eds) *The Legacy of Isaiah Berlin* (New York Review of Books, 2001) 177.

II. Theory/History Distinctions I

We need a clearer understanding of 'history', one that can be used to characterise some legal theories as 'informed by history' and others as not. Is the expertise required for this itself 'theoretical' or 'historical'? Is there a theory/history distinction? It may be easy to slip into seeing academic jurisprudes as to some extent distinguished into theorists and historians. An elementary theory/history contrast, characteristic of its time, was particularly apparent by the 1950s in moral and political theorising, which strongly overlapped with legal theory on at least some interpretations of 'legal theory'. 'Theory' then meant (as under some interpretation it still does) *analysis*, and 'analysis' at that time, particularly in legal theory, characteristically sought clarificatory language rather than the answers to substantive moral or political issues. With respect to legal theory, HLA Hart's 1961 *The Concept of Law* and his and Tony Honoré's 1959 *Causation in the Law* are conventionally regarded as paradigmatic of such an analytical approach.

Apart from analytical clarification, from before the 1950s those wishing to address substantive political issues drew on principles found in Locke, Marx or Mill, for example. In the academic world, this required theorists of such matters to have a sound understanding of the history of political thought. Similarly, it was standard among moral philosophers writing in English to address substantive ethical issues only by recovering, from the history of moral thought, the views of (for example) Aristotle, Kant or the Utilitarians; in substantive legal theory Hart was influenced by Bentham and Mill, exemplified in his opposition to legal moralism. The theory/history contrast hence presented itself here in practical terms as the distinction between clarificatory analysis and substantive evaluation, the latter drawn from history.

In the first half of the twentieth century, analytical moral philosophers and political theorists alike often took the view that, independently of drawing on the past, they were not 'expert' on substantive ethical or political matters. Here I have used the word 'philosophers' as well as 'theorists', in order to use the descriptions they commonly gave of themselves, but any 'philosophy/theory' distinction that might be drawn was not seen at the time as worth noting; they were at one in agreeing that analytical clarification yielded no substantive evaluations. At that time it seemed that all substantive 'philosophy' or 'theory' just *was* history: reflection on the substantive works of past thinkers and the moral or political principles they had advanced. While we might gloss their works, we no longer engaged directly with the foundational tasks they had undertaken. Indeed, political philosophy (so conceived) was 'dead', Peter Laslett (as an observing historian) had said.[8]

However, the entire area of moral, political and legal thinking was revitalised around 1972 with the publication of *A Theory of Justice* by John Rawls. Rawls

[8] P Laslett, 'Introduction' in P Laslett (ed), *Philosophy, Politics and Society* (Basil Blackwell, 1956) vii.

redeveloped political theory in an analytical yet substantive way. Before long, his and others' philosophical pragmatism began to blur the distinctions that had led moral philosophers and political theorists to think that they had no substantive expertise. By the early 1980s 'applied' ethics and substantive intellectual reflection on policy and law had begun their rapid flourishing. By Rawls's time the theory/history contrast no longer mapped on the analytical/substantive contrast and a different theory/history contrast came into being, between those working in either analytical or substantive moral or political theory and those working to recover the history of moral or political thought, with the latter no longer authoritative of substantive results about moral or political principles and yielding only 'historical facts'. This new contrast is one still widely thought to apply.

However, characterising with exactness this later theory/history distinction is not straightforward. Was Rawls's a theory 'uninformed' by history? Rawls's analytical and substantive work certainly was, in one narrow sense, 'informed' by the history of political thought: the main opposition for him was explicitly Mill's utilitarianism, while his first major substantive analytical responder, Robert Nozick, famously drew on Locke. While these substantive moral philosophers and political theorists and their successors often saw themselves as engaging in an ongoing conversation with past substantive theorists in tasks they saw themselves as sharing, such a connection with the historical background of their thought may well be trivial in terms of our present theoretical issues because, using it, we cannot discriminate between theorists 'informed by history' and those not so informed.

This is because no theorising, however analytically abstract and 'unhistorical' or, contrastingly, substantive in its engagement with past (or present) reality, takes place in a historical vacuum. Indeed, it is arguably *impossible* for theory (understanding that here as equivalent to philosophy and indeed to science) to avoid being 'informed' by history in these terms. Hart clearly responded to long-dead John Austin on command theory, but he engaged with Ronald Dworkin too. Theorists all to some extent 'engage in a dialogue with the past',[9] however recently contemporary or far back they go. All theorists, even the most abstract or creative of them, unavoidably live in ongoing social and historical milieux and are validated in terms of their teachers, readers and audiences to address their matters of theoretical concern. On this understanding of a connection with history, there is an interim conclusion: it *must* be true that contemporary legal theory is 'informed by history'; all of it. Theorists all have to take due account of existing published work and without some form of such validation their work would not count as a theoretical contribution at all. The most creative of new subject matters is only so in terms of its recognition as contrasting with what has gone before.

However minimally or maximally substantive such a connection with history might be, we cannot use this to ground a theory/history distinction and we must

[9] See 'In Dialogue with the Past: Reflections on a Metaphor' (2014) 8 *The Journal of the Philosophy of History* (Special Issue).

look elsewhere if we are to justify the widely accepted distinction between those working in theory and those working in the history of relevant thought. Characterising any theory/history contrast depends in large part on what is meant by 'history', and the essence of this cannot depend solely on how far one 'engages in a dialogue with the past'.[10] Yet our earlier criterion is not helpful at this point, either: it is crucial and essential here to observe that, however much they 'engaged in dialogue with' Austin, Mill or Locke, the analytical *methods* used by Hart, Rawls and Nozick to develop their theories did not, or so it appeared, involve much in the way of such professional historical expertise as respect for 'historical accuracy' and 'reference to historical sources'. In this sense history played little relevant part in the test of their theoretical success.

It may nevertheless be thought that 'scholarship' was an essential part of their theorising and that 'historical accuracy' and 'reference to historical sources' were an essential part of scholarship. However, Hart, Rawls and Nozick developed their theories in a particular tradition of analytical philosophy that had cast doubt on this. A clear theory/history contrast had been accepted in much philosophising by the beginning of the second half of the twentieth century. Drawing on a tradition informed by an inheritance of logical empiricism, analytical philosophers often took little notice of past philosophers, while historians of philosophy often felt excluded from live philosophical debates. Most analytical philosophers, however 'scholarly', took for granted the irrelevance of history, including the history of philosophy, and commonly left this matter implicit and unexplained. Unlike them, influential analytical philosopher Peter Strawson, 'historically' informed by his own view of Kant and writing on Leibniz, went out of his way to make helpfully explicit his distance from historians' concerns and hence to make clearly irrelevant possible criticisms from that quarter.

Strawson did so by adding the following qualification to his discussion of Leibniz:

> [T]hat when I refer to the system of Leibniz, I shall not be much concerned if the views I discuss are not identical at all points with the views held by the historical philosopher of that name. I shall use the name 'Leibniz' to refer to a possible philosopher at least very similar to Leibniz in certain doctrinal respects; whether or not they are indiscernible in these respects matters little.[11]

Indeed, within analytical philosophising historical reference or accuracy became irrelevant to the point where thinkers *invented* their opponents: every undergraduate in analytical political or legal philosophy, as in analytical philosophy more generally, was taught to recognise the genetic fallacy, and if one was going to argue with Austin, Mill or Locke then one had better argue with 'Austin', 'Mill' and 'Locke'

[10] For further reflection on this see K Pihlainen, 'There's Just No Talking With The Past' (2014) 18 *Rethinking History: The Journal of Theory and Practice* 575–82.

[11] PF Strawson, *Individuals* (Methuen, 1959) 117. I have presented arguments relating to this quotation in Gorman (n 5) ch 3.

the analytically improved constructs rather than the original straw men (as they were often seen), historically real though they were. Yet for analytical philosophers the utmost care was taken with exactness of expression; 'scholarship' consisted in that and in respect for the other demands of logic also; it did not, however, consist in respect for 'historical accuracy' and 'reference to historical sources'.

While there were other traditions in philosophy for which this was not so,[12] a major element that then defined the tradition of analytical theorising in philosophy was its principled disciplinary and methodological *separation* from history.[13] Of course, one could, as a philosopher, have history or law as one's subject matter, but one would be standing outside that subject matter and using the tools of one's own, separate, discipline. Philosophy, characteristically understood at that time as, like all theory, *essentially* a universalising discipline, could not be grounded in contingent historical occurrences.

Descartes and other rationalists had thought philosophy could be completely foundational, but many analytical philosophers were ambivalent about this and some recognised the possibilities of historical change.[14] Those of a pragmatic persuasion thought that how 'foundational' theorising could be was a matter of degree.[15] We could then perhaps understand philosophy as tending towards the more abstract end of a spectrum, a spectrum that was perhaps itself historically changeable. We could understand 'theory' as ranging from abstract to concrete, from the mathematical or logical to the empirical or scientific, with nothing 'purely' abstract or 'purely' empirical.[16]

[12] We may think of philosophies with roots in German Romanticism, first flourishing in the late eighteenth century with Fichte, Goethe, Novalis, Herder and, in a sense, Kant. A historicist tradition developing by way of Hegel, a recent example is the historical materialism developed in the work of Walter Benjamin, for which see Christopher Tomlins' chapter 'Historicism and Materiality in Legal Theory', elsewhere in this volume. See also D Nassar (ed), *The Relevance of Romanticism: Essays on German Romantic Philosophy* (Oxford University Press, 2014).

[13] This is a summary of material in J Gorman, 'Hayden White as Analytical Philosopher of Mind' (2013) 17 *Rethinking History: The Journal of Theory and Practice* 471–91, where I address this matter further.

[14] Christopher Tomlins helpfully draws our attention to Oliver Wendell Holmes, Jr, like WVO Quine an American pragmatist, who 'invoked history "to tear down the suprahistorical foundations"—logic, morality, and so forth—of law'. See his chapter 'Historicism and Materiality in Legal Theory', elsewhere in this volume.

[15] See, for a denial as foundational of the philosophy/science, otherwise interpreted as the philosophy/theory, distinction, Quine (n 4) 20–46. While Quine's pragmatist philosophy may not look historicist, successors of his such as Richard Rorty drew out the historicist implications of pragmatism; see his *Consequences of Pragmatism* (University of Minnesota Press, 1982). For an account of Quine's 'web of belief' conceived in diachronic and historiographical terms as a rolling web of reality-sorting expressions, see J Gorman, 'The Limits of Historiographical Choice in Temporal Distinctions' in C Lorenz and B Bevernage (eds), *Breaking Up Time: Negotiating the Borders between Present, Past and Future* (Vandenhoeck & Ruprecht, 2013) 155–75.

[16] Legal theorists saw that, while like all theory it had to be 'universal', a legal theory could be 'philosophical' or 'scientific'. See S Coyle and G Pavlakos (eds), *Jurisprudence or Legal Science?* (Hart Publishing, 2005).

However, even those who thought in terms of a historically variable spectrum of theorising presented theorising, whether abstractly philosophical or concretely scientific, as essentially universalising in logical form, and so not to be grounded in contingent occurrences. Historical method involved validation from sources but what, philosophers would once have asked, could any historical work or source tell us about the nature of truth in law or objectivity in history, when such things were a matter of the general relationship between language and the world? In a variation of the problem of induction in science, they asked rhetorically how any historiographical exercise could possibly provide justification sufficient to meet the demands of the epistemological sceptic. It is for this reason that 'history, expelled from the body of knowledge proper by Descartes in part I of the *Discourse*, is still regarded with suspicion by his successors today'.[17]

History—ultimately and inevitably grounded in particular contingencies—could not conceivably answer the problems of philosophical understanding—ultimately and inevitably grounded in universalities, necessities and possibilities; it was inherently irrelevant. Philosophers thus understood with principled clarity that analytical thinking, however substantive it might have become and whatever degree of 'engagement in dialogue with the past' it might have achieved, was fundamentally a different discipline from history and that 'theory' could not be 'informed by history'; at least not so informed in any way other than the theoretically trivial because unavoidable 'taking account of past work' already mentioned. Many philosophers (even Rawls,[18] despite the then climate of developing pragmatism) sought to adopt a standpoint which, in the words of the very influential moral philosopher Thomas Nagel, offered a 'view from nowhere',[19] understanding analytical philosophising in quasi-mathematical terms as assessable independently of any historical context just as mathematics was supposed to be.[20] Many philosophers still seek that. On this understanding of 'theorising', far from the earlier interim conclusion that it *must* be true that contemporary legal theory is 'informed by history', we have a contrary conclusion: it was *impossible* for contemporary legal theory to be informed by history. 'Theory' appeals to the universal; 'history' appeals to the particular. You *cannot* draw the universal from the particular.

Related issues concerning the theory/history contrast were also apparent in philosophy of science in the second half of the twentieth century. Here philosophers

[17] WH Walsh, *Introduction to Philosophy of History* (Hutchinson, 1951) 12.

[18] Rawls's 'original position' is not a version of a 'state of nature' but a history-independent hypothetical construct akin to a Euclidean diagram in theoretical status. With respect to this point, Nozick—as Rawls said of Hobbes's *Leviathan*—'raises special problems'; J Rawls, *A Theory of Justice* (Oxford University Press, 1972) 11, fn 4.

[19] T Nagel, *The View from Nowhere* (Oxford University Press, 1986).

[20] See G Frege, whose *Begriffsschrift: A Formalized Language of Pure Thought Modelled Upon the Language of Arithmetic* was first published in 1879 (various sources and editions). However, see also D Macbeth, *Realizing Reason: A Narrative of Truth and Knowing* (Oxford University Press, 2014).

of science with an inheritance of logical empiricism sought to avoid reference to the history of science because it was seen as relativising science to its social or cultural background, so committing its practitioners to the partisan philosophical position of epistemological relativism. In a parallel but reversed way, historians of science resented and rejected calls from philosophers of science for them to keep abreast of the latest analytical thinking about the nature of science, involving as that so often did issues in mathematical logic and probability theory which were for the historians matters of historical irrelevance. For philosophers of science there was and still is a permanent example which sets the pro-theory and anti-history standard: all physicists know their 'Newton' and 'Einstein', but these are to be unhistorically understood in terms of the received scientific tradition as it is now. Like Rawls's Mill, Nozick's Locke or Popper's Marx, 'Newton' and 'Einstein' are in important part constructs for the sake of contemporary theorising in physics.

III. Theory/History Distinctions II

Our concern is to make sense of the assertion that some contemporary legal theories are informed by history and some are not. The theory/history distinction required for this cannot be a matter of engaging with past theorists, because all theorists must do this, and it cannot be a matter of appealing to historical facts or material, because no theorists can do this. The theory/history distinction is at this point of the argument understood to lie in the distinction between theorists working with 'necessities', 'generalities' and their cognates as opposed to historians working with 'contingencies', 'particulars' and their cognates.

Nicola Lacey in her *Life* of Hart observes that it has been 'pointed out that Herbert's argument is sometimes expressed in terms which invite confusion between analytic and historical claims'.[21] It was JL Austin who was the major philosophical influence on Hart in those first theoretical steps of his at Oxford, while Wittgenstein was less helpful. Lacey says 'The combination of legal experience and philosophical insight equipped Herbert … to make an original contribution to a field which was crying out for someone with insight into the social practices within which linguistic usage develops',[22] and she also observes:

> Wittgenstein circled—in the elliptical style which so alienated Austin—around a problem which Herbert himself never quite confronted. This was the precise nature of the relationship not just between language and behaviour, but more specifically between linguistic usage and the context in which it happens…[23]

[21] N Lacey, *A Life of HLA Hart: The Nightmare and the Noble Dream* (Oxford University Press, 2004) 229.
[22] ibid 145.
[23] ibid 218.

Thus we are asked to think of Hart as investigating a set of ongoing linguistic practices and we are perhaps to conceive that as investigating the ongoing context of law, where 'context' might be understood in 'historical', that is ongoing or time-extended, terms.

Yet, Lacey adds later, although Hart is often thought of 'by followers like Neil MacCormick or Joseph Raz as having had an institutional or social theory of law, his exploration of that institutional framework is relatively thin'.[24] Again, she comments, the reader of *Causation in the Law* 'is given no systematic analysis of the institutional, practical, professional context in which that legal language was used; in Wittgenstein's terms, there is no exploration of the social practices or forms of life within which the causal language game is embedded'.[25] Perhaps we should conclude—with increasing suspicion that this would be an anachronistic judgement—that so clear-minded a person as Hart was offering no more than a poorly developed account of such social contexts, a poorly developed contemporary social history.

Does proper linguistic analysis—a fortiori proper legal theorising, given Hart's approach—then *require* contemporary history? Lacey observes, 'Once the notion of "context" is broadened out, the inexorable conclusion is that illumination of legal practices lies not merely in an analysis of doctrinal language but in a historical and social study of the institutions and power relations within which that usage takes place'.[26] The 'but' here is instructive, for it leaves us with an analysis/history distinction that maps on what seem to be two ways of engaging in analysis: analysis without reference to that historical and social background (what Lacey has called 'context') and analysis with reference to that historical and social background. Is there such a distinction for Hart to have been confused about? Is the theory/history distinction merely a matter of how broad or historical the 'context' is? It may again be observed here that 'breadth of context', however ongoing or time-extended it might be conceived to be, has no essential connection with skills in *historical accuracy* and *reference to historical sources*. It is rather the time-extended nature of the 'context', that is, the social practices or forms of life conceived as subject matter, that makes the appropriate understanding 'historical'.

Elsewhere in her *Life*, Lacey describes how Hart found Harvard in 1956–1957,[27] where law was already discussed in what might be called historical context, with various views about what counted as 'context': thus Rosco Pound had introduced much sociology of law while Lon Fuller advanced historically informed discussion of the merits of the natural law tradition. According to Lacey, Hart saw that bringing law and Austin-style linguistic philosophy together was overly narrow and he came to understand that he and Honoré would need to develop their view

24 ibid 217.
25 ibid.
26 ibid 219.
27 ibid ch 8.

about causation in the law in terms of economic and policy 'contexts'.[28] She quotes Hart's *Listener* BBC broadcast on Christmas Eve 1957 where he said that, 'to many Americans', 'We [in Oxford] stand on the brink, wondering about the meanings of words, while they wish to plunge in and get the drift of whole paragraphs, or some large sense of general purpose, without bothering too much about the precise meaning of what is said'.[29] We should note here the lack of clear connections between 'context' understood as 'economic and policy context' and 'context' as 'drift of whole paragraphs' and such other notions of general 'meaning' or 'purpose' as may be available, quite apart from any further difference between these and 'context' understood as a time-extended form of life or set of ongoing linguistic practices.

Hart differed here from those he called 'the Americans' over how 'meaning' was to be understood and located in practical contexts, with Oxford narrowness contrasted with the American big picture. But Lacey's Hart did not notice that he was not characterising 'America' correctly: 'America' here could only mean *Harvard* where Hart was working at the time and observing the approaches of his immediate contemporaries; by contrast, Wesley Hohfeld of Yale had already offered in 1919[30] a way of theorising about law which, like Hart's, grasped and determined meaning in narrow contexts, one that Harvard people indeed found uncongenial to their own broader tradition. Yale man Arthur Corbin, himself nevertheless committed to the importance of some sense of 'context' in interpreting law, noted a Harvard-style comment in his Foreword to Hohfeld's book: 'Those Yale men say rights-powers-privileges-and-immunities as a single word, the way the rest of us say son-of-a-bitch'.[31]

Hohfeld's analysis of rights and duties is familiar enough to legal theorists. 'Chameleon-hued words are a peril both to clear thought and to lucid expression',[32] he said, and he disambiguated these notions in a table with a newly exact logical structure of four kinds of rights: right; privilege; power; immunity; and four kinds of duties: duty; no-right; liability; disability. Hohfeld said of this analysis:

> Eight conceptions of the law have been analyzed and compared in some details, the purpose having been to exhibit not only their intrinsic meaning and scope, but also their relations to one another and the methods by which they are applied, in judicial reasoning, to the solution of concrete problems of litigation.[33]

[28] Where 'context' might well have a different meaning from 'context' understood as a 'form of life'; it is not clear that 'ongoing' or 'time-extended' are essential to understanding it here.

[29] Quoted in Lacey (n 21) 195–96.

[30] WN Hohfeld, *Fundamental Legal Conceptions as Applied in Judicial Reasoning* (WW Cook ed, Yale University Press, 1919).

[31] AL Corbin, 'Foreword' to Hohfeld (n 30) x.

[32] Hohfeld (n 30) 35.

[33] Hohfeld (n 30) 63.

On the face of it, this might be just the kind of narrow-context linguistic understanding that, in Lacey's view, Hart had not clearly escaped.

Hohfeld's understanding of the meanings of the terms analysed is that they have an 'intrinsic' meaning, and are also those which are actually used in real judicial situations which deal with real legal problems. It is not obvious that they can be both; indeed, it may well be that they cannot be both, for 'intrinsic' meaning suggests a fixedness giving complete independence from time-extended contexts while 'real judicial situations' suggests ongoing forms of life that may change over time. There is a wealth of references by Hohfeld to actual legal usage in support of his analysis, and yet there are also a 'considerable number of judicial opinions' which, as he put it, 'afford ample evidence of the inveterate and unfortunate tendency to confuse…'.[34] Hohfeld, while certainly finding much in the law reports in the way of judicial support for his analysis, also *evaluated* the merits of legal usage by reference to time-independent standards of clarity and consistency.[35]

Hohfeld's theory was an attempt to summarise some features of existing and ongoing social—in particular linguistic—practices, conjoined with a recommendation that certain further refinements be universally adopted by his profession. While there are descriptive elements in his theory, theoretically these amount to little more than a reminder of how selected past judges or jurists had reasoned. Some of this reasoning was 'good' reasoning and some 'bad', by Hohfeld's lights, with his assessment being made not on the authority of the courts in question with respect to how the relevant meanings were to be understood, nor on what the courts counted as good reasoning in the contexts involved, and certainly not in terms of any kind of historical explanation, but on the basis of the need to 'think straight' in relation to all legal problems.[36] Much is stipulation; in effect, stipulation of legal *rules*, clarificatorily analysed to some extent later by Hart and others. However, while Wittgenstein's *Philosophical Investigations* stressed the place of 'social rules' in the understanding of 'meanings,'[37] it does not follow that the stipulation of 'rules' in philosophical analysis is no different from the recovery of rules in the social sciences or history, as Peter Winch suggested,[38] and this may be different again from the nature of rules in the law, where perhaps 'principles' or 'policies' are distinguishable yet essential, as Ronald Dworkin suggested.[39] However such points are to be followed through, the notions of the meaning, type or

[34] Hohfeld (n 30) 27.

[35] I offer an explanation of Hohfeld's argument in J Gorman, *Rights and Reason* (Acumen, 2003) ch 7 and analyse it in ch 8.

[36] Hohfeld (n 30) 25.

[37] L Wittgenstein, *Philosophical Investigations* (GEM Anscombe trans, Basil Blackwell, 1953).

[38] PG Winch, *The Idea of a Social Science and its Relation to Philosophy* (Routledge and Kegan Paul, 1958).

[39] R Dworkin, 'Is Law a System of Rules?' in R Dworkin (ed), *The Philosophy of Law* (Oxford University Press, 1977) 38–65.

breadth of a 'context', and how 'ongoing' that may be, are left undetermined and unexplained.

In his analysis Hohfeld was following a line of philosophy which would have been familiar to logical empiricists in the early twentieth century. It was assumed by many that ordinary or natural usages are inherently vague, and that any claim to exact knowledge which is to be taken seriously—enabling us, for example, to predict what courts will do—needs to be readily translatable into the terms of a rational model, itself best expressed in terms of a formal or mathematically symbolic deductive logical system, preferably classical rather than paraconsistent. Many legal theorists today work in often Scandinavian or Italian traditions of deontic logic which are theoretically independent of any social or historical context. Theorists of law might embrace this as the idea that legal meanings—like the interpretations of mathematical symbols—are in their paradigm form not subject to change, not historicisable, and some theorists might hope that the meanings of statutes and contracts and indeed the existence of human rights are like mathematics in that respect. The analysis of legal rules should then be like the analysis of mathematical rules, involving as Hohfeld wished independent standards of clarity and consistency. It is not in any helpful sense a 'social' or 'historical' investigation. It is likely that Hart saw his analytical work as measurable by just such a context-independent standard: 'legal theory, he insisted, was an autonomous intellectual approach in which philosophy was the appropriate disciplinary resource'.[40]

The philosophical inheritance of logical empiricism, deriving from Gottlob Frege,[41] involved seeking a language of persisting fixed meanings which was reliable for scientific and mathematical use. It was assumed that meanings can be made transparent with nothing but the immediate textual information. To work inside such a language is to work in something like an imagined mathematical space: the historian and theorist of history Nancy Partner has rightly referred to 'the counter-chronological world of philosophical enquiry'.[42] As noted, philosophical analysis was initially modelled on this approach, and many analytical philosophers continue to use it. It was and is assumed that the meanings of words and sentences are determinate and fixed over time, and that this assumption holds in mathematical, logical, scientific and, some theorists will hold, also legal contexts. Said Frege, 'It must be laid down that a letter *retains* in a given context the meaning once given to it',[43] and we need to observe here an essential metalinguistic element: any 'fixedness' of linguistic terms is a matter to be *laid down*. In effect, this is what Hohfeld was doing: stipulating meanings. It is not that the assumptions regarding the determinacy of language in some contexts are in any way self-evident, but

[40] Lacey (n 21) 191.

[41] For original material see P Geach and M Black, *Translations from the Philosophical Writings of Gottlob Frege* (Basil Blackwell, 1966).

[42] N Partner, 'Hayden White: the Form of the Content' (1998) 37 *History and Theory* 168.

[43] Geach and Black (n 41) 1.

rather a contingency whether the linguistic practice involving them has been so set up.

IV. Theoretical versus Historical Stances

There still seems to be a clear if elementary distinction between theory and history as illustrated in the following: theorists ask, say, if Hart's view that 'rules that confer rights, though distinct from commands, need not be moral rules'[44] is true; historians ask if Hart in fact held that view. Each seems to assess the matter in a different way. It is not a disciplinary requirement for historians to have the theoretical grasp required to assess the truth of the claim. It is not a disciplinary requirement for theorists to have the historical skills to know if Hart actually believed it. Both seek 'truth', but each seeks the truth of a different sentence: one seeks a truth about the relationship between law and morality, and the other seeks a truth about who believed what, and each adopts the most suitable method for the purpose.

However, do not both theorists and historians have to know what is *meant* here before they can proceed, so that their disciplines indeed share a common concern and are not so distinct after all? Yet, while 'content' might be 'readily recognised by competent readers or hearers' in everyday matters, what is 'meant' here is problematic: at its simplest, a theorist, in order to assess its truth, might ask what the *sentence* 'rules that confer rights, though distinct from commands, need not be moral rules' means, and will often think of that as a matter—like mathematics, as we have seen—determinable independently of any 'context'; the historian, by contrast, might ask what *Hart* means, and think that to be a matter that depends—perhaps even entirely depends—on the actual 'context' of Hart's saying it, understanding 'context' as including what is likely to be a time-extended dialogue or discourse which arose under certain social conditions.

However, we cannot rely on this sentence/context distinction of 'meaning' to give us a clear theory/history distinction. Often the views about 'meaning' are reversed: many philosophers will think 'context' is indeed essential to meaning (it is, after all, however abstract their understanding, the philosophers who usually propound such theories of meaning), while many historians (and lawyers) will think context inessential (some suppose, for example, that they can understand and interpret old documents, statutes, constitutions, legal deeds and other archival remains perfectly well without the need for any theories of language or interpretation or any grasp of the historical background).

Rather than suppose that what a person meant by uttering certain words was no more or less than the meaning of the words in that utterance, as had been

[44] HLA Hart, 'Positivism and the Separation of Law and Morals' in Dworkin (n 39) 21.

thought pre-war,[45] some philosophers of language developed 'speech act theory'. As explained by Strawson in referring to JL Austin: 'Given that we know … the meaning of an utterance, there may still be a further question as to *how what was said was meant* by the speaker, or as to *how the words spoken were used*, or as to *how the utterance was to be taken* or *ought to have been taken*'.[46] While JL Austin and indeed Hart did not go very far in developing the notion of linguistic context, it was clear to them that mere 'textual' meaning, as we would recognise that in Frege's or Hohfeld's works for example, was not enough. But merely 'textual' meaning was still there; they did not take the more radical step of holding that we do *not* know 'the meaning of an utterance' unless we know how what was said was meant, or how the words spoken were used, or how the utterance was to be taken or ought to have been taken.

With or without that more radical step, understanding language in this 'thicker' way required us to imagine a speaker-hearer situation or analogues of it, and the approach was notably applied to the history of ideas by Quentin Skinner.[47] Such situations can be variously described as 'practical', 'real' or 'everyday' ones, and, whatever the details of the theories of meaning involved, 'meanings' were certainly not to be understood as fixed quasi-mathematical objects appropriate for more abstract theorising. The philosophically often and variously used metaphor 'thick' suggests here some degree of temporal extension to meaning to match the temporal extension of the 'context' involved, with perhaps some opportunity for variation over time. This may well seem to open the door to a full historicising approach, but most analytical philosophers shunned any risk of relativism and did not pass through that door; they did not notice or think relevant any temporal duration of speech acts, usually continuing to suppose that the sentences uttered in such a context had some fixed meaning, while where they also had some 'wider' meanings—such as in Austin's 'performative utterances'[48]—they were thought to be atemporally analysable in such terms as an utterer's 'intention' or a hearer's 'uptake', notions which were themselves atemporally analysable. It was difficult to find analytical philosophers or even concerned historians moving beyond the temporally immediate where 'meaning' was concerned.

What was often striking about much theorising was that it involved philosophising only about the meanings—even 'thick' meanings involving intentions and the like—of those short examples with which analytical philosophers and speech-act theorists most characteristically dealt. 'Context' for many speech act theorists was very limited. It was as if our central concepts take so little time to think that

[45] AC Ewing, 'Two Kinds of Analysis' (1935) *Analysis* vol 2, issue 4, 60.

[46] PF Strawson, 'Intention and Convention in Speech Acts' in JR Searle (ed), *The Philosophy of Language* (Oxford University Press, 1971) 24.

[47] Q Skinner, 'Meaning and Understanding in the History of Ideas' (1969) 8 *History and Theory* 3–53.

[48] JL Austin, 'Performative-Constative' in Searle (n 46).

they are allowably analysable as if they take no time at all to think, so that, once we have got our theory right, their meaning is completely and instantaneously manifest. However, we have seen that it is a *contingency* how far meanings can be 'fixed' and it is a contingency how extensive is the temporally extended 'context' required for understanding.

While for a full theoretical understanding of legal concepts we would need, as Lacey put it, to understand linguistic usage in 'the context in which it happens',[49] from a philosophical perspective 'context' has been shown to be indeterminate: first, there is what one might think of as the *non-verbal* context in which the words were used. With respect to the traditional understanding of history, this might be assumed to be the 'religious, political, and economic factors' involved.[50] However, in our common law system, even the most ancient of statutes has to be interpreted according to rules of statutory interpretation which prioritise what the text means rather than what the author of the text meant. Only when the literal meaning is completely indeterminate might the author's (Parliament's) intentions or beliefs be sought, and even then any wider justificatory context might well be eschewed as a matter of substantive public policy: 'It was a public mischief, [Gladstone] said, to look beyond the walls of Parliament for the influences that were to determine legislation'.[51] In other words, we can *decide* how much, and what kind of, 'context' is required.

There remains the *verbal* 'context' of an utterance, where we once again concentrate on the text itself. In many cases the immediate text may still be taken as the primary bearer of meaning; indeed, perhaps the pen would never have become mightier than the sword unless this were sometimes so. Nevertheless, while we may well continue to accept the importance of, for example, authorial intention and other aspects of the immediate speech-act situation and so recognise that the text is not 'autonomous' in its meaning, in terms of 'verbal context' being essential we are to think of utterances as being interpreted, not as free-standing sentences, but in the light of *the surrounding sentences in which they appear*.[52]

For a full theoretical understanding of legal concepts in these terms it is a contingency whether we can limit ourselves to the immediate speech-act situation, or whether it is in some circumstances essential to analyse particular sentence-meaning in terms of surrounding paragraphs, or in terms of a 'discourse' where we have to think of some form of ongoing time-extended conversation or meaningful

[49] Lacey (n 21) 218.

[50] Skinner (n 47) 3.

[51] J Vincent, *The Formation of the British Liberal Party 1857–68* (Penguin, 1966) 260 (letter from Gladstone to Russell). There is a contrast between statutory interpretation and contract law. For the latter the intentions of the parties are crucial, although the text is nevertheless regarded as the best evidence for what those intentions were. Richard A Posner, thinking about the United States Constitution, says 'people who are sophisticated about interpretation know that text does not come first in any illuminating sense': RA Posner, *Overcoming Law* (Harvard University Press, 1995) 175.

[52] J Gorman, 'Objectivity and Truth in History' (1974) 17 *Inquiry* 373–97; J Gorman, *The Expression of Historical Knowledge* (University of Edinburgh Press, 1982).

dialectic,[53] or in terms of an entire text or genre of texts. Each of these presents us with a meaningful object of shared thought which inevitably has a duration well beyond the immediate and permits substantial change. Indeed, 'at any given time, in any given place, there will be a set of conditions—social, historical, meteorological, physiological—that will ensure that a word uttered in that place and at that time will have a meaning different than it would have under any other conditions';[54] this, however, is no more than a testable assertion.

Once we conceive the situation as involving an object of thought which has a duration well beyond the immediate and permits substantial change we are no longer in the traditional world of theory but in the world of history. This involves adopting a *temporal stance*, in that what one is thinking about as a historian is essentially mentally 'observable' as enduring, continuing, changing or becoming, perhaps with temporally distinct parts. A historical stance is a temporal stance, although not every temporal stance is a historical stance. This is because the object of one's thinking when one adopts a temporal stance may be something of very short as well as of very long duration, while a historical stance characteristically has as its object something which takes an indeterminately longish period.

However, one does not have to be a historian to adopt it, for it is an everyday stance appropriate to the experienced temporal continuity of our everyday lives. In order to think of what are traditionally taken as abstract atemporal matters like mathematics or logic we may have to be educated or trained out of this temporal stance. The theory/history distinction then arises in the world of *imagination* or *consciousness*; despite the Cartesian thought that imagination and consciousness are private to the individual, here they are not private but essential features of our shared world, just as meaningful language itself is.

Those theoretically inclined to traditional philosophical analysis imagine a shared world of meanings that are fixed (or at least comparatively determinate in any flexibility they are supposed to have). This unchanging world is immediately available to us at any and every point in time just because it is eternal, in much the same way as the objects of mathematics are imagined to be. By contrast, those inclined to the 'historical' imagine a shared world that is temporally extended and structured in terms of concepts that can cover change and can themselves change, even change in some revolutionary way.

Such changes are contingent; they structure *our* world, and we can change what we count as our world within limits that current pragmatic philosophy investigates. Our world is what we count it to be, and we experience it and sort it linguistically as time-extended. The beginnings of an appropriately developed theory

[53] Think of Robert Alexy's position, helpfully reflected upon in G Pavlakos (ed), *Law, Rights and Discourse: The Legal Philosophy of Robert Alexy* (Hart Publishing, 2007).

[54] MM Bakhtin, *The Dialogic Imagination: Four Essays* (M Holquist ed, C Emerson and M Holquist trans, University of Texas Press, 1981) Glossary, 428.

of meaning in pragmatic terms can be found in the Quinean web of beliefs[55] understood diachronically and not synchronically.[56] This web is a shared object of historical thought that has and is understood to have extended duration. Contingently, our language community has organised our ongoing shared world so that on the whole we can get on with each other.[57] This involves tacit agreement, analogously with the understanding of social contract theory in political science: we may be with hindsight deemed to have agreed with each other in virtue of our compliance with the ongoing relevant norms governing our shared language. The security of our understanding depends on such compliance, and is as little or as much at risk of evolutionary or revolutionary change as are our most fundamental legal or political institutions.

If there is merit in legal theory being informed by history, then it needs to be informed by history as theorised, by a philosophy of history. To imagine or think historically—to have 'historical consciousness'—is to think *contextually*, a view adopted by many theorists of history since propounded in detail in 1973 by historian of historiography and theorist of history Hayden V White, who had an intellectual influence far beyond his predecessors.[58] The characteristic mode of historical consciousness involves imagining a substantially temporally extended subject matter, a temporally stretched social context which can cover the past, which we can share as the experienced temporal continuity of our everyday lives, and which can cover the future.[59]

While it is true that 'at least some historical work is not particularly diachronic',[60] the world described and referred to by historians is inherently diachronic and the characteristic mode of expressing time-extended historical meaning is narrative; arguably, even non-narrative or 'analytical' histories[61] presuppose an object essentially structurable in narrative form just because it is substantially temporally extended. Narratives are normally how we understand and express time. Central to narrative understanding, according to White, are narrative plot structures which organise such historical contexts.[62] Narrative texts express historical consciousness,[63] that is, the appropriate linguistic structure to express lengthy

[55] Quine (n 4) 20.

[56] This is explained in the necessary detail in Gorman (n 5) and in J Gorman, 'The Presuppositions of Writing the History of Historiography' (2011) 59–60 *Storia della Storiografia* 198–208.

[57] J Gorman, 'The Grammar of Historiography' (2010) 3 *Epistemology and Philosophy of Science: Journal of the History of Philosophy of the Russian Academy of Science* 44–53.

[58] HV White, *Metahistory: The Historical Imagination in Nineteenth-Century Europe* (The Johns Hopkins University Press, 1973).

[59] I give further analysis in Gorman (n 15).

[60] See M Del Mar's chapter 'Modelling Law Diachronically: Temporal Variability in Legal Theory', elsewhere in this volume.

[61] For example, J Huizinga, *The Waning of the Middle Ages* (1924; Penguin, 1955). Compare RW Southern, *The Making of the Middle Ages* (Hutchinson, 1953).

[62] White (n 58).

[63] HV White, 'The Historical Text as Literary Artifact' in G Roberts (ed), *The History and Narrative Reader* (Routledge, 2001) 221.

temporal duration is the story. Not only is the object of historical thought temporally extended, it also takes time to think those concept or concepts only expressible in narratives, that is, it takes time to follow a story.

While both philosophers and historians invite us to imagine their different worlds as they present to us their objects of thought, it does not follow that what we imagine is *imaginary*. These worlds are not fictional. While 'viewed simply as verbal artifacts histories and novels are indistinguishable from one another',[64] the truth of the narrative content cannot depend on the presence or absence of such literary or poetic structures as it shares with fiction. As David Davies argued with respect to art, the 'facts about an object's or structure's history of making *do* play a crucial role in the interpretive appreciation and artistic evaluation of works',[65] and the same answer applies to assessing the truthlikeness of other imaginings. Just as it is the history of a painting's making that makes it distinct from a forgery (however outstandingly identical the forgery), so, for example, it is the history of either a geometrical proof's making[66] or a historical narrative's making that makes it distinct from a work of fiction.[67]

As theoreticians of law we may have to allow that legal consciousness is a form not just of temporal consciousness, for the time extension of that might be short, but of historical consciousness. Given that, what Hohfeld called 'fundamental legal conceptions' are not plausibly briefly summarisable in his terms but only analysable in an appropriate time-extended context-dependent way. There is a Nietzschean saying of such centrality here that another influential theorist of history, Reinhart Koselleck, adopted it as his motto: 'only that which has no history is definable'.[68] By 2001 one of the most distinguished twentieth century analytical moral philosophers, Bernard Williams, had come to recognise the merit of this view.[69] Referring to this remark of Nietzsche's, he said, 'This seems to me profoundly true. The values that we are concerned with here—values such as liberty, equality, and justice—all have a very significant history, and that history stands in the way of their simply having a definition'.[70] '[M]y own view is that the question

[64] HV White, 'The Fictions of Factual Representation' in RM Burns and H Rayment-Pickard (eds), *Philosophies of History: From Enlightenment to Postmodernity* (Blackwell Publishing, 2000).

[65] D Davies, *Art as Performance* (Blackwell Publishing, 2004) 23.

[66] See Macbeth (n 20).

[67] For more detail see J Gorman, 'History as Fiction: the Pragmatic Truth' in A Macfie (ed), *The Fiction of History* (Routledge, 2015) 13–30.

[68] EJ Palti, 'The "Theoretical Revolution" in Intellectual History: from the History of Political Ideas to the History of Political Languages' (2014) 53 *History and Theory* 389, referring to F Nietzsche, *On the Genealogy of Morals*, II, 13.

[69] In about 1971, when I was a PhD student working in the philosophy of history at Cambridge, Bernard Williams told me that the kind of philosophy of history explained here (and which I was then trying to address) could not be done.

[70] B Williams, 'Liberalism and Loss' in Dworkin, Lilla and Silvers (n 7) 91.

of how we should think about the identity and the structure of such concepts is one that philosophy has scarcely even addressed'.[71] That continues to be true.

In general, we should think of those forms of life that are characteristically legal as time-extended processes. It is appropriate as we conclude here to suggest, if only in brief outline, some points about the ways in which concepts that resist timeless definition in the manner so far described can impact on our understanding of law and so the nature of legal theories. One point that has already been clearly implied is that it would not be appropriate to think that a theory such as Hohfeld's, or even a sophisticated system of deontic logic, could be *true*; it is, rather, a conceptual stipulation about how we ought to think in the relevant legal terms, and its relation to the real world would depend on how far its stipulations were understandable and applicable in time-extended social practices. That would not mean only the judicial or juridical practices from which Hohfeld in part, and probably inconsistently, thought he was deriving his theory, since law has in broad terms to be understood by those who are bound by it as well as by those who apply it.

The idea of applying what may appear to be the same legal concepts at different dates also needs careful analysis, one that plausibly would require historical study. Those who are alert to the arguably inevitable fluidity of legal concepts will not seek to express a 'view from nowhere' about what form they take and what their logical associations and implications might be; they will not produce theories analogous to Hohfeld's, they will not seek to write constitutions that are intended to set principles in stone and they will not seek to 'gold-plate' interpretations of, for example, European Community legislation when that is often developed in terms that follow legal traditions where the fluidity, even historicising, of legal concepts is more readily recognised than it is in common law systems.

In order to understand 'process' better, we should remind ourselves of the distinctions made by John Rawls between perfect, imperfect and pure theories of procedure.[72] Perfect and imperfect procedures are explained by Rawls as sharing the same two-stage structure: for each, we specify, first, a situation which we seek to achieve, and for each we seek, second, a procedure which will enable us to achieve that situation. In a perfect process we have a procedure which guarantees the specified outcome,[73] while an imperfect process is less certain to do so. Importantly, a pure procedure contrasts with both of these because it is not a two-stage structure at all. We do not specify an outcome and then seek a procedure, whether perfect or imperfect, to achieve it. Rather, we merely specify a procedure, and the

[71] ibid 92.

[72] Rawls (n 18) 85. That the theories are of procedural justice is not relevant to the current argument and the position is treated in more general terms.

[73] Background assumptions may be involved; for Rawls's own example involving dividing a cake equally, rationality and desire-maximising assumptions are made.

outcome of that procedure is taken to specify what we seek no matter what it is, so long as the procedure is followed.

We could hold legal 'truth', involving in some clear way the legal concepts that we might initially find problematic, as specified by the outcome of a process. We could then seek a procedure, hopefully perfect rather than imperfect, for achieving that truth. However, given a historical stance, that is not the correct way to perceive the process. Rather, we should think of the process as a whole as specifying what *we count legal truth to be*, and the outcome of that procedure then gives us legal truth *no matter what that outcome is*. However, we cannot grasp this outcome as valid or meaningful independently of the process. Getting at a legal 'reality' conceived as independent of the appropriate process, or even solely the conclusion of that process, would not be available to us, on this approach. Suppose, to illustrate, we hold that 'dialectical exchanges constitute the essential component of legal procedures'.[74] Dialectical exchanges are time-extended states of affairs. We might think our problematic legal concepts are clarified in the outcome of the exchange, but a historical stance would involve looking at the exchange as a whole as an extended temporal object, with legal 'truth' constituted by the exchange as a whole and not to be specified merely by the conclusion of the exchange.

To exemplify in a slightly different way, a judicial decision does not give legal truth by itself, for the reasoning for it is an integral part; yet, trying to summarise that reasoning in terms of a ratio decidendi risks ignoring the temporality of the exchange. In general, summaries falsify with a spurious attempt at exactness: as the British empiricist FH Bradley (whose philosophical idealist holism was so close to Quine's pragmatism) put it:

> It is a very common and most ruinous superstition to suppose that analysis is no alteration, and that, whenever we distinguish, we have at once to do with divisible existence. It is an immense assumption to conclude, when a fact comes to us as a whole, that some parts of it may exist without any sort of regard for the rest.[75]

To learn legal truth, to learn the meaning of the legal concepts involved, is to learn the time-extended exchanges that alone constitute it.

It is a contingency what concepts are involved in a historical understanding of legal consciousness, but normative concepts are plausibly paradigmatic. Bernard Williams rightly concluded that 'how [such concepts] determinately work out in different contexts, in different cultures, in different societies, is something that will require a historical story'.[76] As legal theorists who may well have respect for the 'rule of law', we may prefer to value our secure compliance with the ongoing relevant norms governing our shared life and language and may well see that as requiring concepts that are, as Frege saw it of mathematics, 'fixed' in virtue of being

[74] G Sartor, 'A Teleological Approach to Legal Dialogues' in Pavlakos (n 53) 266.
[75] FH Bradley, *The Principles of Logic, vol I* 2nd edn (Oxford University Press, 1928) 95.
[76] Williams (n 70) 93.

laid down as best we can and not freely subject to changes. In so far as such concepts are *established* in our society, it is the stories or time-extended exchanges that express those concepts that are established. While contemporary legal consciousness and the theories that express it would then require historical consciousness, they would not require the kind of historical revision that is also characteristic of study in the discipline of history. That can be left to the academic study of the history of law, now clearly distinct from the theory of law even when the latter is 'historically informed' in the way now explained.

7

Modelling Law Diachronically: Temporal Variability in Legal Theory

MAKS DEL MAR*

> In the study of social facts what is needed is not a convenient technique for cutting down the number of variables, but a means of accommodating as many as possible.[1]

I. Introduction

This chapter seeks to set the scene for and offer some initial answers to the following question: what unique insights can be generated by thinking about law diachronically (ie in brief, treating law as an inherently temporally extended phenomenon)? To seek those allegedly unique insights does not mean that we can or ought to isolate thinking about law diachronically from, say, thinking about law comparatively, sociologically, economically, critically, aesthetically, spatially, materially, and so on. Indeed, it may be that thinking about law diachronically allows us to balance these different ways of thinking about law—the diachronic then being the framework within which we can articulate the largest number of variables affecting the character of law. But this possibility still leaves open the question: what is it that is special about thinking about law diachronically? Put another way: what comes into view about law only when one thinks diachronically?

As indicated, I will be offering some initial answers, but before I do that, I need to say something about how this question fits in to debates about the methodology

* Some of the ideas in this chapter were presented in draft form at the Centre for Legal Theory, National University of Singapore in May 2015. My thanks to Andrew Halpin and Nicole Roughan, and all who attended for discussion. Some related remarks were also presented at a half-day workshop with Brian Tamanaha (whom I also thank) at Queen Mary University of London in June 2015. My sincere thanks to Michael Lobban for many discussions and on-going support, not only with regards to this chapter, but the project as a whole.

[1] R Needham, 'Polythetic Classification: Convergence and Consequences' (1975) 10(3) *Man* 349, 362.

of jurisprudence.[2] This is because it would be difficult to expect insights generated by thinking about law diachronically to be universal in character—there is something, it seems, about thinking diachronically that pushes one in the direction of much more modest, necessarily revisable, generalisation. In this, thinking about law diachronically arguably goes beyond thinking about law empirically, at least where that means taking just one state of affairs at a particular time as one's relevant data. In other words, thinking about law diachronically brings along with it a greater modicum of theoretical modesty: when we study law over and across time, we become keenly aware of how difficult it is to generalise. This is just an initial comment—more will be said below, in Part II, about the place of this question in the context of the methodology of jurisprudence.

Having set the scene for the question, my next task will be to offer some possible ways of answering it: this is attempted in Part III. My aim here is to brainstorm the possibilities, offering as many avenues for future work as occur fruitful to me. I will do so by considering different kinds of temporalities, and offering some initial, cursory suggestions for how they could correlate to thinking about law. In Part IV, I then zoom in on three specific contexts of theorising about law: theories of legal reasoning, theories of the relations between legal traditions, and discourse about law, applying some of the possibilities raised in the previous part.

II. History and General Jurisprudence

I have chosen to use the term 'diachronically' rather than historically, and this requires some explanation. The first reason is related quite simply to my own limitations: to write about thinking 'historically' about law is take seriously the history of the profession of writing historically. This history is, of course, itself complex and contested.[3] Equally complex and contested are debates within historiography and the philosophy of history. A number of other chapters in this collection look more closely at the possible lessons of historiography and the philosophy of history for theorising about law,[4] and there is of course a great deal that can, and ought to, be done by considering where these bodies of literature meet (but by those more competent than I am in those domains!). A second reason, and a more controversial one, is that at least some historical work is not particularly diachronic—it does not analyse its object over time or in time, but instead

[2] I also attempt this, though in a slightly different way, in my introductory chapter to this volume: 'Beyond Universality and Particularity, Necessity and Contingency: On Collaboration between Legal Theory and Legal History'.

[3] See for example J Burrow, *A History of Histories* (Penguin, 2007).

[4] See the chapters by C Tomlins and J Gorman, as well as the chapters in the introductory section of this volume.

provides a portrait of a state of affairs at a particular time. In his fascinating little chapter on 'The Braided Narrative', David Hackett Fischer gives an example:

> The first volume of Perry Miller's *New England Mind* … has no narrative in it. It is a study in arrested motion—a snapshot, so to speak, of the Puritan Mind, and not a moving picture. Its architecture is of the most perfect palladian symmetry. It is divided into four parts, each with four chapters, none of which tell a story. Each of them is an analysis of an aspect of puritan thought, not as it changed in time but as it existed in a moment of time.[5]

Fischer's overall argument is that social history cannot choose between a-diachronic (snapshot) analysis and diachronic narrative—it has to combine both. The best history, he says, does exactly that. He urges us to recall the work of the Annales School, and their balancing of what they call 'structure' and 'conjoncture'. The latter term has no easy English equivalent, but means something like 'tendency' or 'patterns of change', ranging from '*la movement court*' to '*la longue durée*'.[6] 'Conjoncture' is a contested term, with some French historians confining it to a particular temporal model—cyclical—specifically contrasted with a process of growth or seasonal variations.[7]

The general lesson, for my purposes, is this: to think historically about law is not necessarily to think diachronically.[8] To think historically may involve providing a portrait of a particular phenomenon at a particular time—thinking diachronically could involve taking such a snapshot and considering links between it and subsequent or prior events (taken to be commensurable),[9] or it could of course involve questioning the very possibility of taking a snapshot.

What, then, is at stake jurisprudentially in thinking diachronically about law—in treating law as a phenomenon that is inherently, necessarily, temporally extended? The first point to make is that thinking diachronically about law may not be as absent from the last 50 or 60 years of legal theory as one might think at first blush. Of course, one's assessment in that respect depends on how generously one defines 'diachronicity', but consider these examples: HLA Hart's genetic,

[5] D Hackett Fischer, 'The Braided Narrative' in A Fletcher (ed), *The Literature of Fact* (Columbia University Press, 1976) 117.

[6] ibid 119.

[7] ibid.

[8] But see WH Sewell Jr , *Logics of History: Social Theory and Social Transformation* (Chicago University Press, 2005), who argues that although historians may not have often explicitly reflected on their constructions of time, the theoretical value of historical literature (his focus is on history's value for social science) is its implicit repository of different ways of thinking about time. Obviously, this requires considerable excavatory work of the kind that Sewell patiently undertakes. See also P Burke, *History and Social Theory* 2nd edn (Cornell University Press, 2005).

[9] This is part of the point of thinking diachronically: it forces us to treat certain objects as commensurable. Interesting insights can be generated from this, even if one ultimately concludes that the objects were not really commensurable at all. Notice, though, that it would not be enough (to count as thinking diachronically) to simply compare two snapshot portraits at different times: that would be to think comparatively, not diachronically.

imaginary tale[10] about the defects of a system composed exclusively of primary rules, which is designed to generate insights about the unique functions of secondary rules, thereby forming (in Hart's account) the central case of a developed, municipal legal system;[11] or Joseph Raz's idea that any snapshot account of what is valid law at any particular moment is dependent on a story about validity-over-time;[12] or Neil MacCormick's account of legality as a process of institutionalisation, changing as the thickness of institutionalisation changes;[13] or, more recently, Gerald Postema's attempt to convey the inherent, un-sliceable character of legal normativity, for which he uses the model of melody.[14] All of these, on a generous interpretation of diachronicity, incorporate some element of treating law as inherently temporally extended.[15]

And yet, there are two misgivings one might have about this literature. First, when it comes to offering general definitions or concepts of law, these and other jurisprudes tend to present them without any particular reference to diachronicity, for example the central case of a legal system just is the union of primary and secondary rules (rather than, say, a temporally extended process of 'unionisation'), or law is institutional normative order (rather than a process of the institutionalisation of normative order), or law is the practice of a particular kind of practical reason, and so on. Second, there is the issue of what is claimed for the status of jurisprudential insights about law: universality, or at the least such a high level of generality that it is difficult to see how it could ever be acknowledged to be misleading.

Let me, briefly, develop the second misgiving here. At one level, it might seem that there is no necessary contradiction between thinking about law diachronically and claiming a universal status for the insights so generated. After all, a concept of law that, treating law as inherently temporally extended, asserted that law is the process of institutionalisation of normative order could claim that we can only

[10] See HLA Hart, *The Concept of Law* (Clarendon Press, 1961); see also J Gardner, 'How Law Might Emerge: Hart's Problematic Fable' in L Duarte d'Almeida, J Edwards and A Dolcetti (eds), *Reading HLA Hart's The Concept of Law* (Hart Publishing, 2013).

[11] Compare this to, for instance, Bernard Williams' imaginary genealogy in his *Truth and Truthfulness: An Essay in Genealogy* (Princeton University Press, 2002)—it would be difficult to argue that this is not a diachronic approach.

[12] See J Raz, *The Concept of a Legal System* (Clarendon Press, 1970).

[13] For my elaboration on this characterisation of MacCormick's theory, see M Del Mar, 'Legality as Relative Institutionalisation: Neil MacCormick's Diffusionism and Transnational Legal Theory' (2014) 5(2) *Transnational Legal Theory* 177.

[14] See G Postema, 'Melody and Law's Mindfulness of Time' (2004) 17(2) *Ratio Juris* 203. See also his most recent general statement on the importance of history for jurisprudence: G Postema, 'Jurisprudence, the Sociable Science' (2015) 101(4) *Virginia Law Review* 869.

[15] Of course, I do not here discuss the efforts of the last few years, which have arguably seen a reflowering of 'historical jurisprudence'—these include the chapters of this volume, and a number of other collections (see the introduction and conclusion of this volume), as well as the forthcoming monograph by Brian Tamanaha. For one look back at important papers at the intersection of legal theory and legal history in the last 30 years, see M Del Mar and MJ Lobban (eds), *Legal Theory and Legal History* (Ashgate, 2014).

ever justifiably assert to see law where we see that process. For example, imagine that your account of institutionalisation links it to two variables: professionalisation and abstraction of the expression of norms. What you claim is that we can justifiably assert there is law wherever (and only when) we see a certain process[16] of professionalisation and abstraction—everything else is something other than law (eg bureaucracy, governance, administration, custom, convention or everyday morality).

Although such a claim is possible, it appears at odds—at least to me—with the temperament or attitude entailed by thinking diachronically (about law or anything else).[17] To think diachronically is—as the epigraph to this chapter suggests—to increase (if not maximise) the amount of variables one indexes to what one claims we can know about law in general. One can possibly imagine an incredibly complex concept of law that includes all the variables (about what affects the nature of law) that have been generated by thinking about law diachronically. But what is possible is of course not necessarily useful or workable. It is, therefore, at least more likely that, insofar as thinking about law generates a good amount of variables, the status of those insights will be modestly general (always revisable in light of new data) and only ever produce a polythetic concept, ie an index of variables (affecting, one ought to say, different characters law can have, rather than one nature) that one can group together in different and contingent ways. Thus, for example, if one's pool of variables includes the degree of professionalisation, the degree of abstractness of norm expression, the degree of systematicity of norm relations, the degree of population size, the degree of division of labour, and so on, then, in order to justifiably assert that there is law, one might require some overlap between some of the variables (but not any one necessary constellation of them).

Such a view arguably chips away at universalistic claims, but might still not be particularly threatening to them: one could still insist that there is universality in such a polythetic concept of law, albeit with some inbuilt contingency as to the particular constellation of variables in play. Therefore, one should—and I think

[16] Notice that it would not be thinking diachronically to say that there is a certain minimum threshold at which law comes into the picture—one would need to assert that there needs to be a process that occurs over time. This would also mean that there would be points at which one would simply be unsure whether there is law or, say, administration only: one would have to wait ('only time will tell!').

[17] See also the arguments made by Nicola Lacey as to how essentialism is antithetical to the very enterprise of historical scholarship: N Lacey, 'Jurisprudence, History and the Institutional Quality of Law' (2015) 101(4) *Virginia Law Review* 919. A key figure in any more thorough attempt to discuss how a historical sensibility affects, or should affect, a philosophical one is Michel Foucault. It suffices to recall, for instance, his stance on existentialism: there is no essence of a subject, just a history of subjecthood. Some might take this to be an anti-theoretical stance, but it is not: it is a way of doing theory that is historically sensitive. One contemporary scholar who has recognised this is Saskia Sassen—when she says, in her *Territory, Authority, Rights: From Medieval to Global Assemblages* (Princeton University Press, 2006), that her 'concern is not historical evolution but developing an analytics of change using history' (27), she echoes the spirit of this chapter.

one can—go further. To do so, one needs to show that—specifically in the case of diachronicity—there are multiple, incompatible or incomplete models of the diachronic. In other words, there are so many different ways of constructing temporality (of, we might say, 'modelling' it)—and thus also of saying exactly how law (or any other object) is temporally extended—that it is simply impossible to combine them. Each model will generate different insights about law. Therefore, conceptual fragmentation about law is unavoidable. And further, one might add, this is a cause for celebration rather than depression.

A die-hard universalist might still have an answer to this war-cry for diversity—they might say that the very possibility of such fragmentation depends on the universal claim that law is inherently temporally extended. But this too can be pushed back, though not without sacrifice: thinking diachronically about law is on a par with thinking in many other ways about law, all of which will be incomplete and partial, and sometimes incompatible with each other. Thus, for instance, some ways of thinking about law comparatively may treat law as inherently a-temporal (eg comparing some state of affairs at time x with a state of affairs at time y, with no temporal relation between them), and this will be incompatible with thinking about law as something that cannot be described at a particular time but only over time. But, of course, this requires one to assert the contingent value of insights generated by thinking about law diachronically—and why not? To be scared of reaching this conclusion means that one is somehow denigrating insights reached by contingently valuable methods—but only a universalist would be scared of such a conclusion. There is, one might say, diversity, contingency, theoretical humility the whole way, up and down!

One final word on the link between diachronicity and the methodology of jurisprudence: why, one might ask, cannot one go the whole way to particularism, and say that there really are no grounds for claiming any level of generality for one's insights? Instead, what we can only have are particular descriptions generated by any one constellation of thinking about law (imagine a constellation comprised of thinking about law diachronically, aesthetically and materially) and the particular models of those ways of thinking (ie a particular model of the diachronic, aesthetic and material). Here, I think, we must argue that it is possible—and desirable—to reach a certain middle ground between the universalist and the particularist. This middle ground is the modest generalist: someone who realises their theoretical tools are only ever instantiated in particular descriptions, but one who also realises that it is useful (even if ultimately somewhat fictional) to think that theoretical tools can potentially travel from any one description to another (at least until they prove to no longer be useful). A full defence of such an admittedly ambiguous methodological stance must await another day,[18] but I wager that it is a stance that will have much to do with pragmatically-grounded fictionalist modelling as a viable methodology not only in legal theory, but in science and other domains of

[18] Again, I say more about it in my opening chapter (n 2).

intellectual endeavour.[19] Anticipating such a full defence, I use for the remainder of this chapter, and as signalled in the title, the terminology of 'modelling'.

III. Varieties of Temporality

My aim in this part of the chapter is to brainstorm—admittedly very impressionistically—different ways of constructing time, or put differently, to identify different factors thanks to which different constructions of temporality can be proposed. In so doing, I am avoiding the temptation to offer a review of the possibilities already identified in the scholarship on time,[20] including previous attempted classifications of time in legal scholarship.[21] This exercise would no doubt need to be done more rigorously and systematically—but, as I hope to show, even if done impressionistically (and thus also without any claim to originality), there are potential fruits to be garnered.

Perhaps the first factor to consider is what we might call 'the shape of time', that is how one spatialises temporality, including whether one constructs it as linear or cyclical or any other shape (eg zigzagging or cascading). An illustration of an effective use of the cyclical shape of time in recent historical work is Charles Tilly's idea that there is a cycle of extraction-coercion that is repeated over and over, resulting in ever-greater centralisation of political power (and comprising, ultimately, the

[19] Much of this has been inspired by H Vaihinger's, *The Philosophy of 'As If'*' (trans CK Ogden, Brace and Company, 1925).

[20] This includes philosophies of time, naturally, but also analyses of time in literary criticism—see, eg M Sternberg, *Expositional Modes and Temporal Ordering in Fiction* (Indiana University Press, 1978), and of course the work of Mikhail Bakhtin.

[21] There is a sizeable literature on relations between time and law, including in different areas of the law. I am not discussing this literature here as it is more about time in law, or about how particular laws or areas of law construct time—and not about the possibility of theorising about law diachronically. Nevertheless, there is no doubt that some of this literature would be useful in further developing the implications of diachronic sensitivity for general jurisprudence. Consider, for example, the classifications of time offered by R French, 'Time in the Law' (2001) 72 *University of Colorado Law Review* 663; and AJ Wistrich, 'The Evolving Temporality of Lawmaking' (2012) 44(3) *Connecticut Law Review* 737. French proposed a classification based on 1) attributes (eg whether time is a social construction and is culturally-dependent); 2) forms (eg industrial time, transcendent time, physicists' time); and 3) models of time (eg linear, bipolar, cyclical). Wistrich, in turn, spoke of the different 1) directions; 2) speeds; and 3) purposes of time. A particularly interesting application—and an example of a case of thinking about law both diachronically and ethnographically—is the von Benda-Beckmanns' notion of how some rules and principles 'linger on … beyond their formal validity as remembered concepts, standards or rules' (F von Benda-Beckmann, 'Trust and the Temporalities of Law' (2014) 46(1) *The Journal of Legal Pluralism and Unofficial Law* 1, 5; and see F and K von Benda-Beckmann, 'The Dynamics and Change and Continuity in Plural Legal Orders' (2006) 53–54 *The Journal of Legal Pluralism and Unofficial Law* 1. This notion of 'lingering on' can reveal the limitations of a general jurisprudence that has too rigid a definition of validity. See also the papers in J Bjarup and M Blegvad (eds), *Time, Law and Society* (Steiner, 1995).

state).[22] This is a cycle in which armies are set up, the cost of which requires imposition taxes, which in turn requires armies to enforce the tax collection. Indeed, and thus looking ahead, one can see this model as the combination of three factors: shape (cyclical), speed (variable, but accelerating), and degree of occurrence (the cycle is repeated).

A second factor is indeed speed. The first choice here would be whether it is variable or stable—for example consider the difference between an account of the process of professionalisation that presents it as starting out slowly, but then accelerating over time, and one that sees it as being set up swiftly but taking a long time for a culture of professionalisation to set in. The second choice has already been mentioned: literally the speed of the process, whether fast or slow, or however one cuts up the cake of speed. It is important to see the potential rewards of a rich language of speed: think, for instance, of the work by terms such as 'gradual' and 'incremental' in the histories of the common law.

A third factor is the degree of occurrence: whatever the variable one is working with may be (eg degree of abstraction in the expression of norms), does one see it as recurring or as only occurring once? In the case of some variables, even asking this question can be helpful, for example in the case of abstraction, one might, in the face of this question, allow for a model of legal development in which some parts of the law have achieved a certain level of abstraction while others have not, pushing further to identify causes for the differences in abstraction.

A fourth factor will be the direction of time: is one committed to progression, or does one allow for regression, and if so, does one allow for a complex mixture of the two ('two steps forward, one step back')?[23] The difference that allowing for regression can make is considerable—think, for instance, of the dynamics of juridication and de-juridification, or criminalisation and de-criminalisation.[24] Again, one can combine this factor with others: for example with speed, where one can have a model in which criminalisation is quick, but de-criminalisation is slow. Allowing regression is, of course, vital if one takes seriously (as one should) claims about Western bias in comparative and world histories of yore—including in sociologically-sophisticated histories of law (such as Max Weber's, and the histories produced by thinkers in the Scottish Enlightenment).

A fifth factor—related to speed, but not quite the same—is duration. This factor can also be thought of as a matter of temporal framing or lensing. Thus, does one focus on relatively short-term, temporally-bounded events (a micro frame or lens) and the links between them, or does one look more macro, at temporally-extended

[22] See C Tilly, *Coercion, Capital and European States AD 990–1990* (Wiley-Blackwell, 1990).

[23] Indeed, constructing time in these various ways is a bit like choreography. There might, then, be scope for an interesting multi-disciplinary study at the crossroads of dance, music and a diachronically-sensitive legal theory.

[24] Another way to make the point is that this factor picks up on the difference between a model of change (which allows for regression) and a model of development (which does not).

processes that take longer (the way, say, the anger of the masses 'festers'), or even longer than that (eg certain climate conditions, say, or the existence of a document whether relied upon or not). One is inevitably reminded here of the work of Fernand Braudel, who offered the long term of geo-history, the medium term of economic systems, states, societies and civilisations, and finally the short term of events.[25] The application of this factor can be quite dramatic in the legal context: think, for instance, of the idea that law is something that takes time (let us say, a long time) to make. This might make one look closely at minutiae of practice not normally paid attention to, for example the lifecycle of certain documents in the process of making law.[26] Or, thinking in terms of duration (and thus temporally extending processes one normally takes to have happened in an instant) might make one see the importance of something one would not otherwise have noticed, for example if one pays attention to how long it took to write certain legal documents, one might see the importance of the training of certain legal officials in certain cultures in calligraphy (which in turn brings to the fore the aesthetic dimensions of lawmaking).

A sixth factor will be how subjectively, phenomenologically or perspectivally, one approaches time. One can see this at work, for example, in the context of the factor of direction: does one's model include awareness on behalf of the relevant actors that one is approaching something or working towards something? For instance, AJ Arnaud has spoken of the '*avant dire-droit*' character of certain norms in the global context, ie the sense in which certain norms are taken to be 'waiting' for their classification or labelling as law.[27] Roger Cotterrell has suggested that this should make us think of the broader category of the 'juridical', as distinct say from the 'valid', but either way, it seems productive, especially in the transnational context, to think of some norms being 'nearly legal', queuing up before the gates of legality.[28] Perhaps one could flip this around as well: think of norms thought of as legal, but also considered to be on their way out—out-dated, outworn, nearly non-legal norms. This is but one example of incorporating phenomenological factors into one's constructions of time, and the examples here can be easily multiplied: for example many thinkers have argued that we ought to think of time via certain cultural references, such as 'bucolic time' (contrast that with 'London time'), or 'summer time' (and contrast that with 'English summer time'!). Analytically, it may be that one can seek to break these down into the above categories (eg bucolic time is slower and London time is frantic; and the 'legal' / 'nearly legal' / 'nearly not legal' can perhaps be broken down into duration, as to whether it is short and

[25] See Burke (n 8) 158.

[26] See B Latour, *The Making of Law* (trans M Brilman and A Pottage, Polity, 2010).

[27] AJ Arnaud, *Critique de la raison juridique 1. Où va la sociologie du droit?* (LGDJ, 1981) 369–87. See also AJ Arnaud, 'From Limited Realism to Plural Law: Normative Approach versus Cultural Perspective' (1998) 11 *Ratio Juris* 246. I thank Roger Cotterrell for these references.

[28] See R Cotterrell, 'Transnational Communities and the Concept of Law' (2008) 21(1) *Ratio Juris* 1, 10.

provisional, or long and persistent) but it may very well be that something (precisely phenomenological) is lost in such an analytical deconstruction.[29]

This is just a rough indicative list, but one can see how things can become very complex very quickly. For example, one can model the temporality of the variable of professionalisation in one way, and the variable of the abstraction of norm expression in another way, and include them both in one (necessarily incomplete) diachronic model of law. One can run certain variables at the same speed, and others at different speeds. One can say some regress, while others can only be thought of as uni-directionally developmental. Each particular constellation of variables, including each particular temporalisation of the variables in any one constellation, will thereby count as a different model of law—and will generate different descriptions, and thus offer different insights about law.

To add to this complexity, one might need to notice that variables themselves can come in different kinds. It is relatively easy to see how a variable such as population size or even professionalisation can come in degrees. With other variables, that is less easy, for example think of technology or a mode of production.[30] Thus, if one includes in one's model both kinds of variables—ie variables of degree, and variables of kind—then each might be more susceptible to different kinds of temporalisation.[31]

Consider, also, variables such as the following, commonly taken into account in general jurisprudence: law's relations to morality and power. Thus, it is common to see a legal theorist proceeding on the basis that a concept of law will be yielded by articulating in what way law differs from—even if in some other ways it resembles—morality and power. Neil MacCormick, for instance, conceives of law as institutional normative order, thereby distinguishing it but also relating it to both morality (which is normative but not institutional) and power (which is institutional but not normative). What MacCormick does not do—and in this he is hardly alone—is consider whether those relations between law, morality and power ought to be modelled temporally. He treats them, instead, as timeless, universally applicable to all times and places. By contrast, we might ask, are there times—let us say at the outset of a legal system—where law is closer to morality (and thus more normative than it is institutional) and more distant from power, and times (later down the line, say) when it is the other way round (and when, thus, law is quite removed from the everyday morality of a community, or lags

[29] See recently M Valverde, *Chronotopes of Law* (Routledge, 2014), drawing on Mikhail Bakhtin. There are close links here with literary criticism.

[30] Arguably, it is easier to see how one can have different kinds of technology—writing / printing / digital—and harder to think of technology as a matter of degree.

[31] I am not, however, sure whether this distinction holds up. Perhaps any variable of kind can be broken down into a variable of degree. Think of the technology of writing: we can translate it into degrees of literacy in which we include moving from basic ability to communicate to the ability to communicate elegantly.

behind it)? Of course, to make this rather banal point is not to suggest that these are the only relations one might consider—we can imagine a model of law where law's relations with religion, the environment, fashion, literature and others are all taken into account, and all constructed temporally in different ways.

I hope I have here given a glimpse into the possibilities, which are astoundingly rich. The point I want to stress—and that I need to stress given what was said in the first part—is that many (if not all) of these choices (which variables, how to temporalise them) will generate very different descriptions, and therefore also very different insights about law. Thus it seems to me we have to bite the bullet and accept the necessary incompleteness of models of law, and thus the contingent value of any insights generated by thinking diachronically about law.

IV. Applications: Reasoning, Relations, Discourse

I have already, in the third part, offered some very initial, cursory applications of constructing temporality in different ways. In this part, I offer three further—though still brief—applications of some of the above ways of constructing temporality: first, to a theory of legal reasoning; second, to a theory of relations between legal traditions; and third, to discourse (popular and theoretical) about law.

A. Legal Reasoning

At one level, you might argue, this diachronic sensitivity in theories of legal reasoning is entirely familiar.[32] The one point that theorists of legal reasoning have insisted on is that legal reasoning, unlike other kinds of reasoning, is committed to justifying the present by interpreting (and re-interpreting) the past. We have, of course, famous images that correlate with that view: most prominently, the chain novel, where the accumulation of chapters over time generates arguably ever greater constraints on subsequent authors.[33] Not only are theories of legal reasoning backward-looking—they are also forward-looking: consider, if only, the views of the legal realists and the law-and-economics movement, and the related debate on the role of policies (and more broadly predicting possible consequences

[32] I have previously attempted to consider the importance of history to theories of legal reasoning in M Del Mar, 'What Does History Matter to Legal Epistemology?' (2011) 5 *Journal of the Philosophy of History* 383.

[33] See R Dworkin, *Law's Empire* (Hart, 1986) 228–38. Stanley Fish famously denied (in response to Dworkin) that constraints accumulated over time, saying that each author (even the first one) was just as equally constrained as the ones that followed.

of decisions) in judicial reasoning.[34] Surely, then, the entire literature on legal reasoning and legal interpretation is already highly diachronically sensitive?

There is some merit in this plea, but where it falls short is in the continued focus of theories of legal reasoning on the quality of the justification of the instant decision. The problem upon which theorists of legal reasoning have bestowed by far the greatest amount of attention has been: how or to what degree does and ought the past and/or the future inform, guide or even determine the justification of the decision in the present case? What is missing is precisely attention to legal reasoning as an inherently temporally extended activity—as something that cannot be understood, let alone evaluated, when it is not taken as occurring over time. Let me illustrate.

In some previous work, I have defended the role of legal fictions in legal reasoning on the basis that some of their function, and also their value, only become visible when one sees how they work over time.[35] If evaluated only in the context of the present case, fictions are at best seen as a dubious alternative to a more appropriately principled justification for the present decision—and that is precisely how they are most often evaluated.[36] However, if one looks at their operation over time, and thus as communicative devices from the present court to future courts, one sees that not only do they enable a decision in the present case, but they also serve as flexible resources for future courts, who are thereby given freedom to either quarantine the previous case on its facts or to de-fictionalise the past case and establish a new principle or an explicit exception to the previous rule (or indeed to continue the fiction for the time being). Legal fictions thus exist both in 'decisional time' (of the present case) as well as transitionally, as ephemeral phenomena—in 'provisional time'. By existing transitionally in this way, legal fictions can serve a distinct purpose, contributing to the gradual experimentalism of the common law. Put another way, rather than considering the value of fictions solely from the perspective of the present court, one can and ought to consider their value from the perspective of a future court, or indeed a series of future courts.

This approach—treating legal reasoning as, in part, communication across time—can be extended to other modes and devices of legal reasoning. In particular, consider how what is classified (of course, at a particular time) as obiter in a case appears—thanks to this diachronic frame—as a valuable form of hinting, suggesting, and again generally offering flexible cognitive resources to future courts. This includes references to solutions to the problem in other jurisdictions

[34] Indeed, one might argue that what theorists of legal reasoning have pursued is the appropriate balance between backward- and forward-looking considerations that both have vital, but limited roles in justifying decisions. For a theorist who sought to combine both aspects, see N MacCormick, *Legal Reasoning and Legal Theory* (Oxford University Press, 1978).

[35] See M Del Mar, 'Legal Fictions and Legal Change in the Common Law Tradition' in M Del Mar and W Twining (eds), *Legal Fictions in Theory and Practice* (Springer, 2015).

[36] Even in legal history, where fictions tend to get more of an airing, they tend to be seen (eg by Sir Henry Maine) as markers of an immature system—constituting a particular mode of legal change that a legal system best leaves behind.

(which may, on reflection, be adopted by future courts, in part or in whole, or even simply allow courts to understand better their own proposed solutions), and the use of various examples and hypotheticals that are not strictly speaking part of the justification but allow future courts to see certain potential dangers in stretching the scope of a rule or principle in some way. Indeed, the language of courts fizzes with a different kind of energy when one approaches it diachronically: one sees, for instance, certain expressions of hesitations by judges less as self-serving expressions of doubt or anxiety and more as suggestions to future courts or lawmakers and legal scholars.

But thinking about legal reasoning diachronically can be more dramatic still. One of the questions that diachronic modelling raises is whether it is possible, and indeed desirable, to have one theory of legal reasoning, allegedly applicable to all kinds of courts in all kinds of political or economic or cultural contexts, supported (or indeed frustrated) by any kind of technological facilities and resources, and to all areas of the law at any moment in the development of that law—or, whether, it is better, and also more accurate, to have a variety of distinct models of legal reasoning, indexed to variables (temporalised in different ways) such as the architecture of the courtroom, the state and organisation of any archive of past decisions, the state and level of training of advocates and other representatives, the state of assistance in the form of clerks and other resources (eg libraries), and many others besides. Once again, what we see here is that even raising the issue of a diachronic frame brings to bear a whole series of possible variables that arguably affect the character of legal reasoning.

Consider the following comment from legal historian Antonio Manuel Hespanha:

> Recent development in the history of science, as a history of material artefacts, namely of these instruments of communication we call books, help me to illustrate my point that knowledge is also a result of a material social process of production, where the traditional personage we used to call 'author' shares the creative process with the state of communicative technique, the available intellectual devices, not to speak of factors more directly related to social interests and expectations about law. In such terms, the traditional author—if he still exists—appears in a marginalised position, sharing authorship with: technical processes, social arrangements, economic opportunities, intellectual styles or conditions, or the way readers receive the message and rebuild its meaning. By stressing the impact of form on content, I reinforce my thesis of the need to write legal history with less characters and more context.[37]

Following Hespanha, one might thus index legal reasoning—its styles, the kinds of argument employed and seen to be strong or weak, the modes and devices utilised, the manner in which and the degree to which past authority / future consequences

[37] AM Hespanha, 'Form and Content in Early Modern Legal Books' (2008) 12 *Rechtsgeschichte* 12, 38. See also I MacLean, *Interpretation and Meaning in the Renaissance: The Case of Law* (Cambridge University Press, 1992).

are engaged with—to developments in the history of the book. This would include, for instance, the page layout of judicial reports, for example whether they use the agora model of the text in the middle surrounded by annotations, or whether they use no annotations at all, or whether they use a layout which has the key text at the top and then hierarchically-organised annotations at the bottom. Indeed, the very invention of cross-referencing—even, for instance, in the form of a contents page with links to various other parts—or other forms of visualisation of how one part of the law relates to another (and we have these of course already in Blackstone),[38] would surely have had an impact on what kinds of legal reasoning suddenly became possible.[39] Similar points can be made at the level of the availability, accessibility and state of an archive (including whether there were competent librarians to help)—it is these that could be said to be the real cause of the doctrine of precedent,[40] and not any high-sounding principled commitment to justifying the coercion of the state by past political decisions. What thinking diachronically is doing here, then, is allowing a theorist of legal reasoning to see how the practice of legal reasoning changes in relation to, say, typography, aesthetics, material practices (such as archiving), economic practices (such as availability of assistance to judges), and so on. What comes into view is the material art of legal reasoning changing over time.

Notice that I have hardly incorporated the various factors outlined in the second part of this paper—when this is done, complex models of legal reasoning can arise. For instance, we might think that the variable of typography impacts slowly on practices of legal reasoning (some habits die hard), whereas the presence of competent aid (in the form of clerks and librarians) has immediate, rapid effects. We might, in addition, group together certain variables into a cycle—perhaps there is some correlation between the size of a court (the number of judges and assistants, but also whether there is room for a public gallery) and the kinds of arguments and justifications deployed and how adventurous or conservative decisions tend to be. Perhaps certain kinds of arguments tend to, once begun, accumulate rapidly, but then die-off quickly,[41] whereas others may begin slowly, but come to be eventually recognised as valid (eg consideration of the mischief addressed by a statute).

[38] See eg C S Martinez, 'Blackstone as Draughtsman: Picturing the Law' in W Prest (ed), *Re-Interpreting Blackstone's Commentaries* (Hart, 2014).

[39] Think here of the impact of footnotes, margins, headings, and many other typographical inventions. There are of course many wonderful historical studies of these devices (eg see A Grafton, *Footnote: A Curious History* (Harvard University Press, 1999)), but arguably less so as applied to the legal context.

[40] See P Halliday, 'Authority in the Archives' (2014) 1(1) *Critical Analysis of Law* 110.

[41] Policy arguments might be of this kind: it is easy to kill off claims by fearing floodgates, but if resorted to too often may be denounced and suddenly disappear from practice.

B. Relations between Legal Units

Twentieth century legal theory has focused intensely on the identity of legal systems—on how they hang together and form one, unified, complete legal order.[42] This is not the same as saying that the focus has been on the state—for some of what has been argued for in the name of the identity, unity and systematicity of law is compatible with possibly even a strong version of pluralism that allows for the co-existence of multiple legal systems on any one territory.[43] Indeed, some of the most interesting work on what we might broadly classify as the study of relations between legal units[44] has been done within the context of the state, for example on relations of federalism,[45] and on how a central authority variously acknowledges, recognises, authorises, delegates to, authorities it treats as subordinate to it.[46]

However, something more radical occurs when one adds the diachronic frame. Seen from the perspective of the long view, even if initially with a focus on the state or one legal unit, what one sees as vital are the various interactions over time that any one political community has with other communities. In other words, the diachronic frame, perhaps like no other (eg comparison alone would not do it), brings into view the importance, for the change or development of any one legal unit, of interactions with other legal units.[47] These can take a very great variety of forms, including a very thin awareness of the existence of another unit; an acknowledgement and recognition of that existence; borrowing from that unit; more wholescale incorporation of the norms of that unit; the destruction of that other unit; and many others besides. Of course, soon enough one sees the need for an analysis of the interactions from both perspectives: so there may be symmetrical interactions (with both sides borrowing from each other), or asymmetrical ones (one side actively seeking to take over the jurisdiction of the other, and the other side seeking to stake out its own autonomy), or, as will typically be the case, some complex mix of symmetrical and asymmetrical interactions. Further, both sides may have very different attitudes to each other, and these attitudes will also

[42] It is sufficient here to name Hans Kelsen, HLA Hart and Joseph Raz as protagonists.

[43] See N Barber, 'Legal Pluralism and the European Union' (2006) 12(3) *European Law Journal* 306.

[44] By referring to 'units' I am aiming to use as neutral a term as possible, and in preference over order, system, tradition, institution, and so on.

[45] Think of the work of Robert Cover and others in his wake on dialectical federalism.

[46] Here we ought to add the debate from the early twentieth century between the English pluralists and the sovereigntists (see eg D Runciman, *Pluralism and the Personality of the State* (Cambridge University Press, 1997); C Laborde, *Pluralist Thought and the State in Britain and France 1900–25* (Palgrave Macmillan, 2000); and M Bevir (ed), *Modern Pluralism: Anglo-American Debates Since 1880* (Cambridge University Press, 2012)), which is all too often forgotten in contemporary legal theory. An important recent exception is: J MacLean, *Searching for the State in British Legal Thought* (Cambridge University Press, 2012).

[47] A stand-out recent work in that respect is the late Patrick Glenn's *The Cosmopolitan State* (Oxford University Press, 2013).

typically change over time: what begins as a threat to the very existence of another unit might develop into a productive dialogue, and the other way round.[48]

These relations, especially as they change over time, have been surprisingly little studied in legal theory. There are, of course, enormous literatures on colonial legal practices, but it is surprising how little of these—especially those that are diachronically sophisticated, and thus for instance see the contingency of the growth from pluralism to statism in colonial contexts[49]—have informed general theories of law, which have tended to imagine the municipal legal order as autonomous, both internally and in its external relations with other orders it recognises. There is now, certainly, a burgeoning literature on constitutional pluralism in Europe and, more generally, transnational legal pluralism, and theorists here study the interactions—especially between courts—intensively, but little of this literature is diachronically sensitive, and if it is, it tends not to go back further than a few decades.[50]

There exists, at the moment, no real analytical framework of relations between legal units within general jurisprudence. This is likely to change, and indeed is slowly changing.[51] What I would like to stress here is the need for this framework to be diachronically sensitive—we must study not only relations between legal units, but those relations modelled diachronically. It may be, for instance, that we can identify cycles within those relations over time, or perhaps there are mixtures of both progressive and regressive dynamics. Perhaps some kinds of relations only occur once and slowly over long periods of time, while others are multiple and rapid. Without modelling those relations diachronically, we risk collapsing them into an unhelpful a-temporal dichotomy of hierarchy and hetararchy, thereby missing the much more subtle qualities of possible relations, some of which may occur simultaneously but at different speeds (eg there may be instances of rapid, but ephemeral enmity between the executive of two units, and long-standing collaboration between members of the judicial arm). In this context, the diachronic goes hand in hand with the relational,[52] and indeed the former may help develop

[48] Think here of the changes in attitudes between courts in Europe, including between the ECJ and national constitutional courts, and between courts involved in the interpretation of European human rights.

[49] See L Benton, *Law and Colonial Cultures* (Cambridge University Press, 2002).

[50] See N Krisch, *Beyond Constitutionalism* (Oxford University Press, 2010).

[51] See, eg K Culver and M Giudice, *Legality's Borders: An Essay in General Jurisprudence* (Oxford University Press, 2010); N Roughan, *Authorities: Conflicts, Cooperation and Transnational Legal Theory* (Oxford University Press, 2013); and the forthcoming collection of papers on *In Pursuit of Pluralist Jurisprudence* by A Halpin and N Roughan (eds) (Cambridge University Press, forthcoming).

[52] For my take on the relational, see M Del Mar, 'Legal Reasoning in Pluralist Jurisprudence: The Practice of the Relational Imagination' in A Halpin and N Roughan (eds), *In Pursuit of Pluralist Jurisprudence* (Cambridge University Press, forthcoming); and M Del Mar, 'On the Hinges of History: For a Relational Legal Historiography' in C Tomlins and J Desautels-Stein (ed), *Contemporary Legal Thought* (Cambridge University Press, forthcoming).

the language of the latter: think of how much more we learn about friendship or marriage when we look at how they change over time.

Modelling relations between legal units diachronically has the potential to change the practice of legal theory rather dramatically. We no longer ask: how can we determine that this norm belongs to such and such a system? Instead, we ask: how has this norm affected relations between these two institutions, or how has the history of disagreements about what some norm requires reflected how those institutions have related to each other over time? We become less interested in locating some allegedly autonomous, walled-off space within which a norm is said to belong, and instead we study the diachronic dynamics of interactions, for example at the level of linguistics (is there usage of common terms, or are terms frequently invented in a bid to remain autonomous?), or at the level of argument (are arguments repeated, translated, transformed, or dismissed and ignored?), or at the level of rhetoric (including emotional expression).

No doubt we can push this 'diachronic relationalism' quite far: for instance, we could argue that it points to a model of law in one which takes law to be precisely that which allows self-identified units (whether individuals, communities, traditions, institutions) to negotiate their co-existence with other units. Law so modelled, we could say, is inherently relational—but never stably so, or even coherently so: it is a set of (precisely incompatible, contradictory) argumentative resources that creates a space in which we can continually debate how we ought to relate to one another, and this again at various levels (as above, from the individual to the institutional). That, we could say, is the only way we can create a space that is sufficiently resourceful to allow us to manage the complexity of relations as these change over time. Law, on this view, cannot be systematic, consistent and coherent—if it was, it could not effectively serve as a diachronically-relational resource.

C. Discourse about Law

Finally, let me continue in the vein of provocative remarks by considering how we could 'temporalise' the study of discourse about law.[53] This could equally concern both popular and professional discourse about law. For example in the case of the former, one could temporalise popular attitudes to and opinions of law, along the lines of the study of mentalities as in Marc Bloch's *The Royal Touch* or Keith Thomas's work on magic and religion.[54] And one could do the same no doubt

[53] For another attempt to do this—at the level of theories of authority—see M Del Mar, 'Imaginaries of Authority: Towards an Archaeology of Disagreement' in R Cotterrell and M Del Mar (eds), *Authority in Transnational Legal Theory: Theorising across the Disciplines* (Edward Elgar, 2016).

[54] See M Bloch, *The Royal Touch* (McGill-Queen's University Press, 1973) and K Thomas, *Religion and the Decline of Magic* (Harmondsworth, 1971).

for official and academic attitudes and opinions, seeing how, over time, all three relate to each other (for instance: do popular opinions filter down, and slowly or quickly, to official and academic ones, and if so with what effects?). In fact, here too the relational dimension adds an important ingredient, for one can study the changing trajectories of discourses about law between many different kinds of groups: citizens, non-citizens, scholars and different kinds of officials, and of course amongst them too (eg trajectories of disagreements between officials).

Taking this broad approach, we could say that we would be treating law not as an object with properties (whether universal or polythetic), but as the movement of a piece in a chess game, and thus as an intervention in a debate that occurs over a certain period of time. Notice that this is not the same as saying we want to take law to be whatever it is that people call it at a particular time. Instead, we treat statements about law as pragmatic utterances situated in complex relational contexts, these being utterances—and this is the crucial part—which are almost inevitably going to be in tension with other such utterances made by others. Thus, statements that such-and-such an action or state of affairs is legal or illegal, or that this is law and this is not law, are part of a scene of disagreement, of clashes of interests and outlooks, inter-mixed no doubt with other kinds of utterances (say about what is good, appropriate, correct or conventional). One would then not assume that law is something about which there can be consensus—but, on the contrary, one would say that although some partial consensus can be temporarily achieved, what is much more common is that there are many different kinds of contests, with many different kinds of things at stake (eg not only economic, but other kinds of capital), in the game of utterances of 'law' (including other related terms).

What arguably comes more into view when one thinks diachronically about law modelled by way of these 'situated games of discourse' are the variety of reasons and causes for why people might disagree. In other words, by studying these disagreements over time—these different clashing uses—one could identify a greater range of possible factors of disagreement, for example everything from reliance on particular imagery (metaphors, spatial ways of thinking, typical examples), ethical and political orientations, and an enormous range of possible aims and purposes (including everything from preserving the economic interests of the profession to making it easier to teach and examine the subject). A certain way of using the term 'law' in a certain community over time may be the result of the hold of a particular picture (eg of a monotheistic God and an obedient people) which may come into contact and clash with a community in the grip of a very different picture (eg of artisans collaborating in a guild)—and, furthermore, result in a very interesting and complex hybrid compromise of law as, say, in part command and in part custom.

Similarly, by thinking diachronically about discourse about law, one would not only look back at the reasons and causes of disagreements, but forwards at what is at stake (even if the participants do not see this) in such disagreements, thereby considering, for instance, what the results are of a certain usage becoming dominant, or what are the effects of certain usages being kept in tension (and whether over short or long periods of time). Certainly, some trajectories of disagreement (some clash of images for example) may be long-standing, and others may be short-lived, and some may recur in cycles (eg one moves from emphasising will to emphasising reason to emphasising custom, and so on in ever-recurring displacement of one by the other). Some disagreements (and I am thinking here more of those within academia) may be based on holding on to what one takes to be the central contrast pool for law (eg morality and coercion, or religion and literature), and these may correspond to very different things at stake: for example relations between Church and State, or relations between the judiciary and the executive, and so on.

I do not claim any originality for the above suggestions and provocations: they have been raised and debated in the history of ideas and the history of discursive formations, including obviously via Marxist-oriented methods. My point is simply to bring into view a smattering of the possibilities for modelling law diachronically if one treats it as a move in contested discourses over time—discourses whose trajectories can, and ought to, be temporalised in a great variety of ways.

V. Conclusion

My aim in this chapter has not been to preach and prescribe—to say that all theorists of law ought to think about law diachronically. Instead, it has been to indicate some of the possible insights that can be generated by modelling law diachronically. Modelling law diachronically—or, even just raising the possibility of a diachronic dimension to any analysis—is, I propose, a very effective method for generating variables that affect the character of law. This is partly because there is nothing like foregrounding change over time as a solvent for conceptual habits. Further, it may be because modelling law diachronically allows us to keep our senses close to the ground—it forces us to look for details upon which we can hang the hooks of change. All this of course complexifies our task as legal theorists—it makes it harder, more time consuming, it requires us to read more and learn from many other disciplines (aesthetics, architecture, drama, to mention but three still too neglected in legal theory), and it might even require us to invent new disciplines (eg relationalism). But, surely it brings us closer to the complexity of the deeply social phenomenon that is law. To return to where I began: diachronic modelling of social facts may just be the best means we have for accommodating as many variables as possible that affect the character of law.

8

Is Comparative Law Necessary for Legal Theory?

JOHN BELL

In the *Cambridge Companion to Comparative Law*, Mathias Reimann states that

> It is now a banality that comparative law and legal history are closely related ... Legal philosophy is not as routinely discussed in its relation to comparative law. Yet it is worth at least brief consideration. This is not because there is so much interaction between these two disciplines but because there is so little and because there should be more.[1]

William Twining is a legal theorist who is also very keen on a substantial connection between comparative law and legal theory. In his book on globalisation, he wrote:

> Comparative law and legal theory are interdependent. Foreign and comparative legal studies provide much of the essential raw material for developing a new general jurisprudence. Comparison is a crucial step on the way to generalisation.[2]

In his view, legal theory needs to build on the contribution which comparative law makes to the understanding of legal systems across the world. Comparative lawyer David Gerber has pointed out the consequences of the failure to take such information into account:

> To generalize about law on the basis of experience with a single system is a common enough form of entertainment (particularly in the US) but hardly of great analytical value. Only when theoretical propositions can be tested in more than one legal system can they legitimately claim any degree of validity, and the more often they are used and the more rigorously and successfully they are tested, the stronger those legitimacy claims become.[3]

In this chapter, I support the request for legal theory to have regard to existing knowledge about a variety of legal systems in formulating both questions and

[1] M Reimann, 'Comparative Law and Neighbouring Disciplines' in M Bussani and U Mattei (eds), *The Cambridge Companion to Comparative Law* (Cambridge University Press, 2012) 13 at 22, 27.

[2] W Twining, *Globalisation and Legal Theory* (Butterworths, 2000) 256.

[3] D Gerber, 'Towards a Language of Comparative law' (1998) 46 *American Journal of Comparative Law* 719, 734.

answers in jurisprudence. At the same time, I want to take issue with Twining's ambition. It is not just providing data, as if analytical jurisprudence were the only ambition of comparative law. It can also contribute to normative jurisprudence.

First, I will give a brief account of why comparative law and legal theory may have drifted apart. Second, I will suggest that comparative law is often useful not merely in providing information, but also as part of the debate about what are worthwhile questions for legal theory. Third, I will point to some of the difficulties for jurisprudents in using the results of comparative law and suggest a form of collaboration may be a valuable way forward.

I. Introduction: The Separation of Comparative Law and Legal Theory

Twining argues that comparative law and legal theory have drifted apart in modern times[4] and Reimann's comment confirms this. In many ways, this has been happening since 1900, the moment of the formal foundation of comparative law as a discipline in Europe. In the 1860s, John Austin defined 'general jurisprudence' as 'the science concerned with the exposition of the principles, notions and distinctions which are common to systems of law'.[5] He justified this approach by saying, 'Though every system of law has its specific and characteristic differences, there are principles, notions, and distinctions common to the various systems, and forming analogies or likenesses by which such systems are allied'.[6] At much the same time, Jhering wrote that:

> If law is seen functionally as a regulator of social facts, the legal problems of all countries are similar. Every legal system in the world is open to the same questions and subject to the same standards, even countries of different social structures or different stages of development.[7]

The method of generalisation from the data of particular legal systems provided a distinctive character to Austin's form of jurisprudence and to Jhering's scientific comparative law, and legal theory asked whether we draw conclusions about the nature of law by generalising from the way in which different legal systems confront similar problems. In the nineteenth century, such a method would rely on illustrations from particular legal systems, especially Roman law, with which all legal scholars from a variety of countries were familiar.

[4] Twining (n 2) 176–78.

[5] J Austin, *Lectures on Jurisprudence* (Murray, 1885) 1073.

[6] ibid 1072.

[7] Quoted in K Zweigert and H Kötz, *An Introduction to Comparative Law* 3rd edn (T Weir trans, Oxford University Press, 1998) 45.

Since then, in jurisprudence the method of abstraction, favoured by Salmond, has focused on drawing out arguments from the nature of particular notions and the connections between them. He rejected the approach of Austin. Jurisprudence was not the science of those principles which legal systems had in common, rather it is a science of the first principles of civil law, abstracted from contingent and particular content.[8] Even if a topic, such as binding precedent, were not common in many legal systems, he said that it would be an appropriate subject of jurisprudence. In the various editions of Salmond and other textbooks of jurisprudence down to the time of Dias in the 1970s, topics such as the concepts of rights and property would be studied with significant illustrations drawn from national laws. But the agenda was driven by the search for abstract, universal concepts. In more recent years, most works of jurisprudence have become even more abstract and use hypothetical or stylised facts. They have become concerned with questions of the conditions of validity of a legal system. The connection between empirical information about the law and jurisprudence has become more distant.

By contrast, as Twining points out, comparative law has drawn away from legal theory and generalisation. In 1900, comparative lawyers sought to find universal principles of law from the data of specific legal systems. Since then, and especially since 1945, comparative lawyers have increasingly focused on small-scale, detailed comparisons of a few systems, what Twining caricatures as 'the Country and Western tradition'—a comparison of a few countries, drawn mainly from western legal traditions[9] (predominantly because of the ability of researchers to read materials in the original language.). Conclusions of a general character drawn from this sort of data are rarer. In that sense, the approach has been described by Lemmens as 'comparative law as an act of modesty', something which it is possible to do, even if it is by no means perfect, but factoring in powerful critiques of self-awareness.[10] In *The Oxford Handbook of Comparative Law*,[11] there are several chapters on the contributions which particular legal theories can make to comparative law research. Law and economics or critical legal studies help to direct the attention of lawyers to particular research issues. But the *Handbook* does not feature legal theory specifically as one of the many disciplines to which comparative law is related.

Twining has tried to suggest that comparative law can, nevertheless, be bolder and, in its turn, contribute to legal theory. Tur preferred to see the two subjects as two moments in a legal endeavour: the combination of form and content. He said that 'There is an interplay of general jurisprudence and comparative law which operates to refine the conceptual frame [developed by jurisprudence] as well as

[8] JW Salmond, *Jurisprudence or The Theory of Law* (Stevens and Haynes, 1902) 5.

[9] Twining (n 2) 184–89.

[10] K Lemmens, 'Comparative Law as an Act of Modesty: A Pragmatic and Realistic Approach to Comparative Legal Scholarship' in M Adams and J Bomhoff (eds), *Practice and Theory in Comparative Law* (Cambridge University Press, 2012) 304.

[11] M Reimann and R Zimmermann, *The Oxford Handbook of Comparative Law* (Oxford University Press, 2006).

to order the empirical data [developed by comparative law].'[12] It is this approach which suggests that the conclusions of comparative study may feed into legal theory: 'the jurisprudence enterprise involves a systematic knowledge of the possible, supported and dialectically modified by an investigation of the actual.'[13]

But three questions can be asked: *why is it important to look at comparative law? Can a jurisprudent really treat the results of comparative law research as scientific data? How should a jurisprudent work?*

II. So Why is it Important for a Jurisprudent to Look at Comparative Law?

The first reason for using comparative law is to test out whether a research question is really about the nature of law in general, or merely a generalisation within a particular legal family. Claims about law are usually about 'law in general'.

One example is the topic of legal reasoning, Dworkin made his classic distinction between 'arguments of principle' and 'arguments of policy' in 1977:

> Arguments of principle attempt to justify a political decision that benefits some person or group by showing that the person or group has a right to the benefit. Arguments of policy attempt to justify a decision by showing that, in spite of the fact that those who are benefited do not have a right to the benefit, providing the benefit will advance a collective goal of the community.[14]

He later repeated the argument in relation to his fictional judge *Hercules*.[15] Dworkin's distinction between rules and principles was enthusiastically adopted in continental Europe. (I suspect mainly because it was actually found in the work of Esser published some 12 years before Dworkin in a language which he did not read).[16] The same was not true of the distinction between principles and policies.

Let us take two European legal theorists who took Dworkin's work seriously. François Ost imagined Hercules as operating within a codified system, not a common law system.[17] Unlike Jupiter who decided simply according to the Code within which all solutions were hierarchically structured, Hercules is seen as being more pragmatic, solving practical problems to which the Code text provides no clear answer, operating more freely in the interpretation of the law in relation to individual cases. The legitimacy of the decision comes not from the citation

[12] R Tur, 'The Dialectic of General Jurisprudence and Comparative Law' (1977) *Juridical Review* 238, 248.

[13] ibid 249.

[14] RM Dworkin, 'A Reply to Critics' in *Taking Rights Seriously* revised edn (Duckworth, 1978) 294.

[15] RM Dworkin, *Law's Empire* (Fontana,1986) 221–24, 243–44, 310–12.

[16] J Esser, Grundsatz und Norm in der richterlichen Fortbildung des Rechts (Mohr Siebeck, 1956).

[17] F Ost, 'Jupiter, Hercules, Hermes tres modelos de juez' (1993) 14 *Doxa* 169, 178–81.

of the provision of the Code, but from a sense of the unity of the law, viewed as a coherent whole. The decision of Hercules is rational and far from being simply decisionistic or pragmatic:

> His ideal (*religion*), in effect, is the unity of the Law which has to be strengthened by his decision in an individual case: unity in the double sense of the narrative coherence of which is better adapted to the past and present state of the Law, and in the most satisfactory ordering of the principles of political morality shared by the community in that moment of its history.[18]

Dworkin is fitted into the tradition of 'free legal research' going back to Gény in 1899 and Eugen Ehrlich in 1903,[19] who first set off a debate about the rational limits of judicial freedom in the interpretation of the law. But the subtlety of the distinction between arguments of principle based on rights and arguments of policy based on non-rights considerations is completely lost. This is most obvious when Ost links Dworkin's approach to that of the American Realists Holmes and Frank.[20] For Dworkin (and for any American), the intellectual ambitions of the Realists is radically different from that of Dworkin. They introduced the kind of scepticism about the rational basis of legal argument that Dworkin castigates. One of the important features for Ost is that Dworkin's emphasis on the reasoning of judges has to be broadened to include any legal actor.[21]

Writing at much the same time, Robert Alexy accepts the notions that there is a distinction between principles and rules, and rights have a significant place in constitutional adjudication.[22] But for him rights are based on principles which are optimising norms and which can be balanced off against each other in a proportionality argument. His paradigm is German constitutional court reasoning. There are specific rights which are applicable as rules, reasons for decisions in an all-or-nothing way, but most rights function as principles. By this he means that it can be appropriately cited as a prima facie reason for or against a decision.[23] But

> [t]he principles relevant to constitutional adjudication do not include those related to individual rights, that is, prima facie constitutional rights, but also those relating to collective interests and which can be used above all as reasons against prima facie constitutional rights, sometimes also as reasons for them.[24]

He then illustrates the way in which principles of the social state, democracy and 'relative public interests' can be used by courts (and are used in Germany) to

[18] ibid 180 (my translation).

[19] J Bell, 'Continental European Jurisprudence 1850–2000' in M Lobban and J Moses (eds), *The Impact of Ideas on Legal Development* (Cambridge University Press, 2012) 110–12.

[20] F Ost, above n 17, 177–78.

[21] ibid,171 fn 3.

[22] See R Alexy, *A Theory of Constitutional Rights* (Oxford University Press, 2002, German original 1986) 57–58.

[23] ibid 80.

[24] ibid.

define the scope of rights.[25] Alexy accepts the ideas of rules and principles,[26] but rejects a 'one right answer' thesis as intellectually unachievable,[27] which was not how Dworkin intended to present it. He saw it much more as a kind of regulative ideal.

The point of these illustrations is to show how jurisprudents from different legal traditions can end up misunderstanding each other and not engaging in a fruitful debate. Dworkin wrote against a background of common law type reasoning and justification which had been grafted onto the practice of interpreting a very rigid constitution. The constitution was given life by judicial re-interpretation. Ost, by contrast, wrote against a background of French and Belgian judicial reasoning which is very short (perhaps half a page) and the supreme authority of legislation (and not yet the Constitution). Judicial and scholarly re-interpretation adapted the old civil code of 1804 to modern conditions. Alexy, over the border in Germany, wrote in the light of both the authority of legislation over case law and the supreme authority of a modern, but flexible, judicially interpreted Constitution. If jurisprudence is to be a theory of law applicable to a large variety of legal systems, then any theory which is developed must be able to speak clearly to lawyers from different traditions. That requires sensitivity to one's audience—an awareness of how concepts and language will be understood within different legal traditions. But it also requires a willingness to test out one's arguments with lawyers from different legal traditions.

The illustrations also show why it is important to look at how a legal theory is explained. Dworkin's archetypal judge Hercules operates within a classical American legal institutional context. But the quality of Dworkin's core ideas can be extended further. In his comparative study of legal reasoning, Mitchell Lasser has shown the way in which the preoccupations of Dworkin reveal themselves very differently in the judicial justifications presented in different systems. In his book, *Judicial Deliberations*,[28] Lasser gives an account of the French and American judicial discourses on the justifications of judicial decisions in difficult cases. He identifies two discourses in which French judges engage. The first, 'official', portrait is the formal judgment, which is backed up by a theory of the sources of law. Judges make decisions according to law and judicial decisions, in themselves, have no legal binding authority. The judgment cites the legal text and then seeks to draw the solution deductively from it. This style of the discourse conveys a particular message consistent with the official portrait that judges are not being creative. But the second, 'unofficial' portrait is different.[29] Here Lasser has

[25] ibid 80–82.
[26] ibid 57–58; R Alexy, *A Theory of Legal Argumentation* (Oxford University Press, 1989, German original 1978) 243–44.
[27] Alexy (n 22) 385.
[28] M Lasser, Judicial Deliberations. A Comparative Analysis of Judicial Transparency and Legitimacy (Oxford University Press, 2004).
[29] ibid 30–38.

read the actual files of cases, and has seen the typically unpublished reports of the reporting judge, who leads the discussion in a collegial court, and the arguments of the *avocat général*, who, in the French system, is seen as a judicial adviser. In addition, there are published scholarly notes. The character of the debate in the scholarly commentaries, the arguments of the reporter judge and of the *avocat général* is fully and individually engaged in the issues of social and legal principle and policy.[30] There is a 'bifurcation' in justification between what is presented through the published judgment and what occurs both in the internal discussions of the court (as evidenced by the arguments of the reporter and *avocat général*), and in scholarly writing.[31] French judges are not formalist, but they do not justify their decisions publicly in substantive terms. Lasser's basic argument is that these two radically different portraits can be adopted rationally because of a series of mediating institutions. Accountability of the decisions of the Cour de cassation is also maintained by the hierarchical and collegial character of the judicial profession and their close connection to a wider circle of scholarly writers and the small number of *avocats à la Cour*. None of this group misunderstands what is being said in judicial decisions—they know the interpretative freedom of the judge and are aware of the arguments under discussion. Judicial decisions are of limited authority unless they become widely accepted as appropriate by this wider group of the legal community. Judicial accountability comes principally not through the public reasoning, but through the private reasoning, the public annual report, and the debate with doctrinal legal writers. In order to understand the bifurcation of justification, it is necessary to look at the complex framework within which decisions are made and presented.[32] Lasser complains that leading US scholars such as Dawson and Duncan Kennedy[33] simply dismiss this structure of discourse as formalistic without adequately understanding how it really works.

By contrast, Lasser explains, in US judicial decisions, both the interpretative and policy-oriented discussions take place within the same extensive common law judgment. The US legal style is open about the judicial lawmaking in that the style of the decision attempts to justify the solutions reached in an explicit way. At the same time, the creativity is limited by being focused on interpretation. In the US, 'formalism' and 'policy' are used as pejorative terms to describe unacceptable judicial arguments. The US judicial decision is not apparently formalistic in the way a French judgment might appear, but nor is it as openly personal and policy-oriented in the way that the arguments of the French *avocat général* can be. For Lasser, the key to understanding this is the central place of the judiciary, especially of the Supreme Court, within the US system. There is no control by a judicial

[30] ibid 49–60.

[31] ibid 30, 47–60.

[32] ibid 200–02.

[33] ibid 28–29, citing D Kennedy, *A Critique of Adjudication* (*Fin de siècle*) (Harvard University Press, 1997) 36–37 and 107; JP Dawson, *Oracles of the Law* (Michigan University Press, 1968) 415.

hierarchy or by scholarly writers or by the resistance of lower courts. The authority of its precedents and the immunity of the Supreme Court from external controls force on it the need to be accountable through judicial reasoning.

Lasser takes the local lawyers as fundamentally acting in good faith when they say they believe in justification and legitimacy, rather than following Dawson and Kennedy and dismissing their approach because it does not fit into an alternative paradigm well developed in American jurisprudence.[34]

Lasser effectively shows why jurisprudential reflection benefits from comparative scholarship. Like the American theorists and comparative lawyers that Lasser criticises, Dworkin comes to the conceptual question about the role of the judge with presuppositions drawn from the institutional practices of his own legal system. Instead of producing a general theory of law, at best he produces a general theory of the common law legal family, which leaves members of other legal families completely bemused and unengaged. Lasser shows that there does need to be sensitivity to different institutional settings and not just to the different legal rules that apply in different jurisdictions.

III. Comparative Law as 'Data' for Jurisprudence

Two contributions from legal theory stress the way in which the so-called 'data' of comparative law is a construct and that it is significantly interpreted. As a result, jurisprudents have to be aware of the way in which comparative law cannot be used uncritically as the basis for generalisation. At the same time, it provides a useful check.

A. The Construction of Legal Facts

Neil MacCormick's account of law explains the importance of 'institutional fact'.[35] An 'institutional fact' is a fact which we invest with meaning within a particular set of social relations because it performs a particular function. The law is not a set of 'natural facts', but a set of facts that become of significance within a legal context. As I have written elsewhere,[36] a visitor to England might observe one person sitting on a raised platform and wearing robes who is talking to another person in

[34] See B Goetschalckx, '"In Good faith": Re-imagining Comparative Law Discourse' in N Huls, M Adams and J Bomhoff (eds), *The Legitimacy of Highest Courts' Rulings. Judicial Deliberations and Beyond* (TCM Asser, 2009) ch 6.

[35] N MacCormick and O Weinberger, *An Institutional Theory of Law* (Kluwer, 1986) ch 3; this draws on JR Searle, *The Social Construction of Reality* (Penguin, 1995) 47. Also RS Summers, *Form and Function in a Legal System: A General Study* (Oxford University Press, 2006).

[36] J Bell, *French Legal Cultures* (Butterworths, 2001) 5.

a box flanked by two men in uniform. Those are fairly close to 'natural' facts. But they become scenes from a 'trial' when they are seen as a court process by actors within the legal system. The art of Jonathan Swift's *Gulliver's Travels* or Kafka's *The Trial* is to represent to us those 'natural facts' from the point of view of someone who does not share the institutional and internal point of view. Now the institutional character of law arises from the function of law in reducing complexity in life. Social life is very complex with a multiplicity of issues and concerns. There are lots of things going on in a court room, but we need only to focus on some of them in order to understand the idea of a 'trial'. The institutional character of law not only gives us a perspective which invests meaning on reality, it reduces the number of 'relevant' features. Legal routine and structure help to reduce complexity and reduce the number of new things of which a legal actor needs to take account. When I convey my house to another person, I fill out forms that prompt me to certain key questions—do I have title to the house? Are there outstanding mortgages to be paid off? And so on. From the legal point of view, questions such as whether the garden is overgrown or the roof tiles need replacing are irrelevant. No purchaser of a house would ignore them, but they are not, as such, *legally* relevant.

The institutional character of law explains the argument of Geoffrey Samuel that facts do not exist independently of legal categories.[37] The legal rule conceptualises reality in certain ways. Law is not a 'fact', but a contested construct. Lawson suggested that 'Law is not just fact. It is thought applied to fact.'[38] People are presented as 'defendants', 'tortfeasors', 'trustees', and the like. The natural facts become, in this way, 'facts in law'. The law is only concerned with applying legal rules to 'facts in law'.

Lawyers in different legal systems will look at particular phenomena and decide whether they are legally relevant and how they are to be categorised. For example, a doctor is called by a patient at night and the doctor decides not to go to visit the patient. The patient then dies that night. In France, this is a subject for the criminal law, failing to help a person in danger. In England, possibly a matter of tort law, breach of a duty of care or even just of medical discipline.

Another important aspect of the institutional approach to law is the stress on procedure: how do the facts present themselves? Legal rules may explain whether actions are brought and thus the role law plays in a society. To take the example of exploding boilers in the nineteenth century, the victim of a boiler explosion was usually an employee. Under English and German legal rules, the employee victim would find it very difficult to bring an action against his employer. As a result, there were almost no actions brought for boiler explosions, even though hundreds of people were killed each year.[39] It is only by understanding the legal procedures

[37] G Samuel, *Epistemology and Method in Law* (Ashgate, 2003) 125–48 and 173–91, 196–200.

[38] FH Lawson, *The Comparison—Selected Essay, Vol II* (North Holland, 1977) 75–76.

[39] M Martín-Casals, *The Development of Liability in Relation to Technological Change* (Cambridge University Press, 2010) 15–16.

by which claims might be brought that we can understand the questions with which the law is dealing.

Explaining these different ways of constructing legal problems inevitably involves a historical dimension. Especially for developing a theory of law, it is necessary not only to document that different legal systems approach similar problems differently, but to understand the reasons why this is the case. For classical comparative lawyers such as Zweigert and Kötz, historical development is one of the major reasons why legal systems are different.[40] They have in mind the idea, contested by Tomlins in this collection,[41] that it is important to situate legal rules and institutions in the context in which they arose. In fact, they have in mind something closer to Gorman's idea that historical consciousness is a matter of thinking contextually.[42] When looking to understand whether differences between legal systems are fundamental or accidental, then it is necessary to probe beyond the surface of the use of different concepts and procedures to see whether lawyers in the different countries are trying to undertake different tasks. Drawing on Rabel and in harmony with much legal theory, Zweigert and Kötz believe that lawyers operating within different legal traditions and with different legal concepts and procedures are fundamentally trying to do similar things—this is what they call the presumption of similarity: 'as a general rule developed nations answer the needs of legal business in the same or in a very similar way'.[43] They consider that this serves as a heuristic principle. It allows the comparative lawyer (and by extension the legal theorist) to argue that differences between legal systems are fundamentally superficial, rather than part of their deep structure. Thus general legal theory is possible. Understanding history provides a corrective to the apparent contemporary diverging results of legal systems. History is a vector in understanding both the differences and the commonalities in the way in which the law works in society. But comparative law would reject historical determinism. The fact that law now operates with legal concepts and institutions which are inherited from the past does not mean that it is unable to cope with new or old problems in new ways. An illustration is the work of Bobek on contemporary legal reasoning in supreme courts. He explains how a number of Central and Eastern European courts have inherited procedures, concepts and ways of handling legal issues from the Communist era, but have been able to adapt. For example, he argues that judiciaries in the Czech Republic and Slovakia share a long common history, but operate differently today.[44] This approach to comparative law does support the universalising

[40] Zweigert and Kötz (n 7) 68–69.

[41] See C Tomlins, 'Historicism and Materiality in Legal Theory', above ch 5.

[42] J Gorman, 'Legal Consciousness: a Metahistory', above ch 6, p 102.

[43] Zweigert and Kötz (n 7) 40. This is a contested area of comparative law theory, see M Siems, *Comparative Law* (Cambridge University Press, 2014) 30 and 110–12.

[44] M Bobek, *Comparative Reasoning in European Supreme Courts* (Oxford University Press, 2013), esp 189–91.

enterprise of legal theory. At the same time, it does encourage a contextualisation of specific language and illustrations. It also encourages legal theorists to understand the historical context in which the law develops. Comparative law encourages legal theory to articulate some of its assumptions about the way in which the social institution of 'law' has grown up in different countries. It asks legal theory to justify the assumption of universality in the statements which it makes. To that extent, comparative law both embodies aspects of historical method and shares some of the relativising ambitions of historical research.

Facts are thus not neutral. They come as packaged in relation to legal institutions, in particular, they are categorised according to particular legal interests and in the light of the way they will present themselves within legal procedures, such as court proceedings. They need to be analysed in their context, including their historical context.

B. Interpretation of Facts

This therefore raises the important issue of interpretation. There is also a major interpretative function in relation to the legal rules and principles. As McCrudden points out, among others:

> If legal academic work shows anything, it shows that an applicable legal norm on anything but the most banal question is likely to be complex, nuanced and contested. Law is not a datum; it is in constant evolution, developing in ways that are sometimes startling and endlessly inventive.[45]

Lawyers often talk as if there is a 'text' out there in a canonical form that has just to be interpreted. But, in reality, the text has to be constructed in the light both of its original context and of the context of the amending statutes, and it also speaks out of a body of law with which it interacts. The interpreter has to hold all this together in the act of interpretation.

For all these reasons, the act of interpretation is the art of constructing an appropriate text and its meaning. Now one conclusion that Sacco draws from this is that no statement of the law is complete or fully accurate. He would argue that statutes, judicial decisions, academic treatises and articles are all versions of the law or 'formants' which are then used in an interpretative fashion by the judge or lawyer in coming to a decision or writing an account of the law.[46] The result is that any judicial decision or academic writing is a creative act. It does something that is new.

[45] C McCrudden,'Legal Research and the Social Sciences' (2006) 122 *Law Quarterly Review* 632, 648.

[46] R Sacco, 'Legal Formants: A Dynamic Approach to Comparative Law' (1991) 39 *American Journal of Comparative Law* 1.

Now, if this is true of the national lawyer, then it is true a fortiori of the comparative lawyer. Elsewhere I have drawn attention to the methodology of communicating comparative law results. They are destined for an audience different from the national lawyer. As a result, the communication by comparative lawyers is bound to be significantly different in expression and even in content than the communication by the national lawyer to an audience within her own legal community.[47] Even if many of the steps of the methodology of enquiry are similar between the national lawyer and the comparative lawyer, the methodology of communication must necessarily be different. As Lemmens suggests, the comparative lawyer is a translator, making a personal synthesis in order to aid comprehension by the intended foreign audience.[48]

So, if we look at the so-called 'data' Twining and Tur want the jurisprudent to use as the basis for generalisation in legal theory, it comes pre-packaged. It has been selected for its 'legal interest', shaped into legal categories which arise from legal institutions and legal procedures, and then it has been communicated in ways which the comparative lawyer thinks will be effective to say an English-speaking, common law audience.

The consequence is that the jurisprudent must be aware of the theorising that goes into the characterisation of foreign legal systems. Any sensible user would interrogate the comparative lawyer or even work alongside them. Twining rightly singles out the work of MacCormick and Summers on *Interpreting Statutes* and *Interpreting Precedents* as a good example of comparative law.[49] It is work that the jurisprudent can use, because legal theorists themselves acted as the comparative lawyers and ensured a proper interplay between the concerns of the comparative lawyer to communicate effectively and of the jurisprudent to analyse appropriately.

IV. So How Should a Jurisprudent Work?

As Twining remarked, one way to avoid falling into the trap of unjustified universalism is for jurisprudents to work comparatively. Of course, many jurisprudents come from one legal system and work in another, particularly in the US and the UK. As a result, they have an in-built comparative approach, but for others, it is necessary to undertake this in a more structured way.

Collaboration does not have to be the way in which comparative insights are gained. But there does need to be awareness of relevant jurisprudential and comparative literature which does take this perspective. A way forward, it seems to me,

[47] J Bell, 'The Acceptability of Legal Arguments' in DN MacCormick and P Birks (eds), *The Legal Mind* (Oxford University Press, 1986) 45–65.

[48] Lemmens (n 10) 325.

[49] D Neil MacCormick and Robert S Summers (eds), *Interpreting Statutes. A Comparative Study* (Dartmouth, 1991) and *Interpreting Precedents. A Comparative Study* (Dartmouth, 1997).

is illustrated by Neil Duxbury's book, *The Nature and Authority of Precedent*.[50] In his Preface, he writes:

> In so far as this book is concerned specifically with judicial precedents, it is not supposed to present the law relating to precedent in any particular jurisdiction. Rather, it is an exercise in understanding precedent as a jurisprudential concept. In undertaking this exercise I have relied mainly on English law illustrations and problems, though quite often I have used examples from other systems, particularly American law, when those examples point to difficulties and insights that are not immediately apparent from the English sources.[51]

He is aware that much of his work focuses on common law pre-occupations, particularly with stare decisis, but he sees the need to situate that practice in relation to the practices of other legal systems.[52] Accordingly, in an area which Salmond recognised as a most peculiar preserve of the common law, there is still clear awareness of how the statements he makes might apply in non-common-law systems.[53] He has limited his claims as a legal theorist and he stresses the distinctive features within the common law world without making claims that take his theory beyond the evidence. In his parallel work, *Elements of Legislation*,[54] Duxbury solves his problem by writing essentially about English law and then drawing occasionally on the practices of other jurisdictions.[55] He thereby avoids having to engage with the huge literature, particularly in German and Italian on legal method, though he does miss out discussion of Professor Vogenauer's magisterial 1334 page work on statutory interpretation in England, together with Germany, France and the EU, which is helpfully only available in German![56] At the very least, Duxbury has armed himself with an awareness of comparative law, even if he does not engage with it, and he has defined the scope of his claims and research accordingly. That awareness helps him identify his questions and his claims more precisely.

An illustration among legal theorists is Mark Van Hoecke. He is able to review the claims of Dworkin and others about rules and principles in legal reasoning taking account of a substantial amount of both comparative law and also legal theory written in a number of different European languages. That enables him to test out the theory in relation to legal provisions of different legal systems. The result is a more sophisticated and complex picture than that which Dworkin elaborates.[57] His work proves the point that if you want to generalise, then you need

[50] N Duxbury, *The Nature and Authority of Precedent* (Cambridge University Press, 2008).

[51] ibid ix.

[52] ibid 12–13 and fn 33.

[53] ibid 56 fn 109, 117 fn 19, and 136–37 fn 93.

[54] N Duxbury, *Elements of Legislation* (Cambridge University Press, 2013).

[55] ibid ix–x and examples of reference to non-common-law systems on pp 12 fn 33, 72 fn 52, 73 fn 56, 88 fn 127, 136–38, 151 fn 90, and 178–79.

[56] S Vogenauer, Die Auslegung von Gesetzen in England und auf dem Kontinent (Mohr Siebeck, 2001).

[57] M Van Hoecke, *Law as Communication* (Hart, 2002) ch 7.

to scope the phenomena on which you want to generalise. The jurisprudent has to ask herself 'is my theory compatible with what happens in legal systems other than my own?'

Comparative law also helps in the framing of questions about law and what it does. Legal theorists have a rightful autonomy in designing their questions. The questions about the nature of law and the relationship of law to other normative orders arise because of the interdisciplinary connections of legal theory to philosophy, ethics and moral sciences. These provide standards for evaluation of what ought to happen in society. The comparative lawyer is sensitive to local context for two particular reasons: does law operate in solving this problem in societies generally, and secondly does law offer normative solutions? First the legal theorist will claim that the law is part of the solution to problems more in one society than in another. Legal systems may agree that law claims to be the superior reason offered to citizens for action, but there remains a question of how particular problems are handled and whether this is by the law at all. I have always found useful the discussion by Jean Carbonnier of the place of law and non-law within society.[58] The issue is about the source of the norms which govern conduct—how far is *law* the determinative reason for action in a particular problem area and in a particular country. For a start, before talking about law in general, one might question one's assumptions about the issues in which the law is typically or ought to be involved. For example, Anglo-Saxons might assume that the law does not regulate how people dress in public spaces, provided it is not indecent. They might equally think that whether a minimum service is maintained during the next tube strike is not a matter for the law to prescribe. Yet the French would see both as matters on which there should be (and are) legal rules.[59] The boundary between what the law does and what non-law normative rules do is not universal, even within western legal systems. One of the important features of comparative law has been the functional method, which it shares with sociology. It asks 'what task is the society trying to perform, and where does the law fit in?' It is not always the case that law will be the way in which normative solutions to problems are found. Many legal theories contain implicit assumptions about the principle functions which law performs: regulating conduct, providing facilitating structures and so on. Comparative law is a way of helping to clarify whether the functions are always to be related to law. Are they intrinsic to the idea of law or are the accidental in a particular society? Comparative thinking helps the jurisprudent to clarify the question which her theory is addressing.

Another issue about the role of law might be why laws are enacted. The general assumption of Razian positivism is that the law is normative and serves to provide people with reasons for action. Yet a study of the legislative practices of a number of countries might lead one to question whether this is adequate or even right. If

[58] J Carbonnier, *Flexible Droit* 7th edn (Presses Universitaires de France, 1992) Pt 1.

[59] See D McGoldrick, *Human Rights and Religion: The Islamic Headscarf Debate in Europe* (Hart, 2006) ch 2; J Bell, *French Constitutional Law* (Oxford University Press, 1992) 161–62.

we take France again, there are about 10,500 criminal offences of which only 500 are regularly prosecuted.[60] Many legal rules are enacted not to change behaviour but to make a serious public statement about social values. For example, in debating the telecommunications law in 1986, the Conseil d'Etat asked the Ministry what the purpose of article 1 was. It stated 'Telecommunication is free', and the question was what was the normative impact. There was none intended, but it was a way of marking a change in the way telecommunications were regulated. If one is aware of what the different purposes of legislation might be, it is possible to come to ask a better jurisprudential question.

Thus, the approach of involving comparative lawyers, makes one inevitably wary of generalisation. Jhering and Austin were assuming that law (at least in mature societies) does roughly the same things. The comparative law emerging from the dominant micro-comparisons undertaken over the last half a century doubts whether this is right. There are a number of contingent features of a legal system which may determine what role the law plays. Generalisation has to be proved inductively and tested against what is known about legal systems.

Whether comparative lawyers are part of a jurisprudential project or provide background against which jurisprudents undertake their projects, they do more than provide 'data', their interpretations are already part of the jurisprudential enterprise.

V. Comparative Law and the Normative Ambitions of Jurisprudence

There is much writing on the nature and intellectual ambitions of jurisprudence as a legal discipline. This is not helped by the divergence of label adopted in the Anglo-Saxon world and in continental Europe. The Europeans tend to distinguish between 'legal theory' (*Rechtstheorie*) and 'legal philosophy' (*Rechtsphilosophie*).[61] The latter is closely connected to moral and political philosophy and is concerned with the purposes which law ought to serve. The former is concerned with analysing the concepts and techniques which the law (in general) typically does serve. The word 'jurisprudence' in Anglo-Saxon terminology covers both. Nigel Simmonds notes that trends within the Anglo-Saxon world have tended in recent years to draw a distinction between 'analytical' jurisprudence and 'normative' jurisprudence: 'It is taken as more or less obvious that a theory of the nature of law calls for careful description and conceptual clarification, rather than moral enquiry into

[60] Bell (n 36) 103.
[61] M Van Hoecke, *What is Legal Theory?* (ACCO, 1985).

questions of legality and justificatory force.'[62] Both Simmonds and Gardner have criticised this distinction. Gardner is concerned that the analytical and descriptive ambitions turn legal theory merely into a form of sociology, describing and classifying the systems which exist.[63] At the most extreme end of the spectrum, Tamanaha suggests that 'Law is whatever people identify and treat through their social practices as "law" (or Recht, or droit, etc).'[64] Most legal theorists would at least provide a stipulative definition of what ought to be treated as law for analytical purposes. Such an analytical approach might seem to fit alongside both historical and comparative work. Gardner comments that Tamanaha would reduce the study of legal systems to what is very contingent and specific. But Gardner believes that it is possible to develop a general theory of law that is normative. It may be that law is not a universal phenomenon, but it is still possible to say things that are 'interesting and true' about law in general. Furthermore, there is a connection between the social phenomenon of law at the level of description and the normative idea of legality.[65] That idea of legality constitutes a moral ideal, so it is possible and proper to talk about the moral purposes as law, at least in its core connotation. This idea of legality is instantiated in particular legal systems, but not exhausted by those particular instances. Simmonds too argues that the idea of law involves a moral idea. The force of the criticism that someone has broken the law is greater than that the person has just failed to comply with a state-enacted rule.[66] Law may sometimes appear as a set of rather mundane arrangements governing what people can do in society. But law also appears as an elevated aspiration of proper governance: 'governance by law is regarded as being in itself a virtue of a just political community'.[67] It is a special form of having an agreed way of living together that respects the individuality of people. So even though the law exists in different countries in the form of very distinct social practices and with distinct socially enacted rules, there is something more to it:

> Even though law is closely bound up with the existence of such practices, we should not assume that law can unproblematically be *equated* with those practices. For the concept of 'law' is not one that simply *describes* a distinctive type of practice: the concept also has a role within the relevant practices.[68]

The idea of law serves as a regulative ideal within the actual practices of legal institutions. 'Law' is not the sum of the rules of the different legal systems. It is an ideal to be achieved, rather than something fully realised in a particular legal system.[69]

[62] NE Simmonds, *Law as a Moral Idea* (Oxford University Press, 2007) 3.
[63] J Gardner, *Law as a Leap of Faith* (Oxford University Press, 2012) 270.
[64] B Tamanaha, *A General Jurisprudence of Law and Society* (Oxford University Press, 2001) 194.
[65] J Gardner, 'Hart on Legality, Justice and Morality' (2010) 1 *Jurisprudence* 253, 261.
[66] Simmonds (n 62) 10.
[67] Simmonds (n 62) 37.
[68] ibid. See also P Allott, *The Health of Nations* (Cambridge University Press, 2002) 43: 'Legislative texts and reported cases are not themselves the law. They do not even contain the law. The law is somewhere else and something else.'
[69] Allott (n 68) 14.

Now research on a *general* theory of law which is *normative* in the sense that Simmonds has explained might seem to be well beyond the realm of comparative law research. In his recent textbook on comparative law, Mathias Siems[70] does not have a distinct section on legal theory, but does try to connect what comparative law does with jurisprudence. He first considers the place of comparative law and universalism in the sense of concepts common to all legal systems or human communities. Within comparative research, there is a tendency to equate the search for universals with functionalism (the idea that there are some common needs of peoples which are realised in different ways—not always through law—in different social communities). Going further, there is an ambition among many comparative lawyers, as we have seen, to find common standards that can be established from commonalities within the system.[71] The common code or set of principles is offered predominantly as a clarification of the ideals with which people already aspire. There are similarities with the methodology of Rawls in trying to establish principles of justice from what people already accept.[72] Rather like Simmonds, Siems suggests that the ambition of the comparative lawyer is to find the normative standards that are instantiated in social practices, albeit at a much lower level of abstraction than Simmonds or Rawls. A deeper level of comparative law looks not just at rules and practices of different legal systems, but reveals the jurisprudential principles underlying them. As Simmonds suggests, there is critical reflection between theory and the examination of individual instances of law. We want to develop a theory that is properly grounded, but the theory is not just a summary of the detail on the ground, but has underlying reasons which can be justified in terms of theories such as the rule of law. In this case, the jurisprudent is able to work with the material information of particular legal systems and provide insight into these internal principles and beliefs that underlie law in general.[73] So, to this extent, there are some complementarities between the work of comparative lawyers and the ambitions of normative and general jurisprudence.

All the same and like many comparative lawyers, Siems is also concerned to defend comparative law by showing that it does pay considerable attention to social context.[74] Law operates in specific social contexts and this does introduce limitations on how far generalisation about law is possible, at least at the level of specificity within which most comparative lawyers (and legal anthropologists) operate. Jan Smits argues that legal science does aim to be normative, but in a special way. Specific legal systems are often struggling with similar issues, such as balancing the free market as a space for innovation with the protection of consumers against market abuses. In looking at what should be the normative principles

[70] Siems (n 43).

[71] See ibid 28–31.

[72] See TM Scanlon, 'Rawls and Justification' in S Freeman (ed), *The Cambridge Companion to Rawls* (Cambridge University Press, 2003) ch 3.

[73] Siems (n 43) 98–101.

[74] ibid 34.

governing such situations, he sees an important place for comparative law and legal anthropology:

> Existing jurisdictions should be considered as providing empirical material on how to deal with conflicting arguments. The academic method then consists of bringing these arguments into the open and discussing the consequences of choosing one argument over others. In this new perspective, case law and legislation are no longer authoritative statements about what is law within a certain jurisdiction but rather, a source of information about the power of a particular normative argument.[75]

If choice has to be made between the competing arguments, then it is one which has to be justified.[76] In his view the methodology is 'empirical-normative' because the normative argument is developed by looking at what happens in specific legal systems. It seems to me that if one of the functions of jurisprudence is to bring out and debate the normative principles which underpin existing practices (often incoherently and inconsistently), then it does need the contribution of knowledge and analysis of existing legal systems which comparative law provides. Although its ambitions are more theoretical and engage with other disciplines of a very abstract kind, jurisprudence is not exempt from the refinements of the 'empirical-normative' method of law in general.

Importantly, the results of this kind of study may stress the variety of forms in which the same value may be instantiated in particular legal systems. Smits[77] argues:

> The realm of legal science consists … of identifying and re-thinking arguments, and of demonstrating how these arguments might fit the normative setting of a specific jurisdiction. The accompanying method is he empirical-normative one: existing jurisdictions can be seen as laboratories for how to manage conflicting normative positions. The eventual adoption of one argument as the stronger can only take place in the context of a particular jurisdiction. The way in which this decision is made is best described as an application of practical wisdom.

Whereas Simmonds is arguing that valid normative conclusions about law in general can be derived from understanding existing practices, Smits is arguing conversely that the normative conclusions of jurisprudence have to be applied in the concrete settings of particular legal jurisdictions, and this may lead to different practical outcomes. One of my former research students, Lorne Neudorf,[78] has argued for a 'context-sensitive' approach to the study of a legal value such as the 'rule of law'. Whereas there may be a general concept of the rule of law which meets Simmonds' desire for a normative value, its instantiation through

[75] J Smits, The Mind and Method of the Legal Academic (Edward Elgar, 2012) 76.
[76] ibid 96.
[77] ibid 97–98.
[78] L Neudorf, 'Judicial Independence in Context: A Comparative Study of Malaysia and Pakistan' (PhD dissertation, Cambridge, 2014) 33–34.

the conceptions adopted by individual legal systems may vary widely.[79] As Siems suggests, a distinctive contribution of comparative scholars (and also of historical scholars) is in the understanding and analysis of the contextual features of a legal system. This is not a rival to the jurisprudential ambition as sketched by Simmonds and Gardner. Rather, comparative law can contribute both to the formulation of general jurisprudential ideas and to the evaluation of the application of those ideas to concrete situations.

[79] ibid 234–35.

Part III

The History of Theory

9

Reading Juristic Theories In and Beyond Historical Context: The Case of Lundstedt's Swedish Legal Realism

ROGER COTTERRELL*

I. Introduction

Two and a half decades ago *The Politics of Jurisprudence*, a short introduction to juristic theories of law, suggested that the progression of those theories might be understood in new ways by systematically presenting them in historical context. The book argued that they should be considered, in part, 'as responses to political conditions and … conditions of legal professional practice in the time and place in which they emerged'.[1] The book disavowed any aim to *reduce* ideas to their socio-political context (that is, to use context to explain them away as having no significance outside it) but it claimed that this contextual approach could give essential insight into their aims, meaning and scope; it could change understandings of them, sometimes in fundamental ways. The book was concerned only with the Anglo-American context, however, so its cultural comparisons were limited; its focus was on changes in this context in the nineteenth and twentieth centuries.

This chapter attempts to extend and further apply that approach, which was influenced partly by Quentin Skinner's writings about problems of interpreting classical political theory. Skinner originally argued (i) against assuming the *autonomy* of texts as 'self-sufficient object[s] of inquiry and understanding' but also (ii) against their *reduction* to a 'context of other happenings' that might be

* I am grateful to Mauro Zamboni, Maksymilian Del Mar and Michael Lobban for helpful comments, to Jørgen Dalberg-Larsen for supplying some materials, and to Thomas Lakhall for translations from Swedish. I have also benefited from discussion with Sverker Oredsson on matters of historical background. This is a substantially extended and revised version of an article originally published in (2015) 28 *Ratio Juris* 1–14.

[1] R Cotterrell, *The Politics of Jurisprudence: A Critical Introduction to Legal Philosophy* 2nd edn (Oxford University Press, 2003) vii.

thought to 'explain' them.[2] For Skinner, the 'contextual' approach cannot explain a text's meaning (only the conditions of its production), yet it denies that the text itself can explain this meaning. By contrast, the 'autonomy' approach implies timeless, universal meanings of the text, but cannot really solve the problem of how 'timelessness' and 'universality' are to be recognised and established. In practice, 'we' readers in 'our' cultural context may decide what is timeless for 'us'—but an author's questions and the context that inspires them may well be different from ours. Classic texts 'help to reveal … not the essential sameness, but rather the essential variety of viable moral assumptions and political commitments'.[3] For Skinner, they address not timeless, universal problems but historically and culturally specific ones. A study of context cannot explain an author's meaning but it can show the range of possible meaning available to an author in time and place.

Most contemporary scholars of legal theory are surely mainly interested in how they can use theoretical literature to address current theoretical issues. Given such aims a familiar temptation is to *ignore* the specific historical, socio-political context of that literature and to assume an aspiration to timelessness and universality in its arguments and conclusions. Another temptation is to assume that literature, from another time or place, addresses essentially the *same* context of problems and assumptions as that which the reader inhabits. So, one could simply read the literature as if it had *no significant context* other than that familiar to the reader, or one could deliberately take the literature out of context and impose on it a meaning intelligible to the reader in terms of *the reader's own context*. In each of these cases, the text is read as if it is 'autonomous', outside history; yet at least part of the author's meaning is likely to be lost in such approaches to reading.

This chapter argues that it is certainly not illegitimate to seek, in a text from an earlier historical time or written in a different culture, meanings that can transcend that time or culture; but those meanings are unlikely to be found unless context is taken seriously into account in interpreting the aims, meaning and scope of the text. By identifying how much of a work of juristic theory can be best understood by locating it in the socio-political conditions of its time and place, it becomes possible to understand what can legitimately be thought of as *transcending* particular contexts of the text's production: what can speak across time and distance to have meaning in the reader's own world of experience. It could be said that all juristic theory reflects and expresses the characteristics of a socio-political context and a context of established legal institutions and practices, and that nothing can be truly timeless. Whether or not this is so, the most insightful and imaginative theoretical literature can surely sometimes have a range of reference broad enough to address the experience and assumptions (the cultural contexts) of readers distant in place or time from the author. But it is important to reject any assumption that theoretical ideas are *routinely* able to do this or should be expected to.

[2] Q Skinner, 'Meaning and Understanding in the History of Ideas' (1969) 8 *History and Theory* 3, 31, 39.

[3] ibid 52.

How can these abstract ideas about interpreting theory be explored in a more concrete way? This chapter uses the very distinctive theory of the Swedish legal realist Vilhelm Lundstedt to illustrate such an interpretive approach and show how it might help in understanding a particular body of thought. Lundstedt's theory is chosen here specifically because it has been so widely dismissed (at least by non-Scandinavian interpreters) as 'extreme', intemperate and deeply puzzling—even 'impenetrable',[4] with the consequence that it is now almost entirely neglected internationally. This chapter argues that, contrary to these negative assessments, Lundstedt's key arguments—which at one time had very considerable and wide-ranging theoretical and practical influence in jurisprudence and politics in his own country—are *readily intelligible* in the particular Swedish socio-political context in which they were developed. From a certain viewpoint, they appear as a reasonable response to that context.

However, it also seeks to illustrate—by reference to Lundstedt's work—that a contextual study of juristic ideas can facilitate a better assessment of what in those ideas can properly travel *beyond immediate context*: in other words, what enduring insights about the nature of the jurist's task can legitimately be taken from them for more general application. Contrary to prevailing views, I argue that Lundstedt's work, despite having never really been admitted into the international juristic canon, has something of value to offer here. By identifying aspects of it requiring explanation by reference to a specifically Swedish context it becomes possible to see what other aspects might be separated out as transcending that context. The very process of contextualisation may be able to clarify what has more general significance. Thus, the chapter argues that this approach shows Lundstedt's theory as having a much wider relevance for international debates than has previously been recognised. More generally, the chapter seeks to illustrate how ahistorical interpretations of a theory may offer only a partial and, in some respects, distorted or impoverished understanding of its significance.

II. The View from Afar: Lundstedt Abroad

Scandinavian scholars having access to the wide range of literature by and about Lundstedt in Swedish have written extensively on his theory and the context in which it was developed. But his ideas were presented in detail to the English-speaking world mainly through just two books: *Superstition or Rationality in Action for Peace?*[5] published in 1925, and *Legal Thinking Revised*[6] published posthumously in 1956. Information about the socio-political context of his work

[4] R Wacks, *Understanding Jurisprudence: An Introduction to Legal Theory* 3rd edn (Oxford University Press, 2012) 154.

[5] AV Lundstedt, *Superstition or Rationality in Action for Peace? Arguments against Founding a World Peace on the Common Sense of Justice—A Criticism of Jurisprudence* (Longmans, Green, 1925).

[6] AV Lundstedt, *Legal Thinking Revised: My Views on Law* (Almqvist & Wiksell, 1956).

and about his non-English writings is now available in English but is not always conveniently accessible.[7] Lundstedt gained notice in the world outside his own country almost entirely through his two English books,[8] both of them written as general treatises on jurisprudence for an international audience and not presented as tied in any way to Scandinavian legal experience.

The earlier book sets out a lengthy summary of his general views on the nature of law (focusing on criminal law and tort) together with a fierce denunciation of international law as then existing. Reactions to the book ranged from modest interest in his fresh ideas ('There is much that is timely in Lundstedt's criticism of jurisprudential theories')[9] to curt rejection, especially focused on his combative approach ('a shriek is not an argument … cogency of reasoning is not enhanced by loudness of voice').[10] In general, criticism was of the book's seemingly intemperate language rather than of its arguments, with which few reviewers engaged in depth. Reaction to *Legal Thinking Revised* three decades later was more uniformly hostile, both as to the book's content (with its apparently complete rejection of almost all orthodox legal concepts and almost all theories except the author's) and its style, seen as strikingly aggressive and opaque. For most foreign readers, it has been impossible to see behind the disconcerting and often alienating facade that Lundstedt's English texts seemed to present.

His ideas, like those of other Scandinavian legal realists, were mainly judged internationally as an engagement with legal philosophy's perennial conceptual debates. Insofar as these debates addressed such seemingly timeless matters as the nature of rights, duties, responsibility, liability and justice, Lundstedt's contribution, like that of Scandinavian realism generally, appeared largely *negative* and *destructive*. This is because he devoted so much effort to denying the 'reality' of all such established juridical ideas, suggesting not only their lack of practical relevance, but also the serious danger of basing legal practice and legal theory on such 'fantastic', 'irrational' and 'superstitious' thinking.

In relation to the concept of justice, and its invocation as a basis for legal decisions, it is not especially difficult to understand Lundstedt's main arguments, especially as set out in *Superstition or Rationality*.[11] Assuming that justice requires fair or equal treatment, he claims that any law truly aimed at doing justice would need to examine an infinite range of personal circumstances of offenders or litigants to assess their relative position justly, as regards guilt, blame or liability. It would need to inquire into moral perceptions and commitments, states of mind and life conditions, pressures controlling practical choices, inequalities between rich and

[7] In fact much information has become available only since Scandinavian realism has declined in prominence in international juristic debate.

[8] However, LB Orfield, 'A Survey of Scandinavian Legal Philosophy, Part II' (1956) *Wisconsin Law Review* 585, 603–11, summarising his work, draws on his English articles as well as his books.

[9] E Lindsey, 'Book review' (1926) 74 *University of Pennsylvania Law Review* 520, 521.

[10] HJ Randall, 'Book review' (1926) 42 *Law Quarterly Review* 420, 420.

[11] Lundstedt (n 5) 23–27, 48–49.

poor, personal histories and experiences, the differential effects of legal sanctions on individuals, and a host of other matters.

To do all this would make law unworkable; so the appeal to justice as a basis for law is a *chimera*—a mystification and misrepresentation of a working legal system that in practice usually aims not at 'doing justice' or pursuing other 'metaphysical' ideals of traditional jurisprudence but at promoting general security and the welfare of society. Insofar as ideas of justice are practically important they are not the basis and shaping force of legal decisions and policies. In fact, the relationship of cause and effect is reversed: ideas of justice are, to a considerable extent, shaped by law's operations and classifications; they are given substance by normative judgments imposed by the legal system on citizens' actions and relationships, judgments that decide their legal (and, gradually over time, moral) meaning. Insofar as law succeeds in providing long term general security, perceptions of justice will follow it.

As regards criminal law and punishment, for Lundstedt all orthodox justifications for legal action against offenders fail insofar as they focus on deterring, reforming or exacting retribution. The reason is that these justifications operate by attaching ideas of guilt, blame, responsibility or liability to the offender but all such ideas are subject to the same criticisms as those levelled at the concept of justice itself; law has no way to make these concepts refer to objective social conditions but only to a subjective selection of considerations. They refer only to value judgments about offenders and their acts that cannot ultimately be defended because these cannot and do not attempt to take into account all variables (possibly an infinite number of them) that could be considered relevant to the offender's situation. The real function of criminal law is thus not to establish and address offenders' guilt but to identify acts harmful to general welfare; it designates such acts as offences, and connects these offences with 'the general moral instincts' of the public, helping thereby to support and organise these instincts. And the function of punishment is to affirm, through its consistent and predictable use, the existence of criminal law as in force and effective.[12]

This brief summary may be enough to indicate both the negative and positive sides of Lundstedt's theory: the negative side involves sweeping aside all traditional juristic thought as he understands it—what in *Legal Thinking Revised* he calls the method of justice, but which encompasses most orthodox conceptual thinking about law. The positive side involves replacing this with a focus on what is referred to, in *Superstition or Rationality*, as public welfare or the welfare of the community and, in *Legal Thinking Revised*, as the method of social welfare. In Anglophone commentary the reaction to each of these sides of his thought has been different but ultimately equally dismissive. But it is the *negative* side that has often been labelled 'extreme'.

To label theoretical ideas in that way may be to imply that they are outside the acceptable parameters of debate.[13] This judgment seems to have been specially

[12] Lundstedt (n 5) 49–53; Lundstedt (n 6) 166, 218.

[13] cf CR Munro, 'The Swedish Missionary: Vilhelm Lundstedt' (1981) *Juridical Review* 55, 76.

attached to Lundstedt as 'the most extreme' of Scandinavian realists.[14] Yet it is not obvious that he takes a more extreme view of the unreality of legal concepts than does, for example, the usually more respectfully considered Karl Olivecrona.[15] Both writers, closely following Axel Hägerström's anti-metaphysical philosophy, see these concepts (including ideas of rights and duties) as mainly significant only for the psychological feelings that can attach to them, and not as representing a 'reality' (any existing state of affairs relating to law) in themselves.[16] And Lundstedt seems entirely content to accept the use of many basic legal concepts for practical purposes as long as it is recognised that juristic foundations for them linked to the method of justice are chimeral.[17] Thus, it has been said that his 'own works on contract and tort law do not differ much from the works on these topics by other legal scholars'.[18]

The reason for the special judgment on Lundstedt as (unacceptably) extreme may be as much to do with the style of argument of his English books—especially *Legal Thinking Revised*—as with his rejection of established juristic ideas.[19] Critics note his 'polemical tirade', 'tortuous style', 'rambling … badly organised' work,[20] 'arrogance of statement', 'obscurity and incoherence',[21] 'impenetrable thoughts', 'breathtaking conceit and self-importance',[22] and 'naïve and professorial' approach.[23] It seems that, in Anglophone academic cultures not accustomed to Lundstedt's kind of blunt, wounding assessments in which scant respect is paid to the integrity of any views opposed to his own, critics have rarely been in the mood to engage with him or to try to understand what could lie behind the ferocity of his attacks on established juristic ideas.[24]

[14] See eg GW Paton, *A Textbook of Jurisprudence* 4th edn (Clarendon Press, 1972) 39; AH Campbell, 'Book review' (1958) 21 *Modern Law Review* 566, 566.

[15] For a brief recent general comparison of the ideas of the two writers see T Spaak, *A Critical Appraisal of Karl Olivecrona's Legal Philosophy* (Springer, 2014) 268–71. For a discussion of aspects of Olivecrona's legal theory in historical and socio-legal context see R Cotterrell, 'Northern Lights: From Swedish Realism to Sociology of Law' (2013) 40 *Journal of Law and Society* 657. TT Arvind, 'Beyond "Right" and "Duty": Lundstedt's Theory of Obligations' in D Nolan and A Robertson (eds), *Rights and Private Law* (Hart, 2012) suggests that inadequate access in the Anglophone world to Hägerström's ideas may have prejudiced reception of parts of Lundstedt's jurisprudence. But this situation does not seem to have undermined Anglophone appreciation of Olivecrona's thought, which is similarly much indebted to Hägerström.

[16] Lundstedt (n 5) 38, 126–27; K Olivecrona, *Law as Fact* 1st edn (Einar Munksgaard, 1939) ch 3; K Olivecrona, *Law as Fact* 2nd edn (Stevens, 1971) 184.

[17] Lundstedt (n 5) 117–18; and see S Ljungman, 'Vilhelm Lundstedt 11.9.1882—20.8.1955' (1955) 68 *Tidsskrift for Rettsvitenskap* 352, 356–57; Olivecrona 1971 (n 16) 176–77; J Bjarup, 'The Philosophy of Scandinavian Legal Realism' (2005) 18 *Ratio Juris* 1, 11–12.

[18] T Spaak, 'Realism about the Nature of Law' *Ratio Juris*, forthcoming.

[19] One review of *Legal Thinking Revised* suggested that, faced with Lundstedt's 'remorseless analysis', specialists in private law 'may find themselves hard put to find the exact words for a fully effective defence of their most cherished working concepts': see HW Jones, 'Book review' (1958) 58 *Columbia Law Review* 755, 757.

[20] W Friedmann, *Legal Theory* 5th edn (Columbia University Press, 1967) 307, 309.

[21] CK Allen, *Law in the Making* 7th edn (Oxford University Press, 1964) 50.

[22] Wacks (n 4) 154.

[23] HLA Hart, *Essays on Jurisprudence and Philosophy* (Clarendon Press, 1983) 161.

[24] For thoughtful exceptions see Jones (n 19) and (much more critical) Campbell (n 14).

In international context Lundstedt might seem to be debating abstract philosophical positions about the nature of legal ideas; purely academic issues that ought not to justify such intense heat and passion. But, seen in a different, specifically Swedish context, could it be that Lundstedt's 'scorched earth' approach to jurisprudence reflects his impatient sense of an urgent need radically to reshape national legal outlooks to fit them for socio-political conditions requiring new uses of law? I shall argue later in this chapter that this is a fruitful way to see this side of his legal theory.

As regards Lundstedt's *positive* proposals about social welfare, these have been described as abstract, empty of content, wholly unclear, or no less metaphysical than the ideas he rejects.[25] The most incisive sympathetic discussion of them by an Anglophone writer[26] distinguishes Lundstedt's two uses of the idea of social welfare: first, to propose a realistic theoretical explanation of the basis of law, which would avoid all metaphysics, and, second, to advocate a 'constructive jurisprudence' to guide all juristic activity, giving it the practical task of developing law solely on the basis of what is 'useful to the community'.[27] But even Munro concludes that Lundstedt's claims for the method of social welfare 'are significantly limited'.[28] Why then did the Swedish theorist attach so much importance to this idea?

Lundstedt says of the method of social welfare: 'I mean in the first place the encouragement in the best possible way of that—according to what everybody standing above a certain minimum degree of culture is able to understand—which *people in general actually strive to attain*'.[29] He stresses the words 'in the first place' because lawmakers (legislators, judges) might not be able to make these actual strivings the sole guide. They might justifiably see some of them as based on 'false conceptions', and some might be unidentifiable, non-existent, or still in process of formation in the population. Ultimately lawmakers must, as their role requires, make valuations of social welfare to benefit society as a whole.[30]

Lundstedt admits that lawmakers' views or decisions could be distorted by the 'method of justice' but he makes no allowance for any influence on them of prejudice or special interests. Instead, he claims that it is difficult in practice for modern democratic lawmakers to make laws blatantly favouring particular private interests or classes: 'the pressure exerted on the law-maker by the community interest must always be very great' and, in a modern democracy of educated citizens vigilant to watch the lawmaker's actions, '*it is generally impossible to make any*

[25] MDA Freeman, *Lloyd's Introduction to Jurisprudence* 8th edn (Sweet & Maxwell, 2008) 1050; Wacks (n 4) 155; Paton (n 14) 40; Campbell (n 14) 567; but cf TT Arvind, 'Vilhelm Lundstedt and the Social Function of Legislation' (2013) 1 *Theory and Practice of Legislation* 33.

[26] Munro (n 13).

[27] Lundstedt (n 6) 131–36, 193.

[28] Munro (n 13) 76.

[29] Lundstedt (n 6) 140.

[30] ibid 145.

other laws than those which in purpose appear to benefit, broadly speaking, everyone in the community'.[31] Social welfare is obviously a matter of valuations but these are not justified by any overall moral or political philosophy. They will concern the maintenance of social peace and general security, including the security of transactions and the promotion of society's economic well-being through 'the common production of wealth and common exchange of commodities'.[32]

Most critics have seen the method of social welfare as providing little guidance[33] or as simply making ex cathedra judgments about the communal good. Because Lundstedt offers no governing principles but only suggestions of specific goods that social welfare is likely to require, the tendency has been to conclude that the method must ultimately rely on metaphysical commitments (to abstract systems of moral or political principle) which Lundstedt cannot admit, given his claim to reject all metaphysics.[34] So critics have often assumed that what is involved is, despite Lundstedt's explicit denials, some kind of Benthamite utilitarian justification of lawmaking, or a theory of the balancing of interests like Roscoe Pound's.[35]

Taken solely on the basis of what is said in Lundstedt's English books, and without reference to the specific socio-political context in which the method of social welfare is developed, these reductions of it to philosophies of law's purpose that are familiar in international juristic debate are understandable. Correspondingly, Lundstedt's refusal to recognise any fellowship between these approaches and his own becomes incomprehensible. Nevertheless, as will appear, his position is clarified when related to its socio-political context. Not only can it then be seen as based on different assumptions from those informing Poundian or utilitarian jurisprudence but its seeming complacency about the influence of special interests and its total lack of detailed content become readily explicable.

III. Lundstedt in Swedish Context

At least outside Sweden, what has seemed most distinctive about the substance of Lundstedt's theory, most clearly marking him out from the other internationally best known Scandinavian realists, has been his advocated 'method of social welfare'. Olivecrona's most prominent writings say little about it;[36] the Danish realist

[31] Lundstedt (n 5) 133.

[32] F Schmidt, 'The Uppsala School of Legal Thinking' (1978) 22 *Scandinavian Studies in Law* 149, 161.

[33] J Hellner, 'Legal Philosophy in the Analysis of Tort Problems' (1958) 2 *Scandinavian Studies in Law* 149, noting (at 163) the lack of clarity and limited scope of Lundstedt's method, nevertheless offers a careful assessment of its relevance in specifically private law contexts. See also the valuable discussion of Lundstedt's ideas on the law of obligations in Arvind (n 15).

[34] cf M Zamboni, 'Law and Legal Politics: Vilhelm Lundstedt and the Law-maker Function' (2002) 6 *Associations* 35, 57, citing criticisms to this effect.

[35] J Rawls, 'Book review' (1958) 44 *Cornell Law Quarterly* 169, 170; Munro (n 13) 74; Friedmann (n 20) 309; Randall (n 10) 421; cf Hellner (n 33) 164; Jones (n 19) 757.

[36] Olivecrona 1971 (n 16) 45, 84.

Alf Ross explicitly rejects any such idea.[37] Can this seemingly empty theoretical notion of social welfare—presented by Lundstedt as distinct from all other ideas in the international juristic literature—be given greater content and meaning by an appeal to context?

Some well-known facts should be noted. Lundstedt 'is widely known as the most "politicised" legal scholar', writes Mauro Zamboni, 'not only because he was for many years an active member of the [Swedish] Social Democratic Party and the Swedish Parliament. His "political" character is also derived from his legal philosophy'.[38] It has been said that Lundstedt 'very often based his political points of view in his views on law',[39] but it might equally be suggested that his politics and his immersion in the political currents of his time influenced the direction of his legal thought.[40] In the small, closely integrated, Swedish elite of lawmakers, opinion-formers, politicians and academic leaders, Lundstedt was well connected, and was himself an active legislator, a powerful influence in academic life, a prominent legal and political campaigner and an eloquent contributor to the press on matters of legal reform and policy.

My copy of *Superstition or Rationality* offers a simple illustration of such connections. Inscribed in fountain pen ink on its first blank page are the words 'to Rickard Lindström with the author's kindest regards'. Lindström was a journalist and a leading 'modernising' politician in the Social Democratic Party in the 1920s and 1930s[41] when the party was shaping its policies to become the dominant unifying voice of Swedish politics, a position it would seek to maintain through 40 years of uninterrupted government from 1932. This process involved transformation from a socialist class-based party to a national one emphasising solidarity and unity throughout Swedish society, encapsulated in the idea, strongly promoted from 1928, of Sweden as a 'people's home' (*folkhem*)—a kind of homogeneous national family in which class conflict and 'privilege or backwardness' would be dissolved away in an overall national interest, a common social welfare.[42] On such foundations 'a new society marked by good sense, rationality and planning' would be built.[43]

[37] A Ross, *On Law and Justice* (Stevens & Sons, 1974) 295–96. On Ross' persistent negative criticism of Lundstedt, see J Evald, *Alf Ross: A Life* (DJØF, 2014) 226–28.

[38] Zamboni (n 34) 39.

[39] J-O Sundell, 'Vilhelm Lundstedt: A Biographical Sketch' (2005) 48 *Scandinavian Studies in Law* 465, 466.

[40] Lundstedt is said to have referred to his legal realism 'as a Social Democrat legal theory': see Evald (n 37) 227. He joined the Social Democratic Party in the mid-1910s, and his conversion to a realist jurisprudential outlook, under the strong influence of Axel Hägerström, took place around the same time: K Molin, 'A Vilhelm Lundstedt' (1982–84) 24 *Svenskt biografiskt lexikon* 376; Sundell (n 39) 465–66.

[41] K Zetterberg, 'K A Rickard Lindström' (1980–81) 23 *Svenskt biografiskt lexikon* 649; L Trägårdh, 'Crisis and the Politics of National Community: Germany and Sweden, 1933/1994' in N Witoszek and L Trägårdh (eds), *Culture and Crisis: The Case of Germany and Sweden* (Berghahn, 2002) 81.

[42] CE Schall, '(Social) Democracy in the Blood? Civic and Ethnic Idioms of Nation and the Consolidation of Swedish Social Democratic Power, 1928–1932' (2012) 25 *Journal of Historical Sociology* 440.

[43] F Sejersted, *The Age of Social Democracy: Norway and Sweden in the Twentieth Century* (Princeton University Press, 2011) 47.

In fact an idea of *folkhem* had been circulating from early in the twentieth century.[44] Lundstedt's concept of social welfare (*samshällsnyttan*) was present in his writings from 1920.[45] In 1925, while treating it as more or less self-evident, he emphasises that it requires both capitalist 'haves' and proletarian 'have-nots' to renounce irreconcilable demands; each side will have to give way for the benefit of the social and economic wellbeing of the whole national community.[46] At just this time the Social Democratic party was in the process of adopting an ideal of class-free national solidarity and convictions about its necessary policy supports that came to seem entirely self-evident for it; as self-evident as Lundstedt's method of social welfare was claimed by him to be.

There is no need here to postulate directions of influence between Lundstedt's thinking on social welfare and the political currents in which he operated. It is enough to recognise their very close compatibility and the ease with which, in such a climate, the largely empty juristic shell of the method of social welfare could be filled by a political programme seen, in its general shape, as indisputably appropriate by those promoting and supporting it. In other words, socio-political context remedies the 'abstract', 'empty' and 'unclear' character of the method. Lundstedt strongly rejected the claim of some Swedish critics that his legal theory was a cover for his 'social democratic prejudices',[47] and he did not see the requirements of social welfare in exactly the same way as his own political party did.[48]

The essential compatibility between his legal theory and its social democratic political context lies not in an identity of social welfare valuations in each but in the uniform assumption that the meaning of social welfare could be rationally and objectively determined and consensually legitimated in normal political processes. For Lundstedt the everyday refinements of policy derived from the political process are what guide social welfare; and what unifies these policy developments is a political valuation that social solidarity and the economic wellbeing of the society as a whole are supremely important.

In this context it seems reasonable to see Lundstedt's denial of a metaphysical underpinning of social welfare as based on his conviction that conscientious lawmakers will follow this valuation in solving problems as they arise. And because the valuation focuses on the welfare of the national community *as a whole* this is not a matter of a utilitarian counting of how many individuals will benefit, and by how much, from any particular legal policy; nor is it a matter of a Poundian balancing of interests which presupposes individual claims in opposition to each

[44] Trägårdh (n 41) 84.

[45] Schmidt (n 32) 161.

[46] Lundstedt (n 5) 136–37.

[47] Whatever the merits of this claim it misses the point here, which is not that one should read off the legal theory from its author's politics or vice versa, or that one 'caused' the other, but that a direct correlation exists between Lundstedt's approaches to legal theory and to politics; common presumptions underlie the conceptualisation of each field. A similar correlation seems, to me, to exist between Karl Olivecrona's legal theory (insofar as it is seen as a speculative sociology of law) and his published wartime political positions: see Cotterrell (n 15); cf Spaak (n 15) 175–76.

[48] Arvind (n 15) 178.

other and in confrontation with social interests. Lundstedt's 1925 book argues that individual and community cannot be set against each other: the community exists for the benefit of all individuals and cannot be treated as distinct from them; to raise claims against the communal interest would be to undermine the very conditions that provide the individual's guarantee of security and welfare.[49]

The purpose of this chapter is not particularly to defend Lundstedt's views, which in Sweden and elsewhere[50] have been criticised for their potential for authoritarianism.[51] But it is to suggest that they are readily understandable in terms of a specific relation to the political ideologies and cultural experiences that complete them and which they seem strongly to support and confirm. Lundstedt's social welfare presupposes and perhaps idealises very specific socio-political conditions:

— the possibility of building consensus in a small essentially homogeneous population
— a tightly integrated and public-spirited governing elite
— a paternalistic political tradition in which it could be seen as natural for the lawmakers to fix valuations for society as a whole, and
— an assumption of the deep-rootedness of democratic and liberal instincts ('in the blood')[52] tempering any theoretical possibility of governmental authoritarianism.

Criticisms in Sweden of Lundstedt's ideas, or of Scandinavian realism in general, often focus on the attenuation of some of these crucial conditions or assumptions.[53]

Do these considerations then merely 'explain away' Lundstedt's thought by reference to its historical context—which I suggested earlier a contextual approach should not do? Zamboni has suggested that legal realist approaches present the relationship between law and politics as an 'intersecting' one, rather than as reducing the former to the latter; on this view, law has a 'partial rigidity' (an identity) not reducible to political context.[54] Something important remains about the idea of law after it has been confronted 'realistically' with its specific socio-political contexts. But, in the context of Lundstedt's theory, that enduring identity of law

[49] Lundstedt (n 5) 34–35.

[50] See eg Campbell (n 14).

[51] During World War II Lundstedt defended governmental controls on the distribution of some newspapers and other publications, seeing such limitations on the free circulation of ideas as necessary to protect the country in a time of emergency from communists and others who, he thought, sought to destroy it; laws aimed at saving the nation from destruction could not be regarded as unconstitutional. He also advocated control of anti-democratic political parties: see Molin (n 40); cf more generally, P Mindus, *A Real Mind: The Life and Work of Axel Hägerström* (Springer, 2009) 171ff.

[52] cf Trägårdh (n 41) 77.

[53] eg Zamboni (n 34) 52, on change in relation to lawmakers; and J Sundberg, 'Scandinavian Unrealism' in E Kamenka, RS Summers and WL Twining (eds), *Soziologische Jurisprudenz und realistische Theorien des Rechts* (Duncker & Humblot, 1986) 315, on change in relation to liberal traditions.

[54] M Zamboni, *Law and Politics: A Dilemma for Contemporary Legal Theory* (Springer-Verlag, 2008) ch 4.

has to be brought to light, one might say, from the interstices of the theory; from the concepts that still remain important in his thinking even after its relentless attack on metaphysics, and from certain assumptions that enable him to continue to speak of law when so much of the focus of his theory is on policy. Following this line of approach, Lundstedt's method can be seen, I shall suggest, as a way of talking about law that may help in understanding, *in general terms*, what could be an appropriate juristic involvement with issues of legal policy or governmental purpose. But, as a prelude to addressing such matters, the 'negative' side of his theory, his attack on the method of justice, needs also to be linked to its socio-political context.

Realist attacks on metaphysics were heavily attacked as 'value nihilism' (*värdennihilismen*)—a reckless sweeping away of all moral foundations for law, setting it adrift without a moral rudder.[55] One way to interpret Lundstedt's polemic against the 'method of justice' is as a deliberate cultural ground-clearing exercise: a relentless effort to destroy old ways of thought to make way for fresh ideas of law as an instrument to steer a rapidly changing, secularising, modernising society. When his work is examined carefully it is clear that the idea of justice does not disappear from it but is *reinterpreted sociologically* and pressed into service to serve social welfare. On this view, widely accepted ideas of justice cannot guide law securely but are nevertheless needed to support the machinery of the legal system and cannot be ignored by it. A 'common sense of justice' is present in society—a broad consensus on right, wrong and fairness. This originates in primitive social instincts refined and shaped by the operation of the legal system as a mechanism of coercion and persuasion over centuries. And although the common sense of justice is, on this analysis, very largely a consequence of the stable, regular, long term application of law, the working legal system must take this consciousness of justice as a value into account, if its operations are to be effective.[56]

Thus, seen in socio-political context, Lundstedt's attack on metaphysics in law involves reinterpreting all orthodox, 'irrational' juristic ideas in *functional* terms. The recognition of 'rights', 'justice' and other such ideas is a necessary means of securely connecting the attitudes of the citizenry to the tasks of the legal system. Lundstedt's campaigning on many occasions to correct miscarriages of justice can be seen in this light; so can his efforts to bring about the decriminalisation of homosexual acts between consenting adults and his campaign against alcohol prohibition legislation, both of which can be understood as action against pointless legal victimisation of or interference with otherwise law-abiding citizens.[57] In the

[55] J Strang, 'The Scandinavian Value Nihilists and the Crisis of Democracy in the 1930s and 40s' (2009) 19(1) *Nordeuropaforum* 37; Mindus (n 51) 104–06.

[56] Lundstedt (n 5) 132, 189–91; Lundstedt (n 6) 169–70; AV Lundstedt, 'The Responsibility of Legal Science for the Fate of Man and Nations' (1933) 10 *New York University Law Quarterly Review* 326, 335.

[57] Sundell (n 39); J Rydström, *Sinners and Citizens: Bestiality and Homosexuality in Sweden, 1880–1950* (University of Chicago Press, 2003) 161–69.

minds of those to be protected and defended through such campaigns, the issues could readily appear as ones of creating or asserting private rights or promoting civil liberties. At the same time, however, his support for the state's power of expropriation of landed property affirms that, in his thinking, social welfare ultimately has to trump incompatible public attitudes to private rights.[58]

Lundstedt's idea of a common sense of justice assumes a special socio-political context: first, a history of relative peace and stability allowing the consistent maintenance of fundamental legal rules 'over centuries' to shape this sense[59] and, second, that a consensus on ideas about law and morality does, indeed, exist within the regulated population. The assumption of such a consensus seems broadly consistent with the Swedish social democratic outlook on national homogeneity in the period when Lundstedt wrote (1920s to 1950s); one might say that the movement for modernisation and social development presupposed a moral substratum that would provide stability in this process of change. Perhaps unsurprisingly, one of the earliest Swedish empirical studies in sociology of law, carried out in 1947–48, was designed to examine how uniform and wide-reaching the common sense of justice was. It found differences between social groups, but within a broader picture of significant uniformity.[60]

While, for Lundstedt, justice ideas must be taken into account in the operations of the legal system, the 'negative' side of his theory emphasises that they can never be allowed to direct it. This is far from being purely a position in philosophical debates about the epistemology of legal concepts. In his view, an effectively functioning legal system *controls* justice ideas as it makes use of them; it harnesses them to social welfare and prevents the emotional claims associated with them from getting out of hand.

It is in his arguments about international law in *Superstition or Rationality*[61] that Lundstedt shows most clearly why he sees the method of justice and its associated juristic concepts as not merely irrational but dangerous. In a functioning municipal legal system claims of right are successfully managed, limited and directed by the operation of law. But he considers that on the international stage, 'legal' claims of right made by states are subject to no such constraints and there are no adequately effective means to manage them; without an international judicial system backed by immense coercive power to enforce its judgments against mighty states, states' claims of right become excuses for war or for the subjection of weak states to stronger ones. Juridically empty rights-talk by states is significant only for the feelings of entitlement it encourages, fuelling demands for satisfaction by other states.

[58] Lundstedt (n 5) 89; J Strang, 'Two Generations of Scandinavian Legal Realists' (2009) 32 (1/12) *Retfærd* 62, 66; Sundberg (n 53) 316.

[59] Lundstedt (n 6) 169; Lundstedt (n 5) 132, 191.

[60] TT Segerstedt, with G Karlsson and BG Rundblad, 'A Research into the General Sense of Justice' (1949) 15 *Theoria* 323.

[61] Lundstedt (n 5) 161ff.

Unsurprisingly, Lundstedt's views were quickly criticised for ignoring the positive achievements of international law and its potential for development;[62] otherwise, being so negative, they were simply ignored. Politically, Lundstedt supported Sweden's policy of neutrality in the first half of the twentieth century in a situation where, as he saw it, opting out of defensive international ties offered better prospects than relying on the hopelessly weak structures of the League of Nations to police them.[63]

IV. A Wider Context: The Jurist's Role

So far, this chapter has developed two main arguments. First, Lundstedt's idea of social welfare must be understood in relation to a specific socio-political context at a particular time; attention to this context completes the meaning of his otherwise puzzling idea by reference to a political programme and a set of cultural factors treated as its objective foundation. The judge or legislator 'resolves his policy doubts'[64] by awareness of these factual conditions (the desires and understandings of citizens filtered through the political process) which make appeals to metaphysics redundant.[65] Second, attention to context also shows that ideas of justice, and, more generally, most of the apparatus of familiar juristic thought which Lundstedt criticises so heavily, are not actually abolished in his thinking but reappear as significant in it when they are reinterpreted in functional terms and treated as important characteristics of the social environment in which law must operate.

These contextual interpretations do not, however, 'explain away' his juristic theory. They make it possible to see more clearly what in it might properly be transported to a wider international arena of debate. Indeed, perhaps they can show it as more relevant to that arena than it has usually been thought to be. A starting point for such an argument is Olivecrona's seemingly casual comment that 'Lundstedt used to say that he was not a philosopher but a jurist', his practical aim being 'a complete reorientation of legal science'[66]—that is, of the jurist's specific field of concern. This raises the question of what this field is and what idea of law must inform it. It also raises the question of how far the *role of the jurist* can be envisaged in international perspective, beyond the context of any particular legal culture.

[62] FS Dunn, 'Book review' (1926) 26 *Columbia Law Review* 1050.

[63] Sundell (n 39) 467; Lundstedt 1933 (n 56) 337. Later, unusually among Swedish social democrats, he argued in favour of Sweden joining NATO: Sundell (n 39) 468; Arvind (n 15) 179. Seemingly he was again refusing to put his faith in international law and now placed it instead in the effectiveness of an international pragmatic alliance of political and military power against what he saw as the threat of communism.

[64] Jones (n 19) 757.

[65] Lundstedt (n 5) 145.

[66] K Olivecrona, 'The Legal Theories of Axel Hägerström and Vilhelm Lundstedt' (1959) 3 *Scandinavian Studies in Law* 125, 137.

Lundstedt's approach assumes that such a role is, indeed, not that of a professional philosopher, insofar as the latter is seen as concerned to prioritise abstract and universal philosophical problems rather than issues about relating an operational concept of law to its contexts of application. For this practical application jurists may need not a fully developed philosophical system but a more provisional or adaptable idea of law serviceable in addressing legal issues in their time and place and perhaps in trying to preserve and protect and promote values with which law is generally associated.

The international relevance of Lundstedt's thought may lie in helping to point towards such a flexible, juristically useful idea of law. He often refers to law in descriptive, sociological terms as a governmental 'machinery' of control,[67] an idea which in itself offers no general *juristic* view of it in terms of normative concepts or values. But Lundstedt's theory surrounds this skeletal, behavioural conception of law with substantive ideas intended to guide the operation of the legal machinery and give it normative content. Thus, the idea of law's necessary *purpose* (its governing policy) of serving citizens' actual common needs and wants expressed as social welfare clearly dominates his theory. Beyond this, one of his most constant references in discussing social welfare is to *security* as a pervasive value. He stresses the importance of the security that citizens seek through the predictable, consistent operation of the legal machinery.[68] But he also refers to the security of the social order: the reliability of transactions and trading arrangements, and the security for social life provided by a successfully functioning economy.[69] The method of social welfare seems largely directed to (i) framing legally a stable socio-economic order and (ii) protecting law's own order and reliability as regulatory machinery.

It has been seen that alongside these closely related concerns with law's (fitness for) purpose and with security, a focus on *justice* remains central to Lundstedt's thought, even after his rejection of the method of justice. He recognises that, in the democratic legal systems that his theory assumes, ideas of justice cannot be dispensed with. They are a major part of the historical, social and psychological bedrock on which modern law's effectiveness depends. Thus despite his radical critiques, the 'irrational' and 'superstitious' ideal of justice remains important in his jurisprudence.

Thus, ideas about law's purpose, about security as a value, and about demands for justice must be seen as the central organising elements of Lundstedt's juristic thought. Alongside the minimal conception of law as 'machinery', these elements—related but distinguishable pointers to law's essential value concerns—together encompass the entirety of the general idea of law expressed in his juristic theory.

[67] See eg Lundstedt (n 6) 8, 18. cf D Black, *The Behavior of Law* (Academic Press, 1976), conceptualising law simply as 'governmental social control'.

[68] Lundstedt (n 5) 26–27, 135–36.

[69] ibid 131; Schmidt (n 32) 161.

Law is 'the very life of mankind in organised groups and the conditions which make possible ... peaceful co-existence ... and ... cooperation'.[70] So it expresses—through its focus on purpose, security and justice—all the values that enable it to have this character.

But Lundstedt insists that none of these values have any metaphysical foundations. Justice is no more than a popular sense, rooted in instinct and shaped by law; security is merely what people everywhere demand; law's guiding purpose is simply what makes sense in cultural and political context. There are no ultimate philosophical justifications to underpin these valuations. Their content can only be what the jurist, in support of the lawmaker, identifies as relevant for the time and place. In this light it is possible to see why Lundstedt distinguished the jurist's role from the philosopher's. The jurist works with valuations rooted in and validated by specific historical conditions of legal practice. Law, it might be said, is an affair of distinct values—justice, security, efficiency for purpose. Yet the content of these is not developed in or from abstract philosophical systems, but out of the exigencies of juristic work. It is the need to interpret and reconcile these values constantly in practice that gives the jurist a distinctive role.

It seems appropriate to draw a comparison here with Gustav Radbruch's view[71] of the jurist's role, despite fundamental differences between his and Lundstedt's theories. Like Lundstedt, Radbruch recognises the need for a general but flexible idea of law to guide practical juristic activity but sees no need for (or perhaps the impossibility of) a comprehensive philosophical system adaptable for juristic purposes. He similarly emphasises a triangle of values informing the idea of law: security, justice and 'fitness for purpose' (*Zweckmassigkeit*)—that is, law's adaptability to goals set for it culturally or politically. These values are to be interpreted in relation to time and place, the triangular relationship between them shifting with a kind of variable geometry.[72] Like Lundstedt, Radbruch sees the jurist's role as one of working flexibly with shifting conceptions of security and justice as values sought as *social* goods, but also as values sought in law's own operations.

But Lundstedt, unlike Radbruch, does not see justice as ultimately the fundamental element in the idea of law; his purely functional view of it subordinates it to claims for (economic and legal) security and order. Nevertheless, his writings leave open many questions as to how the common sense of justice and the popular demand for security may interact; it seems that this could vary with time and place. And it can be assumed that part of the jurist's task, in Lundstedt's view, is to observe and assess these values, and manage the expression of their practical interaction in legal doctrine.

Lundstedt surely affirms that law's purpose is not capable of being fixed theoretically in some timeless manner: it is a theoretical (and political) given that

[70] Lundstedt (n 6) 8.

[71] G Radbruch, 'Legal Philosophy' 3rd edn (1932) in EW Patterson et al (eds), *The Legal Philosophies of Lask, Radbruch and Dabin* (K Wilk trans, Harvard University Press, 1950).

[72] R Cotterrell, 'The Role of the Jurist: Reflections around Radbruch' (2013) 26 *Ratio Juris* 510.

this purpose must be social welfare, but the detailed content of social welfare in any particular context is to be set by *political* strategies interpreted in the light of *cultural* understandings. Within this purposive framework, concerns for security and for (the popular sense of) justice can be assumed to be prominent. Juristic work involves reconciling these elements successfully in the form of law. From this perspective, law retains its juristic identity (what Zamboni terms its 'partial rigidity')[73] because it faces both ways—it faces towards the political authority that it serves instrumentally and that guarantees its effectiveness, but it faces also towards the cultural authority that it depends on for its roots in popular acceptance and understanding. Putting this in different terms, law is partly a mere machinery of control to secure governmental aims, and partly the repository of values, aspirations, needs and interests rooted in the character and culture of the society it must regulate.

In a particular local context (such as the Sweden of Lundstedt's time) the dialectic of politics and culture plays out in its own distinctive way through law. But the dialectic itself and the tasks of balancing the values of security and justice, as understood in their varied historical and social contexts, might be seen as fundamentals of the juristic idea of law. Seen in this perspective, the pursuit of certain intertwined and sometimes competing values of justice and security, understood in different ways in different times and places and coloured by cultural presuppositions and expectations, provides an essential dynamic of juristic practice.

However, legal forms, as contrasted with legal values, may be less fundamental juristically, especially in a world in which juristic practice is faced with new challenges in conceptualising law in new forms for practical purposes. While the particular positive forms that law takes and the specific institutions and agencies that serve it in a given environment will be of central concern to jurists in pursuing their practice in that environment, they may not need general or comprehensive theories to explain the forms, institutions and agencies of law in some universal or timeless way. Lundstedt was, it seems, content merely to label them collectively as the 'legal machinery' without theorisation. And other pragmatic, provisional working conceptions of law are possible. Thus, positive law in a simple, minimal sense might be seen merely as normative doctrine (of some sort) with specific agencies (of some sort) existing to manage it.[74] In practice, of course, the jurist must understand law in any particular jurisdiction in far more sophisticated terms. But the combination of a minimal conception of legal 'machinery' and a tenacious commitment to the pursuit of basic legal values might be a realistic starting point to allow jurists to begin to address theoretically many new, unfamiliar regulatory phenomena, for example in the diverse, burgeoning fields of transnational regulation.

[73] Zamboni (n 54) 88.

[74] R Cotterrell, *Law's Community: Legal Theory in Sociological Perspective* (Clarendon Press, 1995) 37–40; R Cotterrell, 'What is Transnational Law?' (2012) 37 *Law & Social Inquiry* 500, 506–08.

Lundstedt's theory has to be understood as strongly coloured by the experience of a particular society at a particular time. That necessarily puts many limitations on its relevance as general legal theory applicable beyond the context in which it was developed. Nevertheless, sympathetically interpreted, it may suggest some fundamental, irreducible elements in a juristically useful idea of law that can transcend context. It may also help to reveal general parameters of the jurist's role as that of balancing, through the *time-bound* forms, precepts and processes of law, *enduring* aspirations for justice and security as legal and social values.

10

Legal Realism and Natural Law

DAN PRIEL AND CHARLES BARZUN*

I. Introduction

Legal realism and natural law? The very juxtaposition sounds odd. In the popular academic imagination natural law is all about eternal principles discoverable by pure reason while legal realism is about 'law in flux'.[1] Natural law is the legal theory of Aristotle, Cicero and Aquinas, whereas legal realism has been associated with American pragmatism, logical positivism, behaviourism, psychoanalysis, modern anthropology, even quantum mechanics—all ideas firmly embedded in the twentieth-century psyche. It is these associations that have led one commentator to say that 'with its emphasis on empirical and functional methodologies and its thoroughgoing skepticism about moral or epistemological absolutes, [legal realism] would seem to be a quintessentially modernist jurisprudence'.[2] What could such a view of law have in common with the most un-modernist of legal theories, an approach that more than any other is associated with the affirmation of moral and epistemological absolutes?

The apparent disparity is not merely a matter of competing philosophies; it is also part of history. When the realists came to prominence in the 1930s, their fiercest critics were Catholic scholars, who often contrasted legal realism with natural law. One of them wrote that:

> Realism by taking God, soul, mind, will, innate dignity, and innate *de jure* independence away from man, makes man the pawn of might, and breaks the neck of democracy. Godless Behaviorism and Pragmatism are the head hunters, with Democracy and popular sovereignty the victims.[3]

* We are grateful to Maks Del Mar and Michael Lobban for their comments on an earlier draft.

[1] See KN Llewellyn, 'Some Realism about Realism—Responding to Dean Pound' (1931) 44 *Harvard Law Review* 1222, 1236.

[2] GE White, 'Recapturing New Deal Lawyers' (1988) 102 *Harvard Law Review* 489, 514.

[3] See, eg FE Lucey, 'Natural Law and American Legal Realism: Their Respective Contribution to a Theory of Law in a Democratic Society' (1942) 30 *Georgetown Law Journal* 493, 526, 531–32. Many additional examples are cited in EA Purcell, Jr, *The Crisis of Democratic Theory: Scientific Naturalism & the Problem of Value* (University of Kentucky Press, 1973) 160–72; N Duxbury, 'The Reinvention of American Legal Realism' (1992) 12 *Legal Studies* 137, 164–73.

He associated legal realism with fascism and declared that in the battle of the day 'Democracy *versus* the Absolute State means Natural Law *versus* Realism'.[4]

Moving to the present, the gulf between legal realism and natural law still appears vast. Especially in the American context, natural law is these days typically invoked in defence of conservative causes;[5] by contrast, the realists' most immediate association is with the New Deal, a political agenda that remains anathema to many on the American right. The association of legal realism with natural law theory will also sound odd to those versed in contemporary debates in legal theory. Those who see the realists as early precursors of the critical legal studies movement will agree with Joseph William Singer that the 'legal realists removed the possibility of answering ... questions [like how we come to our normative commitments and how we should question them] by appeal to natural law or to the logical implications of abstract concepts'.[6] Finally, even among the narrower confines of analytic jurisprudence the association of legal realism with natural law flies in the face of an influential recent interpretation of legal realism according to which legal realism presupposes the truth of 'hard' legal positivism.[7] This reading places legal realism as the polar jurisprudential opposite of natural law theory.

And yet, in spite of all this, when one looks at the works of the people who called themselves 'legal realists', matters look less clear cut. Hessel Yntema stated that 'the classification of American legal realism in the category of positivism along with Austin, Kelsen, etc, is so superficial as to border on the perverse'.[8] This does not yet show that the realists saw themselves as natural lawyers—after all, they might have seen themselves as a *new* kind of approach to law—but it already somewhat destabilises the association between realism and positivism. When one turns to the works of the two most famous legal realists one finds in them clear affirmations of a positive connection between legal realism and natural law. As early as 1938 Karl Llewellyn wrote that 'it is difficult for me to conceive of the ultimate legal ideals of any of the writers who have been called realists in terms which do not resemble amazingly the type and even the content of the principles of a philosopher's Natural Law'.[9] Even more surprisingly, Jerome Frank, usually considered among the most extreme realists, the one whose views are sometimes thought to border

[4] Lucey (n 3) 533; to the same effect see B. W. Palmer, 'Natural Law and Pragmatism' (1948) 23 *Notre Dame Law Review* 313, 339-40. 62–63; cf R Pound, 'The Revival of Natural Law' (1942) 17 *Notre Dame Lawyer* 287, 315, 322–23, 325.

[5] See, eg M Worthen, 'The First Principles of Rick Santorum' *New York Times* (9 February 2012) available at http://campaignstops.blogs.nytimes.com/2012/02/09/the-first-principles-of-rick-santorum/.

[6] JW Singer, 'Legal Realism Now' (1988) 76 *California Law Review* 465, 541.

[7] See B Leiter, *Naturalizing Jurisprudence: Essays on American Legal Realism and Naturalism in Legal Philosophy* (Oxford University Press, 2007) 73, 134–35. For critiques of Leiter's position (independent of the arguments developed here) see D Priel, 'Were the Legal Realists Legal Positivists' (2008) 27 *Law and Philosophy* 309; D Priel, 'Jurisprudence between Science and the Humanities' (2012) 4 *Washington University Jurisprudence Review* 269, 307–16.

[8] H Yntema, 'Jurisprudence on Parade' (1941) 39 *Michigan Law Review* 1154, 1164.

[9] KN Llewellyn, 'One "Realist's" View of Natural Law for Judges' (1939) 15 *Notre Dame Lawyer* 3, 8.

on nihilism,[10] stated: 'I do not understand how any decent man today can refuse to adopt, as a basis of modern civilisation, the fundamental principles of Natural Law.'[11] As these words do not fit the image of Frank as the 'bad boy' of legal realism, they are often simply ignored. When they are mentioned, they are explained away as reflecting the views of the 'later', mellower Frank (by then a federal appellate judge), recanting the folly of his youth after the horrors of World War II.[12]

We will address this claim in more detail below, but already here we will note some difficulties with it. In the same year Frank wrote the words just quoted, he published *Courts on Trial*, which is hardly a complacent look at the law. On the other hand, as early as 1932 Frank dismissed the idea that the realists are '"positivists" who are exclusively devoted to whatever is now happening in the legal world'. The realists, he said, were all 'eager … to improve the judicial system, to make it more efficient, more responsive to social needs, more "just", if you like that word'.[13]

One aim of this chapter is to make sense of these seemingly odd statements, to explain how some legal realists think of themselves as natural lawyers. We will argue below that rather than demonstrating some radical shift in the views of Llewellyn and Frank, they reflect ideas that can be found in even their earliest, and seemingly most 'destructive', works. Before we proceed, however, we must add an important caveat. While Llewellyn and Frank were—and remain—among the best-known legal realists, we do not claim that they are necessarily representative of all legal realists, let alone of some abstract construct called 'legal realism'. Both Llewellyn and Frank often warned that the 'Schools' approach to jurisprudence tends to lump together different thinkers who are in fact quite different.[14] And indeed, there were some self-described legal realists who expressed scepticism about natural law ideas.[15] Moreover, as our argument unfolds, it will become apparent that even Llewellyn and Frank understood the term 'natural law' somewhat differently. One incidental aim of this chapter is thus to serve as reminder that all attempts to identify what legal real*ism* is should be treated carefully. Such efforts are often illuminating, but they must be understood as constructs created out of the views of numerous individuals who on many things held quite different

[10] See, eg HLA Hart, 'American Jurisprudence through English Eyes: The Nightmare and the Noble Dream' (1977) 11 *Georgia Law Review* 969, 974; LP Francis, 'Law and Philosophy: From Skepticism to Value Theory' (1993) 27 *Loyola of Los Angeles Law Review* 65, 73.

[11] J Frank, *Law and the Modern Mind* 6th printing (Anchor Books, 1949) xx.

[12] Perhaps the first to make this claim is MP Sharp, 'Realism and Natural Law' (1957) 24 *University of Chicago Law Review* 648, 655–57.

[13] J Frank, 'Mr Justice Holmes and Non-Euclidean Legal Thinking' (1932) 17 *Cornell Law Quarterly* 568, 586.

[14] KN Llewellyn, Law in Our Society: A Horse-Sense Theory of the Institution of Law (unpublished course materials, 1950 edition) 82–83; J Frank, *If Men Were Angels: Some Aspects of Government in a Democracy* (Harper, 1942) 277–79.

[15] See WW Cook, 'Scientific Method and the Law' (1927) 13 *American Bar Association Journal* 303, 306; JW Bingham, 'Law Schools and the Future' (1954) 6 *Journal of Legal Education* 486, 496–97 fn 3; cf OW Holmes, 'Natural Law' (1918) 32 *Harvard Law Review* 40.

views. In this essay we eschew such grand claims and limit our focus to an analysis of the views of two legal real*ists*.

One stumbling block to any meaningful discussion of a possible relationship between legal realism and natural law is that it requires some clarification of the possible sense(s) in which Llewellyn and Frank saw themselves as natural lawyers and (if this is any different) as opponents of positivism. In so doing, we must begin by setting aside several possible interpretations of these terms as inadequate. To begin, neither Frank nor Llewellyn believed that consistency with true morality was a condition of legal validity (or, more colloquially, that an unjust law was no law at all). From the vantage point of contemporary jurisprudence, this may seem odd, as the divide between legal positivism and anti-positivism is often defined in terms of legal validity. But from a historical perspective, the absence of a discussion on the matter of legal validity is unremarkable. If one looks at the long history of natural law thinking, one finds the conditions of legal validity rarely discussed. In fact, in English one is hard-pressed to find *any* discussions that pit legal positivism against natural law before the 1930s.[16] Even today, some natural lawyers deny that 'natural law theory' is committed to the view that an unjust law is not law.[17] Since many prominent natural lawyers profess a decided lack of interest in the question of legal validity and are willing to countenance the possibility of unjust laws, the absence of a discussion of this question in the writings of Llewellyn and Frank does not undermine our suggestion that they endorsed versions of natural law.

After setting aside the question of legal validity, is there any remaining sense of natural law that can illuminate the legal realism of Llewellyn and Frank? Even if so, is this link of more than antiquarian interest today?[18] Our answers are, yes and yes. With respect to the first question, Frank and Llewellyn were natural lawyers in two senses. First, by appealing to natural law Frank and Llewellyn signalled their commitment to the reality of value and the possibility of reasoning about it. Even if they could not come to accept everything said under the banner of natural law, they maintained a faith in *some* notion (however vaguely specified) of

[16] The very contrast between natural law and legal positivism, as two opposing jurisprudential schools is of a much more recent provenance than is often assumed. In Germany it begins to appear in the late nineteenth century and in France some years later. In the English-speaking world one begins to see it only in the 1930s in writings of scholars well-versed in European jurisprudence. See eg K N Llewellyn, 'On Philosophy in American Law' (1934) 82 *University of Pennsylvania Law Review* 205, 206–08; L Fuller, *The Law in Quest of Itself* (Foundation Press, 1940) 4–6. At the time the debate is not treated exclusively (or even primarily) as a debate about legal validity.

[17] See J Finnis, *Natural Law and Natural Rights* 2nd edn (Oxford University Press, 2011) 363–66. Even those who do think that natural law theory entails the idea that unjust law is not law think this is only a small component of natural law theory.

[18] We explore (but don't resolve) some of the more general questions related to the relationship between the history of jurisprudence and its contemporary relevance in C Barzun and D Priel, 'Jurisprudence and (Its) History' (2015) 101 *Virginia Law Review* 849. On this question see also R Cotterrell, 'Reading Juristic Theories in and Beyond Historical Context: The Case of Lundstedt's Swedish Legal Realism' (this volume).

moral reality. Second and related, that moral reality was connected in their work to a broadly 'humanistic' conception of law, one that rejected the idea—popular among some other legal realists—that an empirical approach to legal studies could resolve the need for engagement with moral questions. In this way, their embrace of natural law aligned them in some ways with the historical tradition of law, which stressed the inseparability of legal questions not only from moral ones, but also from social and political questions.

The answer to the second question follows from the first. This understanding of natural law is of continuing relevance because it is similar to understandings still advanced today under that name. Llewellyn and Frank believed that one could not clearly distinguish between legal and other sorts of norms, and they saw their views about law and jurisprudence as closely related to inquiries about politics, and especially American politics and American democracy. In this refusal to separate their claims about law from those about democracy, morality and society, they placed themselves in the same tradition as that of several contemporary natural lawyers. Whether it is even possible to discern abstract and general features of law as such—as opposed to merely observing the qualities it exhibits in some particular social and political context—remains a hotly disputed topic to this day. On these questions natural lawyers hold views that are far closer to those of Llewellyn and Frank.

True, not every legal positivist will disagree with some of the elements of this form of natural law. The existence of a moral reality, or at least the possibility of reasoning about values is, these days, accepted by many legal positivists. But taken together, the views of Llewellyn and Frank reflect a position clearly at odds with much twentieth century legal positivist thought, including that of the most prominent Anglophone legal positivist, HLA Hart.[19] Indeed, on most if not all of these issues Llewellyn and Frank can count as allies of Lon Fuller and Ronald Dworkin, Hart's best-known antagonists, and exponents of what has been called a modern natural law theory.[20]

II. Karl Llewellyn: The Romantic Natural Lawyer

In Hart's famous characterisation, American jurisprudence swerves between two extremes he dubbed the nightmare and the noble dream, extreme scepticism of the law on the one hand, and unbridled faith in it on the other. And though Hart

[19] As a moral sceptic (of sorts) Hart may well have disagreed with all three. And he is not alone. Other prominent legal positivists whose legal positivism may be related to a version of moral anti-realism include H Kelsen, J Coleman and B Leiter.

[20] Both Fuller and Dworkin associated themselves, at least on occasion, with natural law. See L Fuller, 'Human Purpose and Natural Law' (1945) 53 *Journal of Philosophy* 697. Dworkin used the term less frequently, but at least once he defined and endorsed natural law as the view that 'insists that what the law is depends in some way on what the law ought to be'. See R Dworkin, '"Natural" Law Revisited' (1982) 34 *University of Florida Law Review* 165, 165.

stated that the nightmare view is most associated with legal realism,[21] he recognised in that essay (in a way he did not before) that at least as far as Karl Llewellyn was concerned, the picture was more complex.[22] The truth is that the more one reads Llewellyn, the more difficult it becomes to imagine a more enthusiastic noble dreamer of the law. Rather than a sceptic, Llewellyn looks more like the law's greatest romantic.[23]

The following words give a sense of Llewellyn's romanticism:[24]

> There is the man who loves creativeness, who can without loss of sleep combine risk-taking with responsibility, who sees and feels institutions as things built and to be built to serve functions, and who sees the functions as vital and law as a tool to be eternally reoriented to justice and to general welfare. There is the other man who loves order, who finds risk uncomfortable and has seen so much irresponsible or unwise innovation that responsibility to him means caution, who sees and feels institutions as the tested, slow-built ways which for all their faults are man's sole safeguard against relapse into barbarism, and who regards reorientation of the law in our polity as essentially committed to the legislature.[25]

This embrace of the virtues of uncertainty did not imply chaos. As early as 1933, Llewellyn wrote that '"free law" is free only within this small space, and in no way threatens a true legal certainty'.[26] At the same time, what stopped the law from calcifying was '[t]he quest of Right Goals [which] … is … an inherent part of any healthy institution of law: a vital part'.[27]

[21] Hart (n 10) 974.

[22] See his reference to Llewellyn in ibid 978–79.

[23] For a sense of Llewellyn's romanticism see NEH Hull, 'The Romantic Realist: Art, Literature and the Enduring Legacy of Karl Llewellyn's "Jurisprudence"' (1996) 40 *American Journal of Legal History* 115, esp 117–23, 140–45; W Twining, *Karl Llewellyn and the Realist Movement* 2nd edn (Cambridge University Press, 2012) 117–23, 143–44.

[24] This is admittedly romanticism of the moderns. See J Lears, *Something for Nothing: Luck in America* (Penguin, 2003) 281–82, 284–85.

[25] K Llewellyn, 'Remarks on the Theory of Appellate Decision and the Rules or Canons about How Statutes Are to Be Construed' (1950) 3 *Vanderbilt Law Review* 395, 397. As we will show below, Frank held a similar view, as did other realists. See WO Douglas, 'The Dissent: A Safeguard of Democracy' (1948) 32 *Journal of the American Judicature Society* 104, 105 (those who believe in the 'democratic faith will rejoice in the uncertainty of law and find strength and glory in it'); M Radin, in *My Philosophy of Law: Credos of Sixteen American Scholars* (Boston Law Book, 1941) 287, 293 (talking of 'the glorious uncertainty of the law'); JC Hutcheson, 'Lawyer's Law, and the Little Small Dice' (1932) 7 *Tulane Law Review* 1, 10–11.

[26] K Llewellyn, *The Case Law System in America* (P Gewirtz ed, M Ansaldi trans, University of Chicago Press 1989) [1933]) 78. Llewellyn alludes here to the German 'free law' movement. It has been argued that the free law movement has been an intellectual source for American legal realism. See JE Herget and S Wallace, 'The German Free Law Movement as the Source of American Legal Realism' (1987) 73 *Virginia Law Review* 399. While we do not deny that there are important similarities between writers in the two 'schools', it is notable that Llewellyn was fairly critical of free law. After stating that the judge's 'freedom of movement' is only within 'a small space', he added that '[t]he only noteworthy contribution of the "free law" movement is…to advocate that [the] freedom of movement be consciously understood and not exercised blindly'. Llewellyn, ibid. As we will show below, Llewellyn had closer affinities to the German historical school, which was one of the free law scholars' targets.

[27] Llewellyn (n 14) 60. Incidentally, it was because Kelsen ignored this aspect of law that Llewellyn thought his work was 'sterile'. Llewellyn (n 26) 78.

The quest of Right Goals and its role in any healthy institution of law points towards the sense in which Llewellyn saw himself as a natural lawyer. On its own, however, it establishes only a superficial link with natural law thinking. Like many enthusiasts for the common law before and after him, Llewellyn was wary of philosophical abstractions, and therefore had another reason to be wary of appeals to natural law. He worried that many natural lawyers committed 'the error' of going on a quest that 'carries the quester into the realm of untestable truth'.[28] It was tempting but dangerous for the committed natural lawyer to end up with nothing but 'a fighting faith, explored and buttressed by his reason, but necessarily inconclusive on the level of testable truth'.[29] Llewellyn therefore distanced himself from the view that judges should turn to their understanding of what right reason required in their quest for identifying the law.[30]

But if natural law was neither abstract reason nor the judge's own reason, what was it and where did it come from? In an early discussion Llewellyn stated tentatively that 'it is to law that we owe the conception of justice', it is the law's 'own perfection',[31] and that it is this idea that provides the main limit and constraint on the judge.[32] This statement reflects a fairly familiar idea of the common law as the source for its own improvement, as a practice that 'works itself pure' by reworking and refining disparate decisions into a coherent set of principles.

A few years later, when Llewellyn began to make more open references to natural law, one sees a subtle but crucial shift in his view. He began to distinguish between the 'philosopher's Natural Law' and that of the lawyer.[33] The former, while significant, is too abstract and general to be of much use for the practical needs of a lawyer who seeks fairly determinate solutions to legal problems. By contrast, when the lawyer is concerned with natural law he is concerned with 'his rules for his society'.[34] Llewellyn's new alternative to the 'untestable truths' of the philosopher was no longer to quarry the law's own materials for answers. Instead, Llewellyn suggested that the source of law's improvement was the people. The more familiar natural law theories focus on 'Goals as the heart of Jurisprudence and on Right Reason as a method';[35] theories that focus on positive law and seek to find answers to novel problems that 'center on the prevailing Rules and Concepts of Law as the structured machinery without which nothing gets done and on formal logic as a method'.[36] This approach, however, ignores '[t]he people whose law Law is and for

[28] Llewellyn (n14) 60.

[29] ibid.

[30] See also KN Llewellyn, *The Common Law Tradition: Deciding Appeals* (Little, Brown 1960) 422.

[31] KN Llewellyn, *The Bramble Bush: Some Lectures on Law and Its Study* (Columbia University, 1930) 121.

[32] '[C]ourts must move within the framework of the given rules. The rules, however socially unjust they seem to [any individual]...are there. The court is in part their mouthpiece. What it can do, all it can do, is to soften a little there and there in a detail the rigor of the general scheme': ibid 80.

[33] Llewellyn (n 9) 3–4.

[34] ibid 4.

[35] Llewellyn (n 14) 72.

[36] ibid.

whom Law is'.[37] It is for this reason that for Llewellyn natural law 'bears a relation to positive law … which is curiously similar to the relation of such positive law to actually prevailing human behavior'.[38] Modifying the familiar image of natural law as higher law, Llewellyn stated that '[i]f in one sense Official Law (and Natural Law) must be above the people to control them, in another sense it must be in and of them, or it ceases to be in society'.[39]

Thus, against the familiar image of natural law as a set of unshifting Archimedean points in a constantly changing world, Llewellyn offered a different conception of natural law as the basis for his risk-taking ideal for the law. Natural law stood for the essential vitality of law, for its openness to critique and change. The courts who adopted such an attitude, courts that worked in what Llewellyn called the 'grand style', often described their jurisprudence in terms of natural law: 'To me … the feature which they treat as "Natural Law" thinking has as its essence a conscious and sustained quest for and accounting to the best reason a court could find'.[40]

Llewellyn took the essence of his view to be the words he quoted from nineteenth century German commercial lawyer, Levin Goldschmidt:

> Every fact-pattern of common life, so far as the legal order can take it in, carries within itself its appropriate, natural rules, its right law. This is a natural law which is real, not imaginary; it is not a creature of mere reason, but rests on the solid foundation of what reason can recognize in the nature of man and of the life conditions of the time and place; it is thus not eternal nor changeless nor everywhere the same, but is indwelling in the very circumstances of life. The highest task of law-giving consists in uncovering and implementing this immanent law.[41]

As Llewellyn intensified his focus on prevailing norms among the people as the source for law's development, he was moved to suggest that even those who spoke of natural law in the sense of timeless, universal principles, were more often talking about what they were familiar with: '[W]hen the natural law philosopher proposes his ideal solutions', Llewellyn wrote, 'he again and again reverts to positive law of his homeland'.[42] On another occasion he warned of the error he attributed

[37] ibid.

[38] ibid 5.

[39] Llewellyn (n 14) 72; see also Llewellyn (n 9) 6.

[40] Llewellyn (n 30) 422.

[41] ibid 122. Of these words Llewellyn said: 'I doubt if the matter has ever been better put than that': ibid. Savigny expressed a rather similar idea when he said: 'we call … the connection of law with the general existence of the people—the political element; and the distinct scientific existence of law—the technical element. At different times … amongst the same people, law will be natural law (in a different sense from our law of nature), or learned law'. FC von Savigny, *The Vocation of Our Age for Legislation and Jurisprudence* (A Hayward trans, Littlewood 1831) 29. Law then is 'natural' when it is connected to 'the general existence of the people'.

[42] Llewellyn (n 26) 77.

to 'fourth-rate Natural Lawyers', the error of treating the conventions of their day as reflecting some self-evident reality.[43]

The standards by which laws are to be assessed, then, were not timeless: 'in regard to matters of change or crisis I am prepared to argue firmly that right timing … also becomes a vital aspect of the rightness … of the relevant portions of *right*-law [ie, what law ought to be]'.[44] This is because what the law ought to be, the idea that the law ought to pursue must be 'so built as to have heavy impact upon its own people, and so upon the people of some one particular time, place and cultural tradition'.[45]

Those who still find odd Llewellyn's suggestion that natural law was implicit in a society's norms and values might try to dismiss it as the product of an idiosyncratic definition of the latter term, which means almost the opposite of the prevailing understanding of the term. But this understanding was not an invention of Llewellyn's wild imagination. If one looks to the intellectual sources on which Llewellyn drew for his views, there seem to be two. One, already alluded to, is German romanticism and its legal counterpart, the historical school of jurisprudence.[46] The other, no less important, is American ideas of self-government and democracy, and *their* relationship to natural law. Llewellyn's embrace of natural law can thus be understood as an attempt to bring together these two strands of thought. Llewellyn did this through his interpretation of the 'common law tradition', especially in its American incarnation.

Llewellyn thus connected together three ideas—historical jurisprudence, democracy and the common law—to 'the people'. He was not the first to draw a link between the first two,[47] but more than those before him he drew an explicit connection between American common law and American democracy. In one of his many discussions of his distinction between the 'formal' and 'grand' styles of adjudication he contrasted a view that seeks to 'discipline society' with the view that seeks to 'follow society'. In this and other respects the formal style 'r[a]n counter' to various ideas 'gathered under the label of "democracy"',[48] at least if democracy was understood, as it was for him, as an '*active* participation of the beneficiaries'.[49] In a similar way he highlighted American common law's 'earthly

[43] Llewellyn (n 14) 4. Curiously, Llewellyn attributed this mistake to both the American Declaration of Independence and the Communist Manifesto: ibid.

[44] KN Llewellyn, 'What Law Cannot Do for Inter-Racial Peace' (1957) 3 *Villanova Law Review* 30, 31.

[45] ibid 30–31.

[46] This interpretation of natural law had already been described (in works familiar to Llewellyn) in R Pound, *Interpretations of Legal History* (Macmillan, 1923) 149–50; R Pound, *Law and Morals* (University of North Carolina Press, 1924) 16–19. On this aspect of Llewellyn's thought see J Whitman, 'Commercial Law and the American *Volk*: A Note on Llewellyn's German Sources for the Uniform Commercial Code' (1989) 97 *Yale Law Journal* 156.

[47] See M Reimann, 'The Common Law Against Codification: Savigny, Carter, and the Defeat of the New York Civil Code' (1989) 37 *American Journal of Comparative Law* 95, 103–07.

[48] KN Llewellyn, 'American Common Law Tradition and American Democracy' (1942) 1 *Journal of Legal and Political Sociology* 14, 34.

[49] ibid 29.

rooting', its distributed nature among the different states, the fact that it was a law that 'voices … the residual *non-expert* horse-sense of the community'.[50]

The idea of self-government or popular sovereignty has been central to the American conception of democracy, and the debates about the structure of the American polity that accompanied the founding of the United States and the adoption of the federal Constitution can, in part, be understood as debates about the problem of reconciling ideas of natural law with ideas of self-government.[51] Whether and how this is to be done has been the subject of numerous studies on the political ideas at the time of the founding of the American republic. For our purposes, what matters is the way Llewellyn blended these ideas to present what he thought was a distinctly American conception of the common law as an essential ingredient of American democracy.

Though not a matter on which Llewellyn wrote at great length, what he did write reveals a political theory of law, one that sees this societal natural law as imposing a constraint on judges and providing certainty to the law that legal texts on their own were incapable of providing. It provided a political limit to the legitimate (and perhaps also feasible) use of the law to promote social change. At the same time, it was a vision of law that opposed government that is 'secret, self-sufficient in judgment and standard, accounting neither to the individual for particular decision nor to the public for general policy'.[52]

All of this calls for some revision of the still-popular image of legal realism, or more accurately of Llewellyn's legal realism, and its place on the map of contemporary legal theory. Hart correctly recognised Llewellyn's views as fundamentally at odds with his, but his explanation of the difference was mistaken because he misunderstood Llewellyn's position. In *The Concept of Law* Hart treated Llewellyn (on the basis of a single sentence taken out of context) as a paradigmatic example of rule scepticism.[53] But, as we have shown, Llewellyn never doubted that rules provided the law with considerable certainty.[54] The difference between Llewellyn and Hart lies elsewhere. In Hart's view, the legal rules are capable of constraining because their 'core' verbal formulations apply clearly to some cases.[55] For Hart

[50] ibid 30, 31.

[51] See E Barker, *Traditions of Civility: Eight Essays* (Cambridge University Press, 1948) 314–18; TN McInnis, 'Natural Law and the Revolutionary State Constitutions' (1990) 14 *Legal Studies Forum* 351, 356–57.

[52] Llewellyn (n 48) 42. Llewellyn attributed these features to the British style of government: ibid. This makes for a parallel contrast between Llewellyn's view of American and British common law. See KN Llewellyn, 'On the Good, the True, the Beautiful, in Law' (1942) 9 *University of Chicago Law Review* 224, 236–37.

[53] See HLA Hart, *The Concept of Law* 3rd edn (Oxford University Press, 2012) 1, 139. Criticism of Hart's presentation of realists' ideas goes back at least as far as EH Taylor, Jr, 'HLA Hart's Concept of Law in the Perspective of American Legal Realism' (1972) 35 *Modern Law Review* 606. But even critics of Hart's interpretation of legal realism typically associate legal realism with a form of rule scepticism. See Leiter (n 7) 73–78.

[54] See text accompanying n 26.

[55] Hart (n 53) 126.

(and many other legal positivists) these clear and uncontroversial applications of rules mark out the limits of law's domain.[56] Hart did not think judges could never rely on moral considerations, but when they did so they were relying on moral or social considerations that stood outside the law.[57]

Llewellyn rejected all this. Law was indeed largely certain, but not because the language of legal rules provided certainty, and definitely not because there was a clearly-defined domain of posited legal rules. Law for him was largely certain precisely because *law was more than legal rules.* In contrast to the positivist picture, both the constraints that fix the content of the law, and the ideals that law should pursue, are part of the law. Thus, for Llewellyn there are no clear boundaries between law and society, and between law and non-law.[58] It is the process of socialisation that provides the limiting constraints fixing not only the law's content but also its ideals. Indeed, in this picture the distinction between the reality and ideal of the law becomes blurred. This may be the deepest sense in which Llewellyn rejected the positivist stance and thought of himself as a natural lawyer.[59]

III. Jerome Frank: Pragmatic Scholasticism

There is admittedly something ironic about ascribing the label 'natural law' to any of Jerome Frank's views. The reason is that Frank himself often shunned the term, concluding it was too malleable and ambiguous to be of much use. Nevertheless, like Llewellyn, he endorsed philosophical views associated with both ancient and modern versions of natural law theory and expressed increasing sympathy for what he took to be its main principles. Frank's commitment to those principles, including his faith in the natural freedom and individual dignity of all humans,

[56] This characterisation of legal positivism as the thesis that 'there is a test which distinguishes what is law from what is not' is first articulated in J Raz, 'Legal Principles and the Limits of Law' (1972) 81 *Yale Law Journal* 823, 842; see also F Schauer, 'The Limited Domain of the Law' (2004) 90 *Virginia Law Review* 1909.

[57] Hart (n 53) 135. Hart elsewhere aligned himself with 'soft' positivism that saw moral norms as part of the law, but only if 'incorporated' by explicit linguistic reference: ibid 250.

[58] KN Llewellyn, 'How Appellate Courts Decide Cases' (1945) 16 *Pennsylvania Bar Association Quarterly* 220, 227; cf Llewellyn (n 52) 246, 248.

[59] This interpretation places Llewellyn quite close to Fuller. This may seem odd, as one of Fuller's critiques of the realists was precisely their mistaken effort to keep is and ought strictly separate. See Fuller (n 16) 60, 64–65. It is true that in early writings, such as Llewellyn (n 1) 1236–37, Llewellyn insisted on a 'temporary' separation between is and ought, but as Fuller recognised, Llewellyn seems to have moved away from this position in later writings, and both cited each other's work approvingly. See Fuller, ibid 61; Llewellyn (n 30) 421–22. On the possible connections between the legal thought of Fuller and Frank link see C Barzun, 'Jerome Frank, Lon Fuller, and a Romantic Pragmatism' (unpublished manuscript).

may seem at odds with the scepticism for which Frank is famous.[60] For that reason, and as already noted, some have been tempted to write off the former set of views as the result of a postwar transformation of sorts, fuelled by a need to distance himself from legal-realist ideas linked by others to the rise of fascism and Nazism. But while it is true that Frank's discussions of natural law mostly occured in the 1940s, we argue that both his faith and his scepticism stem from the same pragmatist philosophical outlook, which one finds in even his earliest writings.

There is no doubt that Frank had trouble with the *term* 'natural law'. In some of his later writings, he criticised it and called for its abandonment.[61] He said he found the term ambiguous, confusing, and susceptible to abuse. He wrote, for example, that even 'Nazidom has its ideals, its own vicious notions of "natural law" and justice'.[62] Closer to home, the language of natural law and natural rights had been used 'to sanctify the most deplorable consequences of the commercial revolution', by which Frank meant social Darwinism and economic laissez faire.[63] But the concern was not just with terminology; Frank also objected to a particular *form of argument* that relied on natural law. Frank vehemently disagreed with the view that it is possible to derive any automatic prescription for human society from nature: 'Nature is no copybook containing precepts for civilized man. Nor is human nature, unartificialized, a sound foundation for a beneficent social structure'.[64] Thus, Frank pleaded:

> It is high time … that we put an end to the process of referring to 'nature' as the justification for any particular social program … The honest approach is to say: 'Here is my program. Whether or not it is "right" depends upon whether it is in accord with, and will promote, values and ideals which you think both desirable and possible of achievement…'[65]

Frank identified another problem with the term. Throughout history it had become mixed up with the *causal* claim that laws of nature determined all events, including human behaviour.[66] Thus, many exponents of natural law had been

[60] J Frank, *Fate and Freedom: A Philosophy for Free Americans* rev ed (Beacon, 1953) 214 (praising the 'humanistic spirit of Erasmus and Thomas More, with its rejection of asceticism, its stress on the individual man's dignity and moral worth in this world, its ideal of developing the best of man's nature in a just society').

[61] ibid 294 (referring to natural law as a 'dangerously ambiguous terminology'); *Biedler v Bookmyer* (1943) 134 F.2d 828, 830 note 7 (lamenting that 'most persons who are not students of Scholastic jurisprudence (and some who purport to be) give, other, and often conflicting, meanings to "Natural Law"').

[62] J Frank, 'Book Review' (1944) 57 *Harvard Law Review* 1120, 1128.

[63] Frank (n 60) 134. Also ibid 136 ('"Natural," to devotees of laissez faire, meant what they considered desirable'). For an example of a book presenting classical economics as natural law, see H Wood, *The Political Economy of Natural Law* (Lee and Shepard, 1894).

[64] Frank (n 60) 141.

[65] ibid 139.

[66] ibid 115 ('[I]n early stages of Greek religion, the belief that fate, law, order, and justice operated throughout the universe represented a reflection of "primitive" ideals of human law, of moral obligations, of order and justice in human society').

complicit in aiding and abetting what was, for Frank, the true philosophical foe, namely scientific determinism (or as he sometimes called it, 'fatalism').[67]

Frank's commitment to human free will is an important theme to which we will return, but it is worth first laying out why, despite his reservations about the terminology of natural law, Frank nonetheless embraced its central tenets. In his 1945 book, *Fate and Freedom*, Frank emphasised that the following ideas and beliefs were 'never more precious than today': 'the ideals of justice and equality, a high regard for non-material values', and 'a belief in the necessity of restraints on absolutism and arbitrariness in government'.[68] He then went on to say that '[n]o decent, intelligent American will disagree' with the repudiation of the idea that 'man's "free will is frozen into muscular behavior," or with a "belief in the brotherhood of man."'[69] Rather, most Americans, Frank explained, would accept the idea that there are such 'basic principles', which are 'derived from man's nature', and that positive law ought to reflect them.[70] In a different essay from the same period he reiterated this view when he praised the 'Scholastic version of natural law [which] symbolizes a noble ideal of minimum human decencies'.[71]

For Frank, Thomas Aquinas represented the best of the natural law tradition. 'Wise and, for his day, tolerant', Frank explained, 'St Thomas taught that there are but a few, and highly general, immutable principles of natural law. Men should do good and avoid evil, good being what is good for man in the light of his "natural" inclinations'.[72] There were also a few secondary principles, such as 'not to kill, not to steal, to return goods held in trust'.[73] Most importantly, Aquinas understood that how these principles applied to actual human problems varied with time and place. Thus, the chief virtue of Aquinas's understanding of natural law was that it was 'exceedingly flexible and relatively undogmatic'.[74] Moreover, Frank endorsed the views that such values as freedom, justice and equality really exist, that one could reason about them, and that judges should make reference to such values when deciding cases. In that sense, then, it seems plausible to characterise Frank as a defender of natural law.

Or does it? Even if one acknowledges that Frank wrote such statements of support for these natural-law views, one might still object that they seem entirely ad

[67] ibid 105 ('Scientific fatalism is but a faith, a dismal and cruel one. We need not accept it. There is no reason why we should forsake the American faith—which rests on the facts of daily experience—that human purposes are real').

[68] ibid 294.

[69] ibid.

[70] ibid 295.

[71] See J Frank, 'A Sketch of an Influence' in Paul Sayre (ed), *Interpretations of Modern Legal Philosophies: Essays in Honor of Roscoe Pound* (Oxford University Press, 1947) 189, 234.

[72] Frank (n 60) 123.

[73] ibid 124.

[74] ibid. In a judicial opinion from around the same time Frank found himself in agreement with the 'much abused [natural law] scholastics' on the binding force of precedents. Like the scholastics, Frank thought that reaching just outcomes required giving less respect to stare decisis and following precedents 'only when shown to be reasonable'. *Aero Plug Co Inc v BG Corp* (1942) 130 F.2d 290, 298.

hoc and thus insufficient to alter our overall impression of Frank's thought. More than Llewellyn, these views seem plainly inconsistent with the extreme scepticism about law and judicial decision-making that made Frank famous.[75]

One explanation for this apparent change in view is a historical one. Frank wrote *Law and the Modern Mind* in 1930, when sceptical views about religion and morality were increasingly common among social scientists and intellectuals in the United States.[76] But by the time Frank was writing *Fate and Freedom*, the Allies were engaged in a war against fascist and Nazi regimes, and the legal realists with whom Frank had been associated were being attacked for having endorsed views that gave philosophical support to such regimes. Thus, some have suggested that Frank's volte face is best understood as an effort to mollify his critics and to pledge his allegiance to Truth, Justice and the American Way. Indeed, many scholars have interpreted Frank's and other realists' writing in something like this way.[77]

There is a morsel of truth in this explanation. Frank himself acknowledged that the experience of confronting the Nazi regime made the recognition of certain basic human values particularly pressing.[78] But the charge that Frank fundamentally changed his views does not hold up under scrutiny, for it ignores both the extent to which Frank's deeper philosophical commitments remained consistent over this time period and the extent to which his understanding of natural law flowed from those commitments.

In particular, from his earlier writings to his latest ones, Frank was a philosophical pragmatist who assessed metaphysical concepts and theories—whether about the nature of the world, of the person, or of law—by how well their practical consequences served human needs and purposes.[79] Frank combined this background philosophical view with a conviction that the most important human purpose in the political or moral sphere was to improve society overall, and that a judge's most important purpose when deciding cases was to ensure that justice is done in the individual case. This combination of philosophical outlook and substantive moral convictions about human purposes help explain the apparent contradictions noted above. For Frank, a properly sceptical attitude, which sees *all*

[75] J Frank, *Law and the Modern Mind* (Brentano's, 1930) 292 (rhetorically asking if Roscoe Pound's endorsement of the view that eternal principles of natural law 'were not merely discoverable, but which, generally speaking, the jurists had discovered' was akin to 'a small boy with a grown-up vocabulary talking of an ideal father').

[76] Purcell (n 3) 41.

[77] See (n 12).

[78] Frank (n 60) 294 (explaining and endorsing the view that natural law has become all the more important to recognise 'now that we have been shocked by the Nazi assault into a realization of the worth of our basic ideals').

[79] See, eg ibid 169 ('What criterion should one use in choosing between the competing assumptions of causality and acausality, neither of which can be "scientifically proved"? The criterion of their respective consequences.'). The argument supporting this pragmatist or 'humanist' interpretation of Frank's early work is developed further in C L Barzun, 'Jerome Frank and the Modern Mind' (2010) 58 *Buffalo Law Review* 1127, 1137–38.

knowledge as partial, ought to stimulate, rather than dampen, efforts to achieve reform and justice.

In the moral and political realm, Frank embraced the quintessentially American idea that the future could be better than the past, together with the more controversial idea that law and government are an important means for achieving that goal.[80] In his view, in order to make good on that possibility, the American people had to recognise that they had control over their own destiny and the freedom to choose wisely. And that meant rejecting the doctrine of scientific determinism. 'The world's future', he wrote, 'depends on human purposes, not on fate'. While some things are inevitable, he explained, others are not, so that

> [w]e must reject the suggestion that we are but molecules in a wave of the future. We must assert our faith in the power of free men to preserve a civilization in which freedom will seem to have been inevitable—because free men have effectively willed that it should persist.[81]

And for Frank, rejecting determinism meant welcoming the inherent unpredictability of life. Frank thought we ought to embrace 'the Renaissance belief in the reality of chance, a belief which the orthodox religion of science regards with horror'.[82]

These quotations all come from *Fate and Freedom*, but there are important continuities and similarities between his earlier and later works. Frank's almost obsessive concern with the need to come to grips with deep epistemic uncertainty pervades his first book, *Law and the Modern Mind*.[83] There, Frank was primarily concerned with attacking the demand for *legal* certainty, which he thought reflected childlike longings for security and comfort. But he found the same immature impulse driving what was, in his view, an equally quixotic effort to uncover causal laws governing the universe.[84] 'Science, wisely considered is no substitute for the all-wise, all-powerful father', Frank insisted. 'The fact of change and chance must be bravely faced'.[85]

We can now see more clearly why Frank both embraced many of the substantive moral and political values associated with natural law but resisted the label itself. On the one hand, he recognised that the core principles of a Thomistic

[80] See J Frank, 'The New Sin', *Saturday Review of Literature* (22 December 1945) 3, 28; Frank (n 60) 38–39.

[81] Frank (n 60) 17.

[82] ibid 138. Compare this to Llewellyn's views in text accompanying (n 25) above.

[83] Frank (n 75) 98 (emphasising the need to develop '*the spirit of the creative scientist*, which yearns not for safety but risk, not for certainty but adventure, which thrives on experimentation, invention and novelty and not on nostalgia for the absolute'). See also Barzun (n 79) 1158–71 (characterising Frank's notion of the 'scientific spirit' as type of moral and intellectual virtue).

[84] Frank (n 75) 287 (denying that the universe will ever be reducible to 'scientific laws').

[85] ibid.

natural law were invaluable as ideals and guides for action.[86] They were sound (if somewhat vague) first principles and for a pragmatist like Frank, that fact was sufficient to justify belief in their existence.[87] But he resisted the ideas that these principles *closed* any inquiry and that any particular *application* of those principles was permanently carved into nature itself because that view needlessly limited man's capacity to improve social and political life. That is why Frank was so concerned with showing how moralistic notions of natural law were, as a historical matter, bound up with the view that physical laws causally determined everything in nature, including human behaviour. By appealing to 'laws of nature' both the normative and the causal versions of natural law had the consequence of limiting the possibilities for, and motivation to achieve, human freedom.[88]

In this way, Frank's scepticism served as a source not of despair but of faith, both in man's dignity and in social progress. If we can only gain knowledge of the world through our (limited, partial) human perceptual and cognitive faculties, then we can never know with certainty what the natural world is really like or how it operates. This means we need not accept the stultifying and depressing assumption that all human behaviour has been causally predetermined. Instead, since believing in free will, human dignity, and the core, eternal principles of natural law helps us bring about a more just and humane world, we are justified in holding such metaphysical and moral commitments.[89] At the same time, remaining humble about our ability to discern what those general principles of natural law require in any particular set of circumstances should make us pause before advocating policies on the assumption that 'nature' requires them. 'Less cocksure about what we know and can know', Frank explained, 'we can be more sure that our choices will be real, not illusions'.[90]

We can see the same kind of dynamic at work in Frank's discussion of legal decision-making, where once again he uses scepticism to motivate and justify the pursuit of justice. In his early work the logic of Frank's argument is as follows: it is impossible to be certain about how judges will decide cases, either by looking to the relevant legal rules (as traditional jurists had argued) or by using the methods

[86] Frank (n 60) 127 (observing favourably that for seventeenth-century social philosophers 'the axioms of a desirable (and possible) well-ordered state, said to be founded upon a study of human nature, were then regarded as "oughts," or norms, or standards, not as inescapable laws with which men could not help complying').

[87] ibid 169 (endorsing the logic of William James's 'faith ladder' according to which one reasons from the possibility of some view of the world being true, to the 'fitness' of it being true, to the conclusion that it 'shall be true').

[88] ibid 129 (criticising those who believe that 'the power of the universe is on their side—that nature itself will compel men to accept the kind of social order which these Inevitabilists deem desirable').

[89] ibid 169 ('If the chance "axiom," with its "free will" conclusion, aids in promoting the human ideals we cherish, we have the right—still remaining thoroughly "rational"—to prefer it').

[90] ibid at 336.

of social science (as other realists had argued).[91] The reason is that a judge's idiosyncratic (and hence unpredictable) biases and prejudices often determine how he finds facts—for example, which witnesses he believes and which he does not—thereby making it nearly impossible to predict how the legal rules will apply to future cases, even when those rules are clear.[92] Thus, there is little point in judges trying to decide cases in such a way as to develop rules for future cases.[93] Instead, Frank argued, such legal uncertainty should encourage judges to focus on the one thing that they can know and can control, namely how the legal materials ought to apply to the parties to the present case. For in Frank's view, the rules were simply instruments whose purpose was to serve justice to the parties in the case, so they should be interpreted accordingly.[94]

Frank was thus hardly sceptical about the possibility of securing genuinely just outcomes in individual cases. He merely thought that to pursue justice judges had to treat legal rules flexibly and to attend primarily to the particular facts of the case. '*The judge, at his best, is an arbitrator*', Frank insisted, 'a "sound man" who strives to do justice to the parties by exercising a wise discretion with reference to the peculiar circumstances of the case.'[95] His task, according to Frank, was to do 'equity' in the Aristotelian sense.[96] Indeed, Frank's only criticism of Aristotle was that he treated equity as distinct from, and even contrary to, 'law', whereas Frank insisted that the two were 'so thoroughly intermingled that it is impossible to divide them'.[97]

In this way, we can see a position that bears important similarities to his later views. He thought that values were more than mere prejudice and that judges should rely on them to reach just outcomes based on the particular circumstances of the case.[98] What distinguished Frank's approach from more traditional views

[91] Frank (n 75) 104–06. See also ibid 362 ('the more accurate description of the judicial process will serve to show that efforts to procure such predictability (via anthropology, economics, sociology, statistics, or otherwise) are doomed to failure').

[92] ibid 116 ('No one can know in advance what a judge will believe to the "facts" of a case'). Frank could say that despite not doubting the existence of rules. In fact, in his preface to the 1949 edition of *Law and the Modern Mind* Frank treated as 'absurd' the suggestion that he 'sneered at legal rules' or 'considered them unreal or useless'. See Frank (n 11) xxvii.

[93] ibid 155 ('Present problems should be worked out with reference to present events. We cannot rule the future. We can only imagine it in terms of the present. And the only way to do that is as thoroughly as possible to know the present').

[94] Frank (n 75) 167 ('We want judges who, thus viewing and *employing all rules as fictions*, will appreciate that, as rules are fictions "intended for the sake of justice," it is not to be endured that they shall work injustice in any particular case, and must be moulded in furtherance of those equitable objects to promote which they were designed.').

[95] ibid 157.

[96] ibid.

[97] ibid 141.

[98] ibid 134 (suggesting that a 'deeper sense' of uniformity in case outcomes is likely to result to the extent that judges are 'the more enlightened, the more quick to detect and hold their own prejudices, the more alive to the fact that rules and precedents are not their masters but merely agencies to be utilised in the interest of doing justice'); ibid 168 (quoting approvingly M Cohen's statement that there can be 'a scientific character to questions as to what the law ought to be').

of natural law, however, was that for Frank, the key to securing just outcomes in adjudication lay not in properly deducing conclusions from the rules, nor in rigorously searching through of the case law for the right rules. It required instead that judges attempt to overcome their own biases and prejudices through a process of introspection and self-analysis in the hope that doing so would enable them to discern in a less distorted way the relevant moral (and legal) considerations.[99]

Though Frank held on to all this throughout his life, one can identify a shift in his views from the highly personalist views of his earlier works toward greater respect for the values held by the people. We identified a similar shift toward this view in Llewellyn's work, although they drew on different intellectual sources in reaching this view. Frank contrasted Plato's conception of natural law with Aristotle's. Plato's version of natural law was eternal and unchanging; Aristotle, by contrast, 'saw unconquerable unruliness, spontaneous chance and change, as part of reality, [and therefore] his notion of "natural law" was not likely to be that of an "absolute standard," permanent and unchanging'.[100] Frank drew an explicit link between Plato's conception of natural law and his totalitarianism and 'contempt for democracy', and one between Aristotle's openness to chance and his support for 'the loose texture of democracy'.[101] In Frank's thinking a central reason *for* democracy is its recognition that certainty is an illusion and that those who claim the right to rule because they have all the answers must be resisted. This is how Frank tied an epistemological thesis to political theory.[102]

Frank drew a similar connection between metaphysics and legal theory in a judicial opinion touching on the question of judicial impartiality. To be impartial judges need not, indeed cannot, become devoid of values. This level of disinterestedness is only available to the dead. To the living, appeal to values is necessary and desirable. But which values? Frank mentioned, once again, the possibility of 'universal values' acknowledged by 'those devoted to "natural law" philosophy', but stated that these values are 'few and highly general' and 'their applications vary with time, place and circumstance'.[103] In a manner not dissimilar to Llewellyn, he

[99] ibid 147 (arguing that properly individualised, just adjudication requires judges to understand the law as 'a portion of the science of human nature' and emphasising that that requires them to 'come to grips with the human nature operative in themselves' in order that they may become 'aware of [their] own prejudices, biases, antipathies, and the like').

[100] Frank (n 62) 1129; cf Frank (n 72) 234–35; Frank (n 60) 295. For our purposes, it matters little whether this is a plausible reading of Aristotle. Interestingly, around the time a rather similar conception of natural law 'whose practical application will change as current notions of society change' was presented as the unacknowledged basis of legal realist Thurman Arnold's work. See EH Levi, 'The Natural Law, Precedent, and Thurman Arnold' (1938) 24 *Virginia Law Review* 587, 611–12.

[101] Frank (n 62) 1127–28 fn 25.

[102] In seeing this connection, Frank was typical of his time. See Purcell (n 3) 205 (observing that for many intellectuals in the postwar period 'only social theories that recognized all truths, including ethical truths, as tentative, changing, and uncertain could support and justify democratic self-government').

[103] *In re JP Linahan, Inc* (1943) 138 F.2d 650, 652 fn 6.

argued that what determines their content and application in particular circumstances were the values of the community:

> [E]very human society has a multitude of established attitudes, unquestioned postulates. Cosmically, they may seem parochial prejudices, but many of them represent the community's most cherished values and ideals. Such social pre-conceptions, the 'value judgments' which members of any given society take for granted and use as the unspoken axioms of thinking, find their way into that society's legal system, become what has been termed 'the valuation system of the law.' The judge in our society owes a duty to act in accordance with those basic predilections inhering in our legal system (although, of course, he has the right, at times, to urge that some of them be modified or abandoned).[104]

The values that underlie the law may be indefensible from the perspective of the cosmos, but that does not make them less real, and—in a democracy—less binding on the judge. Frank recognised that this was no panacea. He openly admitted that even in a particular period there is never perfect uniformity of opinion among all people,[105] which meant that uncertainty, in both law and fact-finding, could not be completely eradicated. But just like in his earlier, more individualistic, perspective, Frank argued that these values should not be hidden or ignored. That was the kind of pragmatic constraint that was appropriate for an open, democratic society.

This view about how judges ought to go about resolving disputes was related for Frank to his views about the nature of law, and to the extent that we can find in them similarities to contemporary position, here too his views reveal clear continuity and seem to fit contemporary natural law theory (or at least versions of anti-positivism) much more than legal positivism. In *Law and the Modern Mind* Frank dismissed the positivist thesis about the limits of law: 'what Pound calls law and what he calls non-legal cannot be separated. They are so thoroughly intermingled that it is impossible to divide them'.[106] Some 15 years later, in discussing 'the relation of the natural law thesis to judicial activities', Frank stated, in a manner that would not be out of place in Fuller: '"Thus the ideal is constantly becoming the positive" and "in the evolution of the common law system the opposition between positive and natural law is constantly overcome"'.[107]

[104] ibid 652 (footnotes omitted).

[105] See ibid 652 fn 8; *Perkins v Endicott Johnson Corp* (1942) 128 F.2d 208, 217 fn 25. Rather surprisingly, in *Courts on Trial: Myth and Reality in American Justice* (Princeton University Press, 1949) ch 25, Frank expresses doubts about this approach, characteristically, largely because it ignores the indeterminacy of fact-finding. For the most part, however, he was sympathetic to it. In addition to other sources cited here see also J Frank, 'The Scientific Spirit and Economic Dogmatism' in J Nathanson (ed), *Science for Democracy* (King's Crown, 1946) 11, 12, where he speaks of '[t]he art of government' as 'a branch of anthropology, the so-called "science of custom."'

[106] Frank (n 75) 141.

[107] Frank (n 72) 234, quoting F Kessler, 'Natural Law, Justice and Democracy—Some Reflections on Three Types of Thinking about Law and Justice' (1944) 19 *Tulane Law Review* 32, 57; cf L Fuller, 'Reason and Fiat in Case Law' (1946) 59 *Harvard Law Review* 376, 379–80. Elsewhere, Frank characterised Fuller's natural law position as follows: that 'ideals of justice should be an acknowledged vital

IV. Conclusion: The Philosophy of Reconstructing the Past

'We are all realists now', as the saying goes, but what does that mean? 'We', after all, hold very different views on almost every topic that bears on realist themes: law, morality, society, politics, and the relationships among them. If, despite all our differences, we are all realists now, this must mean one of two things. Either the realism that we all share is so thin and banal that no-one could possibly object to it; or we are all realists because by 'legal realism' we mean utterly different things. With regard to some things, it may well be that we are all realists because what we call 'realism' is rather banal and incontestable; but if that were the case, the realists would have little claim to being the seminal figures they are often held up to be.[108] Thus, it seems more likely that scholars are drawing different lessons from the realists based on their own interests, values and purposes.

Nor do we claim to be any different in this regard. No doubt we too are reading Llewellyn and Frank (and perhaps 'legal realism' more generally) through the lens of our interests, values and purposes. This in itself may be one of the core messages both Frank and Llewellyn considered part of *their* legal realism. Nevertheless, while recognising the historical embeddedness of all efforts to theorise about law (or any other social or political phenomenon), two points are worth mentioning. First, in our goal of reconstructing the thought of Frank and Llewellyn, we have above all sought to interpret what these thinkers said on their own terms, rather than simply assume that we can understand them by placing them within a particular historical context or political movement. Second, our own interpretation of realism cannot be explained as merely the product of our historical moment, because in fact it cuts against the grain of the most popular interpretations of realism today. Legal realism is now back in vogue, even spawning a modern reincarnation known as 'new legal realism', in part because there has been renewed interest and confidence in bringing the social sciences to bear on legal issues.[109] Thus, these days scholars—even those critical of the 'empirical turn'—typically treat legal realism as largely an effort to push law and legal scholarship in a more social scientific direction. Morton Horwitz, for example, has criticised '[t]he social

component in the thinking of judges when deciding cases.' Frank's did not think there was anything wrong with it, except that it was unexceptional: 'today most American judges frankly and consciously think in that fashion—endeavoring, within the limits allowed by statutes and well-settled precedents, to make their decisions conform to their ideals of justice': Frank (n 60) 296.

[108] This is, in a sentence, B Tamanaha's central claim in *Beyond the Formalist–Realist Divide: The Role of Politics in Judging* (Princeton University Press, 2010). We think that claim is likely too strong, but we cannot explore this question here.

[109] See, for example, the symposium on 'Empirical Legal Realism: A New Social Scientific Assessment of Law and Human Behavior' (2003) 97 *Northwestern University Law Review* 1075.

science methodology that Llewellyn sought to represent … as the essence of Realism'.[110] But although many of the legal realists certainly did see real possibilities in a more social-scientific orientation in legal scholarship, Llewellyn and Frank were largely unenthusiastic about such efforts. In their different ways, they stressed the sense in which law was not a science but an 'art' or a 'craft'.

This case study also shows us the value and limits of philosophical categories like 'legal positivism', 'legal realism' or 'natural law'. They are useful, perhaps necessary, tools for organising an existing intellectual landscape. But such exercises are perilous because theorists past and present often embrace such labels with a conscious or unconscious desire to inject them with new meanings and implications. The result is that it is often impossible to 'correctly' classify canonical thinkers as belonging to one group or another. Was Hobbes a legal positivist or a natural lawyer? The answer may depend on *when* one asks the question.

Part of why it seems odd at first to think of Llewellyn and Frank as natural lawyers is that we tend to impose our contemporary understandings of the term, which neither easily fits. And yet, their reservations and qualifications notwithstanding, both thinkers made the conscious decision to declare some allegiance to it. Surely that fact alone tells us *something*. The question is, what exactly? Does it tell us something about these particular men—their aims, purposes or interests—in this particular time? Or does it tell us something about *natural law*? In our view, one of the chief purposes of intellectual history is to at least raise such questions, even if it can never answer them definitively.

[110] MJ Horwitz, *The Transformation of American Law 1870–1960: The Crisis of Legal Orthodoxy* (Harvard University Press, 1992) 210.

11

The Role of Rules: Legal Maxims in Early-modern Common Law Principle and Practice

IAN WILLIAMS*

Early-modern common lawyers writing about the common law shared a collection of theoretical ideas or assumptions. One of these was the importance of legal maxims. While Christopher St German wrote that a 'large volume would not suffice' to declare all the maxims of the common law, this did not deter others.[1] These writers were also all practitioners, many of them highly successful, and the language of maxims can be seen in contemporary law reports. One of the major sources for historians' consideration of maxims is itself from a law report, the case of *Colthirst v Bejushin*.[2] Literature devoted to maxims was a feature of early printed law books, suggesting a market amongst practitioners.[3]

Maxims themselves have been the subject of considerable discussion amongst historians of the common law, considering the different theories of maxims which were enunciated and the relationship between maxims and other elements of the law.[4] This chapter takes a different approach and seeks to investigate the

* Spelling has been modernised in all quotations and law-French has been translated. The following abbreviations are used: BL MS Add (British Library Additional Manuscript); BL MS Harg (British Library Hargrave Manuscript); BL MS Stowe (British Library Stowe Manuscript); CUL MS (Cambridge University Library Manuscript); HEH MS El (Henry E Huntington Library Ellesmere Manuscript).

[1] C St German, *St German's Doctor and Student* (TFT Plucknett and JL Barton eds, Selden Society volume 91, Selden Society 1974) 59.

[2] *Colthirst v Bejushin* (1550) 1 Plowden 21, 75 ER 33. Plowden's *Commentaries* are generally taken as fairly accurate reports of proceedings, although Cromartie has raised the question of whether more attention should be directed to Plowden's own views as shaping his reports (A Cromartie, *The Constitutionalist Revolution* (Cambridge University Press, 2006) 109).

[3] In addition to the works cited through this paper, see, eg Anonymous, *Principia sive Maxima Legum Anglie* (Richard Lant, 1546).

[4] eg, P Stein, *Regulae Iuris; from Juristic Rules to Legal Maxims* (Edinburgh University Press, 1966); MS Neustadt, *The Making of the Instauration: Science, Politics, and Law in the Career of Francis Bacon* (PhD dissertation, John Hopkins University, 1987) 35–61; JW Tubbs, *The Common Law Mind: Medieval and Early Modern Conceptions* (John Hopkins University Press, 2000), especially 66–68, 166–78; Cromartie (n 2).

relationship between early-modern common law theory and legal practice.[5] The chapter sets out common features in the various theoretical discussions of maxims, comparing these to the use of maxims in practice. Four topics are considered: the identification of maxims; their incontrovertibility; the content and scope of maxims; and the relationship between maxims and equity.

Broadly, the use of maxims in practice was compatible with the theory of maxims and in some cases the influence of theoretical literature on practice seems clear. However, the prominence of maxims in legal theory was not reflected in legal practice. Law reports suggest that whatever their theoretical importance, maxims were not sufficient to resolve actual cases.

Investigation of maxims in legal practice raises several methodological problems. First, early-modern law reports were not generally intended to be verbatim transcripts of proceedings and were often written by someone other than the lawyer whose argument is reported, so it cannot be assumed that the language used in the report was also that used in court.[6]

Second, there was diversity in the language associated with maxims, a problem of which some early-modern writers were well aware.[7] For example, some writers argued for differences between 'maxims' and 'rules', while others regarded these terms as referring to identical concepts. When considering the theoretical discussions this difficulty can usually be overcome: writers make their preferred usage explicit or can be seen using a range of vocabulary in a manner which enables some assessment of whether different words functioned only as synonyms or as different concepts. Practitioners do not seem to have been concerned to distinguish these clearly, a point recognised by John Dodderidge.[8] For example, in two of his draft arguments Thomas Egerton explained that royal patents are interpreted against the patentee and favourably to the king, describing this as both a 'rule'[9] and a 'maxim'.[10] The substantive point was the same, and it seems legitimate to infer that rules and maxims were interchangeable for Egerton.

[5] For purposes of this chapter, 'early-modern' covers the period 1528–c1650. The start date was determined by the first printing of *St German's Doctor and Student*. As will be noted below (text to n 42), there seems to be a change in the practice of maxims after the first decade of the sixteenth century and there is good evidence that St German's work influenced subsequent practice. After St German discussion of maxims seems to be more heavily influenced by civilian ideas about *regulae iuris* than is the case in the fifteenth century.

[6] DJ Ibbetson, 'Report and Record in Early-Modern Common Law' in A Wijffels (ed), *Case Law in the Making, the Techniques and Methods of Judicial Records and Law Reports (Vol I)* (Duncker and Humblot, 1997) especially 57–58.

[7] For the differences in language and attempts by writers to clarify their terminology, see I Williams, 'English Legal Reasoning and Legal Culture, c1528–c1642' (PhD thesis, University of Cambridge, 2008) 27–28.

[8] J Dodderidge, *The English Lawyer* (Miles Flesher, 1631) 151.

[9] *The Dean and Chapter of Chester's Case* (1578) HEH MS El 482, fo 34.

[10] *Hawes v Hynge* (undated) HEH MS El 482, fo 249.

Third, the modern assumption is that legal maxims are short Latin statements.[11] This has caused considerable problems for some historians, who have identified maxims wherever Latin appears in law reports.[12] Neither early-modern writers on maxims, nor references to 'maxims' in law reports, are limited to Latin statements. Early-modern lawyers seem freely to have stated maxims in both Latin and the vernacular, sometimes in the same work.[13] Not only could maxims be expressed in the vernacular, but not all statements in Latin should be regarded as maxims. Common lawyers might quote material originally in Latin,[14] or in the case of Edward Coke simply summarise arguments with a pithy Latin statement.[15]

This chapter takes a conservative approach. Maxims are only identified where they are specifically identified as such in the report, but given the diversity of language used, this includes any references to 'rules', 'principles', 'grounds' or 'maxims'. Where such language is used, either the lawyer in court, or the reporter, associated the argument with the idea of maxims. One consequence is that the chapter may underestimate the use of maxims in practice.[16] This approach also avoids the difficulties in the use of Latin or the vernacular.

[11] eg, JM Gest, 'The Writings of Sir Edward Coke' (1909) 18 *Yale Law Journal* 504, 529–30; SE Thorne, 'Sir Edward Coke: 1552–1952' in *The Selden Society Lectures, 1952–2001* (William S Hein & Co, 2003) 7; TG Barnes, 'Introduction to Coke's "Commentary on Littleton" in AD Boyer (ed), *Law, Liberty and Parliament: Selected Essays on the Writings of Sir Edward Coke* (Liberty Fund, 2004) 2–3.

[12] A good example of the difficulty is CM Gray, *The Writ of Prohibition: Jurisdiction in Early Modern English Law* 2nd edn (e-book: www.lib.uchicago.edu/e/law/gray/, 2004), vol 2, 25 and 322 and vol 3, 130. Gray's analysis is flawed in identifying any Latin statement as a 'maxim'. The reports of *Bennet v Shortwright* (1590) and *Brooke v Parson of D* (1600) cited by Gray do not refer to a maxim, although most do include the Latin statement '*transeunt decimal in catalla*' in relation to tithes. In context this is simply a conclusion rather than a maxim. The Latin statement was probably used as it also features in the 'statute' Articuli Cleri 1316 (9 Edw 2 c 1) and so the common lawyers sought to use the 'statute' to justify their exercise of jurisdictional control. Similarly, most of the reports of *Cullier v Cullier* (1590) refer to the civil and canon law rule that *nemo tenetur seipsum prodere*. Gray interprets this as a 'maxim' of the common law which other courts could not contradict, but the better interpretation seems to be that the common law courts thought that they were holding the ecclesiastical courts to the canon law's own rules (see generally RH Helmholz, 'The Privilege and the *Ius Commune*: The Middle Ages to the Seventeenth Century' in RH Helmholz, CM Gray, JH Langbein, E Moglen, HE Smith, AW Alschuler (eds), *The Privilege Against Self-Incrimination: Its Origins and Development* (University of Chicago Press, 1997) 43–45.

[13] eg, BL MS Harg 207.

[14] See (n 12) above.

[15] eg, *Slade v Morley* (1602) 4 Co Rep 92b, 76 ER 1074, where Dodderidge's argument is summarised in Latin. Other surviving reports of the case show that Dodderidge delivered a much fuller argument which did not include the Latin statement in Coke's report (see JH Baker and SFC Milsom, *Sources of English Legal History: Private Law to 1750* 2nd edn (Oxford University Press, 2010) 460–66). Thomas Ashe, *Fasciculus Florum* (G Eld 1618) is a collection of Latin statements taken from Coke's *Reports* which Ashe never describes as maxims.

[16] eg, the cases discussed about maxims and equity below, text accompanying nn 66–68. Gray not only refers to cases where a 'maxim' is explicitly mentioned, but other cases where the same substantive issue arose. However, the reports do not demonstrate that the lawyers in those cases considered the issue in terms of maxims.

I. Identifying Maxims

Both theorists and practitioners needed to develop ideas about how maxims were to be identified, an issue which raised considerations about the nature of maxims themselves. There were two different strands of thought in the theoretical literature, strands which were sometimes woven together from 1579 onwards.

The older tradition simply assumed the existence of maxims in a legal system; no source was given for these maxims. The fifteenth-century writer Fortescue stated that there was no 'rational ground' for 'principles', which could be known only through 'sense and memory'.[17] This position was a necessary part of Fortescue's Aristotelian view of maxims as principles used in a logical reasoning process. To consider the source of maxims might provide a means to dispute principles. St German similarly did not explain the existence of particular maxims, or maxims in general. Instead, he linked maxims and customs, the basis for both of which was not explained. According to St German, while customs were known to all, maxims were known only to the learned.[18]

An alternative approach to maxims can be found in Serjeant Morgan's argument in *Colthirst v Bejushin*, as printed in Plowden's *Commentaries* in 1571.[19] According to Morgan, rather than simply being known, maxims are 'conclusions of reason'.[20] In the 1579 printing of Rastell's law dictionary, this idea of maxims as conclusions of reason was combined with Fortescue's inductive approach to maxims, changing Fortescue's language of maxims being learned through 'sense and memory' to knowledge from 'experience'.[21]

Most later writers chose one of these two positions. Both Edward Coke and Francis Bacon, in a rare moment of agreement, described maxims as 'conclusions of reason', although Bacon also thought it 'undue and preposterous to prove rules and maxims', a position like that of Fortescue.[22] However, Noy regarded maxims simply as rules which are known.[23] Like St German, Noy expressly linked maxims and customs and limited knowledge of maxims to the 'learned'. Noy took this

[17] J Fortescue, 'In Praise of the Laws of England' in S Lockwood (ed), *Sir John Fortescue: On the Laws and Governance of England* (Cambridge University Press, 1997) 15. Fortescue's work was first printed in 1543.

[18] St German (n 1) 57–59.

[19] E Plowden, *Les comentaries, ou les reportes de Edmunde Plowden* (Richard Tottel, 1571).

[20] *Colthirst* (n 2) 27v, 75 ER 44. However, Morgan may have been acknowledging the earlier tradition when he described maxims as 'authorities in themselves'.

[21] J Rastell, *An Exposition of Certaine Difficult and Obscure Words, and Termes of the Lawes* (Richard Totell, 1579) fos 150v–151. The law dictionary was first printed in 1523 (as the *Exposiciones terminorum legum anglorum*) and periodically amended. The 1579 printing was a major alteration.

[22] Co Litt (Societie of Stationers, 1628) fo 10v; F Bacon, 'Maxims of the Law' in J Spedding, RL Ellis and DD Heath (eds), *The Works of Francis Bacon vol 7* (Longmans, 1857–1874) 320 and 322.

[23] W Noy, *A Treatise of the Principal Grounds and Maxims of the Laws of the Kingdome* (W Cook, 1642) 20.

position a little further, explaining that 'which is a maxim and which is not, shall always be determined by the judges, because they are known to none but to the learned'.[24] The role of the judges in determining what is and is not a maxim was recognised by St German, but the addition of 'because' by Noy suggests that he saw only the judges as being the 'learned'. Henry Finch, who differentiated between 'rules of reason' and 'maxims', regarded maxims as derived from existing laws, which suggests that maxims are a form of conclusion.

John Dodderidge's discussion was arguably more sophisticated, trying to bring together the two different strands of thinking about maxims as well as ideas from the civilian and Aristotelian traditions. In many respects Dodderidge follows St German. Dodderidge described 'principles' as known to all (like St German's customs) through the 'light of Nature'.[25] By contrast, '[s]econdary principles … are not so well known by the light of Nature, as by other means … and are peculiarly known, for the most part, to such only as profess the study and speculation of Laws'.[26] The limitation on who knows these secondary principles echoes St German's description of maxims. However, Dodderidge also referred to maxims as 'conclusions of reason', a departure from St German's ideas about maxims.[27] According to Dodderidge, 'secondary principles' were 'derived out of the general customs, and maxims, or principles of the law of nature or primary conclusions'.[28] Secondary principles were therefore conclusions of a reasoning process. This seems to be an attempt by Dodderidge to integrate the view of maxims as 'conclusions of reason' and as known to the learned.[29]

In legal argument the situation appears to have been different. However much theorists claimed that maxims were known by all the learned, in argument maxims were very rarely asserted without reference to some other 'authority'.[30] It was not assumed that the judges knew a particular maxim. Either lawyers thought that maxims were not known by all the learned, or that judges were not especially learned. Not only was this a divergence from theoretical writings, it was also a change from practice seen in medieval law reports.

[24] ibid.

[25] Dodderidge (n 8) 191.

[26] ibid 194.

[27] ibid 153.

[28] ibid 194.

[29] Dodderidge's discussion of the derivation of 'secondary principles' seems to follow St German's concept of the law of reason secondary particular (St German (n 1) 35), not only suggesting St German's influence but also indicating a degree of conceptual confusion by Dodderidge.

[30] The concept and language of authority was difficult in this period. Here I take authority to mean simply any text or case which had some force in legal reasoning. An example of a 'maxim' for which no authority was provided is that used in *Beverley's Case* (see (n 69) below). In fact, the 'maxim' seems to be taken from T Littleton, *Tenures* (Richard Tottell, 1581) fo 95v (Lib III c 6 §406), where it is not stated to be a maxim. 'Maxims' stated in argument in the medieval period are not associated with authorities (eg (1440) YB Pas 18 Hen 6, fo 1, pl 1, at fo 2b, per Newton CJCP), but as citations of authority are very unusual in medieval law reports, this should not be given much weight.

Occasionally, a 'maxim' would be taken from a law book, although this technique seems to be associated principally with Edward Coke.[31] More typically, assertions of maxims were associated with cases. In all of these instances where I have been able to identify the earlier case with which a maxim was associated, the earlier case does not expressly state that a maxim was involved. The identification of a maxim in a case was consequently an interpretation of these cases by lawyers.

There were different techniques in using cases to find maxims. In some instances lawyers would discuss a selection of cases, deriving a single maxim from the collection. Serjeant Saunders in *Colthirst v Bejushin* did just that, extracting from the cases he cited a 'principle in law'.[32] In others, a lawyer would state a maxim and argue that the maxim explained various cases, even if they were not directly on point, before then applying the maxim in a different context.[33] These approaches may explain the use of cases in maxims literature too.[34]

A different approach was taken in *Lodsham v Labourne*, where Walter said that he 'learned for a rule often times in this court' before putting forward a rule applicable to the facts.[35] This language of learning something through presence in court suggests a type of experience, indicating a relationship with Rastell's definition of maxims. Thomas Egerton used an alternative approach in *The Dean and Chapter of Chester's Case*, where he put forward a 'maxim' agreed by the all the judges in a single prior case.[36] That approach is closer to the ideas of St German and especially Noy's later contribution, of relying upon the judges to determine what is a maxim. One use of a single case to establish a maxim is possibly linked to theory in another way. In *Eaden v Marshe* Popham CJ and Gawdy J observed a maxim that was 'put for a rule' in an earlier case, and then applied it.[37] In fact, the prior case does not refer expressly to a rule, simply stating that 'in all these cases, the commencement of this must of necessity be alleged', explaining that to require otherwise would be 'against reason'.[38] The attribution of this statement as a maxim might have been reinforced by the language of reason, as it could be interpreted as meaning that the requirement of stating commencement amounted to a 'conclusion of reason', integrated into the theory of maxims as a result.

[31] *Ratcliff's Case* (1592) 3 Co Rep 37a, 40a; 76 ER 713, 726 (a 'maxim' from Littleton's Tenures (ibid)); *Hallyocke v White* (1599) BL MS Add 25203, fo 53 (a 'rule' from *Bracton*). *Hallyocke v White* is useful in showing that Coke's use of legal texts was not an editorial addition to his own reports, but observable by others in Coke's curial arguments. A 'maxim' was asserted in *Sharington v Strotton*, seemingly as an extension from a set of facts discussed in Littleton's *Tenures* ((1566) 1 Plowden 298, 305; 75 ER 454, 464).

[32] *Colthirst* (n 2) 28v, 75 ER 46.

[33] eg, Croke J in *Lord Hastings v Douglas* (1634) CUL MS Gg.2.19, fo 509.

[34] See text to (n 40) below.

[35] *Lodsham v Labourne* (1602) BL MS Add 25203, fo 445v.

[36] *Dean and Chapter of Chester's Case* (1578) HEH MS El 482, fo 34.

[37] *Eaden v Marshe* (1600) BL MS Add 25203, fo 214v.

[38] *The Dean and Chapter of Bristol v Clerke. The Serjeants' Case* (1553) 1 Dyer 83a, 85b; 73 ER 181, 185.

The use of cases in relation to maxims in legal practice can therefore be associated with particular aspects of theoretical discussions about maxims. While none of these discussions explicitly provided a role for cases in relation to maxims, both the model of maxims as known only to the learned, and maxims as conclusions of reason, provided a role for prior cases in determining maxims. If maxims are learned through 'sense and memory' or 'experience', prior cases provide a means of acquiring the necessary experience. If maxims are conclusions of reason, prior cases are a means to learn these conclusions of reason, an intellectual short cut. As Dodderidge put it, the efficient cause of maxims is reason 'tried and sifted upon disputation and argument', which is (arguably) a description of what can be seen in law reports.[39] Although Francis Bacon thought it was 'preposterous' to prove maxims, this remark occurred in an explanation as to why he had not cited cases in his discussion of each maxim, suggesting that he did recognise a role for cases in identifying maxims, even if he did not approve of it. However, no theorist insisted upon prior cases as a necessary element in identifying maxims. Several discussions of maxims do feature references to prior cases, but always seemingly as examples of the application of the maxim.[40] Several of these examples therefore suggest a link between the theory and practice of maxims, albeit in relation to cases which were rarely themselves mentioned in the theoretical discussions (or, in fact, in common-law theory generally in this period).

II. The Incontrovertibility of Maxims

A significant agreement between the theory and practice of maxims was their incontrovertibility, a theoretical position upon which all writers about maxims agreed. This position was clear in the writings of Fortescue, St German and the Henrician judge Anthony Fitzherbert and adopted by later writers.[41] Indeed, according to one Elizabethan manuscript collection of maxims, the incontrovertibility of

[39] Dodderidge (n 8) 242. Dodderidge discussed the civilian practice of collecting maxims from cases and seemingly rejected it (ibid 153), although he did acknowledge that maxims contain 'in a short sum the reason and direction of many particular and special occurrences', which looks somewhat casuistic.

[40] Bacon (n 22) (although it is not clear that these references were included in Bacon's original text); Co Litt fo 10v and the cross-references there; Finch, *Nomotexnia* (Societie of Stationers, 1613); Noy (n 23). Similarly the collections of maxims in BL MS Harg 207 and BL MS Harg 318.

[41] Fortescue (n 17) 15; St German (n 1) 57–59; Fitz NB (Thomas Barlett 1534), preface (unpaginated). Later references include Finch, ibid fo 2v (although see text to (n 46) below for the interaction between Finch's idea of 'rules of reason' and 'maxims'); Co Litt fo 10v; Dodderidge (n 8) 37 and 196; Noy (n 23) 20 (the text here closely follows *Doctor and Student*). Thomas Hedley's speech in Parliament, 26th June 1610, in Elizabeth R Foster (ed), *Proceedings in Parliament 1610, Vol 2, House of Commons* (Yale University Press, 1966) 186.

maxims was itself a maxim.[42] This incontrovertibility appears to be a change in practice. Assertions of a relevant maxim were challenged into the first decade of the sixteenth century.[43] The change may be a consequence of the influence of both Fortescue (whose views on maxims were first printed in 1543) and St German (*Doctor and Student* was first printed in 1528).

Although it is difficult to prove satisfactorily by absence, no instances have been found of an asserted 'maxim' being challenged as substantively incorrect in legal argument from the reign of Henry VIII onwards, nor have any instances been discovered where lawyers ever challenged the assertion that a particular rule was a maxim. The only positive evidence which seems to point towards incontrovertibility in legal practice comes from Thomas Egerton's report (or possibly draft) of his argument in *Hawes v Hynge*. An argument made by Coke was criticised by Egerton as an examination of the 'reason' of a maxim which Egerton had put in argument.[44] Although not directly concerned with the unchallengeable status of maxims, the fact Egerton could complain about any examination of the maxim at all suggests that challenges would be unacceptable. If this is correct, then assertions of a maxim would perhaps be the strongest argument available to common lawyers.

Some theoretical writers considered the potential of challenges to the use of particular maxims in particular cases on the basis that individual maxims existed within a broader system of maxims and were consequently limited by other parts of the system. For these writers, ultimately all of English law could be set down as a system of maxims.[45] These writers differed from St German, who identified maxims as only one of the types of law in England. As a consequence, they needed to address potential conflicts in a way which those writers who saw maxims simply as one source of law or type of legal argument did not—for lawyers in the latter group conflicts might be avoided or resolved by the use of alternative arguments or sources of law. Finch distinguished between 'rules of reason' and 'maxims' with

[42] BL MS Harg 207, fo 6.

[43] (1496) YB Hil 11 Hen 7, fo 15, pl 11, where serjeant Kebell said 'there is no ground or erudition as you say'; (1504) YB Mich 20 Hen 7, fo 6, pl 17, fo 8, where Fyneux CJKB said that 'there is not in our law any such general maxim or ground for the showing of deeds, but that such maxim may be disproved'.

[44] *Hawes v Hynge* (undated) HEH MS El 482, fo 249. It should be noted that Egerton continued to criticise Coke for examining the reason of the maxim without any book or authority to support him, suggesting the matter may not have been quite so simple, but nevertheless Coke's attempt to subvert the maxim by examining its justification was decidedly unwelcome. Coke did examine the 'reason' behind maxims on a number of occasions (eg, *Pinchon's Case* (1611) 9 Co Rep 86b, 86-87a; 76 ER 859, 860). However, no instances have been found of Coke doing so outside of his own printed reports, and it may be that such justifications were added as pedagogical devices.

[45] Such a model of law, which he associated with positivism, was rejected for the common law by Simpson (AWB Simpson, 'The Common Law and Legal Theory' in AWB Simpson, *Legal Theory and Legal History* (Hambledon Press, 1987) 359–82. Simpson described the common law as a customary system, but the use of custom here is different to that in early-modern sources.

maxims being inferior and giving way to rules of reason.[46] According to Dodderidge the 'Rules, Axioms, and Propositions of the common Law' were

> restrained by exceptions; which are grounded upon two causes. The one is Equity: the other is some other Rule or Ground of Law, which seems to encounter the Ground or Rule proposed: wherein, for conformity's sake, and that no absurdity or contradiction be permitted, certain exceptions are framed, which do not only knit and conjoin one Rule in reason to another, but by means of their equity, temper the rigour of the Law, which upon some certain circumstances in every of the said Rules might happen and fall out.[47]

Bacon described some rules as 'worthier and to be preferred'.[48] More generally, Serjeant Morgan suggested that in legal argument seemingly competing maxims could be 'conferred and compared, the one to the other' 'by reason'.[49]

No applications of these ideas of a system or hierarchy of maxims (or even seemingly conflicting maxims) have been found applied in legal practice, despite Serjeant Morgan's remark occurring in a reported case. While practitioners seem to have accepted the theoretical idea of maxims as unchallengeable, they did not develop any particular tools for addressing situations where different maxims may have been applicable, leading to different outcomes. One explanation for this may be the influence of St German's legal theory, rather than the theoretical models which regarded the entire law as a system of maxims.[50] St German did not raise the possibility of disagreement amongst maxims, regarding maxims as only one part of English law.

The incontrovertibility of maxims did not mean that in practice arguments which referred to maxims were automatically successful. Many were not. However, counters to maxims were never challenges to the maxims themselves. Rather they were disputes about the application of the maxim to the particular facts of the case in question. In the preface to his *Maxims*, Bacon explained that he included cases applying maxims after the statement of each maxim for 'light and direction' as a means of 'opening their sense and use and limiting them with distinctions'.[51] For Bacon, uniquely in the theoretical literature, cases were crucial for understanding the real sense of maxims and their use in legal reasoning.[52]

In legal practice practitioners relied not on theories about maxims, but on cases. Cases provided an important means by which maxim-based reasoning could be

[46] Finch (n 40) fo 2v.

[47] Dodderidge (n 8) 209–10.

[48] Bacon (n 22) 336.

[49] *Colthirst* (n 2) 27v, 77 ER 44.

[50] See text to (n 65) below for a situation where the best explanation for the use of maxims in legal practice derives from the work of St German.

[51] Bacon (n 22) 323.

[52] Dodderidge did use cases to explain maxims ((n 8) 157), but never refers to the possibility of the scope of the maxim being limited.

weakened.[53] Even Serjeant Morgan's well-known explanation of a theory of maxims in *Colthirst v Bejushin* was criticised on this very ground. Serjeant Saunders put forward cases with an outcome contrary to that suggested by Serjeant Morgan, who was relying on maxims.[54] Saunders argued that by ignoring these cases, the opposing lawyers 'commend the maxims in words, yet they deny them in fact'.[55] For Saunders, a simple reliance upon maxims without association with cases was not truly to understand and apply maxims at all. This meant that arguments involving maxims rapidly became very similar to other types of common-law reasoning: strongly casuistic and analogical.

III. The Content and Scope of Maxims

Theoretical writers agreed that maxims had a significant role in the common law. Most writers also agreed that individual maxims could have a wide scope. Several lawyers observed that some maxims could be very specific, but others were very broad, potentially encompassing a range of situations. Dodderidge, Bacon and Henry Finch even sought to classify maxims on the basis of their breadth.[56] For such writers, the maxims with wider scope, at least, were applicable to most, if not all, of the common law.

The situation in legal practice seems to have been very different. Typically, 'maxims' put in argument were narrow rules of law and were predominantly concerned with property law alone.[57] In *Colthirst v Bejushin* three maxims were suggested. The first was that when a remainder was appointed to someone, the recipient must be capable of receiving the remainder; the second that 'a bar is good if it is certain to a common intent'; third that 'livery of seisin shall not be taken most strongly against him that makes it'.[58] None of these are broad general principles, two of them are limited to real property law. In *Eaden v Marshe* it was stated as a rule that where someone seeks to establish title to a thing, the commencement of their title

[53] 'Cases' could be real or hypothetical in this period, although genuine cases were becoming predominant (I Williams, '"He Creditted More the Printed Booke": Common Lawyers' Receptivity to Print, c1550–1640' (2010) 28 *Law and History Review* 39, 47–48).

[54] *Colthirst* (n 2) 28v, 77 ER 45–46.

[55] ibid.

[56] See generally Neustadt (n 4) 38–40, 43–44 and 53–54 (Bacon distinguishing between 'maxims' and 'placitata juris'). Finch's *Nomotexnia* (n 39) distinguishes between 'rules of reason' and more narrow legal learning (fo 2v).

[57] CM Gray ('The Boundaries of the Equitable Function' (1976) 20 *American Journal of Legal History* 192, 207), reached a similar conclusion but limited it to real property law and only from cases involving jurisdictional disputes between common law courts and courts of equity. The discussion here covers a wider range of cases.

[58] *Colthirst* (n 2) 27v–28, 77 ER 44–45.

must be expressly alleged, another narrow point of property law (and of pleading).[59] In two seventeenth century cases, the rule of survivorship in situations of joint tenancy of land were identified as maxims.[60] Not all examples concerned real property law, for example in *Lodsham v Laborne*, a rule was stated as to what amounted to a conversion of goods.[61] Maxims, whether substantive, interpretative or concerned with pleading rules, almost always related in some way to issues concerning property.

A good demonstration of the difference between theoretical writers and lawyers in practice can be seen in the arguments of Thomas Egerton. All the 'maxims' discussed by Egerton in his notes of cases concerned the interpretation and application of documents such as deeds and royal charters. One such maxim was that deeds are to be interpreted strongly against their maker.[62] By contrast, in Francis Bacon's *Maxims*, a more general maxim was stated, 'that a man's deeds and his words shall be taken strongliest against himself'.[63] Bacon's discussion incorporated the maxim of Egerton, categorising it as an example of the broader maxim.

The one exception to the narrow scope of individual maxims found in legal practice is another maxim used by Thomas Egerton. His notes do not provide the facts or legal context, but the case seems to be an appeal of felony, a process by which victims of felonies (or their surviving relatives, in the case of homicide) could bring criminal proceedings against the alleged perpetrator. Egerton, when arguing about the acceptability of the appeal in this case, states as a maxim that the common law is 'in favour of life'.[64] Given the mandatory death penalty for felony convictions, this was an argument against any appeal of felony. The same maxim was recognised in a manuscript collection, where it was part of a largely familiar triad. According to this collection, the common law was in favour of life, liberty and marriage.[65]

Practitioners may have only described narrow rules of law as maxims because such precise rules were more useful at deciding particular cases. However, given the acknowledged theoretical strength of maxims, arguing that a wide principle was applicable in a given case would provide some added strength to an argument. Application of such a wider principle would probably require the use of cases, but this occurred in relation to narrow rules of law too.

[59] *Eaden v Marsh* (1600) BL MS Add 25203, fo 214v.
[60] See (n 68) below.
[61] *Lodsham v Laborne* (1602) BL MS Add 25203, fo 445v.
[62] *Saunders and Starkey v Stanforde* (undated) HEH MS El 482, fo 73v.
[63] Bacon (n 22) 333.
[64] *Anon* (undated) HEH MS El 482, fo 84.
[65] BL MS Harg 207, fos 10, 12v and 124v. The author of this collection repeats that the common law is in favour of life on three occasions, once in combination with liberty and 'dower', the other in combination with 'liberty'. As the author also refers to the common law favouring marriage (fo 8), the reference to dower in the triad seems to be a mistake.

If maxims in practice were regarded as narrow rules of law, this might explain the focus on property law. One would expect to find precise rules in the more developed areas of the common law. The most sophisticated body of learning in the medieval common law was property law. Other areas of law, such as contract, were subject to considerable change in the early-modern period and it might have been difficult to describe any of the emerging ideas as 'maxims' which could not be challenged.

The narrowness of maxims, and the focus on property law, may also be a consequence of the dissemination of particular ideas about maxims. A focus on maxims as narrow and concerned with property law can be seen in St German's *Doctor and Student*. St German listed 28 maxims, of which four were not somehow connected with land law issues.[66] If lawyers were learning much of their legal theory from St German, then their understanding of maxims would be of narrow rules of property law.

IV. Maxims and Equity

One use of maxims in legal practice is largely unaddressed in the early-modern theoretical literature, namely the role of maxims in jurisdictional disputes between the common law courts and inferior courts of equity such as the Court of Requests.[67] In the first three decades of the seventeenth century, common law courts prohibited courts of equity from proceeding with cases where equitable intervention would infringe a 'maxim' of the common law. These maxims were usually narrow rules of law. In two cases the maxim in question was the rule of survivorship in joint tenancy of land.[68] In the third case, the 'maxim' concerned whether someone could rely upon their own incapacity to avoid a bond upon which money was owed.[69]

The principal difficulty with the application of the common law in this way is that the contemporary, essentially Aristotelian, theory of equity, accepted that the application of general rules might lead to hardship in particular cases. Such hardship was a legitimate basis for equitable intervention.[70] John Dodderidge's

[66] St German (n 1) 59–65. The four maxims which are not connected with land are 'if an exigent of felony be awarded against a man: he hath thereby forfeited his goods to the king'; 'if a man steel goods to the value of xii.d. or above it is felony'; 'he that is arraigned upon an indictment of felony shall be admitted in favour of life to challenge xxxv jurors peremptorily'; 'he that recovers debt or damages in the king's court by such an action wherein a *capias* lay in the process may within a year after the recovery have a *capias ad satisfaciendum* to take the body of the defendant and to commit him to prison and he shall not be released till he have paid the debt and damages'.

[67] The use of maxims in this field was first discussed by Gray (n 57).

[68] *Anon* (1612) BL MS Add 25210, fo 4 and *Portington v Beaumont* (1624) BL MS Harl 5148, fo 15v.

[69] (1603) *Beverley's Case* 4 Co Rep 123b, 124a; 76 ER 1118, 1119–20.

[70] JL Barton, 'Introduction' to St German (n 1) xliv–li.

discussion of maxims appreciated this difficulty, accepting equity as an exception to the application of maxims.[71]

Gray suggests that maxims might have justified preventing equitable intervention on the basis that such maxims were not 'expressions of those deep and fruitful value-choices that deserve to be called fundamental and so to control Aristotelian equity.'[72] Applying a maxim was not unconscionable, and unconscionability was the basis of equitable intervention.[73] Gray's analysis is therefore based in the theory of equity, not of maxims. The difficulty with this is that one of the 'maxims' which justified prohibiting the intervention of equity was that 'a man would not be permitted to stultify himself' and so could not use equitable intervention to be relieved from liability on a bond created when he was *non compos mentis*. However, the report shows that the maxim would permit someone else to plead the incapacity of the creator of the bond, demonstrating that even the common law considered the obligation created in such circumstances to be unacceptable. This seems to be just the sort of rule of pleading or proof, rather than substance, from which equity provided relief in other contexts.[74]

If this explanation is deficient, might the theory of maxims assist in providing a justification for the common law position? In his report of *Beverley's Case*, Coke made it clear that equity could not intervene 'for this should be in subversion of a principle and ground in law'.[75] This was the only attempt at an explanation which Coke provided. For Coke, the fact that equitable intervention would contradict a maxim in itself justified interference in the proceedings of the equity court. This suggests that it is ideas about maxims which provide the justification for Coke's conclusion. Coke does not provide any explanation as to why equity could not interfere with the application of a maxim, but the theoretical literature on maxims provides a solution, specifically the work of Christopher St German.[76] Like Coke, St German stated that equity could not be used to interfere with the application of a maxim of the law.[77] The only explanation, such as it is, for this assertion is that

[71] Dodderidge (n 8) 209–10.

[72] Gray (n 57) 218.

[73] See generally, DR Klinck, *Conscience, Equity and the Court of Chancery in Early Modern England* (Ashgate, 2010).

[74] A standard early-modern example of equitable intervention was of a debt owed on a sealed bond. If the debtor paid the debt, but the bond was not destroyed or defaced, or the debtor given a written acquittance, at common law the creditor could sue on the bond twice due to the evidential rule that the only defence to such a bond was an acquittance. It was universally accepted that equity could intervene in such a context.

[75] *Beverley's Case* (n 69) 124a, 76 ER 1120.

[76] The reliance on St German would explain why other writers on maxims did not raise this issue. These writers were concerned with maxims, or the common law more generally. By contrast, St German wrote about the appropriateness and limits of equitable intervention in the English legal system.

[77] J Guy (ed), *St German on Chancery and Statute* (Selden Society Supplementary Series vol 6, Selden Society, 1985) 116. This is a reference to St German's *Little Treatise* concerning writs of subpoena, a work which only exists in manuscript. Aside from St German's autograph copy, the surviving copy is

equitable intervention would render the maxim void, a comment similar to that made by Coke. St German was influenced by Thomas Aquinas. Aquinas raised the argument that *epieikeia* was not a virtue, because it 'judged' a law.[78] In his *Little Treatise*, St German similarly refers to the idea of judgment of a law, saying that 'there lies no subpoena directly against a statute, not directly against the maxims of the law, for [if] it should lie, then *the law should be judged* to be void, and that may not be done by no court, but by the parliament'.[79] Coke's position, and perhaps that in the other cases, may be attributable to the ongoing influence of St German's exposition of legal theory.[80]

V. The Relationship Between Theory and Practice, and the Prominence of Maxims

The evidence presented in this paper suggests relatively close correspondence between the early-modern common law theory of maxims and the use of maxims in legal practice, but with certain important differences. Theory and practice seem to have been aligned in identifying maxims and both recognised the incontrovertibility of maxims, but the two seem to have diverged with regard to the content of maxims and theory was largely silent on the interaction between maxims and equity.[81] This section attempts to explain both the similarities and differences between theory and practice.

A recurring comment in this paper has been the seeming influence of the work of Christopher St German on maxims in legal practice. St German's influence seems to have been particularly significant, not only in identifying maxims with narrow rules of property law, but also in stressing the protection of maxims from equitable intervention and perhaps in changing the approach of lawyers in practice to render maxims incontrovertible, unlike the position in late-medieval law.[82]

from later than 1576. Four of the five remaining copies of St German's *Replication* (to which the *Little Treatise* was a reply) are also mid-Elizabethan. This suggests that St German's work was still regarded as current in Elizabethan England.

[78] Aquinas himself rejected this criticism, but it may have influenced St German nonetheless. T Aquinas, *Summa Theologiae*, (TC O'Brien ed, Cambridge University Press, 2006) vol 41, 277–78 (IIaIIae, Q.120, a.1).

[79] Guy (n 77) 116 (emphasis added). On this issue and possible influence see J Guy, 'Law Equity and Conscience in Henrician Juristic Thought' in A Fox and J Guy (eds), *Reassessing the Henrician Age: Humanism, Politics and Reform 1500–1550* (Basil Blackwell, 1986) 186.

[80] For *Anon* (1612) BL MS Add 25210, fo 4 and *Portington v Beaumont* (1624) BL MS Harl 5148, fo 15v, St German's influence may have been mediated by Coke, whose report of *Beverley's Case* was printed in 1604.

[81] The exception is the work of John Dodderidge, whose views are opposite to practice (see text to (n 71) above).

[82] See text to (n 43) above.

Doctor and Student may have been influential for a few reasons. Most obvious is perhaps its accessibility. *Doctor and Student* was available in English from the early-1530s, making it a suitable work for students early in their legal studies. Furthermore, St German's work served both as a discussion of legal theory, and as a source of cases for use in legal argument.[83]

Most importantly, perhaps, *Doctor and Student* was printed.[84] Many of the other discussions of maxims were unprinted until late in the period under discussion, most only in the reign of Charles I. Of the various writers concerned with maxims discussed in this paper, only St German, Fortescue and the remarks reported in Plowden's *Commentaries* were printed before 1600. There is one piece of evidence which suggests that practitioners who were not themselves writing theory made use of ideas from other theorists to inform their legal arguments. As was shown above, there is plenty of evidence that in practice cases were used to prove the existence of particular maxims. However, in one case, a maxim was used to argue against particular cases. In *Lord Mountjoy v Sir Henry Mildmay*, Rolle argued that individual cases providing 'precedents' were inferior to an established 'rule of law'.[85] Rolle's position was to rely upon the higher nature of maxims to diminish the strength of precedents, arguing that cases incompatible with a maxim were invalid. The only writer who hints at this role for maxims is Francis Bacon, who suggests that maxims, as conclusions of reason, could 'correct' erroneous cases.[86] For considering the relationship between legal theory and legal practice, the important evidence is that Bacon's *Maxims* were first printed in 1630.[87] It seems plausible that Rolle's argument was informed by the recent publication of Bacon's views.

Finally, St German's theoretical discussion of the common law purported to be descriptive of what common lawyers did.[88] Aside from the incontrovertibility issue, St German's discussion of maxims looks fairly consistent with late-medieval practice as seen in the law reports. These late-medieval reports were the most printed law reports of the sixteenth (and possibly seventeenth) century and were printed in a cycle which suggests a regular student audience.[89] This made St German a means to interpret the cases which students were expected to read, a

[83] A late case to use *Doctor and Student* as a source for a case is *Miller and Jones v Manwaring* (1634) CUL MS Gg.2.20, fo 621v.

[84] See (n 77) above for the difficulty in this regard in relation to maxims and equity, where St German's views only existed in manuscript until 1985.

[85] *Lord Mountjoy v Sir Henry Mildmay* (1632) CUL MS Gg.2.19, fo 295.

[86] Bacon (n 23) 322.

[87] In *The Elements of the Common Lawes of England* (Robert Young, 1630).

[88] St German (n 1) 31–32.

[89] DJ Seipp, 'Introductory Tables and Notes' in DJ Seipp (ed), *Year Books Edward V, Richard III, Henry VII, and Henry VIII: 1483–1535* (2011, Lawbook Exchange, Clark, New Jersey) iii; I Williams, 'A Medieval Book and Early-modern Law: Bracton's Authority and Application in the Common Law c1550–1640' (2011) 79 *Tijdschrift voor Rechtsgeschiedenis* 47, 54.

suitable tool for explaining what students and lawyers encountered early in their training. This does not mean that St German did nothing more than describe; he provided a theoretical language and some ideas to lawyers which they could use. Furthermore, the yearbooks do not demonstrate the incontrovertibility of maxims, or the relationship between maxims and equity, subjects upon which St German may have been influential. But by seeming to provide a theory based upon what could be found in the books of legal practice, all of St German's views could be interpreted as accurate statements of English law.

VI. Postscript: Why did Theory Diverge from Practice?

This provides some explanation of the nature of maxims in practice, but not to the divergence of theory from practice. Why did theoretical writers, who were themselves practitioners, insist upon a model of maxims which was different to that seen in practice?[90] The answer lies in understanding what the theorists were often setting out to do. Not all writers on maxims were concerned with accurately representing contemporary legal practice. Francis Bacon even criticised lawyers who 'argue upon general grounds, and come not near the point in question', but still thought such general maxims were worth recording.[91] Several Elizabethan and Jacobean writers on maxims, including Bacon, were concerned with the role of maxims in legal education and learning the law, rather than legal practice. Others were concerned with the related issue of the status of the common law as a 'science'.

By setting out maxims, writers could provide some degree of method to the common law.[92] In early-modern thought, method was an important route to learning and understanding. Both Henry Finch and John Dodderidge were writing works for students and used their understanding of broad maxims and narrower rules to provide structure to the law. Finch's book purported to be a methodical exposition of the entire common law, while Dodderidge attempted to show how any particular legal topic could be set out methodically. There was no claim on the part of these authors that simply learning the individual maxims would answer particular legal questions. Maxims were a route to memory and understanding which would then enable questions to be answered.

[90] One possibility is that the conservative approach to identifying 'maxims' in practice adopted in this paper misrepresents the position.

[91] Bacon (n 22) 320.

[92] Although not all lawyers concerned with maxims as a route to learning the law approved of this (eg, Bacon (n 22) 322).

Another concern grounded in education was to establish the common law as a 'science'.[93] This could be associated with memory and method.[94] However, rather than being concerned with the efficacy of legal education, claims to scientific status were based upon disciplinary competition and prestige, originally in the university context. Maxims provided the means to establish claims that the common law was a 'science'. As a science the common law would be a higher discipline, equivalent to medicine, the civil and canon laws and theology.[95] To claim status as a science, a discipline needed to fulfil the Aristotelian criterion of being based upon known principles. Maxims provided these principles for the common law.

By establishing the common law as a science, its prestige would be enhanced. Justifying the law and enhancing its prestige is a recurring trend in speeches given in readings (lectures) at the Inns of Court.[96] Demonstrating that the common law was a science was a means to establish the common law's equivalence or even superiority over other bodies of learning. According to Francis Bacon, it was a matter of 'majesty' to show the 'concordance' between the broad maxims of the common law which he set out and those of the civil law. Edward Coke and John Davies took this further. In Coke's report of *Ratcliffe's Case* it is stated explicitly that 'rules and principles' can be, and are, set out because the common law is like 'every art and science' in having and using such rules, a remark which precedes criticism of the civil law (another science) for its uncertainty.[97] Similarly, in the preface to John Davies' *Reports*, Davies explains that the principles of the common law are not only certain like those of other sciences, but hyperbolically 'more certain'.[98] The common law was more science-like than recognised sciences, its superiority demonstrated.

Legal theory about maxims was consequently not always directed to legal practice, but to the practicalities of legal education and the status of the common law as an educational discipline. In this regard maxims may have achieved some success.

[93] The first reference to maxims in connection with the common law as a science is found in Fitz NB, preface (unpaginated). Later references, in the context of maxims, include Dodderidge (n 8) 244 ('in the Law (as in other sciences)'); E Coke, *Le tierce part des reportes del Edward Coke* (Thomas Wight, 1602), sig Cii (in the common law 'as in all other Arts and Sciences').

[94] W Fulbeck, *A Direction or Preparative to the Study of the Lawe* (Thomas Wight, 1600) fos 4–5v.

[95] On this issue in European universities, I Maclean, *Interpretation and Meaning in the Renaissance: the Case of Law* (Cambridge University Press, 1992) 22–29.

[96] I Williams, 'The Tudor Genesis of Edward Coke's Immemorial Common Law' (2012) 43 *Sixteenth Century Journal* 103, 106.

[97] *Ratcliff's Case* (n 31) 40a, 76 ER 726.

[98] John Davies, *Le Primer Reports des Cases and Matters en Ley resolves & adjudges en les Courts del Roy en Ireland* (John Franckton, 1615) sig *2v. Davies' concern may have arisen because his collection of reports was largely concerned with the establishment of English rule in Ireland, including the imposition of the common law in place of native Irish custom. By demonstrating that the common law was better than Irish custom (which the relevant cases in the volume all concluded) and other sciences (including the civil law), Davies showed that the common law was the best law to be implemented in Ireland.

Finch's elaboration of the common law was dependent upon his theory of maxims and according to Blackstone, Finch's 'method is greatly superior to all that were before extant'.[99] Blackstone noted 'how great are the obligations of the student to him … in reducing the elements of law from their former chaos to a methodical science'.[100] As Blackstone was recommended to read Finch when he was learning the common law, this was informed praise from a scholar over a century after the first appearance of Finch's work.[101] How legal education in general, and the role of maxims within education, affected legal practice is a much more difficult question to answer, but may perhaps be the more significant.

[99] W Blackstone, *An Analysis of the Laws of England* (Clarendon Press, 1756) vi.
[100] ibid.
[101] W Prest, *William Blackstone: Law and Letters in the Eighteenth Century* (Oxford University Press, 2008) 68.

12

Theory in History: Positivism, Natural Law and Conjectural History in Seventeenth- and Eighteenth-century English Legal Thought

MICHAEL LOBBAN

Contemporary jurisprudence can be very tribal. Rival schools compete with each other to show that they have the best answers to fundamental questions about the nature of law and legal reasoning. Their answers may appear incompatible, in part because they focus on different aspects of law. Positivists such as HLA Hart and his followers, who seek to identify what counts as law, find its systematic unity in the fact that it derives from an identifiable source which is distinct from morality. Hart's critics, notably Ronald Dworkin, focus on the question of how judges develop the law in the process of adjudication, arguing that the law develops not with the discretionary diktats of the judge acting as a kind of subordinate legislator but though a form of moral reasoning engaged in by the judiciary. While such theorists may not be particularly interested in seeking analytical systems in the law, other schools of thought—such as corrective justice theorists in private law—seek to find a logical unity within areas of legal doctrine, by using both conceptual analysis and moral philosophy. Few of these schools now make much use of history in their argumentation—in contrast to nineteenth-century jurists such as Savigny, who both argued that law reflected the people's consciousness, or *Volksgeist*, and that it was jurists dealing with legal concepts who articulated that consciousness. Where history is drawn on, it is rather by sociological or instrumental theorists, who wish to challenge the assumption of those theorists who take an 'internal' view and consequently concentrate their analysis on the language of jurists.

In their academic disputes, the combatants often seem to suggest that the law student needs to be persuaded that only one view accurately describes the world he inhabits. Yet it may be suggested that no single theory has the monopoly of truth. Neither does it have a monopoly of usefulness. Indeed, it is hardly to be expected that it would, given that different theories focus on different aspects of law, and that few now would attempt to create a holistic theory encompassing both law in general and the substantive rules it enforces. To understand law in its totality, we may find each of these theoretical approaches to be useful, while not necessarily definitive.[1] We may also find that it is useful, perhaps necessary, to look to history to understand the shape of the law. To illustrate this, we will in what follows explore how theory was used in the century and a half after the English civil war when a number of jurists did try—for the first time since the composition of the *Bracton* treatise—to create a holistic theory of the common law. The writers we will explore were not abstract theorists—they were seeking to draw on theory for the very practical purpose of making sense of the law of their era. As shall be seen, they had great difficulty in making a single theory explain all that needed to be explained.

This was a novel enterprise. Although jurists before the civil war certainly thought deeply about the nature of legal reasoning and legal practice, they did not develop systematic theories of law and its content. For them, the common law was a system of special professional knowledge, or 'artificial reason', best manifested by legal argumentation in the courtroom.[2] As Sir John Dodderidge explained in 1629, the common law was 'not left in any other monument, than in the mind of man'. Its content was 'to be deduced by discourse of reason; *when occasion should be offered*, and not before.'[3] However, in the century following the civil war, a number of English lawyers sought to emulate their continental and Scottish counterparts in writing 'institutes' of national customary law on the model of Justinian's textbook.[4] Their task was significantly different from that of the Europeans, whose aim in writing such works was to give unity to a variety of formerly autonomous customary systems, or to assert the national system's autonomy from a dominant *ius commune*. A unitary national legal system had existed in England since the era of Henry II (1154–89), when the royal justice dispensed by the king's judges began to displace local jurisdictions. But if her system of judicature was much more unified than those of her continental neighbours, England had a much more

[1] See also Steve Hedley's arguments on corrective justice in this collection.

[2] For Coke, difficult cases could be solved by 'no one Man alone with all his true and uttermost labours, nor all the actors themselves by themselves out of a Court of Justice, nor in Court without solemn Argument'. S Sheppard (ed), *The Selected Writings and Speeches of Sir Edward Coke* (Indianapolis, 2003) vol 1, 307 (preface to Part 9 of the *Reports*). See further, M Lobban, *A History of the Philosophy of Law in the Common Law World* (Springer, 2007) ch 2.

[3] J Dodderidge, *The Lawyer's Light* (London, 1629) 90 (emphasis added). Quoted in M Lobban, 'Common Law and Common Sense' (2008) 21 *Ratio Juris* 542. Dodderidge went on: 'therefore there is nothing of more force and effect touching the making and framing of a good Law, then the present occasion offered, sith thereby it brought to light, that which otherwise would not asmuch (many times) as be thought upon, and giveth occasion to dispute that which none would have thought ever should gave come in question. And therefore not without due consideration among the Romans, *Disputationes fori*, and with us *Demurrers* have ever beene allowed as originalls of Law.'

[4] See K Luig, 'The Institutes of National Law in the Seventeenth and Eighteenth Centuries' (1972) *Juridical Review* 193–226 and JW Cairns, 'Blackstone, an English Institutist: Legal Literature and the Rise of the Nation State' (1984) 4 *OJLS* 318–60.

fragmented substantive law. For the new generation of 'institutists', the aim was to show that English law as a whole could be put into as rational a framework as Roman law, to refute the commonly held view (as Thomas Wood put it in 1720) that 'there was no Way to attain to the Knowledge of them, but by a Tedious Wandring about, or with the Greatest Application and Long Attendance on the Highest Courts of Justice'.[5]

In doing so, different jurists used different theories for different purposes. Although each of the jurists we will study saw himself as writing in a natural law tradition, this was an ambiguous heritage, for the law of nature could be seen either as the commands of a divine legislator, or as a set of principles of justice accessible to right reason.[6] It could be seen either as *lex*—a form of commanded rule—or as *ius*[7]—a sense of justice, generating a will to live honestly, not to harm others, and to give them their due.[8] As shall be seen, the first model was used particularly by those writers who sought to explain the nature of the state, and the rules of distributive justice which derived from that constitution. The pioneer in this field was Sir Matthew Hale, whose model was also followed by the first man to publish a complete set of *Commentaries on the Laws of England*, Sir William Blackstone. The second model was useful for those who were less interested in the state, and more interested in how to resolve the problems of corrective justice faced by judges. This view of law was more favoured by Sir Jeffrey Gilbert, who planned (but did not complete) a large-scale overview of the English law, in far greater detail than Blackstone's lectures. As shall be seen, each 'school' used the model which was most useful for answering the questions it regarded as most important. At the same time, as shall be seen, neither school found that abstract theory answered all the questions. Instead, theory needed to be supplemented by history.

I

William Blackstone's *Commentaries on the Laws of England* began with a chapter 'On the Nature of Laws in General'. His decision to commence his discussion of

[5] T Wood, *An Institute of the Laws of England* (E Nutt and R Gosling, 1720), vol 1, Preface. For the educational impulses behind this, see D Lemmings, 'Blackstone and Law Reform by Education: Preparation for the Bar and Lawyerly Culture in Eighteenth-Century England' (1998) 16 *Law and History Review* 211–56.

[6] cf *Digest* 1.1.9.

[7] The ambiguity can be seen in the phrasing of a passage at the start of Gratian's twelfth century *Tractatus de Legibus*: 'The *ius* of nature is what is contained in the *lex* and the Gospel. By it, each person is commanded to do to others what he wants done to himself and is prohibited from inflicting on others what he does not want done to himself.' Quoted in K Pennington, 'Lex Naturalis and Ius Naturale' in SE Young (ed), *Crossing Boundaries at Medieval Universities* (Brill, 2010) 228.

[8] *Digest* 1.1.10.1.

the legal system with an analysis of the concept of law was not dictated by the institutional model he was using. Three decades earlier, the civilian lawyer John Ayliffe began his *A New Pandect of the Roman Civil Law* not by discussing *law*, but by discussing the concept of *justice*, which was not only the parent of law, but set limits to it.[9] For Ayliffe, jurisprudence was the study 'of that which is just, and that which is unjust': justice was the constant and perpetual will of giving each his due, and was encapsulated in the precepts (taken from the beginning of both the *Digest* and the *Institutes*) to live honestly, not to hurt another and to give every one his due.[10] By contrast, Blackstone's initial focus was on law, which he defined in a particular way. '[T]he general signification of law,' he stated at the outset of his discussion, '[is] a rule of action dictated by some superior being'.[11] If natural law was God's will, municipal law was 'a rule of civil conduct prescribed by the supreme power in a state, commanding what is right and prohibiting what is wrong'.[12]

The notion that law was to be seen in terms of the will of a superior was hardly new, having been discussed extensively in the seventeenth century by a number of writers who had influenced Blackstone, including Thomas Hobbes, John Selden, Samuel Pufendorf and Sir Matthew Hale. Hale had himself planned to write an institutional overview of the laws of England, an outline of which was published posthumously in 1713 as *The Analysis of the Law*.[13] He did not complete this work, but he did leave behind an unpublished treatise on the nature of the law of nature, in which he discussed law in terms of commands and rules. In Hale's view, law was

> a Rule of Morall Actions, given to a being endued with understanding and will; by him that hath power or authority to give the same, and to exact obedience thereunto *per modum imperii*, commanding or forbidding such actions under some penalty expressed or implicitly contained in such law.[14]

Consequently, in any legal system, obligations arose 'from the Party to whom the Law is given unto the Party by whom it is given to observe and perform it.'[15] Elsewhere, he explained that:

> A Law or Rule is not in it self effective or active, neither can it subsist or exist without an Agent that either gave it, or works by or according to it. The Laws of a State are the Rules

[9] J Ayliffe, *A New Pandect of Roman Civil Law* (Thomas Osborne, 1734) 1–5.

[10] Thomas Wood similarly began his *New Institute of the Imperial or Civil Law* (Richard Sare, 1704) by stating that 'The Law is an *Art directing to the knowledge of Justice*,' the 'constant and perpetual desire of giving to every one his due'. Only after having discussed the nature of universal and particular justice, and the distinction between commutative and distributive justice did he define law as '*the precept of the supreme power*, (or power derive from it) *obliging the Subject to act or not act under a Penalty*.'

[11] W Blackstone, *Commentaries on the Laws of England* (Clarendon Press, 1765–69), i: 39. Law, he added (i: 43) 'always supposes some superior who is to make it'. Blackstone's theorisation was influenced by JJ Burlamaqui, *Principles of Natural Law* (J Nourse, 1748) 77–78.

[12] Blackstone, ibid i: 39, 44.

[13] M Hale, *The History and Analysis of the Common Law of England* (J Nutt and J Walthoe, 1713).

[14] M Hale, *Of the Law of Nature* (ed D S Sytsma, CLP Academic, 2015) 6. See also Lobban (n 2) ch 3.

[15] Hale, ibid 15. Indeed, the subject of the law was under two distinct obligations: '1. An antecedent obligation; whereby the Subject is bound to obey such Law's as are Justly made. 2. An Obligation

> of its Government, but this Law must be given by some Power, and some Power there must be that must act according to it, otherwise a Law is a stupid, dead, unactive, and unconceivable thing.[16]

Hale's elaboration of this theory might not have been well known in the eighteenth century, but many other writers did define law in similarly positivist terms. The idea that the law of nature was imposed by God's will—an idea elaborated by Selden and Hale as well as numerous other natural lawyers—was repeated by several eighteenth-century English writers, including Blackstone.[17] They also saw human law in such positivist terms. One of Blackstone's successors in the Vinerian chair, Richard Wooddeson, argued that laws 'cannot be abstracted from the authority of a lawgiver'.[18] In his view, '[t]he giving of laws to a people forms the most exalted degree of human sovereignty; and is perhaps in effect, or in strict propriety of speech, the only truly supreme power of the state'.[19] Similarly, in his *Considerations on Criminal Law* of 1772, Henry Dagge gave this definition: 'Law is that faculty whereby some lawful superior prescribes rules of action, which those in subjection are obliged to perform, under certain penalties, express or implied.'[20] Dagge added that every subject was bound to observe every law made by lawful authority, whatever he thought of it, 'for he has given up his right of judgment to the legislature'. Furthermore, anticipating an argument which was to be particularly associated with John Austin, he wrote that 'the supreme magistrate is not himself bound by the laws of the land: For as he acknowledges no superior, no one can command him; since such a power would induce the absurdity of *Imperium in Imperio*.'[21]

secundary or subsequent, whereby the Subject in case of disobedience is obliged to the penalty or sanction of the Law'; ibid 29.

[16] M Hale, *The Primitive Origination of Mankind, Considered and Examined According to the Light of Nature* (William Godbid, 1677) 344. Elsewhere, he wrote that 'Without a power to exact obedience and to inflict punishments for breach, the Law were ridiculous and vain'; M Hale, *A Discourse of the Knowledge of God and of our Selves* (William Shrowsbury, 1688) 23, quoted Hale, *Law of Nature* (n 14) 6n. Following his mentor, John Selden, he wrote that the law of nature itself derived from God's commands. Hale, *Discourse* ibid 23.

[17] Blackstone wrote that the state of man's dependence on God obliged 'the inferior to take the will of him, on whom he depends, as the rule of his conduct … [t]he will of his maker is called the law of nature'; Blackstone (n 11) i: 39. John Taylor noted that if 'legal necessity must come from a superior and directing hand … Then I can gather, that a Being of infinite Wisdom, who contrived that Fitness, should be willing to demand the Execution.'; J Taylor, *Elements of the Civil Law* (Cambridge University Press, 1755) 126. By contrast, Richard Wooddeson wrote that Selden's 'very learned work' in tracing natural law to the Praecepta Noachidarum 'is not in equal estimation with the writings of those who have paid more attention in their researches to the pure dictates of reason'; R Wooddeson, *Elements of Jurisprudence* (J Moore, 1792) 4. At the same time, he wrote that God, '[t]he sovereign legislator hath … exercised his consummate authority. He hath ordained certain measures of human conduct' (ibid 10).

[18] Wooddeson, ibid 10.

[19] ibid 71.

[20] [Henry Dagge], *Considerations on Criminal Law* (T Cadell, 1772) 2–3.

[21] ibid 5.

These writers' concept of law was closely tied to the concept of a sovereign body acting within a state. Civil law was the product of a civil society. Human legislators had been created by men who had been driven into society as a means of self-preservation,[22] or out of a '*sense* of their weakness and imperfection'.[23] In Blackstone's view, once society was formed, 'government results of course, as necessary to preserve and to keep that society in order'. Any society therefore needed a superior whose commands all were bound to obey—'a supreme, irresistible, absolute, uncontrolled authority, in which the *jura summi imperii*, or the rights of sovereignty, reside'—as well as a judge who could 'define their several rights and redress their several wrongs'.[24] There could be no provision in law for resistance to the established authorities, even if there might be times when resistance was required.[25] Wooddeson also argued for an illimitable legislative sovereign, which had been created by the consent of the people. Echoing views which could be found in Hooker and Hale, Wooddeson added that this consent was not revocable by the people alone 'for that would be making a part of the community equal in power to the whole originally, and superior to the rulers thereof after their establishment.'[26] He also drew a distinction between moral fitness and political authority: 'We cannot expect that all acts of legislators will, or can be entirely good, ethically perfect; but if their proceedings are to be decided upon by their subjects, government and subordination cease.'[27]

In the view of these writers, legislators were needed to flesh out, give shape to and enforce natural law. As Hale explained, human laws were necessary, not only to regulate matters which were indifferent,[28] but also because the detail of some obligatory laws of nature needed to be determined by positive authority,[29]

[22] Hale (n 14) 77.

[23] Blackstone (n 11) i: 47. By contrast, Wooddeson (n 17) 44, quoting Coke (*The King v Marsh* (1615) 3 Bulst 27) stated that 'magistracy is by the law of nature, reason assuring men that they cannot well subsist without civil society, nor civil society without government'. He also argued (at 73) that the existence of political power was God's will.

[24] Blackstone (n 11) i: 48–49; cf i: 91.

[25] cf [Dagge] (n 20) 10: 'it is not for an ignorant and factious multitude, misguided perhaps by a few needy and interested leaders, to determine what is, or is not, a violation of the laws, in either prince or people. The common and statute law can only determine in cases where subjects resist the supreme magistrate; and the united voice of the whole people can only decide upon the crisis when resistance may be justifiable'.

[26] Wooddeson (n 17) 36.

[27] ibid 81.

[28] Hale qualified this, however, saying that it might be difficult to find any particular action 'in the concrete' which was purely indifferent; 'yet we are not presently thereupon to conclude that all these are under the precise Command or prohibition of the Law of Nature'; Hale (n 14) 192.

[29] Hale pointed out that the laws of nature 'cannot be certainly and definitively enumerated in their uttermost extent' because of 'the great variety of Circumstances which Accompany moral actions which strangly diversify the application of the Generall Laws which we may suppose naturall whereby those that perchance subscribe to the same universall Laws of Nature, yet are contradictory in their Conclusions touching particular Moral Actions'; Hale (n 14) 46.

given the 'great variety and the great diversity that ariseth by the Exygencies and Conveniencys of several people'.[30] Blackstone—who argued that the law of nature was binding of itself, but that positive law was needed to regulate indifferent matters—added that 'the main strength and force' of *any* law—whether regulating natural or indifferent matters—'consists in the penalty annexed to it. Herein is to be found the principal obligation of human laws.'[31] Wooddeson also argued that human laws were needed to give form to the law of nature. Although individuals could 'comprehend whatever may possibly be known to be the duty of all men by necessary consequence, deduced out of clear and manifest principles', they 'must not descend to conjectural probabilities, as to what is convenient, for that is a field of arbitrary determination, and the province of positive law.'[32] In making the point that a human legislator was needed to work out the specific details of what natural law required, Wooddeson drew on the distinction (made by Pufendorf) between the 'absolute' and 'hypothetical' (or primary and secondary) law of nature, the first of which regulated man is a state of nature, and the second of which dealt with the necessities created once men were organised into civil societies, the most important of which was property. Furthermore, he noted that although cases had to be decided on the principles of natural law where positive law was silent, '[t]he necessity of recurring to primary principles of right and wrong is avoided, where the municipal institutions are express: it is then, in general, concluded, that they are founded on the law of nature, or contain nothing repugnant to it.'[33]

Writers from Hale to Wooddeson praised the apparently complex English law for the detail of its provisions. As Hale explained:

> The Common Laws of England are more particular than other Laws, and this, though it render them more numerous, less methodical, and takes up longer time for their study, yet … it prevents arbitrariness on the Judge, and makes the Law more certain and better applicable to the business that comes to be judged by it … It hath therefore alwayes been the wisdome and happiness of the *English* Government, not to rest in Generals, but to prevent arbitrariness and uncertainty by particular Laws, fitted almost to all particular occasions.[34]

Over a century later, Wooddeson agreed:

> [A] man of the most penetrating understanding would rarely be able to solve an intricate legal question, unless a general acquaintance with the whole law capacitated him to judge of the various relations and dependencies of the case stated for discussion, and of the consequences which his determination might involve, by shaking and deranging the

[30] ibid 196.
[31] Blackstone (n 11) i: 57.
[32] Wooddeson (n 17) 21–22, following Hooker. On Hooker and probabilities, see Lobban (n 2) 66.
[33] Wooddeson (n 17) 134.
[34] Preface to Henry Rolle, *Un Abridgment des Plusieurs Cases et Resolutions del Common Ley* (A Crooke et al, 1668).

juridical system. It must be remembered, how great a part of municipal law consists of positive institutions, having little or no original connexion with the principles of natural law and abstract justice; established at first arbitrarily, because it was necessary they should be in some way settled, and adhered to afterwards for the sake of uniformity of decision, which the welfare of the community demands. As in civil life rules of property must be instituted, they also must be permanent and stable.[35]

Why did these writers build their institutes around this 'positivist' model? Two reasons may be suggested. The first was practical. These writers were seeking to describe the body of the common law as a systematic set of rules which could be identified and described, and to explain their pedigree within the system. Just as political societies needed to have rulers, so they needed to be held together by rules. As Hale put it,

> what a Confusion would there be in the World, if the particular Laws and rules of property were not settled and governed by some established Laws or rules, if all punishments should be equal or none at all, if there were no compuls[ion] for the inforcing of every Man to performe his promise, or make retribution in damages.[36]

These rules could be neatly parcelled out in the institutional division of persons, things and actions. The law of persons—which in Hale's system dealt with 'the Relation of Persons, and the Rights arising thereby', including political, economical and civil relations—provided a ready category to describe the rules of constitutional law. The law of things allowed for the discussion of rules of property ownership, while the law of actions allowed jurists to set out the rules of criminal law. In each of these areas, English law could be described in terms of rules whose origin and pedigree could be identified. The second reason was more political: in the aftermath of the attempts of the seventeenth-century Stuart monarchy to exercise extensive prerogative powers, anti-absolutist jurists sought to describe a constitution which clearly demarcated where legislative power lay in the state. By defining law as the product of the will of a sovereign, and by identifying where sovereignty lay, jurists were able to show which institutions and individuals did not have authority to make law. For this reason, writers from Hale to Blackstone to Wooddeson aimed to set out what powers the crown had, and how constitutional power was allocated to different bodies acting under the law. The jurisprudence they developed consequently served a particular purpose. These 'positivists' were not concerned with making an argument that law had no foundation in morality. Nor were they simply seeking to clarify concepts, so that it would be easier to distinguish the realm of the legal from the non-legal. Instead, they were more concerned in identifying who had the authority to pronounce what that law was, and who did not.

[35] Wooddeson (n 17) 172–73.
[36] Hale (n 14) 196.

II

If a positivist theory of law explained that there had to be a single sovereign power in any state, and showed that the law made by that power was binding, how was it to explain the authority of that sovereign, and the obligation of the people to obey it? How could it explain why the particular constitutional arrangements were authoritative? This was a central question for seventeenth and eighteenth-century writers to address, writing in the aftermath of half a century of constitutional crisis.

In the seventeenth century, Thomas Hobbes had solved this problem by resting the authority of his sovereign on a legalistic social contract theory. His was a normative theory which explained the subject's duty to obey whatever laws the sovereign passed: for each subject was said to have authorised the sovereign by an act of his will when making the social contract.[37] However, since this in effect preached obedience to whatever authority was established, and argued that sovereign power was by nature illimitable, it did not account for how sovereign powers might be limited by law, or how a constitution might change. The Hobbesian route was therefore not one our seventeenth and eighteenth-century jurists wanted to take; for while they agreed with him in wanting to base the constitution on legal foundations, they wanted foundations which might define and limit the powers of constitutional actors, and to allow for constitutional modifications over time.

Nor did they take the approach developed by subsequent generations of English positivists, who did not seek a normative grounding for their theory of law, but instead located the ultimate basis of the sovereign's authority in social facts, either a habit of obedience (in the case of Bentham and Austin) or a 'rule of recognition' (in Hart's case). For such approaches could not show how and why the English constitution had obtained legal authority. In Bentham's theory, it was for each individual to make his own present calculation of the benefits and burdens of obeying the sovereign: and if enough people calculated that there was more utility in obeying than disobeying, the sovereign remained in power. The people's disposition to obey could constrain the sovereign, but (in Bentham's early formulations, followed by Austin) it was not a legal constraint.[38] Hart sought to solve

[37] See further M Lobban, 'Thomas Hobbes and the Common Law' in D Dyzenhaus and T Poole (eds) *Thomas Hobbes and the Law* (Cambridge University Press, 2012) 39–67.

[38] Austin did not have access to Bentham's unpublished manuscripts, but did read Bentham's *Fragment on Government*, where he wrote 'That to say there is any act they [supreme legislatures] *cannot* do, to speak of any thing as their's as being *illegal*,—as being *void*;—so speak of their exceeding their *authority* (whatever be the phrase)—their *power*, their *right*,—is, however common, an abuse of language'; J Bentham *A Comment on the Commentaries and a Fragment on Government* (Athlone Press, 1977) 485–86. Bentham's unpublished work (and his later constitutional writings) showed that Bentham did envisage sovereigns being limited by constitutional laws *in principem*. For a discussion of the relationship between Bentham and Austin's ideas on this, see M Lobban, 'John Austin and

the problem that the Benthamic vision did not appear to allow for legally limited government through his theory of the rule of recognition, which was a power-conferring rule which might limit the powers conferred. However, Hart's rule of recognition—a customary rule of the officials of a system, who in effect made the rule by their customary practices—did not explain where the officials got their power from or how they were themselves constrained, nor did it explain the rules of change of the system itself, rather than the rules within it.

These were the problems which our thinkers needed to provide for, and they found their solutions in history. For them, the original power-conferring rule which gave powers to the constitutional actors had to be in some way a legalistic one: and for that reason, they were often tempted to follow Hobbes to a notion of a social contract. At the same time, in the absence of historical evidence of such a contract, they were often forced to invoke immemorial custom as evidence of an historical consent, which had acquired the status of law. An historical foundational moment was presumed, which in turn created a presumption of the legitimacy of institutions and the legal customs they enforced, which included the rules which determined how the constitution itself could be modified. Like the common law itself, these customs were legal customs *in foro*, in contrast to the general custom of the community, or customs *in pays*.

The notion that there was an ancient constitution, rooted in communal consent, consequently underpinned the constitutional theory of several of these writers. As Hale explained,

> if the original of government appears not, then we must have recourse to the common custom and usage of the kingdom … For custom and usage hath not only a kind of declarative evidence what the original pact was in case there were any, but if it be constant and immemorial, it hath a kind of introductive or institutive power.[39]

Hale traced this history from legal sources. As he explained, in tracing the constitution, one needed to examine 'such customs as have been allowed by the known laws of the kingdom'. These 'legal' customs were to be found not in the community, but 'in the traditions and muniments of the municipal laws, law-books, records of judgments and resolutions of judges, treaties and resolutions and capitulations of regular and orderly conventions, authentical histories, concessions of privileges

Bentham's *Of the Limits of the Penal Branch of Jurisprudence*' in G Tusseau (ed) *The Legal Philosophy and Influence of Jeremy Bentham: Essays on Of the Limits of the Penal Branch of Jurisprudence* (Routledge, 2014) 149–69.

[39] DEC Yale (ed), *Sir Matthew Hale's The Prerogatives of the King* (Selden Society, 1976) 7. In Hale's view, if one could show an original contract, one could establish the duty of subjects to obey, which was rooted in the divine command to keep one's promises. The citizen was bound to keep his faith 'not only by an Obligation between me and the Party, to whom it is given, for then if I could avoid his coertion I may loosen myself again. But I am obliged hereunto by a more soveraigne and uncontroleable Law, the Law of Almighty God who hath given this Law, to me and to all mankind, that *fides est servanda*.'; Hale (n 14) 16–17. cf J Selden, *De Iure Naturali et Gentium Iuxta Disciplinam Ebraeorum* (Richard Bishop, 1640) 106–07.

and liberties'.[40] Looking at such sources—rather than to the 'notions and fancies' of those who might wish to make new models of governments—showed that 'it is the settled constitution and custom of the kingdom, that fixeth and defineth, where the legislative power is lodged.'[41]

Blackstone also took a historical view of the constitution. He was more sceptical about the notion of an original contract by which men emerged from the state of nature into a political society, considering the theory 'too wild to be seriously admitted'. However, he argued that since men's weakness and imperfection kept them in society, an original contract 'in nature and reason must always be understood and implied, in the very act of associating together'.[42] Indeed, the notion that there was a contract 'necessarily implied by the fundamental constitution of government, to which every man is a contracting party' ran through the *Commentaries*.[43] At the same time, it was supplemented by Blackstone's historical vision 'of the Rise, Progress and gradual Improvements of the Laws of England' (the title of his last chapter). This chapter mapped out the gradual progress of 'our laws and liberties', showing the constitution to be a product of time: 'the fundamental maxims and rules of the law … have been and are every day improving, and are now fraught with the accumulated wisdom of ages'. For Blackstone, its very authority seemed to come from its history: 'Of a constitution, so wisely contrived, so strongly raised, and so highly finished, it is hard to speak with that praise, which is justly and severely it's due'.[44]

Writers like Hale and Blackstone were keen to show a continuity in English constitutional history, unbroken by any conquest which might give absolute power to a conqueror. Hale therefore argued that William I had conquered not England, but only the usurper Harold, and consequently had only ever obtained the powers which earlier kings had under 'our ancient government, laws, and rights.'[45] Indeed, William 'did not pretend, not indeed could he pretend, notwithstanding this Nominal Conquest, to alter the Laws of this Kingdom without common Consent in *Communi Concilio Regni*, or in Parliament.'[46] This was to argue that the central institutions which made up the sovereign in the state had derived from some foundational moment, whose authority had been confirmed by a continuing history. Although Blackstone did not share Hale's assumption of the foundational moment, he did take much of his history from Hale, to construct an argument that

[40] Yale, ibid 7.

[41] M Hale, *The Jurisdiction of the Lords House or Parliament* (ed F Hargrave, 1796) 11. At 4, he said the king's power was 'qualified at least in some points of government, as in making of laws and imposing of taxes or altering properties.'

[42] Blackstone (n 11) i: 47–48.

[43] Blackstone (n 11) iii: 158.

[44] Blackstone (n 11) iv: 435–36.

[45] Hale (n 13) 90; Yale (n 39) 10.

[46] Hale (n 13) 105, 108.

while the origins of parliament were hidden 'in the dark ages of antiquity', they could be traced both in Saxon and Norman eras. In his view, the constitution was 'coeval with the kingdom itself,' and had been reaffirmed in several constitutional landmarks, including Magna Carta and the abolition of feudal tenures on the restoration of Charles II, which saw 'our ancient constitution' restored together with 'the complete restitution of English liberty.[47]

Wooddeson similarly sought to trace the roots of the English constitution to Anglo-Saxon times. Drawing on seventeenth-century historians, he argued that the Anglo-Saxon *witan* had been composed of representatives of the people, as well as the crown and nobility. If the Commons had been temporarily eclipsed after the conquest, the ancient constitution was revived in the age of Simon of Montford. His historical survey concluded that

> the English constitution has immemorially been in substance much the same, or has at least born a strong resemblance to the present system, although its influence was impeded, and its lustre obscured, for near two centuries by the obvious effects of the Norman invasion and tyranny.[48]

Like Blackstone, he felt that the constitution had been restored to its ancient purity in later times. For these writers, the turn to history was not merely rhetorical or decorative: rather, an historical understanding of the constitution was essential to explain its authority, and so performed an important theoretical function.

It was not only the constitution which was to be understood by tracing the evolution of rules through particular historical moments. History was also used to explain the rules which made up the common law, which were seen as the product of positive imposition at specific times.[49] If these rules obtained their authority from moments of imposition, the coherence of their content could only be explained by tracing their history. The history employed by writers like Hale or his followers was not a contextual, or sociological one, but rather involved tracing particular rules to their origins either in legislation or in specific case law. It was, in other words, lawyers' history. Lawyers' history was employed, for instance, to explain the law of property, which was agreed by these writers to derive from positive imposition. As Blackstone explained, 'it is impracticable to comprehend many rules of the modern law, in a scholarlike scientific manner, without having recourse to the ancient.'[50] As in their constitutional writings, these jurists drew on a particularly legalistic view of history when discussing property rights: they

[47] Blackstone (n 11), i: 143–45, iv: 431. cf his views of the origins of the common law of the kingdom at iv: 405.

[48] R Wooddeson, *A Systematical View of the Laws of England*, 3 vols (Thomas Payne, 1792) i: 28.

[49] As Hale put it, many of these rules doubtless 'had their Original by Parliamentary Acts', which had then been developed by judges by building on ancient foundations, as cases came for decision. Hale (n 13) 3. See also Lobban (n 2) 88.

[50] Blackstone (n 11) ii: 44.

held that the foundational principles of English land law had been introduced by constitutional consent at a specific moment in time. Blackstone accepted Sir Martin Wright's view that although the principles of the English system of tenures were derived from a pan-European feudal law,[51] the system itself had only been introduced into England by consent after the Norman Conquest, at a precise moment in 1085, when the council of the nation consented to its introduction by William.[52] The English were misled, Blackstone told his auditors, and 'Norman interpreters, skilled in all the niceties of the feodal constitutions' were able to introduce very 'rigorous doctrines' which it would take centuries to prune.[53] It was still necessary to understand the ancient system, he argued, for although 'the oppressive or military part of the feodal constitution' was abolished root and branch, the constitution itself was not laid aside, and it needed to be understood 'to explain any seeming, or real, difficulties, that may arise in our present mode of tenure'.[54]

A similar approach was used to explain criminal law. Although it was acknowledged that many offences were violations of the law of nature—and might not need the signal of legislation to tell people that they were offences—it was generally agreed that positive law was needed to determine sanctions.[55] Hale noted that while many offences were prohibited by the laws of God and nature, all states had varied their punishments from the Biblical ones: 'Penalties therefore regularly seem to be *juris positivi, & non naturalis*, as to their degrees and applications, and therefore in different ages and states have been set higher or lower according to the exigence of the state and wisdom of the law-giver.'[56] In Blackstone's explanation, '[a] crime or a misdemeanor, is an act committed, or omitted, in violation of a public law, either forbidding or commanding it.'[57] Wooddeson argued that the exercise of capital punishment was the greatest exercise of the 'legislative power', and said that it was for the legislature to judge of the necessity of imposing

[51] M Wright, *An Introduction to the Law of Tenures* (E & R Nutt, 1729) 80–81.

[52] Blackstone (n 11) ii: 49, following Wright (n 51) 66.

[53] Blackstone (n 11) ii: 51.

[54] Blackstone (n 11) ii: 78. Wooddeson also drew on Wright's historical discussion of the rise of feudal tenures. Like his predecessor, he argued that the importation of feudal tenures had been assented to be a legislator, which was misled by the use of 'feudal expressions' which were then used 'to aggrandize each feudal superior, and in particular to advance the prerogatives of the crown.' Wooddeson (n 17) 142.

[55] As Hale explained, while many offences were prohibited by the laws of God and nature, punishments were determined by positive law. M Hale, *Historia Placitorum Coronae* (E & R Nutt and R Gosling, 1736) 1.

[56] ibid 13.

[57] Blackstone (n 11) iv: 5. He went on to explain (at 8) that while in the state of nature, all had a power to punish, in civil society this power was transferred to the sovereign. The sovereign also had power to punish for *mala prohibita*, 'upon this principle, that the law by which they suffer was made by their own consent; it is a part of the original contract into which they entered, when first they engaged in society; it was calculated for, and has long contributed to, their own security'.

this penalty.[58] Much of criminal law could therefore be discussed in terms of the development of legislation, tracing which offences had been punished in which way over time.

The positivist/historical model developed by the theorists we have discussed suited their purposes, for it answered the questions which they sought to resolve. It allowed them to set out the parameters of the constitution, and the rules of property law and criminal law. Using this method, Vinerian professors like Blackstone and Wooddeson, teaching English law to a non-professional audience, could set out briefly and clearly the rules which subjects and citizens most needed to know. However, this model of law did not explain everything a lawyer needed to know. In particular, it was unable to explain how judges should resolve disputes where the rules were unsettled, particularly in the law of obligations. Indeed, writers like Blackstone did not devote much time to exploring the nature of contract or tort. In part, this may have been because they saw the law of obligations as essentially ancillary—a law of wrongs (or actions) responding to breaches of rights. For some writers, it was possible to explain the law of torts or contracts in terms of the remedies created by positive institution. As the author of an early eighteenth-century *Treatise concerning Trespasses* explained, it was only 'thanks to our laws, and not the good nature of my neighbour' that anyone was protected in their persons and interests:

> If a man commit a trespass maliciously, I can pardon him and pity him as a Christian; but I ought not to spare punishing him as I am a Member of a Politick Society, when he continues obstinate and perseveres in his Malice; but this punishment must be by Law.[59]

However, this kind of analysis said little about the principles underpinning the law of contract or tort (or unjust enrichment); nor could it show judges how to develop these areas of law. Indeed, it was evident that there were also many areas outside the law of obligations—such as the law relating to criminal capacity—where lawyers developed the law through legal reasoning which went far beyond the application of the rules of positive law. Discussing this issue, Hale explained that humans were liable to punishment by virtue of the fact that they had understanding and will, and consequently had a capacity to obey: 'where there is no will to commit an offense, there can be no transgression, or just reason to incur the penalty or sanction of that law instituted for the punishment of crimes or offences'. Since such a general view might offer too great an opportunity for people to escape punishment, he added, it had 'been always the wisdom of states and lawgivers to prescribe limits and bounds to these general notions' and to define who could claim exemption from incapacity. Yet it was clear that this had not always

[58] Wooddeson (n 48) ii: 489.
[59] Anon, *A Treatise concerning Trespasses vi et armis* (J Walthoe, 1704) Preface.

been done by *legislation*: in the era of Edward III, he explained, the law relating to incapacity of age

> received a greater perfection, not by the change of the Common law, as some have thought, for that could not be but by act of parliament: but men grew to greater learning, judgment and experience, and rectified the mistakes of former ages and judgments.[60]

When it came to explaining how judges were to develop these kinds of principles, the positivist model proved incomplete, and those whose main interest was in exploring how to develop the law of obligations took a different theoretical route.

III

An alternative model of law to the positivist one was invoked by those who were less interested in exploring the nature of the state, and more interested in explaining those areas of law—such as contract and tort—whose principles could not be readily explained by tracing moments of positive institution. This approach was taken by Sir Jeffrey Gilbert, who (like Hale) planned to write a comprehensive work on the laws of England and left behind a large number of manuscripts, many on aspects of law (such as contract) which had not hitherto been given systematic treatment by English jurists. A large number of these manuscripts were published as separate treatises after Gilbert's death, though the works which most clearly revealed his theoretical premises remained unpublished.[61] In common with civilian writers such as Ayliffe, Gilbert was more interested in exploring the nature of law as *ius* rather than as *lex*, considering that the notion of justice preceded the notion of command. Gilbert's treatise of the law of nature began with the following definition:

1. Laws are the rules of justice and injustice made known by supreme power.
2. Justice is the giving every one his right and to do the contrary we call injustice or wrong.
3. Right is what a man hath power to exclude others from the use and command of by the rules of law.[62]

Elsewhere, Gilbert began his discussion of the nature of law with the following phrase: 'Justice is [the] constant and perpetual inclination to give every man his own, and that which can be called a man's own, is what he possesses either by the laws of nature or by the laws of civil society.'[63] For Gilbert, the rules of justice

[60] Hale (n 54) 14–15, 24–25.

[61] A volume of Gilbert's writings on the Law of Nature, and on Property and Contract is currently being prepared for publication by the Selden Society.

[62] J Gilbert, *Treatise on the Law of Nature*, Lincoln's Inn, MS Hargrave 13, f 1.

[63] J Gilbert, *Treatise of Property and Contract*, Arthur W Diamond Law Library, Columbia Law School, MS Singleton 31, ch 7.

concerning rights to property and contract could be figured out from reasoning on natural law: they did not need a state to impose them.

Gilbert was not the only early eighteenth-century writer interested in exploring the nature of justice without invoking the state. However, other writers devoted less attention to the theoretical groundwork. In his institute of English law, Thomas Wood omitted the command-based definition of law included in his civilian work, and stated simply:

> As *Law* in General is an Art directing to the knowledge of Justice, and to the well ordering of Civil Society, so the Law of *England* in particular, is an Art to know what is Justice in *England*, and to preserve Order in that Kingdom.[64]

To know what was justice in England, he turned to English writers predating Hale: Christopher St German and Edward Coke. From the former, he took the six grounds on which English law was built—the law of nature (or reason); revelation; general customs; certain principles and maxims; particular customs; and statutes. From the latter, he took a series of maxims, such as that the common law was 'the Absolute Perfection of Reason', or that 'The Law provides a Remedy for every Wrong'. This was to echo an early seventeenth-century view of law as a system of artificial reasoning to reach just outcomes, rather than developing a new theory of his own.

The author of *A Treatise of Equity*—sometimes attributed to Henry Ballow—similarly began with the statement, 'It is plain that Law is a moral science, since the end of all law is justice'. This writer's focus on notions of abstract justice is perhaps not surprising in a work on equity, whose function was to correct positive law when it was defective:

> [W]e do not intend to confine our Discourse to the municipal Laws only, but to have chiefly in View that natural Justice and Equity, which ought to be the Ground-work and Foundation of all Laws, and which corrects and controls them when they do amiss.[65]

Since the rules of municipal law were finite, cases often occurred for which there was no rule, for which there had to be a recourse to natural principles. In common with many of the civilians, Ballow used Aristotelian language in setting out the subject matter of his treatise, distinguishing between distributive justice ('of Things to be divided amongst those who are united in civil Society') and commutative justice ('that which governs Contracts'). Ballow's main interest was in the latter, not the former, though he did not devote much attention to the theoretical foundations of commutative justice. These foundations were described in broad contractual terms:

> [A]s an Action or Suit, which is the Remedy the Law hath provided for the Obtaining Justice, is but a legal Demand of some Right, and all civil Rights must arise from

[64] Wood (n 5) i: 6.
[65] [H Ballow], *A Treatise of Equity* (London, E & R Nutt and R Gosling, 1737) 1–2.

> Obligations, and these Obligations are founded on Compacts, it follows of Necessity, that the proper subject of Law is Contracts, and that Justice the chief End of Law, which teaches the Performance of them. The voluntary are, Buying and Selling, Letting and hiring, Deposits, the Interest of Money and the like. The involuntary are, Theft; Murder, Rapine, and all other heinous Offences, whether secret or violent.[66]

Ballow borrowed the distinction between 'voluntary' and 'involuntary' contracts, and the accompanying examples, from Book V of Aristotle's *Nicomachean Ethics*, and he borrowed the notion that every right was correlative to an obligation from Pufendorf's *On the Law of Nature and Nations.*[67] However, he omitted to mention Pufendorf's wider explanation of the distinction between voluntary and involuntary transactions, which showed that the latter were not really 'contractual'. Rather, where a party was made to pay damages for a wrong, the obligation rested 'upon that necessity of Restitution, which upon a Settlement of Property, evidently flows from the Laws of Nature'.[68] The flaws in Ballow's exposition were perhaps not particularly important, insofar as he explained that his interest did not lie in analysing the 'involuntary' transactions, but in explaining 'those particular Contracts, which are limited to the Benefit of certain Persons, and presuppose Property and Price';[69] but it was to assume rather than demonstrate a natural law system which underpinned the rules he was to elaborate.

By contrast, Gilbert attempted a more philosophical discussion of the nature of natural law. Like Hale, he considered the law of nature to be the law commanded by God. However, where Hale had seen natural law in terms of the commands given by God to the sons of Noah, at the centre of which stood the command to keep one's promises, Gilbert conceived of natural law as a dictate of reason instructing man in the requirements of justice. The commands and prohibitions of God were very simple, and could be deduced once one recognised the existence of God and his creation of mankind: God commanded whatever led to the preservation of mankind, and prohibited what led to its destruction. In brief, 'all the laws of nature are reduced to this single head, to maintain an universal love to all mankind, and procure as much as in us lies the good of all men'.[70] As Gilbert explained, 'he that acts towards the preservation of the species, answers the primitive design of God Almighty, but he that acts any thing that tends to the destruction of the

[66] ibid 2.

[67] S Pufendorf, *On the Law of Nature and Nations* 2nd edn (B Kennett trans, L Lichfield, 1710) 620–21 (VIII.iii.5).

[68] As Pufendorf explained, Aristotle had called the obligation to make satisfaction an involuntary contract, because the wrongdoer's obligation to pay damages did not depend on the victim's consent.

[69] [Ballow] (n 64) 3. Equally, although Ballow also noted that it was by 'universal Pacts' that 'the Propriety and Dominion of Things was at first established', he was not interested in exploring this area of civil obligation.

[70] Gilbert (n 62) ch 7. Gilbert's formulation was probably influenced by his reading of Richard Cumberland's *A Treatise of the Law of Nature* (J Maxwell trans (1727), J Parkin ed, Liberty Fund, 2005) 300 (ch 1, § IX).

species disobeys the laws of nature.'[71] Since 'the preservation of every individual being' could be shown to be the will of God, it had 'the obligation or binding force of a law'. Furthermore, God had implanted in man not only a power of reasoning, but also 'a natural pity to the innocent, and an aversion to those actions, which if the table were turned would be very uneasy, and grievous to ourselves.'[72] A sense of good and evil thus pre-dated civil laws, which did not themselves generate criteria of right and wrong, but were judged by them. If men disagreed about right and wrong, and fell into discord, it was because they had been given free will, and were prone to be ruled by those appetites which were necessary for their self-preservation, with the result that the appetites might prove too powerful for their reason. But this did not mean that the jurist could not figure out what the law of nature required.

Gilbert used the kind of reasoning which Thomas Hobbes had used in *De Cive*, but to very different effect.[73] Where Hobbes's theory required a sovereign to be the arbiter of citizens' disputes in a civil society—since men in the natural state could never agree on right and wrong—Gilbert suggested that judges could themselves figure out what natural law required through analytical reasoning, commencing from the principle of self-preservation. Since war led to the destruction of mankind (which was against God's will), men had to seek peace with each other. This meant in turn that 'no man ought to take away the life of an other without just cause', and that anyone who did so would commit 'the crime of murder'.[74] The foundations of property were also explained by similar reasoning: since man had a right to preserve himself, and a right to the means of self-preservation, he had a right to cultivate the earth and to keep the fruits generated by his labour. Property arose from occupancy of the means of self-preservation, which was made up of both an act of the mind and an act of the body: no one could have property 'without some act of his own, for nothing can tend to the preservation of any man without some application and relation to him'; and nothing 'can have any relation to him or the means of his preservation without his own judgment and consent'.[75] Once property was occupied with the appropriate intention, a man obtained a right which he could defend. He had a consequent right to defend the property from invasion (or to compensation for harm done to it), and he had a right to transfer it to others. Just as he had obtained property through an act of the will, so he could transfer it through acts of the will, found in contracts or testaments. In this way, Gilbert developed a natural law theory of property, contract and testament, which did not require the existence of a civil society: its rules were rather natural.

[71] ibid.
[72] ibid.
[73] For the relationship between Hobbes's approach and Gilbert's see further Lobban (n 37).
[74] Gilbert (n 61). Other forms of conduct which violated the principle of human preservation included 'the sin of lying', arrogance, ambition, and evil-speaking.
[75] ibid.

Gilbert's writings on contract remained largely unpublished in the eighteenth century, as did his philosophical writings. Nonetheless, the notion that the principles of contract could be figured out through natural reason, without resort to the commands of a legislator, was one shared by other writers, who published the first English works on contract law. Ballow began his exposition of contracts in the *Treatise of Equity* with the notion that, in order for property to be transferred, 'there must be an Union of Minds and Affections'. A contract required mutual agreement and consent, which was 'an Act of Reason, and accompanied with Deliberation'. As a corollary, it meant that 'Creatures void of Reason and Understanding are incapable of giving a serious and firm Assent'.[76] Ballow then explained that in order to protect them, children were regarded as being incapable of contracting (other than for necessaries), and then added that ignorance and error were other impediments to assent. Similarly, in his late eighteenth-century *Essay upon the Law of Contracts*, John Joseph Powell wrote that contracts 'must uniformly be determined by the principles of natural or civil equity'.[77] Noting that '[a]ll reasoning must be founded on first principles,' he argued that:

> The science of the Law derives its principles either from that artificial system which was incidental to the introduction of feuds, or from the science of morals. And, without a knowledge of these principles, we can no more establish a conclusion in law, than we can see with our eyes shut, measure without a standard or count without arithmetic.[78]

Like Gilbert, Powell presumed that property could be acquired and transferred in the state of nature, and he was concerned with teasing out the rules relating to the transfer of property, which did not depend on any rules created by a legislator, but which could be worked out analytically from the nature of the subject. He stated:

> [T]he regular effect of all contracts being on one side to acquire, and on the other to part with or alien some property, or to abridge and restrain natural liberty by binding the parties, or one of them, to do, or restraining them, or one of them, from doing, something which before he might have done, or omitted doing, at his pleasure, it is necessary that the party to be bound, shall have given his free assent to what is imposed upon him.[79]

IV

Those eighteenth-century writers who set themselves the task of explaining the structure of the law of obligations sought to develop abstract models, which

[76] [Ballow] (n 64) 6.
[77] JJ Powell, *Essay upon the Law of Contracts* (2 vols, J Johnson, 1790) preface.
[78] ibid, v–vi.
[79] ibid, vii–viii.

did not depend on positive legislation or on precedent, but on correct moral reasoning. This new methodology was summed up in the preface to Sir William Jones's *Essay on the Law of Bailments*, where he stated that he had sought to explain the subject analytically (tracing 'every part of it up to the first principles of natural reason' or 'the plain elements of natural law'), historically (to show how those principles were recognised by other nations) and synthetically (setting out clear rules).[80] Such writers were often influenced by models taken from civilian texts; and for many civilian writers, reason was always to trump precedent. As the early eighteenth-century civilian John Ayliffe noted:

> In the Business of Deciding Causes by Precedents ... every Judge is a Law-giver, by drawing the Law *de Similibus ad Similia*, as he fancies: But this is a dangerous Way of proceeding, and only serves to confound the Law, and not to do Right and Justice oftentimes.

The fact that one sentence conformed with another 'argues nothing as to Right or Equity, but only concludes a Concurrency in Opinion, both of which may be erroneous and mistaken'.[81] For Ayliffe, the judge should therefore use reason rather than precedent: for 'in Cases which depend upon fundamental Principles, from which Demonstrations may be drawn, Millions of Precedents are to no Purpose.' This was quite a different view from that subsequently taken by Blackstone, who argued that

> it is an established rule to abide by former precedents, where the same points come again in litigation ... because the law in that case being solemnly declared and determined, what before was uncertain, and perhaps indifferent, is now become a permanent rule.[82]

For jurists like Ayliffe, the route to justice was through right reasoning, rather than decisions of authority.

However, if the law of contract or tort might be explained by abstract reasoning, there remained many areas of law which could not be so explained. To begin with, as Gilbert explained in his posthumously published treatise on *Devises*, while the basic principles of the acquisition and transmission of property by contract and will could be figured out by reason in the state of nature, they could not explain the rules relating to English real property: for 'however reasonable this NATURAL notion may seem of transferring property by *testament*, it was *not* admitted into the *feudal* law; the reasons whereof will appear, if we examine into the nature of the old *feuds* and *tenures*.'[83] To explain these areas, jurists like Gilbert turned to history, just as Wright and Blackstone were to do. Consequently, where

[80] W Jones, *An Essay on the Law of Bailments* (J Nichols, 1781) 4, 11.
[81] Ayliffe (n 9) 8–9.
[82] Blackstone (n 11) i: 69.
[83] J Gilbert, *An Historical Account of the Original and Nature as well as the Law of Devises and Revocations* (E & R Nutt, 1739) 4.

Gilbert's projected treatise on personal property and contract began with theoretical conjectures on the state of nature, his projected work on real property began with a 'History of the Feud'. However, Gilbert's brand of history was a rather different one from Blackstone's Whiggish legal history, which served to give historical underpinning to his unitary sovereign state. Gilbert's was a conjectural sociological history, which looked back to the seventeenth-century histories of feudalism written by Sir Henry Spelman and forward to the four-stage theory of the Scottish Enlightenment.[84] For Gilbert, a resort to history did not serve the function of tracing the validity of particular property regimes, or of explaining the authority of the sovereign as the source of all valid laws, as it did for the 'positivist' jurists discussed earlier. One needed an historical understanding, not to grasp why particular rules were valid, but to comprehend the nature and purpose of different kinds of property. This required the jurist to do more than lawyers' history.

Thus, in material published in his posthumous *Treatise of Tenures*, Gilbert traced allodial and feudal property to different sources. Allodial property was 'the old Patrimonial Property revived by the Christian Clergy among the Barbarous Nations'. It derived originally from the first notion of 'regular property' which had developed among the Jews and Egyptians: 'The *Jews* were taught from Heaven, and the *Egyptians* by the Inundations of *Nile*, to settle in regular Neighbourhood; and from the *Egyptians* the Notions of Property came to the *Greeks* and *Romans*.'[85] In this text, Gilbert described the various rules of inheritance found in Biblical sources and in Roman law, describing (for instance) how the Roman *paterfamilias* could disinherit his children by express words in his will and how the Roman rules allocated property in case the father died without making any disposition.[86] Feudal property had a different source. Where allodial property had spread from the Nile to the Greeks and Romans, feudal property was to be traced to the Scythians, the ancestors of the northern Gothic nations, which included the barbarians who had conquered the Roman Empire—Ostrogoths and Visigoths—as well as the Saxons. These nations lived in clans in which possessions were not heritable but temporary or transitory.[87] Feudal property came to be heritable over a period of time, for reasons to be explained more by conjectural history or sociology than philosophy. The military lords who had granted lands 'to such Persons as behaved themselves well in the War, for their Lives only,' sometimes married their daughters to such vassals.[88] When they did this, they limited the lands not only

[84] For a recent reassessment of the importance of his historical writings, see J Rudolph, *Common Law and Enlightenment in England 1689–1750* (Boydell, 2013) 232–34, 258–62. On Gilbert's broader project, see M Macnair, 'Sir Jeffrey Gilbert and his Treatises' (1994) 15 *Journal of Legal History* 252–68.

[85] J Gilbert, *Treatise on Tenures* 2nd edn (E & R Nutt and R Gosling, 1738) 2.

[86] Gilbert explained that these Roman rules relating to intestate succession were subsequently introduced in England: ibid 7.

[87] These views are set out most fully in the 'History of the Feud' in British Library, Hargrave MS 194.

[88] Gilbert (n 85) 8.

to the feudiary, but to the issue of the marriage. In this way, the northern nations developed a notion of succession which was distinct from the Roman one, and one whose detailed rules were to be explained by reference to its original nature. For Gilbert, understanding the nature of English real property law required the jurist to engage in an exercise in historical sociology. Rather than being a framework of rules introduced at a particular moment by the consent of the nation—as Wright and Blackstone suggested—it was a system reflecting the social and military structure of the Gothic nations.

In a similar way, Gilbert also explained the evolution of different political systems in more sociological terms. Rather than seeing the origins of political society in a Lockean social contract dating from one notional past moment, Gilbert saw political society emerging as primitive societies became richer and more refined; and suggested that the structure of the polity which emerged—whether monarchy, aristocracy or democracy—would depend on socio-economic factors, primarily where the greatest concentration of land lay. When he turned to discussing English medieval history, the kind of history he wrote was also less 'constitutionalist' than writers such as Blackstone. In Gilbert's history, two major changes had followed the conquest. The first was that William had converted all allodial holdings into feudal tenures, so that all land was held of the king. The second was the creation of a new system of royal courts which took power away from more communal bodies. The king created a 'constant Court in his own Hall, made up of the Officers of his own Palace', which supplanted the popular Saxon witenagemot, which (Gilbert argued) had also heard appeals.[89] He also granted commissions to sheriffs by writs of justicies, in 'the *Norman* form, by which all power of judicature was immediately derived from the Prince', which gave the sheriff the power to judge cases 'independent of the suitors of the county court.'[90] If these changes had increased the power of the king, the balance was soon redressed. For Gilbert explained that although for some reigns after the time of the Conquest, the barons were kept in subjection by the king—since 'the *Norman* and *English* Barons were a balance one for the other, the *Normans* being dependants upon the crown who had new planted them in the Kingdom'—after some time, the Normans became more Anglicised, and became fond of the liberties they had enjoyed in Saxon times.[91] In the baronial wars of the thirteenth century, they turned against the king, which led to a 'new policy in the kingdom': not only the conformation of

[89] 'Introduction' to *The History and Practice of the Court of Common Pleas* (E & R Nutt, 1737), ix (also printed as *Of the Division of the Courts* in *Cases in Law and Equity with Two Treatise, the One on the Action of Debt, the Other on the Constitution of England* (Catherine Linton, 1760) 449–68.

[90] 'Forum Romanum' in *The History and Practice of the high Court of Chancery* (2 vols, Richard Watts, 1758) i: 2.

[91] ibid 6.

Magna Carta, but the development of a parliament with two houses. For Gilbert, England's balanced, mixed constitution was the product of social forces over a period of time. It was not only the product of Norman barons seeking greater liberties in the thirteenth century, but also the product of the commons growing in power in the sixteenth, thanks both to Tudor attempts to weaken the nobility, and economic changes strengthening the gentry.

V

Each of the writers we have discussed were engaged in the very practical business of attempting to put the law of England into a coherent and systematic order. To assist them in this project, they turned to legal theory, seeking answers both about the nature of law and of legal reasoning. Jurists drew on a wide variety of theories and approaches, including positivism, natural law and 'internal' as well as 'external' legal history. Different theories were better placed to address different questions. As writers such as Hale and Blackstone found, constitutional law, the law of real property and criminal law were easiest to put into a 'positivist' frame, which derived all law from moments of positive institution, which could be traced through legal landmarks—even ones which (like the original contract) were conjectural. By contrast, the principles of the law of contract or tort were much harder to fit into this model, especially in an age with very sparse legislation on these topics, and a relative paucity of reported case law. Those scholars more interested in discovering the principles which lay behind these areas, such as Gilbert, developed natural law theories which did not rest on human legislation, but which could be worked out analytically. Yet their models could not explain the areas that the rival school's theory could—and so, to explain the law of real property or the constitution, they turned to a different model of history.

For each of these theorists, both theory and history operated as tools which could be used to get a better understanding of the law. The tools were far from perfect, and did not suit all the tasks they set themselves. Nor were the theories themselves always convincing. However, they were tools which helped these jurists rethink the law and its organisation in productive ways. If they did not have the last word, it was because there was no last word to be had. Theory turned out to be ever provisional—a useful starting point to organise the law, and a useful model to explain parts of it, even if it proved incapable of explaining the totality.

By the nineteenth century, the ambition to put all of the law of England into a systematic form had fallen out of fashion: in this era, jurists made use of the analytical jurisprudence popularised by John Austin to write coherent treatises on different aspects of law. Nor did the jurists who reinvigorated English jurisprudence after the Second World War seek to revive the grand project of putting all of the law of England into a systematic structure grounded on theory. Such an ambition would have been regarded as utopian, since few would have agreed that there was an inherent unity to be found. Yet despite this scepticism about an innate substantive coherence in law, many post-war jurists remained confident that their theories were uniquely able to answer questions such as 'what is law' and 'what is legal reasoning'? The history we have been engaged with in this chapter might suggest that the aim to find one theoretical answer to such questions is equally utopian. Legal theory offers a box of tools, and different tools may be taken from the toolbox for different jobs.

Part IV

Uses and Limits of Theory in History

13

Legal History and Legal Theory Shaking Hands: Towards a Gentleman's Agreement About a Definition of the State

JEAN-LOUIS HALPÉRIN AND PIERRE BRUNET

One of the distinctive features of the Centre for Legal Theory and Analysis, located at Paris West University (Université Paris Ouest) and the Ecole Normale Supérieure is that it brings together legal theorists and legal historians, whose research is based on positivist postulates and analytical methodology. Building on the theoretical insights of Kelsen, Hart and Ross, we agree that there are neutral (or formal) criteria for identifying legal systems and for distinguishing these systems from other forms of normativity; which leads us to support the arguments developed by Brian Tamanaha and Baudouin Dupret against pluralist theories which find 'law' in all manner of social regulations.[1] By contrast, the question of how to define the state has proved to be much more controversial. As is well known, in attempting this task, the jurist runs the risk of choosing a definition which is inadequate, in that it fails to take into account all the historical situations. Equally, the definition chosen may be too narrow, if it is created with the specific goal of accounting for a determined situation. To overcome these problems, we propose to combine the approaches of a legal historian (Jean-Louis Halpérin in the first part) with those of a legal theoretician (Pierre Brunet in the second part). They can be combined, as the first one focuses on the characterisation of the legal order and the second one on the set of doctrines that has conceptualised the state.

[1] Brian Tamanaha, 'The Folly of the "Social Scientific" Concept of Legal Pluralism' (1993) 20 *Journal of Law and Society* 192–217; Baudouin Dupret, *Droit et Sciences Sociales* (Armand Colin, 2006).

I. The Legal State as a Process of Hierarchisation of Norms

Before deciding if it is possible (that does not mean mandatory) for legal theorists and legal historians to agree about a common definition of the state, we have to explain why a legal definition of the state could be useful, especially with the challenge resulting from the distinction made by historians between law, 'ancient' state and modern state. Then, we would propose the definition of the state for the first stage (ancient state) and some criteria for the passage to the second stage (the modern state).

A. The Choice of a Methodology

Generally speaking, historians are prone to adopt the political and sociological definition of the state given by Max Weber, as a 'human community that successfully claims the *monopoly of the legitimate use of physical force* within a given territory'.[2] They tend to focus (even in legal history) on the development of the state apparatus (such as bureaucracy, army and taxes)—what Weber called the 'means' of the state, as opposed to the 'ends' of the political association. Historians consider generally that there were different stages in the development of this state apparatus. 'Modern' states are opposed to ancient polities and are characterised by a strong reinforcement of centralised powers, developing from the sixteenth century onwards, leading to territorial sovereignty, the development of legislation, the establishment of standing armies and taxes, all these phenomena being supported by the use of the state's vocabulary in political ideology.[3] Besides this sociological and political approach of the state, as a particular form of power, there are of course different ways to stress ideological and theoretical features of the state: from the Marxist histories denying any autonomy of the State as an instrument of the ruling class[4] to Pierre Bourdieu's symbolic vision of the State[5] or Quentin Skinner's studies about the empirical use of the word 'state' as a tool of political theory.[6] However, it seems to us that none of these definitions can eliminate the

[2] M Weber, *Political Writings (The Profession and Vocation of Politics)* (Cambridge University Press, 1994) 310–11 (emphasis added). For a 'classical' use of this definition of the state by historians, M van Creveld, *The Rise and Decline of the State* (Cambridge University Press, 2003) 1–15.

[3] G Poggi, *The Development of the Modern State* (Stanford University Press, 1990); C Pierson, *The Modern State* (Routledge, 1996 and 2004).

[4] N Churchich, *Marxism and Alienation* (Fairleigh Dickinson University Press, 1990) 268 about the contradiction (and the historical perspective) inside the Marxist theory of the state.

[5] P Bourdieu, *Sur l'État. Cours au Collège de France, 1989–1992* (Seuil, 2012).

[6] Q Skinner, 'A Genealogy of the Modern State' in *Proceedings of the British Academy*, vol *162* (London, 2009) 325–70.

association between a form of power and legal elements (as the 'legitimate' use of force in Weber's definition) in the historical emergence of the state.[7]

Paradoxically, this question of the historical emergence of a specific form of power that can (or should) be called 'state' is a relatively recent issue in legal theory. At the beginning of the twentieth century, those writers who tried to develop in Europe a general theory of the state (in Germany, this *Allgemeine Staatslehre* was considered as a subject for many books and even as a kind of special matter)[8] were convinced that the State was a 'universal phenomenon' that was present, like laws, in all societies. For example, Jellinek wrote that the state has existed in the most remote periods of history, its origins being 'impenetrable'.[9] In France, Duguit also thought that the 'fact of the state was always identical' in all periods of history as he wanted to deal with the power of rulers and to take away any 'metaphysical' concept of the sovereign state.[10] His 'rival' in the French legal writing about public law, Hauriou, expressed no doubts about the existence of a 'state' in the Egyptian and Chaldean empires, as well of course as in Greek cities and Roman law.[11] As a legal historian and one of the first specialists of constitutional law in France, Esmein dealt with the word 'state' for ancient polities (like the Roman empire) and conceded only that the notion of 'state' was weakly developed in primitive societies.[12] As an exception confirming the rule, the non-published lectures of Laband in Strasburg were at that time the only legal doctrine, which considered the state as a progressive product of the human culture.[13] If Laband thought that there were societies (or polities) without state, he gave the name 'state' to the Roman republic and empire, as did all his contemporaries.

Kelsen was the heir of this general doctrine of the state that considered the state as old as the law and consubstantial to all societies. As it is well known, Kelsen proposed, from his habilitation thesis in 1911 onwards, an innovative conception of the relationship between state and law.[14] According to Kelsen, the law was not a product of the state, neither the state subordinated to a pre-existing law, but state and law were identical in a legal perspective. However, from the first edition of the *Reine Rechtslehre* in 1934, Kelsen introduced an important historical nuance. If all the states were legal orders, Kelsen has said that could have been legal orders

[7] M Oakeshott, *On Human Conduct* (Oxford University Press, 1991) 201–11 opposing *societas* (as a formal relationship in terms of rule, as the Roman *res publica*) and the *universitas* (as a corporate mode of association with a common goal, as the modern state); M Wenman, *Agonistic Democracy: Constituent Power in the Era of Globalization* (Cambridge University Press, 2013) 210.

[8] M Stolleis, *Geschichte des öffentlichen Rechts in Deutschland. Zweiter Band 1800–1914* (Beck, 1988) 423–60.

[9] G Jellinek, *Introduction à la doctrine de l'État* (French trans G Fardis, A Fontemoing, 1904) 31.

[10] L Duguit, *L'État, le droit objectif et la loi positive* (A Fontemoing, 1901) 22.

[11] M Hauriou, *Précis de droit constitutionnel* (Sirey, 1929) 78.

[12] A Esmein, *Cour élémentaire d'histoire du droit français* (Larose & Forcel, 1892) 43 and 176.

[13] P Laband, *Staatsrechtliche Vorlesungen. Bearbeitet und herausgegeben von Bernd Schlüter* (Duncker & Humblot, 2004) 56 and 99.

[14] H Kelsen, *Hauptprobleme der Staatsrechtslehre entwickelt aus der Lehre von Rechtssatze* (Mohr Siebeck, 1923) 252, 269 and 405.

before the creation of the states.[15] Kelsen opened the door to a historical development leading from 'non-state' legal orders to the 'modern' states identified with legal orders. It does not seem that Kelsen was aware of the progress of the historical science, especially of the *École des Annales* in France, which began in this time to defend the concept of a 'modern State' as a specific form of power appeared in the sixteenth and seventeenth centuries. One of the seminal texts in this way was Lucien Febvre's article '*L'état moderne*' in the *Encyclopédie française* published in 1935.[16] Even in France, one has to wait until after World War II to see some legal writers, such as Marcel Prélot and Georges Burdeau, who take account of this historical distinction between ancient states and modern states. Even today the idea that the state has a history is not common in continental legal writing.

Kelsen's theory does not mean, as it is frequently caricatured, the elimination of the state and of the law from the greatest part of history. In fact, Kelsen created the opportunity for legal historians to propose a kind of scale of different levels of state by the distinction he drew between centralised and decentralised orders, the latter being characterised in three ways by Kelsen: first, by a decentralised process of law-creating based upon custom; second, by the weakness of general norms in comparison to 'individual norms' decided by courts in a discretionary way; and third, by the role of local laws.[17] Nevertheless, there remains a discrepancy between the jurists' and the historians' points of view, because the identification of a legal order with the state is counter-intuitive to the idea that there were legal systems (like 'Roman law') before the emergence of states, even 'decentralised' ones. Secondly, Kelsen's criteria for distinguishing between decentralised and centralised legal systems are not particularly useful for legal historians, especially the idea that individuals could create customary rules independently from the authority of legislative and judicial powers.[18] Furthermore, the 'purity' of Kelsen's theory is based on a strict separation between disciplines and methods. According to Kelsen, the question of the establishment of the state is a sociological and historical problem.[19] Only explanatory or comprehensive sciences can deal with this problem. According to this view, it is not the task of the jurist (or the legal historian claiming also to be a jurist) or of a normative science like jurisprudence to look for legal criteria explaining the foundation of states.

In spite of these objections, we consider that Kelsen himself did propose some criteria for distinguishing polities, decentralised and centralised states that are useful. We also think that Kelsen's works can be a point of departure for a problematic association between legal theory and legal history about a definition of the

[15] H Kelsen, *Reine Rechtslehre* (Deuticke, 1934) 117.

[16] G Giuliana, 'Lucien Febvre et les représentations de l'État contemporain. Le Tome X de *l'Encyclopdie française*' (2002) 163–164 *Cahiers Jean Jaurès* 97–116.

[17] H Kelsen, *Pure Theory of Law* (MKnight trans, Berkeley, 1967 and Clark NJ, 2008) 228, 251, 315.

[18] J Halpérin, 'La détermination du champ juridique à la lumière de travaux récents d'histoire du droit' (2012) 81 *Droit et Société* 403–23.

[19] H Kelsen, *Allgemeine Staatslehre* (Berlin, 1925) 23.

'state'. The first reason is that legal theory needs a definition of the state, which is likely to be used in the description of all legal systems in the present and in the past. The ambition of the legal theory, as exposed in Kelsen's first sentences of the *Pure Theory of Law*, is to be a discourse (what we call now a 'meta-discourse') about all the forms of positive law, independent from any particular legal system, but likely to be used in order to make a science for all the legal systems.[20] From this perspective, any conception of the legal theory accepting this point of departure needs the use of definitions that are acceptable by all the readers (what we call now 'stipulative definitions'). In this sense, the normativist school is in harmony with the analytical school of jurisprudence trying from the epoch of Bentham to find acceptable meanings for legal words. The whole work of Herbert Hart is the proof of these links between a positivist approach of the law and the search for 'formal' definitions of legal concepts. Of course, there is no necessity to be positivist and even with a positivist conception of law, we can choose to limit our science to a purely empirical method. As long as one considers as 'legal' all the systems that declare themselves as 'law' (the problem being the translation of this word in different languages), one can be satisfied with an approach limited to the uses of the word 'state' in the legal discourses. But if we think that legal theory is possible as a 'general theory', we have to look for some agreed definitions as the one of the state.

There are also good reasons for legal historians to search such an agreed definition for the state. First, because legal historians cannot be indifferent to the development of the historical research about the specificity of the 'modern' state and the problems inherent to the use of the word 'state' for ancient polities. Secondly, because legal historians know that the use of modern concepts (or words to determine these concepts, like the one of 'state') to qualify historical situations is not only possible, but in some way inevitable (we use our contemporary language) and often fruitful (as an heuristic method to analyse some phenomena that were not perceived by the contemporaries of the studied period). If we have to prohibit anachronistic facts, we can use 'anachronistic' concepts.[21] Thirdly, legal historians cannot ignore that one (rather important!) aspect of the construction of the state is the legal conceptualisation of the phenomenon called state. One could say that the different 'political' definitions of the state proposed by Marx, Weber or modern scholars studying the history of ideas are quite convenient for historians and consequently for legal historians. If it were the case, legal history (as an attempt to underline the specificity of the history of legal phenomena) would not be useful. If it is possible to make a history of the army or of the finances without legal considerations, how could one imagine a history of the state without law? For all these reasons, we think that legal historians need definitions for 'law', 'state' and 'modern state' (this latter concept being defined as a species of the genre 'state').

[20] For the French translation of the first publishing of the *Reine Rechtslehre*, see H Kelsen, *Théorie pure du droit* (French trans H Thévenaz, Neuchâtel, Editions de la Baconnière, 1953) 25.

[21] M Troper, 'Sur l'usage des concepts juridiques en histoire' (1992) 47 *Annales Économies Sociétés Civilisations* 1171–83.

Now there are two possible uses of Kelsen's theory for our problem, knowing that Kelsen was not an expert in legal history and that his developments about law in antiquity (since the Babylonian times) were questionable, if not erroneous. The first attitude is to adopt the whole system of Kelsen and, in this case, to say that political scientists and sociologists cannot use another definition of the law or of the state than the legal one. It was the interpretation that Kelsen made of Max Weber.[22] Not only is this interpretation questionable and reductionist (Weber has consciously distinguished the legal point of view and the sociological one about legal orders), but the idea that only legal science can define the law and the state is scientifically 'imperialistic'. This aspect of Kelsens' theory is linked with his conviction that the same object (in that case, the law and the state) can be studied only by one science. Kelsen has especially wanted to fight the *Zwei-Seiten Theorie* of Jellinek, which associated a political and a legal science dealing with the state.[23] For this reason, he preferred to consider that the sociological concept of state and the legal concept were two completely different concepts. In this case, again, legal historians need a legal definition of the state and it would be better if this definition is in harmony with legal theory.

The second attitude, which we prefer, is to contest Kelsen's affirmation that the same object cannot be studied according to different methodologies and approaches that could be dependent from separated sciences (as legal science, political science, sociology and history). In this perspective, the historical phenomena qualified as 'state' (with the admission of the dichotomy between 'ancient' and 'modern' state) can be studied with a legal as well as with a political or sociological definition. The legal definition is not, as Kelsen has thought, a pre-condition of all researches about the state, but is one of the possible tools for studying and understanding the state, a tool that legal historians and legal theorists can use with profit. For the reasons we have exposed above, it seems fruitful to look for definitions (of a legal order, of a 'state' and of a 'modern state') that could be acceptable in the same time for legal theorists and historians. It does not mean that the former and the latter should agree on the same definitions, let alone that all scientists (especially historians) had to abandon the other (political or sociological) definitions. The legal definition of the state is conceived as an increase in value for the understanding of a phenomenon, which is not foreign to the law, not as a means to substitute the current hypothesis of the other sciences with a legal holistic definition.

The hypothesis, as a definition of an ideal-type (a concept that simplifies and exaggerates the empirical facts, but can be useful to understand the historical phenomena), we develop in the following paper builds on a first work presented at a

[22] H Kelsen, *General Theory of Law and State* (The Lawbook Exchange, 2007) 175–78.
[23] H Kelsen, *Der soziologische un der juristische Staasbegriff* (Mohr Siebeck, 1922) 116.

symposium organised in Paris on this question in January 2013.[24] The hypothesis we propose corresponds to our respective convictions as a legal historian (Jean-Louis Halpérin) and a legal theorist (Pierre Brunet), but is of course open to discussion and modifications. The hypothesis consists in making the existence of a dynamic and static hierarchy of norms as a legal criterion for identifying a state. This hypothesis consists in re-formulating a problem discussed by Michel Troper, who has proposed to consider the existence of such a static and dynamic hierarchy as a criterion for recognising the existence of a legal order.[25] Contrary to the proposition of Michel Troper, we consider that a legal order could exist without this hierarchy, and that the development of this hierarchy is a legal character for the establishment of a state, then for the transformation leading to the modern state.

B. A First Stage: the Invention of the Legal Order and the Process Towards the State

First, as positivists, we do not think that all societies (or polities) had developed a 'legal system', as defined through Hart's secondary rules or Raz's criteria of 'supremacy', 'comprehensiveness' and 'openness'.[26] Law, as a human artefact, has been 'invented'. As a technology or tool to be used by political powers, it presupposes some specific characteristics, such as its formality or neutrality, ie independence from the content of the rules.[27] If one considers that, on the European continent, this technology was invented by the Romans[28]—with the turning point of the Law of the Twelve Tables (450 BC)—it can be largely accepted that the Roman Republic at its beginnings was not a 'state': the legal order was not very 'thick', it is not certain that it got supremacy over the *mores*, and there was no hierarchy between the norms. What was lacking in the period of the Law of the Twelve Tables is a centralised power governing through laws, or using law (ie legislation and justice) as a means to govern. This absence leads us to our hypothesis of the legal definition of the state as a 'power knowing some kind of hierarchy of norms and using it to transform the legal order'.

With the support of many Romanists, we can say that some processes for creating a hierarchy of norms began at the end of the Republic with the multiplication

[24] 'Formes et Doctrines de l'État: histoire du droit et théorie du droit' (Université Paris I/Université Paris Ouest, 14–15 January 2013).

[25] M Troper, *Pour une théorie juridique de l'État* (Paris, 1994) 194. cf Troper, 'L'opposition public-privé et la structure de l'ordre juridique' (1987) 5 *Politiques et management public* 181, 190: 'In a static hierarchy, each norm is valid because its content is conformable to that of a superior norm, notably because it can be subsumed under that of the superior norm. In a dynamic hierarchy, a norm is valid, whatever its content, simply because it has been expressed in a way prescribed by a superior norm'.

[26] HLA Hart, *The Concept of Law* (Clarendon Press, 1961); J Raz, *The Authority of Law: Essays on Law and Morality* (Oxford University Press, 2009) 115–19.

[27] It can be characterised also, with the vocabulary of M Weber, as a 'rational' set of rules from a 'formal point of view'.

[28] A Schiavone, *Ius. L'invention du droit en Occident* (Belin, 2009).

of statutes (linked in some cases in a legislative programme as for the Gracchi, Sulla and Caesar), leading to a clearer idea of a 'dynamic hierarchy' of norms based on the principle *lex posterior priori derogat*.[29] However, in the late Roman Republic, there was no centralisation of justice (praetors were elected every year and, despite the fact they organised the judicial process with a continuous policy through their edicts, they let individual judges take the sentences without any possibility of appeal). Government by the Senate and the 'people' did not control the exercise of justice, even in Rome (then in Italy after the end of the social war and the extension of the Roman citizenship) and the administration of provinces allowed a large amount of room for the application of non-Roman rules to *peregrini*. The *res publica* had, without doubt, a legal order that was centred on civil law, but it did not have the features we have proposed for a state. The Empire brought contradictory trends: the personalisation of power that was not likely to maintain the idea of an impersonal *res publica*, but also the centralisation of legislation (with true programmes of reforms like the *leges Juliae* decided by Augustus) and of justice (with the creation of an appeal process before the *princeps*).[30] The process, beginning in the second century of our era, for extending Roman citizenship and for subordinating 'municipal', 'provincial' or 'customary' law to the law of Roman citizens[31] allows us to affirm that, for the relatively short period of the Severan Dynasty (193–235 AD), there was a Roman state with a centralised process of law-creating and a kind of 'hierarchy of norms'. For a short period of time (that Justinian tried to imitate with his compilations), the imperial bureaucracy controlled both the judicial process and the legislative one, especially though the use of rescripts, that were likely to impose the respect of Roman law to all subjects (all free men being Roman citizens since the edict of Caracalla in 212) and to all provinces.

Such a hypothetical definition of the state (a form of power knowing the hierarchy of legal norms and using it to govern), based on Foucault's representation of a non-essential state being created progressively by a legal process,[32] can be used to explain other historical situations in Europe and outside Europe. In Europe, the Roman state disappeared long before the 'great invasions', even if its model was preserved and transmitted through Justinian's compilation. Some legal orders—very 'thin' ones—developed in the early middle ages in decentralised polities that nobody would suggest qualify as states, as with the Germanic *leges Barbarorum*,

[29] J Halpérin, 'Lex posterior derogat priori. Lex specialis derogat generali. Jalons pour une histoire des conflits de normes centrée sur ces deux solutions concurrentes' (2012) 80 *Tijdschrift voor Rechtsgeschiedenis* 353–97.

[30] C Nicolet, 'L'Empire romain est-il un État moderne?' in N Coulet, J Genet (eds), *L'État moderne: le droit, l'espace et les formes de l'État* (CNRS Editions, 1990) 111–18.

[31] J Coriat, *Le Prince Législateur* (Bibliothèque des Ecoles Francaises d'Athènes et de Rome, 1997) about this process before and after the Edict of Caracalla, transforming all free men of the Empire into Roman citizens, but preserving for many of them their 'personal status'.

[32] M Foucault, *Dits et écrits* (Gallimard, 1994) vol III, 655.

or in Ireland or in Iceland, far away from the influence of Roman law. Then, the 'papal revolution',[33] the rediscovery of Roman law and the construction of the first centralised kingdoms can be analysed as the development of new forms of states.[34] Ranging from the Papacy to the Holy Roman Empire to Italian cities and to the English or French kingdoms, they varied widely from each other in form. While some were more centralised and some more decentralised, this was not the criterion about the strength of power that is decisive for our purposes. Rather, it was the fact that they were all endowed with an organised 'legal system', notably through a hierarchy of courts, albeit one that was different from modern states.[35] The hierarchy of courts, and the submission of the final solution of litigation to supreme courts, can be considered as a criterion for these pre-modern states. The Church ruled by the Papacy, with the extraordinary development of *decretals*, can be considered (from a legal point of view, which is not the one of Weber focusing on violence and territory) as a state, a very centralised one, but perhaps not a 'modern state' in the absence of a developed hierarchy of norms. At the beginning of the fourteenth century, the papal theocracy failed to impose its supremacy, especially towards secular states like France and England. If one takes the example of England, from Henry II's reforms to the end of the Middle Ages, there was of course a plurality of courts, some of them very independent from the king. But the Crown 'asserted a general responsibility for the judicial work of every secular court in the land'.[36] This hierarchy of courts, and of 'individual' norms produced by judges (according to Kelsen's vocabulary), would have developed before the hierarchy of general norms and could be the main feature of the 'pre-modern' state.

C. The Second Stage: the Modern State

In our hypothesis, the 'modern' state corresponds to another stage and more legal sophistication. It needed the development of something that was still in its embryonic stages at the climax of the Roman Empire: a more rigid 'hierarchy of norms' that tried to incorporate all the sources of law (including local customs or by-laws as well as canon law) into a system ruled by state organs, both legislative and judicial. One can say, for example, that the idea that private contracts were subordinated to general norms (or that they had not to be *contra leges* to be legally binding) was already present in classical Roman law. But this hierarchy was limited to the domain of civil law and the legislative frame was very weak to

[33] H J Berman, *Law and Revolution. The Formation of Western Legal Tradition* (Harvard University Press, 1983).

[34] It could be said that there was no qualitative difference between the 'absolute' powers of Henry II and of Henry VIII in England, or between Philip The Fair and Louis XIV in France: they were all 'legislators' in their kingdom.

[35] JR Strayer, *On the Medieval Orgins of the Modern State* (Princeton University Press, 1973).

[36] AR Hogue, *Origins of the Common Law* (Liberty Press, 1966) 189.

restrict contractual freedom. The pre-modern states of the last centuries of the Middle Ages remained confronted with the pluralism of legal orders depending from the churches, the barons or the town corporations. Based on the legislative power of the princes to create jurisdictions, supreme courts were a strong means to determine what were the legal rules (including customs and rules inherited from Roman law) to apply in a determined territory (this power to make a link between legal rules and territories being something ecclesiastical courts lacked).[37] Of course, the territorial domination (that was a weakness of the 'papal state') was important to intensify this judicial control and one aspect of the modern state is its increasing supremacy on the Church (through Reformation giving the supreme religious power to the prince or through legal ways for quashing legal decisions of the Church, as the *appel comme d'abus* in catholic France).[38] We think that there were other legal criteria that distinguished the modern states from the pre-modern ones. The 'modern' stage consisted in the creation of new ways to ensure that the hierarchy of norms would be respected, both inside the courts (through different forms of judicial review)[39] and outside the courts (through legislative authorities[40] and, later, through constitutions). At the same time, the policy of granting charters to guilds or other corporations (like boroughs or cities) was increasingly coordinated by state legislators during the seventeenth century.[41] These processes began in Europe between the sixteenth and the eighteenth centuries and were as much associated with the 'absolute monarchies' of France or Spain or 'the enlightened despotisms' in Prussia and Austria as with the sovereignty of the Parliament (combined with the royal prerogative) in Great Britain.

As a third possible criterion of the modern state, this implementation of the hierarchy of norms was also linked to the colonial process that set a hierarchy between colonial by-laws, colonial charters granted by the colonisers and the municipal laws of the mother country.[42] Colonial powers had to decide how to delegate sovereignty on overseas territories and how to implement rules from European origin in American and Asiatic contexts (the first generally characterised by a vacuity of indigenous laws, the second ones by the recognition of personal status for non-Christians). It was a new challenge to create hierarchical links between the laws of the motherland and the laws of the colonies and to conceive

[37] °J Hilaire, *La construction de l'État de droit dans les archives judiciaires de la Cour de France au XIIIe siècle* (Dalloz, 2011).

[38] For the differences and similitudes between the French and the English states in their relationships towards the Church between the sixteenth and eighteenth centuries (the extinction of papal jurisdiction in England and the ways to control the jurisdiction of the ecclesiastical courts like the *appel comme d'abus* in France), see R Helmolz, *The Oxford History of the Laws of England. The Canon Law and Ecclesiastical Jurisdiction from 597 to the 1640s* (Oxford University Press, 2004) 240.

[39] MS Bilder, 'The Corporative Origins of Judicial Review' (2006) 116 *Yale Law Journal* 502.

[40] J Hoppit, 'Patterns of Parliamentary Legislation 1660–1800' (1996) 39 *Historical Journal* 109.

[41] M Weinbaum, *British Borough Charters 1307–1660* (Cambridge University Press, 1943) XII–XIII.

[42] L Benton, *Law and Colonial Cultures. Legal Regimes in World History 1400–1900* (Cambridge University Press, 2002) 103–09 proposes a comparison between the Ottoman state and the Spanish empire as two forms of modern states linked with the control of 'colonised' territories.

colonial charters as provincial constitutions subordinated to the 'central' constitution of the kingdom.[43] Take the case of the Netherlands, the so-called Republic of the Seven United Provinces. This can be considered as a weak state, without a high degree of centralised power, lacking a federal legislation or a federal courts system. However, there was a Dutch legal system (including many references to Roman law or customary rules) and a federal law (emanating from the Assembly of the State-General). It is significant that the statutes of the Dutch East and West India Companies were fundamental pieces of this federal law and that the colonised empire of the Netherlands expressed the development of a modern state.[44] In the perspective of English law, the East India Company was a model of a modern government with a kind of delegation (for a surrogated quasi-state) from the 'modern state'.[45] With the North American conflict, this process also provoked the birth of 'modern constitutionalism', which was a powerful factor (with the separation of powers) for developing the legal structure of the modern state.

While Kelsen argued against mixing historical explanations of social phenomena and normative concepts, the point of view of our legal history hypothesis consists in identifying the role of legal techniques in the state's construction, these legal techniques being more concrete than legal concepts like sovereignty or absolutism (which does not mean that these legal concepts are meaningless, for example the definition of sovereignty as an exclusive power likely to impose the legislative norms to all the subjects of law corresponds to the features of the modern state we have proposed).[46] We have thus proposed to distinguish two stages that can be considered as expressed through progressive evolutions, from the first stage of the pre-modern states with a hierarchy of (individual) norms based on the hierarchy of courts, to the second stage of the modern state with a hierarchy of general norms based on judicial review, respect of the 'constitutional' (in some cases customary) frame and in many cases colonial expansion (extending the legal order overseas). The passage from the first to the second stage took different forms in various countries (the English monarchy is not the same as the French one, the Spanish one or the Ottoman Empire, let alone the Chinese Empire for which this transition to the modern state was more problematic).

Two points seem to be particularly important to take from this all-too-brief presentation of this hypothesis focusing on the legal process of the state's construction. The first one is to reject the critics of a 'Western-centred' point of view

[43] On this question, see A George Peck (ed), *The Political Writing of John Adams* (Indianapolis, 1954) 36–46.

[44] J Israel, *The Dutch Republic: its Rise, Greatness and Fall 1477–1806* (Oxford University Press, 1995); JL Price, *The Dutch Republic in the Seventeenth Century* (Macmillan, 1998).

[45] PJ Stern, *The Company-State: Corporate Sovereignty and the Early Modern Foundations of the British Empire in India* (Oxford University Press, 2004) 6 and 9.

[46] M Troper, 'Sovereignty and Natural Law in the Legal Discourse of the Ancien Régime' (2015) 16(2) *Theoretical Enquiries in Law* 315–35.

that would ignore the history of other continents.[47] Using Hart's or Raz's criteria for identifying legal systems leads us, in effect, to distinguish many 'social regulations' (in Ancient Mesopotamia, in India, in Africa) from legal systems; but it does not stand in the way of a recognition of the 'invention of law' outside the Roman sphere, notably in China and in the Muslim world. For the same reasons, the identification of the modern state as a 'legal process' of 'scalability' of norms is not inconsistent with the existence of modern states outside Europe and before the colonisation (for example, the Ottoman Empire).

The second point is to note that this 'legal' process of state construction has been, in large part, the work of juridical thought, or legal scholarship. For example, in Rome, the fact that Gaius began his *Institutes* by inserting Roman civil law in the *jus gentium* (the famous text from Gaius '*Omnes populi*' incorporated in the D.1.1.9) and that Ulpian defined 'public law' as concerning the '*status rei Romanae*' (D.1.1.2) are more than 'simple perceptions' of the state: these doctrinal affirmations themselves played an important part in the construction of the state, a construction developed later in the middle ages and in modern times, that shape the legal mind even today. Arguing in favour of criteria that are written down in laws for recognising the different stages of development of the state does not mean that, from a legal point of view, the state could be understood as something else than a legal abstraction taking account of the use of these techniques. If the chronology of the legal construction and of the intellectual conceptualisation is not completely identical (although they were not so different, with the emergence of the 'modern state' in the seventeenth century in both fields), it could be said that the legal state could not succeed without a set of doctrines to explain and legitimate this artefact.

II. The Legal State as a Set of Doctrines

Saying that state is the work of legal scholarship can be understood in several ways. First, it means that lawyers (even positivist ones) shaped the legal concept of the state and contributed to its emergence. Such a point is quite well known and many historians, especially in the history of ideas, have succeeded in demonstrating that it was legal scholars and lawyers—the legists—who were among the first to shape and formulate most of the main concepts which we are still using today when we want to talk about the state. But the idea should also be understood in another way. The legal concept of the state is the result of many 'legal theories and concepts', which constitute the legal state. This means furthermore that the concept of

[47] Maksymilian Del Mar, 'Beyond the State in and of Legal Theory' in S Donlan, L Heckendorn-Urscheler (eds), *Concepts of Law: Comparative, Jurisprudential and Social Science Perspectives* (Ashgate, 2014) 19–41.

the state is the product of law; though law here must be understood not as a system of mandatory norms (which are always produced by the state and its representatives) but as a set of facts under necessity.

A. The Methodological Problem

Though it sounds old fashioned, it is worth recalling the Realist methodology for analysing the concept of the state, and especially that of the Danish theorist Alf Ross. Ross's objections to the traditional definitions of the state were primarily methodological. According to him, although most political theorists ask 'what is the state?', such a question is not at all fruitful, because it is neither logically possible to refer to only one definition of the word 'state', nor is it logically possible to refer to some descriptive statements by which we are used to defining what we ordinarily have in mind when we are talking about the 'state' or are using the word 'state'. So, there is not any general and universal concept of the 'state', in the way that there is a universal concept of 'water'. The concept of 'state' is the result of a specific activity, and the legal concept of the state cannot be the same as the sociological one.

This is where Kelsen comes in. His analysis of the legal concept of state, as identified with the legal order, is either taken for granted but not used, or (more often) neglected because it is said to be excessively juristic and/or idealistic. It is indeed true that Kelsen rejected the idea that legal concepts have any reference to the real and empirical world, and that they cannot be used to describe any reality. So, from that point of view he was not realistic at all. On the other hand, Kelsen was very much concerned with legal language and the metalanguage of law and the way that his contemporary legal scholars were using the word 'state'; as also was Ross when he studied the use of the word 'state' and 'state organ' in legal language from a metalinguistic point of view. Both were inheritors of Bentham's contextual analysis and methodological claims. And even that kind of realism should not be neglected: it is much more realistic to pay attention to the way words are used than to pretend that words have a universal meaning which may be grabbed by anyone.

Such a realism was neither common to nor diffused in the General Theory of State before Kelsen. Most of the prominent scholars were certainly convinced of their own neutrality but the questions they raised were indeed normative questions. This is particularly the case when they asked whether a non-sovereign state could really be a state, or whether the representatives of the people really did represent the people, or again if the state is a 'person' and what makes the state a 'legal person'.

And some questions were not answered at all. From the point of view of the positivist tradition, the question of the emergence of the state is very often left to history, especially because of the distinction taken between questions of fact and questions of law: the emergence of the state is supposed to be a question of fact and so jurisprudence—legal science—is not required to answer it. Such a position is quite barren. It suggests on the one hand that it is not possible for legal science to ask historical questions and on the other that one cannot use the concepts of legal science in order to investigate historical periods and historical questions. It is also in contradiction with one of the claims of a General Theory of State which is supposed to account for any state. At the end of the day, it raises the main problem: what is the concept of the state that historians are used to employing? As Jean Louis Halpérin suggested in the first part of this chapter, the historians' concept of the state is the Kelsen-Weber's one (or, if I may so designate it, the Kelsweb conception).

B. Constitutive Legal Doctrines of State

If this methodological requirement is relevant, then it seems naïve to ask, for example, whether the 'State' appeared before 'Law' with capital L. Kelsen's well-known theory of the unity of the law and the state means that law is the name for a set of norms through which political power is exercised. But both sides of such an assumption can be understood in two ways. It first refers to the idea that power is exercised through norms, that normative hierarchy is a system of delegation and control over lower authorities. Such a way of thinking is very close to Weber's theory of the state.[48] The word 'state' refers here to specific institutions which are able to exert force against other people. But it must be noticed that this force depends on norms. This is one point that most of the Realists have very well seen, contrary to Austinian and positivist theories which were too prompt to quick that the law 'was' force. As said Olivecrona:

> [T]he traditional relationship between law and force must be discarded. It is impossible to maintain that law in a realistic sense is guaranteed or protected by force. The real situation is that law ... consists chiefly of rules about force, rules which contain patterns of conduct for the exercise of force.[49]

Here is a decisive point: if the use of force can be justified by the law, the law on the behalf of which force is used (in whose name?) cannot be justified itself (only) by force. Here is a constraint in the argumentation that any one faces when he/she makes use of force and wants to justify this use by law.

And this constraint produces another concept of the state: the state as the personification of law as a system of norms.

We may think of the extreme case of revolution and constituent power. From a positivistic point of view, such a power cannot be explained without regard to a

[48] As Bobbio saw it very soon: N Bobbio, 'Max Weber e Hans Kelsen' in R Treves (ed), *Max Weber e il diritto* (Franco Angeli, 1981) 135–54.

[49] K Olivecrona, *Law as Fact* 1st edn (Humphrey Milford, 1939) 134 and A Ross, *On Law and Justice* (Stevens, 1958) 53: 'We must therefore insist that the relationship of the legal norms to force lies in the fact that they concern the application of force, not that they are upheld by means of force.'

positive constitution. As the French constitutional scholar Carré de Malberg put it, constituent power is always under a constitution, though this constitution is not explicitly written.[50] It means that lawyers cannot give an account of any legal power without presupposing that such a power is based on positive norms. But this is not a legal bias which would be considered as a legalist prejudice: that person who wants to act in legal form is constrained to give a legal basis of her action. And she has no other choice but to create the figure of an authorising norm of competence—the norm Kelsen called the Basic Norm and considered as a fiction, because it was a norm in thought and not a positive norm, that is, the meaning of an act of will which was not real but fictitious.[51] This means that the word 'state' does not refer only to institutions using force: in fact, these institutions are under a necessity (and not yet legal obligation) to justify their own power as the power of someone or something else (and then to conceal their power behind objective law, or subjective will behind an objective one). This is the second way in which Kelsen's theory of the unity between law and state appears to be relevant and fruitful for the aim of justifying decisions and also fruitful to conceal the existence of power itself.

Moreover, one of the most important points made by Kelsen's theory of the unity of law and state is to reveal or to shed light on the double phenomenon of personification and imputation, which is the distinctive feature of the legal theory of the state. Such a personification is not the particular object of any specific theory of the state but it results from many theories—one might prefer to say 'arguments'—which are common to any particular state because they are constitutive of the state itself: sovereignty, representation, unity (and or personality) and, last, liability. If one asks how these theories appeared, or when they emerged, or again why did they come out, the answer could not be formulated in descriptive terms. The theory of sovereignty which may be summed up as 'the quality of a power that has no superior' does not describe any empirical phenomenon,[52] though it

[50] RC de Malberg, *Contribution à la théorie générale de l'Etat*, vol 2 (Sirey, 1922) 500.

[51] H Kelsen, 'Professor Stone and the Pure Theory of Law' (1965) 17 *Stanford Law Review* 1128–57, esp 1148: 'The basic norm is not an intellectual "construct" because [...] it is not "created" by juristic thinking, but presupposed in it, if we consider—without referring to a meta-legal authority such as God or nature—the subjective meaning of the acts by which the constitution (in the positive-legal sense of the word) is established and the subjective meaning of the acts established on the basis of this constitution to be their objective meaning, and if we thus consider these meanings (which are norms) as objectively valid.' And *General Theory of Norms* M. Hartney, (trans), (Oxford, 1991) 256: 'the basic norm of a moral order or legal order is not a positive norm but a merely thought norm, the meaning of a merely fictitious, and not a real, act of will."

[52] It may be argued that sovereignty is a descriptive concept at the metalinguistic level, because it is used to identify legal rules or norms—eg by defining a legal rule as a command by the sovereign—while it is normative as a concept of legal language, because it is used to justify the power of an organ who is called the sovereign (see I Turégano Mansilla, 'A vueltas con la noción de soberanía: reflexiones sobre la contribución de Ernesto Garzón Valdés' (2007) 30 *Doxa* 199–203). But even if one concedes that point, it should be recognised that the description is internal to law itself. And Bentham may add that the description is quite circular.

is useful for the state itself: not only (if ever) because it allows us to define a legal rule as a command by the sovereign but also (and more likely) because it is a way of concealing power behind reason. The theory works as a justification for the supremacy of the state and the concentration of power in the state.[53]

The same could be said for 'representation'. Prima facie, and from a technical point of view, representation seems to be useful as a tool to make laws in numerous polities and/or societies. Such a view is less false than flawed and historical materials exist which demonstrate how the fight for legal (if not sociological) 'representativeness' was a tough one between the twelfth and eighteenth centuries.[54] The reason for this is quite simple: as the legal system was built and rights were attributed, it became necessary to create more and more artificial persons whose actions needed real ones. And here again, representation has been used as a way of justifying the action of a real—a physical—person action on behalf or in the name of an artificial—a 'purely legal'—person. First used in private relations, this justification has merged to public sphere when the kings used it to justify their own power, by introducing themselves as the representative of God and later of the nation. When democratic assemblies were elected, they did the same: elected by the people, they claimed to be the representative not of their own electors but of the people as an organic whole. It is also true that the king himself has been called a representative of the nation while, by definition, he was not elected (in France for example, in the constitution of 1791). And one may recall the discussion between the Federalists and the Anti-federalists about the artificial and the real representation.[55] Such a justification is not only made of words without any value. These words cover legal and complex relations and shape a specific way of making decisions, in the name of this specific and legal entity that is called the 'State'.

These two last elements should be put together with other 'mechanisms of organisation' of the legal system as, for instance, the ideas of a 'hierarchy of norms'

[53] Such a supremacy can take several forms. We can here refer to the three meanings of 'sovereignty' that Carré de Malberg (above n 50, vol. 1, 79) had distinguished from legal literature of his time: 'In the original sense, the word "sovereignty" refers to the supreme character of the State's power. In a second sense, it refers to the whole range of the powers included in the State's authority and it is therefore synonymous with that authority. Thirdly, it is used to characterise the position occupied within the State by the highest organ of the State's authority and in that sense, sovereignty is the same thing as the power of that organ'. He noticed that German language has three distinctive words—one for each of these senses—when French has only one. '*Souveranität*' corresponds to sovereignty in the first sense, ie the supreme character of the state on the international as well as on the domestic level. '*Staatsgewalt*' is the power of the state in the second sense. '*Herrschaft*' is the power of domination by an organ (above n. 50, vol. 1, 79). And Michel Troper adds a fourth sense: it is the quality of a being on the behalf of which sovereignty in the first three senses is exercised—the doctrine of sovereignty in this fourth sense is a principle of imputation, see M Troper, 'The Survival of Sovereignty' in H Kalmo and Q Skinner (eds), *Sovereignty in Fragments: The Past, Present and Future of a Contested Concept* (Cambridge University Press, 2010) 132–50.

[54] cf HF Pitkin, *The Concept of Representation* 2nd edn (University of California Press, 1972) and H Hofmann, *Repräsentation: Studien zur Wort-und Begriffsgeschichte von der Antike bis ins 19. Jahrundert* (Duncker & Humblot, 1974).

[55] T Ball, 'A Republic if You Can Keep It' in T Ball and J G Pocock (eds), *Conceptual Change and the Constitution* (University Press of Kansas, 1988) 137–64.

and of 'judicial review'; which developed contemporaneously with each other, even though they were conceptualised in isolation from each other.[56] These different 'constitutive doctrines' can be understood as the progressive steps toward the legal construction of the State, a legal frame—a set of concepts—which it would be difficult if not impossible to get rid of or go beyond. If one can consider that, until now, the state as a set of doctrines gives a correct description of the State as a hierarchised legal order, there is no reason, even in the developments of international law, to reject the concept of legal state as outdated.

If we try, in order to conclude, to bring together the perspectives of the legal historian and of the legal theorist, we can consider that both of them accept some aspects of Kelsen's theories but reject others, especially the distinction between decentralised and centralised legal orders as a definition of a state. We also agree to consider the advent of States and their development as modern States (as distinguished from pre-modern States) are processes in the *longue durée* which cannot be fixed at a precise date. But they are linked with profound ruptures (that we can call 'revolutions') in the way of thinking and making work all together the legal features of the State. It can be said that the historical point of view is focusing rather on objective criteria for identifying the transition from one type of state to another, whereas the theoretical point of view insists on the contemporary set of legal doctrines through which we are thinking of the State. We dare say that the two perspectives are consistent: the former studies a historical process for which it was necessary to invent the state (then the modern state) and to shape it not only on intellectual basis; the latter considers states that are well established and the ways they are maintained through intellectual conceptions of the legal system. The hypothesis remains unique: there could exist a definition of the state and of the modern state, which is based only on legal criteria. It is noteworthy that this definition is not the same as the conventional one of the international law (the links between a territory, a population and a government completed by the international recognition of the state) and that the question still remains over whether states exist without any international recognition.

[56] One might think of the charts of guilds and boroughs in the sixteenth and seventeenth centuries that were standardised and conceived as by laws submitted to the law of the King.

14

Law, Self-interest, and the Smithian Conscience

JOSHUA GETZLER*

This essay examines how law understands and engages with self-interest. After examining the turn to voluntarism and away from a jurisdiction of conscience in recent law and legal theory, it moves attention to intellectual history, and examines the work of Adam Smith in ethics, economics and jurisprudence, where a theory of conscience based on sympathy is used to explain self-interest and to provide the ground of an original ethical system. Evidence is then adduced that lawyers in Chancery in the decades immediately following Smith's theorising came to think in similar terms, perhaps directly influenced by Smith's arguments.

I. How Does the Common Law Regard Self-interest?

Self-interest as a term of art is only seldom found in the records of English and Scots common law. In one of the earliest instances, the Court of Session in 1708 found a 'conflict betwixt the point of honour and conscience on the one side, and self-interest on the other', in a case determining whether words in a letter betokened a mandatory assumption of trust or rather mere words of precation, a benevolent desire that might freely be withdrawn.[1] The phrase 'self-interest' was used more negatively by Lord Chancellor Macclesfield in 1721, as a synonym for 'knavery' and 'dishonesty'.[2] Here was a certain irony, for Macclesfield was impeached for bribe-taking and corrupt sale of offices by Parliament some four years later. This was a judge who knew of what he spoke.

* I thank Maksymilian Del Mar and Michael Lobban for their acute and helpful comments, and also participants at the UK IVR 2013 Annual Conference and my colleagues at the UNSW Law School for lively responses to initial testing of this essay in the lecture theatre.

[1] *Francis Maxwell of Tindwal v Irving of Gribton* (1708) 4 Brown's Supplement 688 (Court of Session).

[2] *Frederick v Frederick* (1721) 1 Peere Williams 710, 716; 24 ER 582, 584 (Ch).

The negative connotations of self-interest recur later in the century. Counsel in a case of 1774 likened self-interest to 'malice'.[3] In 1810 the Admiralty judge Sir William Scott defined self-interest as 'improper bias' as he tested the motives behind declaration of the military status of a captured port.[4] This was within the constitutional principle enunciated by Chief Justice Coke in 1610 in *Doctor Bonham's Case* prohibiting a judge from deciding in his own cause, itself likely a transference of the Roman quasi-delictual action against the 'judge who makes the dispute his own'.[5] In 1830 the Court of Common Pleas characterised fraud as a 'sordid regard to self-interest'. In that case liability attached for untruths spoken with a view to gain, whether it was intended to deceive or not.[6] An interesting usage occurs in the next year in the House of Lords in a case where a broker chose securities on the advice of a trusted financial dealer who secretly profited from the trades by churning his own stock.[7] The dealer, none other than Nathan Mayer Rothschild, was made to account for undisclosed gains derived from a relationship of 'trust and confidence'. In substance if not in name this was a fiduciary relationship, where, in Lord Wynford's judgment, the entrusted person is 'not to raise the slightest suspicion of self-interest'. It is in fiduciary cases that the notion of proscribed self-interest plays out in later law.[8]

Outside the fiduciary principle, modern English law came to abandon the semantic association of self-interest with fraud or oppressive taking of advantage found in cases before 1830. The law reports shows a rival usage appearing from the middle of the nineteenth century, whereby self-interest is equated with rational behaviour in the use of legal powers so as to reach individual ends effectively.[9] But despite the paucity of direct reference in judgments, we may fairly claim that the operation and constraint of self-interest within the law of obligations is one of the abiding themes of the modern common law.

[3] *Cojamaul v Verelst* (1774) 4 Brown 407; 2 ER 276 (HL).

[4] *'Progress'—Barker* (1810) Edwards 210; 165 ER 1085 (Adm).

[5] *Doctor Bonham's Case* (1610) 8 Coke's Reports 113, 118; 77 ER 646, 652 (CP). Coke's *ius commune* sources are explored in RH Helmholz, 'Bonham's Case, Judicial Review, and the Law of Nature' (2009) 1 *Journal of Legal Analysis* 325; for the classical Roman background on judges' liability see DN MacCormick, 'Iudex Qui Litem Suam Fecit' [1977] *Acta Juridica* 149, and PBH Birks, 'A New Argument for a Narrow View of Litem Suam Facere' (1984) 52 *Tijdschrift voor Rechtsgeschiedenis* 373.

[6] *Foster v Charles* (1830) 7 Bingham 105, 108; 131 ER 40, 42 (CP) per Gaselee J.

[7] *Rothschild v Brookman* (1831) 2 Dow and Clark 188, 198; 6 ER 699, 702 (HL).

[8] eg *McPherson v Watt* (1877–88) 3 LR App Cas 254, 266 (HL) per Lord Cairns: 'An attorney … must be prepared to shew that he has acted with the completest faithfulness and fairness; that his advice has been free from all taint of self-interest; that he has not misrepresented anything, or concealed anything; that he has given an adequate price, and that his client has had the advantage of the best professional assistance which if he had been engaged in a transaction with a third party he could possibly have afforded'.

[9] See eg *Oswald v Ayr Harbour Trustees* (1883) 10 Rettie 472, 492 per Lord Craighill (Court of Session, 2d Division); *Mogul Steamship Co Ltd v McGregor, Gow, & Co* (1888) 21 QBD 544, 614 per Bowen LJ (QB); *Herron v Rathmines and Rathgar Improvement Commissioners* [1892] AC 498, 523 per Lord Macnaghten (HL(I)); *Allen v Flood* [1898] AC 1, 64 per Wills J.

II. How Does the Common Law Constrain Self-interest?

The common law courts have used three main theories to explain the controls the law places on self-interest in bilateral relations.[10] The first approach deploys a *voluntarist* or *will* theory of obligations, describing the bonds of law as ultimately based on the consent of the parties, whether that consent is express, implied, or imputed to the parties as a rational inference of their will. Rights and duties constraining self-interest are seen to be chosen self-interestedly by the parties themselves, or at least prudentially accepted as the logical consequence of a system of mutual restraints. Breach of obligation is a defection from those mutually agreed restraints and will typically result in a remedy such as damages which is also seen to be party-designed, a part of the deal as an alternative to performance, and not a remedy ordained from without by the state. The state rather provides an enforcement mechanism for rights generated by party conduct. Much of tort as well as contract can be assimilated to this model as parties voluntarily engaging in conduct are taken to assume responsibility for any risks created by that conduct.

The second approach may be named a *command* or *paternalist* theory of obligations. Here, rights and duties are prescribed by law not to articulate party wills, but in order to apply communal or policy norms to guide conduct. Law can thereby curb the trespasses, opportunism and weaknesses that can trip cooperation and foment exploitation. The constraints imposed by law are the compulsory conditions within which self-interest is permitted to operate. Breach or abuse of obligation summons a police action to restore civility and raise conduct standards.

The third method of control may be described as the theory of *conscience* or *good faith*, expressed most extensively in Chancery's equitable jurisdiction, but by no means confined to that body of doctrines and remedies. Conscience does not provide a foundational theory of legal rights, but rather supplies a concurrent or overlaying jurisdiction, providing an engraftment of obligations on top of those rights and duties that derive from party consent or state prescription. Duties of conscience control the manner in which acknowledged legal rights may be exercised. The court makes a presumption of honesty, a kind of moral counterfactual where the parties, upon being confronted with the full evidence of their conduct and its impact on others, are taken to choose good faith in the exercise of their rights and duties. Based on this presumption, the court will lead the parties to correctly execute all rights and duties (through primary enforcement such as specific

[10] For alternative historical taxonomies see PS Atiyah, *The Rise and Fall of Freedom of Contract* (Clarendon Press, 1979) esp ch 22, 716–79; W Swain, *The Law of Contract 1670–1870* (Cambridge University Press, 2015) esp 153–230; D J Ibbetson, *A Historical Introduction to the Law of Obligations* (Oxford University Press, 1999); M Lobban, 'Contract' and 'Tort', in WR Cornish et al (eds), *The Oxford History of the Laws of England, Vol XII: 1820–1914* (Oxford University Press, 2010) 297–610, 879–1150; M Lobban, 'Contractual Fraud in Law and Equity, c1750–1850' (1997) 17 *Oxford Journal of Legal Studies* 441.

performance or an order of account of assets), or else will undo or block rights and duties improperly conceived or exercised (through inter alia injunction, rescission, estoppel, conveyance by constructive trust, relief against penalties and forfeitures and *restitutio ad integrum*).

Today it is the voluntarist or will theory that is ascendant in the courts. The command theory is now seen as the preserve of legislatures;[11] and the equitable conscience jurisdiction has steadily dwindled, with the most recent step being the uprooting of the primary performance obligation in trust law by judicial fiat.[12] The voluntarist theory was restated in its full force by Lord Neuberger and Lord Sumption in *Cavendish Square Holding BV v Talal El Makdessi*,[13] a Supreme Court case of 2015 concerning the extent of control of penalties clauses in contracts stipulating remedies in excess of the greatest possible harm caused by breach of a primary obligation. Their Lordships noted that the rule was not based on the traditional equitable concern with procedural propriety and good faith negotiation, but acted directly on the primary content of negotiated contracts. They continued:

> The penalty rule is an interference with freedom of contract. It undermines the certainty which parties are entitled to expect of the law… In a negotiated contract between properly advised parties of comparable bargaining power, the strong initial presumption must be that the parties themselves are the best judges of what is legitimate in a provision dealing with the consequences of breach.[14]

The court in that case reluctantly maintained the ancient jurisdiction to control penalties clauses in contract law, but refused to extend the jurisdiction to substantive obligations, as the High Court of Australia had done three years earlier in regulating banker-customer relations.[15] The Australian judges had held that since contingent primary obligations resembled remedies in their effect or function, they too fell to be controlled by the court outside the will of the parties. The English judges in *Cavendish Square* inverted this reasoning, with Lords Neuberger and Sumption making this analysis:

> Modern contracts contain a very great variety of contingent obligations. Many of them are contingent on the way that the parties choose to perform the contract. The potential assimilation of all of these to clauses imposing penal remedies for breach of contract would represent the expansion of the courts' supervisory jurisdiction into a new territory of uncertain boundaries, which has hitherto been treated as wholly governed by mutual agreement.[16]

[11] A Burrows, 'The Relationship Between Common Law and Statute in the Law of Obligations' (2012) 128 *Law Quarterly Review* 23.

[12] *AIB Group (UK) plc v Mark Redler & Co Solicitors* [2014] UKSC 58; [2014] 3 WLR 1367 (Supreme Court of the UK).

[13] *Cavendish Square Holding BV v Talal El Makdessi; ParkingEye Limited v Beavis* [2015] UKSC 67.

[14] *Cavendish Square* (n 13) [31], [35].

[15] *Andrews v Australia and New Zealand Banking Group Ltd* (2012) 247 CLR 205. cf *Office of Fair Trading v Abbey National plc* [2010] 1 AC 696 (UKSC); S Whittaker, 'Unfair Contract Terms, Unfair Prices and Bank Charges' (2011) 74 *Modern Law Review* 10.

[16] *Cavendish Square* (n 13) [42].

Here the judges acknowledge the existence of a 'supervisory jurisdiction', constraining the parties *ex lege*, independently of their will, but this version of command theory was expressed as a subordinate source of rights and duties, to be applied only where there was a special justification. Otherwise voluntarism is the norm.

This tilt to voluntarism is not merely a phenomenon confined to commercial contracts. If we look elsewhere in the modern law of obligations we find increasing resort to putative consent or will to explain the origin and content of obligation. The courts use complex tests for *volenti* in order to determine who should shoulder risk;[17] they engage in elaborate interpretation of contractual intentions looking beyond the formal terms in order to set the level of performance and determine due discharge and remedy;[18] they use implied terms to explain contractual duties such as good faith disclosure in formation or fair dealing and good faith in performance;[19] they look for undertakings or assumption of responsibility or legitimate expectations, rather than relational conduct or status, in order to trigger ascription of responsibility in tort and in fiduciary law.[20] The role of the will in forming obligations can also be inverted, with the *absence* of a causative will being sufficient to trigger a commutative obligation, for example to restore an unjust enrichment or an unjustly negotiated contract because there has been no fully autonomous will authorising value to be transferred in the first place.[21] And voluntary will can be used actively to cut back extant obligations, as where consent to lowered protection in fiduciary or tort law is derived from the circumstances or context of the parties, rendering normally expected rights and duties defeasible.[22] The juridical urge to place all or most obligational rights and duties on a voluntarist basis seems almost an *idée fixe*, as if the judges sense that any legal constraint of the conduct of self-interested actors can be justified only by tying that constraint back to the self-interested intentions of those actors.

[17] eg *The Golden Victory* [2007] UKHL 12, [2007] 2 AC 353; *The Achilleas* [2008] UKHL 48, [2009] 1 AC 61; *Coope v Ward* [2015] EWCA Civ 30.

[18] eg *Daventry District Council v Daventry & District Housing Ltd* [2011] EWCA Civ 1153, [2012] WLR 1333.

[19] Compare *Yam Seng PTE Ltd v International Trade Corporation Ltd* [2013] EWHC 111, [2013] 1 All ER (Comm) 1321 (QB) per Leggatt J, with *Mid Essex Hospital Services NHS Trust v Compass Group UK and Ireland Ltd (t/a Medirest)* [2013] EWCA Civ 200.

[20] eg for tort: *Woodland v Swimming Teachers Association and Others* [2013] UKSC 66, [2014] AC 537; *Michael v The Chief Constable of South Wales Police* [2015] UKSC 2 for fiduciaries: *F&C Alternative Investments (Holdings) Ltd v Barthelemy* [2011] EWHC 1731; [2012] Ch 613); JJ Edelman, 'When Do Fiduciary Duties Arise?' (2010) 126 *Law Quarterly Review* 302; cf J Getzler, 'Ascribing and Limiting Fiduciary Obligations: Understanding the Operation of Consent' in AS Gold and PB Miller (eds), *Philosophical Foundations of Fiduciary Law* (Oxford University Press, 2014) 39–62.

[21] cf PBH Birks and G McLeod, 'The Implied Contract Theory of Quasi-Contract: Civilian Opinion Current in the Century before Blackstone' (1986) 6 *Oxford Journal of Legal Studies* 46; P Birks and NY Chin, 'On the Nature of Undue Influence' in J Beatson and D Friedman (eds), *Good Faith and Fault in Contract Law* (Oxford University Press, 1995) 57–97.

[22] J Getzler, 'Excluding Fiduciary Duties: The Problem of Investment Banks' (2008) 124 *Law Quarterly Review* 15; Getzler (n 20).

The modern voluntarist trend in the law of obligations links back to other theoretical positions long extant in the law. For example English courts will control the methods by which rights are brought into being, protecting the free wills and capacities of interacting parties. But they have tended to exclude not only the idea of substantive fairness in the content of rights,[23] but also any doctrine of abuse of rights, that is, denied any curial control over the manner in which acknowledged rights and associated powers may be wielded by the right holder, notably in the arena of property[24] but also in contract. Jhering made such non-interventionism into a political or moral argument in 1872 in *The Struggle for Law*, claiming that the self-interested absolutism of rights was intrinsic to the legal personality of a free agent; the state was strictly to enforce all rights, but never attempt to curb or balance the free exercise of rights. Jhering's manifesto for legal liberalism must have struck a chord in the English-speaking world: his book was a runaway bestseller and went into a number of English and American editions, as well as translating into 25 other languages.[25] Some theorists go still further and see this non-interventionism as structural, a position instinctive to rights recognition and enforcement, rather than merely a political choice. On this account legal rights only make conceptual sense as zones of untrammelled will or choice. Hence it is part of the definition of a right that the interests of others need not be taken into account in exercising that right within its due boundaries. Hart, for example, argued that the right holder is a 'little sovereign' in control of the duty performance,[26] and a sovereign is not accountable to outsiders as to what it decides within its territory, else it would not be a sovereign. External legal constraint on self-centred exercise of rights may then be re-mapped within a command model as conditions applied to the validity of the right by the recognising or coordinating authority as a condition of their exercise;[27] or alternatively as the resultant of conflicting rights and immunities of others that curb the privileges and powers of the first right holder, a kind of summing or integration of orthogonal wills.[28] Other theorists have described the oscillation between ascription of rights and defeasibility at the instance of counter-rights as the essence of practical legalism, a style of contingent moral reasoning deeply familiar to lawyers in their everyday practice. Hart, for example, propounded a defeasibility model in his earliest general analyses of law and obligation, and Honoré applied a similar model to property law, followed by

[23] cf SA Smith, 'In Defence of Substantive Fairness' (1996) 112 *Law Quarterly Review* 138.

[24] M Taggart, *Private Property and Abuse of Rights in Victorian England* (Oxford University Press, 2002).

[25] R von Jhering, *Der Kampf um's Recht* (Vienna, 1872), translated by JJ Lalor as *The Struggle for Law* (Callaghan and Co, 1879).

[26] HLA Hart, 'Legal Rights' in *Essays on Bentham. Studies in Jurisprudence and Political Theory* (Clarendon Press, 1982) 162, 183–84.

[27] JM Finnis, *Natural Law and Natural Rights* (Clarendon Press, 1980) 276–78; JW Harris, 'Human Rights and Mythical Beasts' (2004) 120 *Law Quarterly Review* 428.

[28] R Stevens, 'The Conflict of Rights' in A Robertson and TH Wu (eds), *The Goals of Private Law* (Hart Publishing, 2009) 139.

Epstein in his theory of tort law as a succession of overlapping pleadings. Parties can scale their obligations up or scale them down at will, and the task of the legal system is to facilitate this free scaleability.[29]

Voluntarism can thus be elaborated to deliver a highly sophisticated law of obligations, that operates to constrain self-interest and balance rights, without much resort to rival norms. But the voluntarist model does not fully capture the phenomenology of rights. It must perforce resort to objectification of consent and imputation of intentionality from circumstances where the parties do not subjectively will their obligations. Moreover, the theory cannot easily protect the interests of weaker parties, especially in complex and continuing relationships where the voluntarist slogans of *caveat emptor* and *volenti non fit injuria* hold increasing sway, for example in markets for financial products and labour supply. When a model departs radically from lived experience, and brings with it a bevy of painful moral and political problems, then it may be time to rethink whether the model is in good health—a question also increasingly asked of modern micro-economics, the partner theory to legal voluntarism.[30]

What is to be done? In a liberal or postmodern world, suspicious of the paternal authority and command of the state and its elites, does the third jurisdiction of conscience offer a possible corrective to the weaknesses of voluntarism? Much has been written by modern jurists about how conscience can operate in today's fused systems of law and equity, sometimes defending, usually attacking the existence of the third jurisdiction, with its apparent moralism and discretion seeming to challenge rule of law ideals.[31] Meanwhile the detailed operation of the Chancery jurisdiction of conscience before nineteenth-century fusion has been subjected to close scrutiny by legal historians, deepening our understanding of how conscience

[29] HLA Hart, 'The Ascription of Responsibility and Rights' (1948) 49 *Proceedings of the Aristotelian Society* (ns) 171, reprinted in A Flew (ed), *Logic and Language* (Basil Blackwell, 1951) 145; AM (Tony) Honoré, 'Rights of Exclusion and Immunities against Divesting' (1960) 34 *Tulane Law Review* 453; R Epstein, 'Defenses and Subsequent Pleas in a System of Strict Liability' (1974) 3 *Journal of Legal Studies* 165; R Epstein, 'Pleading and Presumptions' (1973) 40 *University of Chicago Law Review* 556. The ascriptive approach derives from JL Austin, 'A Plea for Excuses' (1956–57) 57 *Proceedings of the Aristotelian Society* (ns) 1, reprinted in JO Urmson and GJ Warnock (eds), *Philosophical Papers* (Clarendon Press, 1961) 175; Hart later disowned ascriptivism, but philosophical supporters may still be found: eg JR Lucas, 'The Ascription of Actions' (c1975), at http://users.ox.ac.uk/~jrlucas/ascript.html#r-1.

[30] The marriage of legal voluntarism with wealth-maximising microeconomics through the medium of equilibrating shadow markets is expressed notably in RA Posner, *Economic Analysis of Law* 9th edn (Wolters Kluwer, 2014).

[31] See for example the notorious attack levelled against equitable conscience by PBH Birks, 'Equity in the Modern Law: An Exercise in Taxonomy' (1996) 26 *University of Western Australia Law Review* 1; for a more nuanced but still hostile view, see Lord Neuberger of Abbotsbury, 'The Stuffing of Minerva's Owl: Taxonomy and Taxidermy in Equity' (2009) 68 *Cambridge Law Journal* 537. Stern defences of the old discourse of conscience have been issued by the High Court of Australia, eg *Roxborough v Rothmans of Pall Mall Australia Ltd* [2001] HCA 68; 208 CLR 516; *Farah Constructions Pty Ltd v Say-Dee Pty Ltd* [2007] HCA 22; (2007) 81 ALJR 1107; and see JD Heydon, MJ Leeming, and P Turner, *Meagher, Gummow and Lehane's Equity: Doctrines and Remedies* 5th edn (LexisNexis Australia, 2014).

has operated within the common law tradition.[32] It may be useful to supplement these accounts of the third jurisdiction by taking an extra-legal vantage, and examining the thought of the economist and ethicist Adam Smith, who had much to say on the relations of self-interest, conscience, and the law. Smith's ideas on conscience and its jurisdiction are especially interesting on two major scores. The first concerns Smith's contrasting expositions of altruism in ethics and egotism in political economy. Smith postulated that the interactions of individuals in the market-place are driven solely by self-interest or 'self-love', and beneficially so; but he also held to his theory that social relations were sustained by a reflective moral sympathy based on conscience. How did Smith resolve this seeming disjuncture, and what role did he believe law might play in mediating this tension? The second reason to study Smith is that in his highly influential theory of ethics, a model of conscience using the secular language of Enlightenment reason and sensibility is placed at the very centre of his normative system, just at the stage when many conscience-driven doctrines of the modern Chancery jurisdiction are taking form, including the doctrine of presumptive equitable fraud and its twin the remedial presumption of honesty. Reading Smith's thought alongside the law of his day thus offers a new perspective on the development of the third jurisdiction.

Before reviewing Smith's ideas about self-interest and conscience, we will first touch on the utilitarian theorists who preceded and followed him in order to frame his thought within an intellectual tradition. We will then turn to the law of Smith's day to see how the contemporary courts explained the constraints placed on self-interested actors in the exercise of their rights and powers.

III. Self-interest and Its Infirmities: The Utilitarians

It is a commonplace of microeconomics and rational choice theory that the pursuit of self-interest by actors engaging with each other to improve their individual welfare can fail due to collective action problems and the logical limits of strategic bargaining.[33] Moreover individuals may be poor at pursuing their self-interest due

[32] Some of the leading contributions: M Macnair, *The Law of Proof in Early Modern Equity* (Duncker & Humblot, 1999); M Macnair, 'Equity and Conscience' (2007) 27 *Oxford Journal of Legal Studies* 659; M Lobban, 'Preparing for Fusion: Reforming the Nineteenth-Century Court of Chancery' (2004) 22 *Law and History Review* 389, 565; DR Klinck, Conscience, *Equity and the Court of Chancery in Early Modern England* (Ashgate, 2010); R Havelock, 'The Evolution of Equitable "Conscience"' (2014) *Journal of Equity* 128; and J Rudolph, *Common Law and Enlightenment in England, 1689–1750* (The Boydell Press, 2013).

[33] T Schelling, *The Strategy of Conflict* (Harvard University Press, 1960); M Olson Jr, *The Logic of Collective Action: Public Goods and the Theory of Groups* (Harvard University Press, 1965); RM Axelrod, *The Evolution of Cooperation* (Basic Books, 1984); M Piccione and A Rubinstein, 'Equilibrium in the Jungle' (2007) 117 *Economic Journal* 883.

to flaws in their ability to understand and interpret their external environment, and also poor conceptions of their own internal motivations and goals, with time inconsistency and weakness of will as particular curses tripping the individual's setting of goals and priorities.[34] These problems have been discussed for centuries in the utilitarian tradition, and many theorists have proposed that state law is the prime solution. The problem lies in explaining the justification and goals of state coercion that forces actors to pursue their welfare more effectively. A recent instantiation influential in the organisation of United States social policy calls itself 'libertarian paternalism', seeking to 'nudge' actors towards choosing higher welfare paths by improving the salience of superior choice sets, without denying them the experience and responsibility of active choice.[35]

Thomas Hobbes is the *fons et origo* of this tradition. In a striking passage in the *Leviathan* of 1651 he explained the tendency of self-interested men tactically to fail in their transactions due to choosing betrayal and conflict rather than cooperation when left to their own devices, and how authority could provide a cure:

> If a covenant be made wherein neither of the parties perform presently, but trust one another, in the condition of mere nature (which is a condition of war of every man against every man) upon any reasonable suspicion, it is void: but if there be a common power set over them both, with right and force sufficient to compel performance, it is not void. For he that performeth first has no assurance the other will perform after, because the bonds of words are too weak to bridle men's ambition, avarice, anger, and other passions, without the fear of some coercive power; which in the condition of mere nature, where all men are equal, and judges of the justness of their own fears, cannot possibly be supposed.[36]

For Hobbes, authority, whether expressed by law or executive power, was therefore essential to stop rival self-interests nullifying each other. The key problem was to explain how any pact would be upheld by relentlessly self-seeking persons who might be expected rationally to breach the pact if such defection could win advantage. Persons might be driven to breach without opportunism, but rather defensively, in order to forestall the predicted opportunistic defection of the counterparty. In other words we will often betray in order to get in first; not because we are monsters, but because it would be irrational to expose ourselves to the monstrosity of others. Mutual fear feeds mutual threat, creating a downward cycle.

[34] HA Simon, *Models of Bounded Rationality* (MIT Press, 1982); RH Frank, *Passions Within Reason: The Strategic Role of the Emotions* (Norton, 1988); A Tversky and D Kahneman, 'Judgment Under Uncertainty: Heuristics and Biases' (1974) 185 *Science* 1124; G Ainslie, *Picoeconomics: The Strategic Interaction of Successive Motivational States Within the Person* (Cambridge University Press, 1992).

[35] RH Thaler and CR Sunstein, *Nudge: Improving Decisions About Health, Wealth, and Happiness* (Yale University Press, 2008). The 'nudge' theory of state-crafted individual choice was promoted energetically by Sunstein both as head of the Office of Information and Regulatory Affairs, and by writing some 10 sole-authored books exploring the subject since the initial 2008 volume with Thaler.

[36] T Hobbes, *Leviathan or The Matter, Forme and Power of a Common Wealth Ecclesiasticall and Civil* (Andrew Crooke, 1651) ch xiv, 64–71 (spelling modernised).

With the constitutional covenants we make to erect the lawmaking sovereign, we create a force that protects persons, property and pacts by law, repressing all defections, and so self-enforcing the legal order itself. Thus in the coercive state, argues Hobbes with self-conscious paradox, we have the highest creation of self-interest. The natural law schools that followed Hobbes recoiled from his egoistic theory of action, instead seeing the state as the objective enforcer of intrinsic rights that men interacting in the state of nature would otherwise observe or aspire to, but too imperfectly, let down by their partiality as distinct individuals with varying rational judgments. The state, on a Lockean or Kantian account, perfects a mutual network of rights by securing the practical commitment of all subjects to their equal enforcement, and such theories will often emphasise property in goods and personal autonomy or self-ownership as the foundational rights, protected by an adjectival law of wrongs, and prior to contract powers and liabilities.[37]

Jeremy Bentham, writing at the turn of the eighteenth century, likewise recoiled from the bare psychology and logical authoritarianism of Hobbes; yet he also rejected the natural law reasoning of Hobbes' critics.[38] Bentham created his own analysis of the interplay of law with self-interest: like Hobbes he strongly emphasised the role of law in perfecting utilitarian calculation; but unlike Hobbes he gave priority to rule certainty over authority, rejecting the discretionary powers of prerogative rulers and common-law judges, favouring instead the fullest possible codification of the laws to constrain state power and promote predictable ex ante solutions. By insisting on respect for strict legal rights as a counter to opportunism and defection, Bentham argued that the law allowed parties to extend the range and complexity of successful interactions, and helped give individuals the self-discipline to overcome short-term advantage and pursue more ambitious goals.[39] A commitment by state and subjects to respect rights, no matter what the anticipated consequences, thus guaranteed the best ultimate consequences in promoting welfare—a utilitarian strategy that shaded into the rationalist and deontological theories of rights associated with Kantian thought. Here was a new paradox: the optimal strategy to uphold self-interested calculation through application of law was not to apply self-interested calculation to the application of law. In the next generation we find an echo of this approach in John Stuart Mill's psychological insight that individual felicity can often be attained only obliquely,

[37] For the revulsion against Hobbes see SI Mintz, *The Hunting of Leviathan: Seventeenth-Century Reactions to the Materialism and Moral Philosophy of Thomas Hobbes* (Cambridge University Press, 1970); for the distinction of Hobbesian, Lockean and Kantian social contract models pertaining to private rights, see A Ryan, *Property and Political Theory* (Blackwell, 1984); and J Waldron, *The Right to Private Property* (Oxford University Press, 1988).

[38] See JE Crimmins, 'Bentham and Hobbes: An Issue of Influence' (2002) 63 *Journal of the History of Ideas* 677.

[39] J Bentham, *The Theory of Legislation & Principles of the Civil Code* (R Hildreth ed, W Stevens, 1864) esp 97–157.

through dedication to ideals and duties not chosen for their direct capacity to yield happiness, but pursued for some other metric of value.[40] Thus the classical utilitarians accepted that a calculated pursuit of happiness by competing individuals may be self-defeating at both the personal and social levels, unless moderated by respect for other persons, acculturation into social ideals, and obedience to protective rules and institutions promoted by the public order. We may best be utilitarians by trying not to be.

IV. Self-interest and Self-consciousness: Adam Smith

Active chiefly some two decades before Bentham, Adam Smith may be cited within the utilitarian tradition of devising institutions to maximise individual welfare. Certainly like Hobbes and Bentham, he had much to say about how self-interest fitted into welfare calculations. But Smith came from a different intellectual lineage, being a child of the Scottish Enlightenment. He was first educated at Glasgow by Frances Hutcheson in the late 1730s, then from 1743 mentored by Henry Home, Lord Kames in Edinburgh following an unsatisfactory sojourn as a graduate student at Balliol College in Oxford; and then from 1751 to 1763 served as a professor at Glasgow, growing close to David Hume as he cultivated his work in ethics and law. He had contact in 1766 with the great figures of the French Enlightenment in Geneva and Paris, following a year and a half spent in Toulouse as a tutor, giving him time to deepen his reading in political economy.[41] He wrote two great books, on ethics and economics, and planned a third even greater, on the history and theory of jurisprudence, which he regretfully could not complete.

Smith wrote in 1759 in his first book *The Theory of Moral Sentiments* of how the shallowest self-seeking can benefit society:

> The produce of the soil maintains at all times nearly that number of inhabitants, which it is capable of maintaining. The rich only select from the heap what is most precious and agreeable. They consume little more than the poor, and in spite of their natural selfishness and rapacity, though they mean only their own conveniency, though the sole end which they propose from the labours of all the thousands whom they employ, be the gratification of their own vain and insatiable desires, they divide with the poor the produce of all their improvements. *They are led by an invisible hand* to make nearly the same distribution of the necessaries of life, which would have been made, had the earth

[40] JS Mill, *On Liberty* (Parker, 1859); cf *Utilitarianism* (Parker, 1863). On Mill's synthesis of libertarian and utilitarian thought see J Harris, 'Mill, John Stuart (1806–1873)', *Oxford Dictionary of National Biography* Oxford University Press 2004) §18711.

[41] IS Ross, *The Life of Adam Smith* 2nd edn (Oxford University Press, 2010) 40–155, 195–218.

> been divided into equal portions among all its inhabitants, and thus without intending it, without knowing it, advance the interest of the society.[42]

Note that in his 1759 argument it was important for Smith that the rich, through their asocial rapacity, bestow benefits '*without intending it, without knowing it*'. *Unselfconscious* self-seeking turns out to be a positive social force, if not a virtue. By 1776 Smith has further developed this idea in *The Wealth of Nations*, where we find perhaps the most perfect celebration of self-interest in the history of letters:

> But man has almost constant occasion for the help of his brethren, and it is in vain for him to expect it from their benevolence only. He will be more likely to prevail if he can interest their self-love in his favour, and shew them that it is for their own advantage to do for him what he requires of them.
>
> …
>
> It is not from the benevolence of the butcher, the brewer, or the baker, that we expect our dinner, but from their regard to their own interest. We address ourselves, not to their humanity but to their self-love, and never talk to them of our own but of their advantages.[43]

Smith's metaphor of an invisible hand has been deployed ever since to explain how self-interested transactions aggregate to form an efficient market economy ultimately benefiting all, even if greed and unequal rewards drive the mechanisms of production and trade. But Smith is quick to qualify his paean to self-interest, and shows how this spring of action can swiftly produce ambiguous or malign results.

[42] A Smith, *The Theory of Moral Sentiments* (1st edn, A Millar, 1759; 6th edn, 1790 in the *Glasgow Edition of the Works and Correspondence of Adam Smith, Vol 1*, DD Raphael and AL Macfie (eds), Clarendon Press, 1976 & 2014) iv.1, 184–85 (emphasis added) (all subsequent page references to this work are from the *Glasgow Edition*, based on Smith's sixth and final edition of 1790). John Finnis identifies the importance of this passage as an example of moral reasoning about side consequences in 'Allocating Risks and Suffering: Some Hidden Traps' (1990), reprinted in JM Finnis, *Philosophy of Law: Collected Essays Volume IV* (Oxford University Press, 2011) 337, 337–40. The seemingly inegalitarian thrust of Smith's model whereby the demands of the rich for opulence benefit the poor was developed by Thomas Malthus in his *Principles of Political Economy* (John Murray, 1820; 2nd edn, 1836) 322, 398, but Malthus' model in turn was adapted by John Maynard Keynes to justify redistribution to the poor in order to defeat recessions caused by collapses in demand: see JM Keynes, 'Thomas Robert Malthus' in *Essays in Biography* (Macmillan, 1933, 2nd edn, 1972) 71; BA Corry, 'Malthus and Keynes—A Reconsideration' (1959) 69 *Economic Journal* 717; RP Rutherford, 'Malthus and Keynes' (1987) 39 *Oxford Economic Papers* (ns) 175.

[43] Adam Smith, *An Inquiry into the Nature and Causes of the Wealth of Nations* (W Strahan, 1776; 3rd edn, 1784 in the *Glasgow Edition of the Works and Correspondence of Adam Smith, Vol 2*, WB Todd (ed), Clarendon Press 1975–76 and 2014) i.2, 26–27 (all subsequent page references to this work are from the *Glasgow Edition*, based on Smith's 3rd edition of 1784 as the most accurate version of his final intentions, superior to the 4th and 5th editions). Smith's argument that selfish motives can usefully be harnessed to reach individual and social goals, without having to rely constantly on the more fragile motivations of love or altruism, have struck a chord with economists to the present day: eg DH Robertson, 'What Does the Economist Economize?' (1954), reprinted in *Economic Commentaries* (Staples Press, 1956) 147. See further A Offer, 'Self-Interest, Sympathy and the Invisible Hand: From Adam Smith to Market Liberalism' (2012) 2 *Economic Thought* 1.

The 'invisible hand' as presented in the *Wealth of Nations* does not appear as some providential free market mechanism that aligns selfish wills into a greater whole, a beneficial equilibrium; Smith never speaks of *the* invisible hand as a noumenon, a social law or causal mechanism. Instead, in order to illustrate his metaphor Smith uses the example of a businessman who seeks protectionist State support for domestic trades against cheap foreign imports, in order selfishly to maintain his profits. An invisible hand here appears in the guise of a use of public state power to make private gains:

> By preferring the support of domestic to that of foreign industry, he intends only his own security; and by directing that industry in such a manner as its produce may be of the greatest value, he intends only his own gain, and he is in this, as in many other cases, led by *an invisible hand* to promote an end which was no part of his intention. Nor is it always the worse for the society that it was not part of it. By pursuing his own interest he frequently promotes that of the society more effectually than when he really intends to promote it.[44]

Yet another caution against the potential of conscious self-interest to distort the general welfare is added in the final phrase of this celebrated passage:

> I have never known much good done by those who affected to trade for the public good. It is an affectation, indeed, not very common among merchants, and very few words need be employed in dissuading them from it.[45]

The work of an invisible hand, it seems, can only benefit us if it is precisely that—unseen, and perhaps more importantly, *unknown*. Even then it is fallible; private benefit only 'frequently' causes public gain, it is 'not always' harmful. And we are warned that when traders self-consciously assert their interests in the public sphere then self-interest quickly becomes noxious power, with the active few dominating and exploiting the whole. Smith's mistrust of organised monopoly—by which he included most private corporations, the 'visible hand' of capitalism—runs throughout the *Wealth of Nations*, tempering any unalloyed belief in the beneficent power of self-interest. Fear of knowing self-interest exerted consciously through control of state and market is the flip side of Smith's original invisible hand idea. Perhaps his suspicion of state action as an agent of rank self-interest limited Smith's usefulness for the classical utilitarians. Bentham and his circle appreciated Adam Smith's theories of economy and government and approved his pro-market stances; yet Bentham did not use Smith's theories in the details of his own systems, and indeed Bentham opposed Smith quite fiercely for not being utilitarian enough either to abandon state control of interest rates so as to allow

[44] Smith (n 43) iv.2, at 456 (emphasis added).

[45] ibid. The ironies in Smith's position are identified in E Rothschild, 'Adam Smith and the Invisible Hand' (1994) 84 *American Economic Review* 319. A neo-classical economist's angst over the ambiguities of Smith's exposition is set out in WD Grampp, 'What Did Smith Mean by the Invisible Hand?' (2000) 108 *Journal of Political Economy* 441.

money to find its natural price, or to support state intervention such as price controls in order to overcome market imperfections in the food supply.[46]

So we find that Smith the economist was tolerant of self-interest in the private sphere of market transactions, less so in the public sphere of state and corporate power. These elements of his thought were a chief inspiration for Ronald Coase and the Chicago school of law and economics when they constructed a new form of free market utilitarianism in the 1960s and 1970s. In Coase's model, lawmakers should not presume to be able to enhance social welfare by displacing a market allocation of risks and benefits. Any such allocation was likely to be futile, either because public decisions would be misconceived due to lack of information or bias about the relative utilities of actors competing for resources in transitive relationships; or because parties would trade around initial entitlements to a new and superior equilibrium in any case. Coase therefore argued that the role of the state should be confined to creating the best conditions for private market trades through elimination of barriers to transacting, so that the invisible hand of the market could then determine the optimal allocation of resources. Law should be used chiefly to *demolish* laws or any other barriers to free market entry. Only rarely were markets so difficult to construct that public allocations had to be created by law; even supposedly non-rivalrous public goods such as lighthouses, argued Coase, turned out to be profit-making club goods on closer inspection.[47]

Powerful and influential though the Chicago model has proved in the past half-century, it is hardly the case that Coase is Adam Smith's true heir, or that Chicago represents the correct interpretation of the Sage of Glasgow's[48] historical legacy. For one, there were many examples given by Smith where the market, purely as an instrumental device, might fail to provide the goods society needed, hence the need for publicly organised justice, police, revenue collection, utilities and so on. Moreover Adam Smith's thought about the role of self-interest in human affairs was far more complex than the Chicago reading, with its parsimonious view of wealth maximisation as the sole concern of welfare economics.[49] Smith by contrast was deeply concerned with the psychology of self-interest and the nature of hedonic states, explored in *The Theory of Moral Sentiments*, the work he saw as his most important contribution, so much so that he remoulded the original arguments through his life, issuing six editions from first publication in 1759 until his death in 1790. There he argued that the desire to emulate the wealthy and successful and so win the admiration of others was a spur to effort and achievement in a

[46] J Bentham, *Defence of Usury* (1787) and *Defence of a Maximum* (1801), in W Stark, *Jeremy Bentham's Economic Writings: Critical Edition Based on His Printed Works and Unprinted Manuscripts* (Royal Economic Society & Allen & Unwin, 1952–54) i, 121–208, iii, 247–450.

[47] RH Coase, *The Firm, the Market and the Law* (University of Chicago Press, 1988).

[48] The phrase is Charles Bonnet's, the French natural philosopher and lawyer, who befriended Smith in Geneva.

[49] RM Dworkin, 'Is Wealth a Value?' (1980) 9 *Journal of Legal Studies* 191.

competitive market society; wealth was a good status and was not sought simply for the ease and enjoyment that riches bring.[50] Smith also observed that the specialisations and division of labour necessitated by capitalist production and trade could narrow the imagination and intellect and undermine an ethos of higher self-interest involving refined tastes, considered judgments, and deferred gratifications, each qualities that were essential for a free and active citizenry.[51] The danger to market society lay not so much in inequality per se, but rather in a coarsening of conduct amplified in turn by emulation.[52] As a prophet of capitalism (a label he never used), Smith was also its most powerful early critic.

Ever since the publication of *Wealth of Nations*, scholars have debated this ambivalence in Smith's thought: how Smith's political economy of competitive individualism can be made to cohere with the critique of self-interest and the sympathy-driven ethical theories contained in *The Theory of Moral Sentiments*. We cannot say that the 1776 publication supersedes that of 1759, for Smith continued to revise the earlier book up until 1790, the year of his death, whilst the later book was left largely unchanged. One solution to 'Das Adam Smith Problem', as it was dubbed in Germany immediately after 1776, is to see that Smith was

[50] *Theory of Moral Sentiments* (n 42) i.3.2, 50-61, eg at 50: 'For to what purpose is all the toil and bustle of this world? what is the end of avarice and ambition, of the pursuit of wealth, of power, and pre-eminence?...and what are the advantages which we propose by that great purpose of human life which we call bettering our condition? To be observed, to be attended to, to be taken notice of with sympathy, complacency, and approbation, are all the advantages which we can propose to derive from it. It is the vanity, not the ease, or the pleasure, which interests us. But vanity is always founded upon the belief of our being the object of attention and approbation'.

[51] *Wealth of Nations* (n 43) v.1.3.2, at 781-82: 'In the progress of the division of labour, the employment of the far greater part of those who live by labour, that is, of the great body of the people, comes to be confined to a few very simple operations; frequently to one or two. But the understandings of the greater part of men are necessarily formed by their ordinary employments. The man whose whole life is spent in performing a few simple operations, of which the effects too are, perhaps, always the same, or very nearly the same, has no occasion to exert his understanding, or to exercise his invention in finding out expedients for removing difficulties which never occur. He naturally loses, therefore, the habit of such exertion, and generally becomes as stupid and ignorant as it is possible for a human creature to become. The torpor of his mind renders him, not only incapable of relishing or bearing a part in any rational conversation, but of conceiving any generous, noble, or tender sentiment, and consequently of forming any just judgment concerning many even of the ordinary duties of private life. Of the great and extensive interests of his country he is altogether incapable of judging; and unless very particular pains have been taken to render him otherwise, he is equally incapable of defending his country in war. The uniformity of his stationary life naturally corrupts the courage of his mind, and makes him regard with abhorrence the irregular, uncertain, and adventurous life of a soldier. It corrupts even the activity of his body, and renders him incapable of exerting his strength with vigour and perseverance, in any other employment than that to which he has been bred. His dexterity at his own particular trade seems, in this manner, to be acquired at the expence of his intellectual, social, and martial virtues. But in every improved and civilized society this is the state into which the labouring poor, that is, the great body of the people, must necessarily fall, unless government takes some pains to prevent it'.

[52] Smith (n 42) i.3.3, at 61–66, eg at 61: 'This disposition to admire, and almost to worship, the rich and the powerful, and to despise, or, at least, to neglect, persons of poor and mean condition, though necessary both to establish and to maintain the distinction of ranks and the order of society, is, at the same time, the great and most universal cause of the corruption of our moral sentiments'.

an ironist who chose contradiction and dialectic as the truer representation of the predicament of humanity. In other words he well grasped the inconsistency between a fully-functioning market society and the demands of personal morality and character; his task was to investigate the problem, not wish it away.[53] Markets and market individualism were valuable not only for their potential to liberate mankind from material want through enhanced production, but also for their tendency to disabuse humanity of unwarranted respect for authority and hierarchy, thus allowing self-liberation. But with these gains in positive and negative liberty came losses to character, with the avaricious and haughty rich setting a bad example to the repressed and stunted poor. So an enlightened society would have to find new ethical teachings, shorn of the religious and authoritarian pressures of the past, to articulate how moral sentiments could be enhanced in a competitive self-regarding society. Here was one of the great themes of Enlightenment thought—the conflict of modernity and character, the problem of sustaining morale and happiness in a disenchanted individualistic world. It is no surprise that resonances have been found between Smith's *oeuvre* and the great German philosophers of his time and after, as they struggled with similar themes.[54]

In *The Theory of Moral Sentiments* Adam Smith sets out a new model of sympathy and conscience as the foundation of ethics. He draws on Stoic, Christian and natural law theories of conscience, but his theory is original and distinct. Smith states that people are born with a strong natural sense of sympathy for others. We measure the feelings of others by imagining how we might feel in their position. And the strongest of all moral sentiments is the reciprocal desire to feel that others approve of us. For Smith it is the restless desire for regard, recognition and confirmation that chiefly drives our actions. The approbation of others is desired mainly as an objective validation of our own self-worth; indeed our chief desire in life is to feel good about ourselves, but we need to win our own self-approbation by a valid and convincing path. The approval of others helps

[53] See CL Griswold Jr, *Adam Smith and the Virtues of Enlightenment* (Cambridge University Press, 1999) esp 292–301; K Tribe, 'Das Adam Smith Problem and the Origins of Smith Scholarship' in *The Economy of the Word: Language, History, and Economics* (Oxford University Press, 2015) 139-62.

[54] Hegel in particular seems to have read Smith closely before producing his theory of will and reason as a search for recognition by other reasonable creatures, and like Smith he warned of the capacity of competitive individualism to undermine character and intellectual capacity: see L Herzog, *Inventing the Market: Smith, Hegel and Political Theory* (Oxford University Press, 2013); JP Henderson and JB Davis, 'Adam Smith's Influence on Hegel's Philosophical Writings' (1991) 13 *Journal of the History of Economic Thought* 184. Marx too was fond of quoting Smith on the alienation of labour and free personality under capitalism: see RL Meek, *Smith, Marx, and After* (Chapman and Hall, 1977) 14. Kant avowed his philosophical debts to Hume not Smith; yet some have found strong affinities between Kantian and Smithian thought, emphasising the objectivism in Smith's moral postulate of the impartial spectator, eg N MacCormick, *Practical Reason in Law and Morality* (Oxford University Press, 2008) esp 47–68; for critique see J Waldron, 'Legal Judgment and Moral Reservation' in A Menendez and J Fossum (eds), *Law and Democracy in Neil MacCormick's Legal and Political Theory* (Springer, 2011) 107; M Del Mar, 'The Smithian Categorical Imperative: How MacCormick Smithified Kant' (2012) 98 *Archiv für Rechts- und Sozialphilosophie* 233.

us bestow strongly authenticated approbation upon ourselves. But to further authenticate that external approval, we need to convince ourselves that we have rightly earned the approval of others and not fooled them into praising what is dishonest or empty. Even with loud applause the anxiously critical subjective voice inside the individual is not stilled. Smith developed this psychology in a key phrase from the *Theory of Moral Sentiments*, inserted only in the final 1790 edition: 'Nature, accordingly, has endowed him not only with the desire of being approved of, but with the desire of *being* what ought to be approved of.'[55]

The way we handle our anxiety to be deserving of genuine approbation is to route the reactions of others through the postulated mind of the 'impartial spectator' with whom we maintain a constant moral dialogue:

> We endeavour to examine our own conduct as we imagine any other fair and impartial spectator would examine it … We suppose ourselves the spectators of our own behaviour, and endeavour to imagine what effect it would, in this light, produce upon us.[56]

Smith's impartial spectator can be described as a third-party observer sitting in judgment over one's conduct by explaining how it might seem to others. I imagine my internal critic's response as a third person to the conducts I offer to a second person, and then review and adjust my first-person conduct accordingly. This is a secularised rendition of the age-old idea of conscience, the desire to appear well in our own eyes by conduct that we can objectively imagine as morally valid. And indeed Smith makes this assimilation, comparing the 'moral sense' or 'sentiment' which 'Providence undoubtedly intended to be the governing principle of human nature' with 'Conscience', which 'properly signifies our consciousness of having acted agreeably or contrary to [the moral faculty's] directions'.[57]

It is notoriously difficult to pin down just what Smith meant by the intellectual devices of 'sympathy', 'conscience', and the 'impartial spectator'. He is eclectic, blending psychological speculation about the innate quality of empathetic imagination with the philosophical detachment of Stoic tradition, holding the two together with ideas from a deistic natural law. One initial problem is to specify the interior mental operation of sympathy. Smith suggests that sympathy might be derived from empathy, or living the experience of another by taking on their internal perspective; but empathetic feeling quickly blurs into sympathy, or understanding another's experience from the remove of an observer who can imagine similar experiences to self:

> As we have no immediate experience of what other men feel, we can form no idea of the manner in which they are affected, but by conceiving what we ourselves should feel in the like situation.[58]

[55] Smith (n 42) iii.2, at 117.
[56] ibid iii.1, at 110, 112.
[57] ibid vii.3.3, at 326.
[58] ibid i.1.1, at 9.

> That this is the source of our fellow-feeling for the misery of others, that it is by changing places in fancy with the sufferer, that we come either to conceive or to be affected by what he feels, may be demonstrated by many obvious observations, if it should not be thought sufficiently evident of itself. When we see a stroke aimed and just ready to fall upon the leg or arm of another person, we naturally shrink and draw back our own leg or our own arm; and when it does fall, we feel it in some measure, and are hurt by it as well as the sufferer. The mob, when they are gazing at a dancer on the slack rope, naturally writhe and twist and balance their own bodies, as they see him do, and as they feel that they themselves must do if in his situation.[59]

When we shift the sympathetic imagination away from experiences so basic as physical risk or harm, and instead aim to assess moral feeling, the operation of sympathy necessarily shifts, since we can all imagine a like reaction to pain or fear but do not necessarily share in common our experience and judgment of conduct and motive. Smith does seem to think that there was a basic commonality of moral view to set the ball rolling:

> The all-wise Author of Nature has … taught man to respect the sentiments and judgments of his brethren; to be more or less pleased when they approve of his conduct, and to be more or less hurt when they disapprove of it. He has made man, if I may say so, the immediate judge of mankind; and has, in this respect, as in many others, created him after his own image, and appointed him his vicegerent upon earth, to superintend the behaviour of his brethren. They are taught by nature, to acknowledge that power and jurisdiction which has thus been conferred upon him, to be more or less humbled and mortified when they have incurred his censure, and to be more or less elated when they have obtained his applause.[60]

It is at this point that the impartial spectator is invoked as an objectifying device to improve the shared moral sympathies of subjective wills:

> But though man has, in this manner, been rendered the immediate judge of mankind, he has been rendered so only in the first instance; and an appeal lies from his sentence to a much higher tribunal, to the tribunal of their own consciences, to that of the supposed impartial and well-informed spectator, to that of the man within the breast, the great judge and arbiter of their conduct. The jurisdictions of those two tribunals are founded upon principles which, though in some respects resembling and akin, are, however, in reality different and distinct. The jurisdiction of the man without, is founded altogether in the desire of actual praise, and in the aversion to actual blame. The jurisdiction of the man within, is founded altogether in the desire of praise-worthiness, and in the aversion to blame-worthiness; in the desire of possessing those qualities, and performing those actions, which we love and admire in other people; and in the dread of possessing those qualities, and performing those actions, which we hate and despise in other people.[61]

[59] ibid i.1.1, at 10.
[60] ibid iii.1.31, at 128, 130.
[61] ibid iii.1.32, at 130–31.

Smithian conscience thus works in two directions, with the device of the impartial spectator being used to evoke imagination of the effects of one's conduct produced on the second person, but also to create some distance from self so as to assess one's first-person motives and behaviours as if from the outside, imagining how others fairly regard one's behaviour. Smith borrowed heavily here from the Stoics, but he also distances himself from their tradition as too coldly objective, using over-much the idea of external observation to repress the feelings and inter-subjective emotions (that is, the sentiments) that Smith deemed necessary for moral being. Thus the second person in the three-party court of moral conscience is affected not only by the objective conduct offered to him or her by the first person, but also by the motives underpinning the first-person action; the impartial spectator helps the first-person actor look more deeply at both sides of relationships to discover how first-second person relationships are truly operating. Smithian conscience can thus be portrayed as a kind of higher egoism seeking truth about and validation of self:

> It is reason, principle, conscience, the inhabitant of the breast, the man within, the great judge and arbiter of our conduct … It is from him only that we learn the real littleness of ourselves, and of whatever relates to ourselves, and the natural misrepresentations of self-love can be corrected only by the eye of this impartial spectator. It is he who shows us the propriety of generosity and the deformity of injustice; the propriety of resigning the greatest interests of our own, for the yet greater interests of others, and the deformity of doing the smallest injury to another, in order to obtain the greatest benefit to ourselves. It is not the love of our neighbour, it is not the love of mankind, which upon many occasions prompts us to the practice of those divine virtues. It is a stronger love, a more powerful affection, which generally takes place upon such occasions; the love of what is honourable and noble, of the grandeur, and dignity, and superiority of our own characters.[62]

To sum up Smithian conscience: a subjective desire to seem well in the eyes of the self was measured against objectively-won knowledge of the appraisal of others, attained by use of the sympathetic imagination refracted through the eyes of the impartial spectator. Thus Smith melded older theological concepts of *conscientia*, knowledge of one's moral conduct, and *synderesis*, the innate moral desire to act well planted by God and nature, and he translated these Stoic and Christian concepts into a modern theory of ethics based on sentiment and the yearning for approbation.

V. A Sympathetic Law? Smith's Jurisprudence

Smith thought about law as the foundation of civil government and the guarantor of personal security from injury; law thereby provided a foundation for economic

[62] ibid iii.1.4, at 137.

and ethical life in civil society. Smith promised to give the subject full treatment, and his planned history and principles of justice and police seems to have occupied him for decades; yet he could not complete, and he had the long-worked-over drafts burnt at his death. All we have is the evidence of his earlier legal thought contained in detailed student notes of his Glasgow lectures of the 1760s,[63] which some scholars discount as provisional work, and too filtered through the vagaries of second-hand transmission to be relied upon. So we are left with the fact that the third great work, the treatment of jurisprudence as the solvent of the problem of self-interest, was promised but never delivered. It may be that finding the correct juristic or institutional balance between self-interested market freedoms and an ethic of sympathy ultimately defeated Smith. Was this an echo of 'Das Adam Smith Problem' within the master himself?

In the notes we have of Smith's 1760s lectures, he uses the idea of the sympathetic yet impartial spectator to evolve a commutative theory of legal justice. One can suffer breach of perfect or natural rights on the one hand, 'those which we have a title to demand and if refused to compel another to perform', or on the other hand, imperfect or adventitious rights, moral claims that one can hope for but cannot demand.[64] An example of breach of the first category are those actions that injure the security of the self in any setting, the latter those that are an injury due to a social context such as praise to the worthy or charity to the needy. Smith uses the distinction of perfect and imperfect rights to illustrate the various causes of action, the triggers for legal intervention in human affairs. Thus a seriously made promise where no formal contract had been concluded was imperfect; one could expect but not demand performance; but a formal covenant was perfected and exigible.[65] A right to exclusive use of a picked apple or a captured hare was perfected; but if one's friend interposed to snatch a fruit one was about to pick, or likewise took a hare one had long been chasing, then there might be breach of an imperfect right through the lack of courtesy and consideration, but no legal claim. How was one to distinguish the perfect and imperfect rights in these famous examples? In the lectures Smith learnedly explains the different opinions in Roman and medieval law on just such points of doctrine, but concludes that the deeper reason is that an impartial modern spectator would 'justify the first possessor' in defending his occupation, but would not see a grave enough offence to sanction even a bad-mannered taker of goods not occupied.[66]

> The cause of this sympathy or concurrence betwixt the spectator and the possessor is, that he enters into his thoughts and concurs in his opinion that he may form a reasonable expectation of using the fruit or whatever it is in the manner he pleases. This expectation

[63] Adam Smith, *Lectures on Jurisprudence* (RE Meek, DD Raphael and PG Stein (eds), Clarendon Press, 1978).
[64] ibid 9.
[65] ibid 98.
[66] ibid 16–19.

> justifies in the mind of the spectator, the possessor … If I was desirous of pulling an apple and had stretched out my hand towards it, but another who was more nimble comes and pulls it before me, an impartial spectator would conceive this was [a] very great breach of good manners and civility but would not suppose it an incroachment on property.[67]

Smith conceded that the case of an apple picked, then dropped and snatched by another, would be an even worse case of ill manners and 'bordering very near on a breach of the right of property'.[68] He is not very clear on what basis other than assertion of reasonableness one might use the impartial spectator technique to resolve such liminal cases.

The legal system, argued Smith, existed to launch retribution against those who cause unwarranted harm to the security and expectations of others, creating 'resentment' that can overpower social order. For example, 'The whole of criminal law is founded on the fellow feeling we have with the resentment of the injured person'.[69] The legal system chooses the relevant *iniuria* to be regulated by referring the offence to the measure of the impartial spectator, who can judge the level of rightful resentment caused and hence find the proportionate level of legal sanction necessary to restore comity. Hence not all subjective harms will be actionable, for example many expectations to be benefited by others, a distributional concern, must be left to be enforced by religion, morality and politics rather than law. Only those ruptures of expectation that our postulated ideal observer would find egregious will be sanctioned. Since all persons may be taken to agree that the perfect rights should be both respected and enforced, a breach involved a disturbance of commutative justice, of settled expectations, and the ensuing resentment had to be redressed by a restoration of the prior position.[70] In effect, this is setting up a morality based on the objective or shared common sense we would expect from an ideal peer group engaging in moral reflection—the sympathetic juror, the wise judge, the reasonable man. Some have called this 'invisible hand ethics', depending on a social equilibrium of moral thought.[71] It is not entirely clear here whether Smith was concerned to distinguish the viewpoint of his ideal sympathetic observer from the common opinions of average mankind; perhaps we can postulate the impartial observer as the ideal commoner—not that different from the common law's romantic concept of the juror, though Smith's own discussion of the jury is brief and uninformative. It is striking that in Smith's extant theory of law the impartial spectator is used quite seldom, maybe thrice in all the extensive notes of his law lectures;[72] and then not in the sophisticated and discursive manner

[67] ibid 17.
[68] ibid 19.
[69] ibid 277.
[70] ibid 475–76.
[71] J Evensky, 'Retrospectives: Ethics and the Invisible Hand' (1993) 7 *Journal of Economic Perspectives* 197.
[72] Smith (n 63) 421, 459, 475; Smith's lectures also involve a 'bystander' at 19.

evoked in *Theory of Moral Sentiments* as a guide through reflexive sympathy into heightened *conscientia* and *synderesis*. The Smithian spectator in the law appears more as an objective, disembodied third-person standard of reasonableness, not far different from the civilian standard of the *bonus paterfamilias*, the reasonable burgher behaving as like burghers would think fit.

How can one account for the thinness of the Smithian theory of conscience in law? It may be that we simply do not know his developed thoughts, since the notes that make up the *Lectures on Jurisprudence* cannot be taken to be a sufficient guide. Another more speculative interpretation would be that Smith disliked the idea of applying some internal model of conscience by a legal process forcing such conscience on parties as mandatory. Perhaps this seemed too much like state enforcement of natural law norms rooted in religion; indeed all his work, including the lectures, presents an anthropological and relativistic appraisal of religious beliefs including the belief systems of Christians, indicating that any moral-legal standards drawn from such a source would be irrational and unstable. Thus for example he notes that in many times and places Christians, including the American colonists of his own day, and the past Christian emperors of Constantinople, had wholeheartedly supported the institutions of slavery.[73] Religion could only come into legal enforcement if such beliefs could be seen to enter into the appraisals of the impartial spectator as a measure of the common wisdom of the local community; religious norms could not be applied by fiat as this would be a forcing of moral conscience for those who might not believe or accept religious authority.

Indeed the point about not enforcing morals by legal command was placed at the very centre of Smith's jurisprudence. Recalling that duties of benevolence were 'imperfect', because the impartial spectator could discern no reasonable expectation of performance by those hoping to benefit, he went on to explain:

> Imperfect rights, again, refer to distributive justice … rights … that belong not properly to jurisprudence, but rather to a system of morals as they do not fall under the jurisdiction of the laws. We are therefore in what follows to confine ourselves *entirely* to the perfect rights and what is called commutative justice.[74]

This leaves the question whether Smith really did intend to exclude imperfect moral rights 'entirely'. Was there no room for enforcement of duties of good faith or honesty that sounded in morality but yet might attract legal support? We may close our discussion of Smith's jurisprudence by asking what role he found for the equity jurisdiction of the Court of Chancery as a test case for his division of benevolent morality from legal expectation. The answer, so far as we can see from the *Lectures*, lay in remedy. Courts of law might be cramped in their heads of remedy due to their jurisdictional history, and here Chancery could issue fresh

[73] ibid 191.
[74] ibid 9 (emphasis added).

writs modelled on the old but extending the scope of actions. But then the Chancellor began to give remedies 'in those cases which the courts of common law did not comprehend'.[75] For example common law courts saw breach of contract as an injury warranting corrective damages, but the Chancellor went further:

> The first thing he did in this way was to order specifick performance of contracts. These were not sustained by the common law; all they did was to give the pursuer damages but did not think of forcing specifick performance. This however a man was bound in honour to perform, and the Court of Chancery, which was considered a Court of Conscience with the Chancellor at the head who was generally a clergy man skilled in the cannon law, began to give action on this head. Anoth(er) thing was all cases of trust and fraud.[76]

Smith then enumerated the areas where the Court of Chancery intervened in either sole or auxiliary jurisdiction: the enforcement of trusts; the specific performance of contracts for sale of land; the upholding of testamentary trusts and probate of wills; charitable trusts for the church or eleemosynary corporations. He admitted that whilst common law judges are tightly circumscribed by strict law with few powers of interpretation, and are beholden to the jury for fact finding, 'the Chancellor is certainly as arbitrary a judge as most'.[77] But if this could not be defended in principle, it could be tolerated in practice:

> But neither is he [the Chancellor] very dangerous to the liberty of the subject, as he can not try causes besides those which have no remedy at common law. Nor can he in any case act contrary to any method of proceeding laid down by courts of common law. And from this court as from all others appeals may be carried before the House of Lords.[78]

Smith showed no greater interest in applying his own elaborate ideas of conscience to law; indeed he seems to have merely tolerated the application of ideas of conscience, mainly in the realm of specific enforcement of contract and trusts, as a relic of the past, an appendix that was perhaps marginal and exceptional. In his attitude to Chancery jurisdiction, Smith was very far from his mentor Henry Home, Lord Kames, who saw equity as a practical instantiation of natural law, stating that

> the duty of benevolence arising from certain peculiar connections among individuals, is susceptible in many cases of a precise rule. So far benevolence is also taken under the authority of the legislature, and enforced by rules passing commonly under the name of the law of equity.[79]

[75] ibid 474.

[76] ibid 281–82.

[77] ibid 282; also 286 on the historical anomaly of the Court of Chancery having no jury, since at the outset it was not supposed to have the dignity of a court of law.

[78] ibid 282–83.

[79] Henry Home, *Lord Kames, Essays on the Principles of Morality and Natural Religion* 2nd edn (Hitch & Hawes et al, 1758) 102, quoted by M Lobban, 'The Ambition of Lord Kames's Equity' in A Lewis and M Lobban (eds), *Law and History* (2003) 6 *Current Legal Issues* 97, 108.

Kames published his own elaborate treatise on the *Principles of Equity* in 1760, just after Smith issued *The Theory of Moral Sentiments* and just as Smith was writing his *Lectures on Jurisprudence.* Smith can be seen to reference details from Kames' legal treatise on a number of occasions in the lectures; but it can be no accident that he resolutely refused to follow Kames' view that equity legislated natural morality. Smith was not a command theorist of the law; but at the same time he resisted the use of conscience as a moral constraint on self-interested conduct. The record of his lectures in jurisprudence suggest that he can more properly be placed within the *ius commune* tradition, whereby legal professionals use the doctrines of the old civilian jurists to work up solutions agreeable to the sentiments and customs of modern populations. This would make Smith a more conventional and conservative thinker in the law than he ever was in ethics or economics.

VI. The Conscience of Chancery and Smithian Conscience

Can Smith's theories of conscience and self-interest be traced into the legal discourse of his time? It is likely that cultivated lawyers of the mid to late eighteenth century were exposed to Smithian ethics; after all, Smith was read and debated very widely, and he assiduously lectured on his ethical theories alongside his political economy and jurisprudence for over 15 years in Edinburgh and Glasgow up to 1761, to many of the young men who went on to lead the court systems of Scotland and England.[80] Moreover a great number of university-educated lawyers from Scotland pursued advocacy either full time or ad hoc in the English courts.[81] Whether some direct transfer of Smithian ideas into the law can be established or not, it may be shown that lawyers in English Chancery deployed the idea of conscience in new ways that recalled Smith's moral language of sympathy and the impartial spectator. Chancery jurisdiction in fact went further than Smith was prepared to go, and sometimes enforced the so-called 'imperfect' duties of benevolence that Smith saw as outside positive jurisprudence. It is striking that leading Chancery judges and advocates of the 1770s and 1780s used Smithian ethical language as they extended the province of conscience as a legal device to constrain self-interest. The English lawyers were here more Smithian than Smith.

In one important aspect the lawyers of mid-century wholly agreed with Smith: conscience could not be enforced by courts in the form of simple moral command. Judges could not in the latter half of the eighteenth century be conceived as

[80] Ross (n 41) 129–42.

[81] J Finlay, 'Scots Lawyers and House of Lords Appeals in Eighteenth-Century Britain (2011) 32 *Journal of Legal History* 32, 249.

delegates of a confessional state or monarch, as early seventeenth-century lawyers had sometimes argued. For example Lord Ellesmere in the *Earl of Oxford's Case* in 1615 described the conscience jurisdiction of Chancery in terms of political theology:

> The Office of the Chancellor is to correct Mens Consciences for Frauds, Breach of Trusts, Wrongs and Oppressions, of what Nature soever they be ... Law and Equity are distinct, both in their Courts, their Judges, and the Rules of Justice; and yet they both aim at one and the same End, which is, to do Right; as Justice and Mercy differ in their Effects and Operations, yet both join in the Manifestation of God's Glory.[82]

Lord Ellesemere earlier described the judges as 'noe subordinate Magistrates, but absolute Kings', fully as sovereign within their realm of law as the king in any of his prerogatives. If the judges were ordained by the king, yet they were independent of 'the discretion or Conscience of the King'.[83] This independence was a quality required by the king himself, who appointed each judge to decide 'by true reason of the Law', and 'his owne heart and Conscience'; they were to serve as '*Coram Deo & Angelis*', a divine and angelic court. The king's power as '*Pater patriae*, and soveraigne head' constituted the body politic, with the courts as impartial members and treated in return with impartiality by the king.[84]

After the Revolution and Restoration Lord Nottingham marked the shift away from spiritual command theory with his analysis of equitable jurisdiction in *Cook v Fountain* in 1676:

> With such a conscience as is only *naturalis et interna*, this Court has nothing to do; the conscience by which I am to proceed is merely *civilis et politica*, and tied to certain measures; ... for otherwise ... no man need to be confessed.[85]

[82] *Earl of Oxford's Case* (1615) 1 Chancery Reports 1, 6–7; 21 ER 485, 486 (LC) per Ellesemere LC. D Ibbetson, 'The Earl of Oxford's Case (1615)' in C Mitchell and P Mitchell (eds), *Landmark Cases in Equity* (Hart Publishing, 2012) 1–32, argues that Lord Ellesmere gave his celebrated speech many months after the actual judgment, as a polemical defence of the Chancery's jurisdiction to gloss the common law by *in personam* restraint of litigants. The real problem addressed by Ellesmere was how to claim this power for Chancery without rupturing statutory prohibitions against interference with common law judgments, a policy aimed at barring ecclesiastical and especially papal jurisdiction.

[83] 'A Coppie of a Wrytten Discourse by the Lord Chauncellor Elsemore Concerning the Royall Prerogatiue' (c1604), in LA Knafla, *Law and Politics in Jacobean England: The Tracts of Lord Chancellor Ellesemere* (Cambridge University Press, 1977) 197, 198 and 200.

[84] 'The Speech of the Lord Chancellor of England, in the Eschequer Chamber, Touching the *Post-Nati*' (1608), Knafla, ibid 202, 214.

[85] *Cook v Fountain* (1676), reported (1827) 3 Swanston 585, 600–601; 36 ER 984, 990. The case significantly went through some nine hearings in the House of Lords following the Chancery decision: *Journal of the House of Lords: Volume XIV, 1685–1691* (His Majesty's Stationery Office, 1774) 55, 79, 356, 407, 409, 425, 449, 462, 464; but Nottingham's own notes of the case were not published until 1827. See further MR Macnair, 'Coke v Fountaine (1676)' in C Mitchell and P Mitchell (eds), *Landmark Cases in Equity* (Hart Publishing, 2012) 33–62.

A more expansive argument against conscience as discretionary command was made in *Cowper v Cowper* in 1734 by the Master of the Rolls, Sir Joseph Jekyll:

> The law is clear, and courts of equity ought to follow it in their judgments concerning titles to equitable estates; otherwise great uncertainty and confusion would ensue and though proceedings in equity are said to be *secundum discretionem boni viri* [in accord with the judgment of a good man], yet when it is asked, *vir bonus est quis*? ['what man is to be called good?] the answer is, *qui consulta patrum qui leges juraq; servat* [the one who keeps the decrees of the fathers, and who maintains the laws and justice]'[86] and as it is said in *Rook's* case, 5 Rep 99 b, that discretion is a science, not to act arbitrarily according to men's wills and private affections: so the discretion which is exercised here, is to be governed by the rules of law and equity, which are not to oppose, but each, in its turn, to be subservient to the other; this discretion, in some cases, follows the law implicitly, in others, assists it, and advances the remedy; in others again, it relieves against the abuse, or allays the rigour of it; but in no case does it contradict or over-turn the grounds or principles thereof, as has been sometimes ignorantly imputed to this Court. That is a discretionary power, which neither this nor any other Court, not even the highest, acting in a judicial capacity, is by the constitution intrusted with.[87]

Both the above cases involved controversy over whether the benefit of estates could be shifted by secret evidence of motive in transactions, where the court had no direct evidence to expose relevant motive through evidence, but could only extrapolate from context. In *Cook v Fountain* it was acknowledged that a conveyance without consideration or obvious reason might raise a regular presumption that a trust had been intended without the beneficiary having to go to further proof. Because parties knew of this 'violent and necessary presumption'[88] of trust from conduct when they settled property, it was just to hold them to this structure of expectations of right conduct. *Cowper* went on to show that such pro-beneficiary presumptions were not to be invented by the courts merely to solve particular cases. Jekyll MR denied that good conscience required the court to impose a trust 'when such release or conveyance is only supposed or inferred from appearances, out of which that supposition does not necessarily or even naturally arise'.[89] Extrapolating from these instances, the general question for the court of equity was to interpret in which stereotypical situations conduct that was prima facie legal was nonetheless likely to be affected by hidden motives and intentions (including impaired intentions due to problems of position and capacity) warranting intervention by the court on the grounds of conscience. Judges came to describe the 'conscience of the court' in two limiting senses: the court needed good evidence of wrongdoing or fraud, or at least strong presumptive proof of such; and the court was bound to follow Chancery precedents in applying

[86] Jekyll MR is here quoting Horace's *Epistles* i.16.40. This passage in *Cowper* was in turn quoted incessantly for the next hundred years as epitomising the nature of English equity.

[87] *Cowper v Cowper* (1734) 2 Peere Williams 720, 753–54; 24 ER 930, 941–42 (ChD).

[88] *Cook v Fountain* ([1676]/1733) 3 Swanston 585, 591; 36 ER 984, 987.

[89] *Cowper v Cowper* (1734) 2 Peere Williams 720, 753; 24 ER 930, 941 (ChD).

forensic and presumptive rules to interpret conduct.[90] These principles surface in *Heathcote v Paignon*, a 1787 case of sale of an annuity at an undervalue by a family claiming afterwards that they had acted in distressed circumstances. Lord Chancellor Thurlow challenged counsel for the plaintiff, Mr John Scott (later Lord Eldon) to show evidence why the sale was against conscience, stating

> The business of a court of equity is certainly not so much to make people honest, as to obviate the inconveniences of dishonesty. Here is no evidence of distress, nothing but the inadequacy of the value; and if that could be made the rule, the least circumstance which varied the next case which occurred might make the difference.[91]

Scott in the end succeeded in showing the court that such distress existed and was known to the defendant who took an advantage. Setting aside the contract protected the conscience of the defendant by preventing him from carrying through what would have been a fraudulent act.

What was emerging in Lord Thurlow's time was a separate procedural conscience test quite distinct from moral assessment of the parties subject to decision. The court is speaking of the demands of conscience as a duty *on the decision-maker* to find evidence and follow precedents before discovering equitable fraud. This represented a considerable shift from the 'command' equity of Lord Chancellor Ellesmere. It may be that the change reflected the new age of toleration and scepticism where courts began to withdraw from enforcement of religion and ethics. Lord Mansfield said as much in a debate over religious pluralism and liberty in 1767, in language echoing both Smith and Hume:[92]

> Conscience is not controllable by human laws, nor amenable to human tribunals. Persecution, or attempts to force conscience, will never produce conviction; and are only calculated to make hypocrites, or—martyrs.[93]

If the modernising eighteenth-century Chancery's jurisdiction of conscience was not based on command, then what was its *modus operandi*? It may be summed up by the maxim 'equity sees as done that which ought to be done', which may be restated as a presumption of honesty. Equity presumes that every party in court, when all available evidence is discovered, all permitted inferences drawn, and all relevant conduct understood, will seek to perform due obligations and avoid pressing home undue rights, and thereby choose to avoid a conscious breach or

[90] eg *Smith v Evans* (1725) Ambler 834, 835; 27 ER 523 (Ch) per Lord King C.
[91] (1787) 2 Brown's Chancery Cases 167, 175; 29 ER 96, 100 (LC).
[92] Griswold (n 53) 266–92.
[93] *The speech of the Right Honourable Lord Mansfield in the House of Lords, in the Cause between the City of London and the Dissenters [Chamberlain of London v Evans* (1767)] (D Blow 1774) 21; see also *Harrison v Evans* (1767) 3 Brown's Parliamentary Cases 465; 1 ER 1437 (HL). On legal enforcement of religious dogma in England and Scotland in Chancery see further J Getzler, 'Faith, Trust and Charity' in A Burrows, D Johnston, and R Zimmermann (eds), *Judge and Jurist: Essays in Memory of Lord Rodger of Earlsferry* (Oxford University Press, 2013) 559–74.

abuse of rights. The court by uncovering the fullest evidence and confronting the defendant with the quality of his or her actions so guides that party to choose honest conduct. Equity's presumption of honesty on the civil law side was sometimes conceived as an extension of the presumption of innocence in criminal law.[94] The criminal law requires positive proof of guilt before it will adversely interpret the moral quality of a person's ambiguous conduct as a breach of duty. By analogy courts of conscience in controlling civil obligations will look at ambiguous conduct and require proof showing a completed commitment to perpetrate a fraud before finding an actor guilty. Equity will always prefer to avoid such a finding, and instead reinterpret party conduct so as to induce or steer a defendant away from committing a breach in the first place. There are two sides to this equation: an anti-fraud jurisdiction and a primary duty jurisdiction. In the first, the court requires a defendant to foreswear a right he or she ought not to insist upon, for example because the right was attained in circumstances where its unrestricted exercise will turn it into an engine of fraud or wrongdoing. In the second jurisdiction the court will order a party bearing a primary duty, for example of contract relating to specific property, or of fiduciary management or trustee control of assets, to tender specific performance of a finite contractual duty, or to render an account and make a due performance of a continuous stewardship or agency, rather than choose to breach and offer a secondary remedy.[95] This explains the maxim 'a court of equity does not punish':[96] the court of conscience prefers to put the parties out of breach and into performance so they do not need to be punished; punishment as a secondary remedy is not in Chancery's armoury. If a party does insist on carrying through or ratifying a fraudulent breach, this will usually be severe enough to attract actions for tortious and criminal fraud or deceit with dishonest intent, bringing legal damages, forfeiture and imprisonment as sanctions. But this is a jurisdiction of law and police, when equity and conscience fails.

The presumption of honesty measure of conscience is adumbrated early in the writings and judgments of Lord Chancellor Nottingham in the later seventeenth

[94] Interestingly this attitude was deprecated by common law judges after the fusion of law and equity in 1873–75; see eg *Ward v Hobbs* (1877) 3 QBD 150, 166 per Cotton LJ: 'I think it would be too great a refinement to imply, from the presumption of honesty, a representation by every one that there is nothing to his knowledge which makes his acts dishonest'.

[95] J Getzler, '"As If". Accountability and Counterfactual Trust' (2011) 91 *Boston University Law Review* 931.

[96] *Hodgens v Hodgens* (1837) 4 Clark & Finnelly 323, 353; 7 ER 124, 135 (HL, counsel in arguendo). This was a case where a mother who scandalously abandoned husband and children nonetheless could not have her marriage settlement trusts reopened to extract maintenance for her children simply because of her anterior bad behaviour; Lord Brougham C noted that contempt of court could bring imprisonment of the person to coerce obedience, but negative sanctions for bad behaviour did not lie in the normal jurisdiction of Chancery. See further *Harris v Digital Pulse Pty Ltd* (2003) 56 NSWLR 298 (NSWCA), where Heydon JA covers all the significant eighteenth and nineteenth century authorities on equity's aversion to punishment.

century.[97] His theory that neglectful exercise of managerial power over the affairs of another could lead to a primary accounting remedy in turn provided the basis for the eighteenth-century's development of co-trustee and directors' duties of due care and supervision in management roles, notably in Lord Hardwicke's decision in the 1747 case of *Charitable Corporation v Sutton*.[98] On the negative or restraining side of the conscience jurisdiction we have Lord Hardwicke's important 1750 judgment in *Earl of Chesterfield v Janssen*.[99] There Lord Hardwicke explained how equity could find out fraud presumptively, from circumstances that spoke loudly of exploitation or sharp practice, where direct proof of ill motive might not be discoverable. His judgment amounted to a codification of equitable practice, stating a fourfold test of fraud in bargaining:

> The … question is, supposing the … contract to be valid in law, whether it was contrary to conscience, and to be relieved against in this court upon any head or principle of equity? … This court has an undoubted jurisdiction to relieve against every species of fraud. 1. The fraud, which is *dolus malus*, may be actual, arising from facts and circumstances of imposition; which is the plainest case. 2. It may be apparent from the intrinsic nature and subject of the bargain itself; such as no man in his senses and not under delusion would make on the one hand, and as no honest and fair man would accept on the other; which are unequitable and unconscientious bargains;… A 3rd kind of fraud is, which may be presumed from the circumstances and condition of the parties contracting: and this goes farther than the rule of law; which is, that it must be proved, not presumed; but it is wisely established in this court to prevent taking surreptitious advantage of the weakness or necessity of another: which knowingly to do is equally against the conscience as to take advantage of his ignorance: a person is equally unable to judge for himself in one as the other. A 4th kind of fraud may be collected or inferred in the consideration of this court from the nature and circumstances of the transaction, as being an imposition and deceit on the other persons not parties to the fraudulent agreement.[100]

He here identified a double ill—callous disregard by the stronger party, and inadequate consent of the weaker party, fomented or exploited by the stronger. Equity offered two remedial solutions to a bargaining fraud: it might deny the stronger party specific performance and thus leave the party to seek possibly derisory damages; or it might order the stronger party not to enforce the contract, or to rescind the contract and restore the position ex ante.

In this peculiarly English discourse of conscience and the presumption of honesty, where do Adam Smith's ideas fit in? Smith briefly picked up on the

[97] DEC Yale (ed), *Lord Nottingham's Manual of Chancery Practice and Prolegomena of Chancery and Equity* (Cambridge University Press, 1965) 166–67, 196, 200; *Palmer v Jones*, in DEC Yale (ed), *Lord Nottingham's Chancery Cases* (Selden Society vol 79, 1961) 649, no 824 (1678); cf rehearing by North LK at (1683) 1 Vernon's Cases in Chancery 144; 23 ER 376.

[98] (1742) 9 Modern 349; 88 ER 500 per Lord Hardwicke C.

[99] *Earl of Chesterfield v Janssen* (1750–51) 2 Vesey Senior 125; 28 ER 82; 1 Atkyns 301; 26 ER 191 (Ch).

[100] 2 Vesey Senior 125, 155–56; 28 ER 82, 100; 1 Atkyns 301, 351–52; 26 ER 191, 224–25 (LC).

primary performance idea in his jurisprudence lectures, albeit briefly, noting how a 'Court of Conscience' will 'order specifick performance of contracts' where 'a man was bound in honour to perform'.[101] It is interesting then to ask what work the idea of 'honour' performs in his formulation. And here we reach a thoroughly Smithian moment in the history of law and conscience. In the 1778 case of *Gwynne v Heaton*[102] the defendant had sold to a necessitous heir a life annuity for the father for a large sum charged against the family estate, where there was ample evidence that the father was at death's door and the annuity would not amount to much. The plaintiff's case was presented by Alexander Wedderburn. He was a Scottish-educated barrister who had attended Adam Smith's lectures on rhetoric and politics in Edinburgh in 1748, and then became his fast friend.[103] Wedderburn had moved his practice to England in 1757 and became Attorney-General in 1771. After long service as Chief Justice of Common Pleas from 1780 to 1793 he served as Lord Chancellor from 1793 to 1801 as Lord Loughborough and then the Earl of Rosslyn. He was regarded as the most rhetorically gifted barrister in the London of his day, if not the most learned. He participated avidly in the politics of his day, moving from the Tory side to the Whigs over the John Wilkes case, and moving back again during the American Independence crisis. He notably applied Smithian ideas on political economy and Smithian rhetoric to legal problems; for example, when introducing legislation in the House of Lords to contain accumulations in the wake of *Thellusson's Will Case*, Wedderburn stated:

> A fortune in circulation, even if spent in luxuries, waste, and dissipation, did more good to the public, and afforded more emulation to industry, and better encouragement to arts and manufactures, than any useless accumulation of money could do.[104]

As counsel for the plaintiff in *Gwynne v Heaton*[105] Wedderburn began by tactically heading off the possibility that the court might refuse the aid of specific performance or rescission to either party, and let them fight it out at law on the matter of damages—in effect a victory for the defendant. He pressed instead for equitable rescission and *restitutio ad integrum*, or restoration of the position before the contract. The problem he faced was explaining why a self-interested purchase of an asset at a low price must taint the contract and make it vulnerable to court control. To this end he offered a novel theory of the court's jurisdiction in conscience:

> No case puzzles me so much as one where the Court will assist neither party.—It is certainly true, that courts have no censorial authority, but it does not follow from hence,

[101] Smith (n 63) 281–82.

[102] (1778) 1 Brown's Chancery Cases 1; 28 ER 989 (LC).

[103] A Murdoch, 'Alexander Wedderburn' in *Oxford Dictionary of National Biography* (Oxford University Press, 2004) §28954; Ross (n 41) 52–53ff; Finlay (n 81).

[104] *The Parliamentary Register; Or, History of the Proceedings and Debates of the Houses of Lords and Commons* (Debrett, 1800) xii, 77 (HL, 6 June 1797); see further P Polden, *Peter Thellusson's Will of 1797 and Its Consequences on Chancery Law* (Mellen Press, 2002).

[105] (1778) 1 Brown's Chancery Cases 1; 28 ER 949.

> that they can give no relief.—The rules of morals, *honeste vivere, alterum non lædere, suum cuique tribuere*, do not all apply to courts of justice.—*Honeste vivere* is not their object, *suum cuique tribuere* is their proper ground, but they will prevent one man from injuring another: on this foundation stands the action upon the case.—If the bargain is beyond the limitation the law has fixed, it will punish. But there are cases which are not illegal, but which still are unconscientious.—If a man finds another in distress, and supplies him on unconscientious terms, the Court, in relieving him, enforces the rule of morality.[106]

Wedderburn here referenced Ulpian's great statement of the ends of law that stands at the head of the *Institutes* and *Digest* of Justinian:

> *Juris praecepta sunt haec: honeste vivere, alterum non lædere, suum cuique tribuere.*
>
> The following are the precepts of the Law: To live honourably, to harm no one, to give to each his own.[107]

Wedderburn's rhetoric and civilian learning must have been striking to those in court that day; for instance a young John Scott, struggling to establish himself at the bar and spending all hours he could find listening to the arguments of the best London counsel, wrote a *précis* of the speech in his notebook that helps explain what was at stake:

> Courts it is said have no censorial Jurisdiction. Many moral Obligations beyond the reach of Laws.
>
> Honeste vivere beyond Law
>
> Suum cuique tribuere the business of Courts
>
> Alterum non lædere—Courts have always attended to—Not to gain to himself by injury to another —
>
> Money a commodity its Price rises & falls but of so general use that every State in every Age has put the Use of Money and Advantage to be made of [it] under certain Restrictions. There is one case where the use of money is illegal: ~~the~~ another which Law does not reach, where it is unconscionable.[108]

The key phrase identified here is the assimilation of conscience to '*honeste vivere*'. 'To live honorably' encoded the Stoic ethic of concern for others in order to attain tranquillity of mind or good conscience. It was a foundation of the Ulpianic vision of law at the high point of Roman classical jurisprudence.[109] Wedderburn's speech as reported seems at first to argue that honorable conduct, with its connotations of

[106] (1778) 1 Brown's Chancery Cases 1, 6–7; 28 ER 949, 952 *in arguendo*.

[107] *Institutes* 1.3; *Digest* 1.1.10 (*Ulpianus libro secundo regularum*).

[108] John Scott, *Notebook of Chancery Cases*, Saturday 27 June 1778, MS., Lord Eldon Collection, Georgetown Law Center, Washington DC.

[109] AM (Tony) Honoré, 'Ulpian, Natural Law and Stoic Influence' (2010) 79 *Legal History Review* 199.

honest respect for others, was not the business of justice or law: there is no 'censorial' jurisdiction, no power to command good morals; or (in Scott's recollection) 'Many moral Obligations beyond the reach of Laws'. But if conduct within legal bounds was yet so exploitative of a person as to become 'unconscientious', then 'the Court, in relieving him, enforces the rule of morality'. Wedderburn's rhetoric was brilliant because it divided moral standards into two: those standards reserved for moral regulation outside the law—Smith's imperfect obligations of benevolence—and those standards where breach would involve patent dishonesty, living without honour, pursuing self-interest beyond conscience as accepted by any neutral observer or judge, and so disrupting society. These latter moral obligations fell to Chancery to correct. Wedderburn completed his advocacy by concluding that the terms of the deal were so bad on their face, and the powers given to the lender over the family estate so extensive and overbearing in the circumstances, that it was no answer that the lender claimed in his subjective mind to be 'honest' in both acquisition and exercise of rights. Looking at all available facts including the obvious distress of the family and the adverse terms extracted, it was simply implausible to presume other than that this was an 'exorbitant' contract: 'The circumstances put together shew the bargain to be enormous ... I do not desire a casualty to be considered; but what at the time was most probable to happen should be considered.'[110]

Wedderburn won his case. Lord Chancellor Thurlow gave relief against the contract, using *Janssen's Case* as supporting precedent: 'Lord *Hardwicke* treats inequality as a mark of fraud'.[111] The evidence was sufficient to establish that the father's 'dissolution' was notorious and so the security was likely to be called early, so that at the time of transacting the estate was likely be acquired at gross undervalue, greatly overcompensating the lender for any risk ex ante. Lord Thurlow then applied this test of conscience:

> To set aside a conveyance, there must be an inequality *so strong, gross, and manifest*, that it must be *impossible to state it* to a man of common sense, *without producing an exclamation at the inequality of it* ... It then comes to this; that Heaton the purchaser, knowing the actual state of the lives for which he was bargaining, the inequality which that introduced, and the indigence of the man with whom he was contracting, makes a bargain with him, which appears as enormous..., without one circumstance to cast a shade over the case. The deeds must be set aside.[112]

Here the Court of Conscience uses 'a man of common sense' as the third-party observer, the impartial spectator, showing the defendant where the dictates of conscience lay. The honourable or honest course of conduct was not to press home his acknowledged, perfected legal rights, and indeed because the defendant had put

[110] *Gwynne v Heaton* (1778) 1 Brown's Chancery Cases 1, 7; 28 ER 949, 952 *in arguendo*.
[111] (1778) 1 Brown's Chancery Cases 1, 8; 28 ER 949, 953 (LC).
[112] (1778) 1 Brown's Chancery Cases 1, 9, 10–11; 28 ER 949, 953–54 (LC) (emphasis in original).

the plaintiff to the trouble of filing a bill to resist a contract that was clearly pernicious in principle, it was proper that plaintiff's costs should follow the cause.[113]

Gwynne v Heaton was an important milestone in Chancery doctrine, cited continuously into the late nineteenth century with *Chesterfield v Janssen* as a foundation of the equitable fraud jurisdiction. In *Gwynne* Wedderburn and Thurlow elucidated how equitable fraud should be understood, taking the Smithian ideas of impartial conscience and the limits of imperfect moral obligations, marrying these to Chancery forensics, and using Stoic ideas embedded in Roman law to explain why court enforcement of conscience involved a presumption of honesty, and was not some 'censorious' imposition of top-down morality. Lord Thurlow went on to apply the presumed honesty test in the positive cases of accountability, for example ordering accounts against a servant or agent in a fiduciary position and also against a stranger who acquires trust property or assists the agent in breach of retainer;[114] from the same Smithian language came the modern law of fiduciaries.[115]

It remains to note that the language of conscience is also found in common law claims of the age. In the seminal unjust enrichment case of *Moses v Macferlan* in 1760, Lord Mansfield CJ gave an argument for recovery of flawed payments as conscience-driven, using Roman language '*ex æquo et bono*', obligations from equity and good faith:

> This kind of equitable action, to recover back money, which ought not in justice to be kept, is very beneficial, and therefore much encouraged. It lies only for money which, *ex æquo et bono*, the defendant ought to refund: it does not lie for money paid by the plaintiff, which is claimed of him as payable in point of honor and honesty, although it could not have been recovered from him by any course of law; as in payment of a debt barred by the Statute of Limitations, or contracted during his infancy, or to the extent of principal and legal interest upon an usurious contract, or, for money fairly lost at play: because in all these cases, the defendant may retain it with a safe conscience, though by positive law he was barred from recovering.[116]

The notion of conscience is here used in a striking fashion not only to explain prima facie restitution as a unified cause of action,[117] but also to construct an important defence: where monies are paid to a person gratuitously under an

[113] (1778) 1 Brown's Chancery Cases 1, 11; 28 ER 949, 954 (LC).

[114] *East India Company v Henchman* (1791) 1 Vesey Junior 287, 289; 30 ER 347, 348 (Ch) (the name of defendant is a happy coincidence). See also *Bonney v Ridgard* (1784) 1 Cox's Chancery Cases 145, 147; 29 ER 1101, 1102 per Sir Lloyd Kenyon MR, where primary enforcement of trust duties was ordered against an executor who had used a legal power to transact with the deceased estate to retire his own debts; 'common honesty' required an account of profits by the executor lest he commit 'equitable fraud'.

[115] *East India Company v Henchman* is still cited as a foundational fiduciary case in J McGhee (ed), *Snell's Equity* 33rd edn (Sweet & Maxwell, 2014) ¶ 7-054.

[116] (1760) 2 Burrow 1005, 1012; 97 ER 676, 680–81 (KB) per Lord Mansfield CJ.

[117] PBH Birks, 'English and Roman Learning in *Moses v Macferlan*' (1984) 37 *Current Legal Problems* 1.

imperfect obligation, 'payable in point of honor and honesty', then there is no conscience to repay simply because the donor afterwards repents his non-enforceable payment. This seed laid the foundation for much that followed in the common law of unjust enrichment. Now William Murray, Lord Mansfield, had left Scotland behind as a schoolboy and was English-educated, yet he corresponded with Adam Smith and sent him foreign students anxious to learn philosophical jurisprudence.[118] It is difficult to imagine that this learned judge was ignorant of the theories of Smith and Kames on the nature of obligations and the calls of conscience. The language seems closer to Smith.

VII. Conclusion

If lawyers of the stature of Thurlow and Wedderburn, Scott and Mansfield, could each resort to arguments of Smithian conscience to explain the jurisprudence of obligation, and in fact used such ideas to invent much of our modern law, then that leaves us with a tantalising question for the present. Can the judges of today do a better job of constraining self-interest if they dispense with the third jurisdiction of conscience? Can a better explanation be given of how self-interest may be perfected?

[118] Ross (n 41) 32, 158; and see Ross's account of the influence of *Theory of Moral Sentiments* on Mansfield's judgment in Somerset's Case, ibid, 170–71.

15

The Practical Dimension of Legal Reasoning

STEPHEN WADDAMS

'The various necessities of mankind induced also the judges very soon to depart from the rigour and simplicity of the rules of the common law.'

Blackstone (1766)[1]

I. Introduction

Where courts have been called upon to select among legal rules, or to formulate a new rule, they have frequently been influenced by practical considerations. It is a commonplace[2] to say that legal reasoning has practical consequences, but the force of practical considerations in legal reasoning has not always been appreciated (in either sense of the word), and its implications have not been fully explored. In very many instances propositions of law once thought to be firmly established have been displaced by what Blackstone, referring to changes in the law over two centuries in relation to the Statute of Uses, called 'the various necessities of mankind.' Nineteenth-century references to practicalities are frequent. Dr Lushington said, in reference to prize law, that the object was to 'reconcile the abstract principles of justice with practicability.'[3] In the twentieth century Lord Goff said that 'it is, I believe, unhistorical, for us now to castigate our legal ancestors for adopting a doctrine which was widely understood in their time to achieve practical justice.'[4] In the present century Lord Neuberger has said that 'the decision as to which view

[1] W Blackstone, *Commentaries on the Laws of England* (4 vols, Clarendon Press, 1765–69) ii, 334.

[2] 'These observations are almost banal: the public would be astonished if it was thought that judges did not conceive it as their prime duty to do practical justice whenever possible … For my part practical justice strongly militates in favour of an order for disgorgement of profits against Blake.' Lord Steyn in *Attorney General v Blake* [2001] 1 AC 268 (HL), 292.

[3] *The Leucade* (1855) 2 Sp 228, 248.

[4] *Kleinwort Benson Ltd v Lincoln City Council* [1999] 2 AC 349 (HL), 371.

is correct must be based on legal principle, decided cases, policy considerations, and practicalities.'[5] Practical considerations are difficult to weigh, difficult to predict, and are capable of displacing even the firmest legal orthodoxies. Since the force of such 'practicalities' necessarily varies from time to time, judge-made law is always liable to change, and change has usually occurred in response to perceived practical considerations. Law is not only a set of conceptual constructs; it also constitutes a practice, and has been strongly influenced by its anticipated practical effects, both as between the particular parties, and also as affecting future litigants.

The practical considerations that have influenced the courts cannot be precisely defined. They include considerations of policy but are not confined to matters of policy in the usual sense of that word. They include residual considerations of fairness, of convenience, of 'common sense,' and of avoiding results perceived as intolerable. This is, it is suggested, a distinct and characteristic aspect of legal reasoning. It is related to the rhetorical concept of *reductio ad absurdum*, but is not limited to avoidance of what is 'absurd.'

II. Privity of Contract

Many illustrations might be given. One is the succession of reversals of judicial opinion on the question of privity of contract, and is particularly striking in the present context because of the forceful language in which the House of Lords denied the possibility of legal change shortly before such change occurred. In 1962, Viscount Simonds, speaking for a majority of four members of the House of Lords (Lord Denning alone dissenting), spoke in uncompromising terms of the necessity to maintain the position then regarded as orthodox:

> Learned counsel … met [the argument for enforcement of a promise by a third party beneficiary] … by asserting a principle which is, I suppose, as well established as any in our law, a 'fundamental' principle, as Lord Haldane called it, … an 'elementary' principle, as it has been called times without number, that only a person who is a party to a contract can sue upon it. 'Our law', said Viscount Haldane, 'knows nothing of a jus quaesitum tertio arising by way of contract'. Learned counsel … claimed that this was the orthodox view and asked your lordships to reject any proposition that impinged upon it. To that invitation I readily respond. For to me heterodoxy, or, as some might say, heresy, is not the more attractive because it is dignified by the name of reform. Nor will I easily be led by an undiscerning zeal for some abstract kind of justice to ignore our first duty, which is to administer justice according to law … The law is developed by the application of old principles to new circumstances. Therein lies its genius. Its reform by the abrogation of those principles is the task not of courts of law but of Parliament. [Two decisions of Lord Denning were cited here and rejected.][6]

[5] *FHR European Ventures LLP v Cedar Capital Partners LLC* [2014] UKSC 45, [2014] 3 WLR 535, at [12].
[6] *Scruttons Ltd v Midland Silicones Ltd* [1962] 1 AC 446 (HL), 467–68.

This passage, exceeding the forceful, and pressing on the limits of judicial courtesy because of its implied attack on Lord Denning (who was a member of the panel) forms part of a sequence of reversal and reinstatement of orthodox opinion on the question of privity of contract, and the right of a third party to enforce a contract made between two others. In the early case of *Dutton v Poole*,[7] a third party was permitted to enforce such a contract, but this approach was rejected by the Court of Queen's Bench in *Tweddle v Atkinson* in 1861.[8] Courts of equity had sometimes permitted third parties to enforce promises made by other persons for their benefit, and when the Judicature Acts came into effect (in 1875) Pollock tentatively suggested that the equitable rule might prevail,[9] but Anson adopted a dogmatic and uncompromising rule excluding such a possibility,[10] and the House of Lords affirmed a strict rule of privity in *Dunlop v Selfridge*,[11] and again in the *Midland Silicones* case, as already mentioned.[12]

Yet, within a few years, the Privy Council, in *The Eurymedon*, on appeal from New Zealand, on facts very similar to those in *Midland Silicones*, reached what was, in effect, the opposite conclusion.[13] The sequence of changes of judicial opinion, particularly the strong language of Viscount Simonds in *Midland Silicones* followed by *The Eurymedon* supplies an example of an orthodoxy 'as well-established as any in our law' being displaced, in this instance very quickly, by the force of practical considerations.[14] Formal reasons were given by the majority for the result, but these were (to say the least) strained, and can scarcely be reconciled with orthodox views on contract formation or on agency. It is clear that the perceived practical inconveniences of the old rule played a crucial role. Lord Wilberforce, for the majority, summarising the reasons for the result, said:

> It should not be overlooked that the effect of denying validity to the clause would be to encourage actions against servants, agents and independent contractors in order to get round exemptions (which are almost invariable and often compulsory) accepted by shippers against carriers, the existence, and presumed efficacy, of which is reflected in the rates of freight. [Their Lordships] see no attraction in this consequence.[15]

Though formally presented as though it were an afterthought ('it should not be overlooked that…') it is clear from the context[16] that the thought embodied in

[7] *Dutton v Poole* (1689) 2 Lev 210, affd T Raym 302.

[8] *Tweddle v Atkinson* (1861) 1 B & S 393, 30 LJQB 265.

[9] F Pollock, Principles of Contract at Law and in Equity (Stevens & Sons, 1876) 190.

[10] W Anson, Principles of the English Law of Contract and of Agency in its Relation to Contract (Clarendon Press, 1879) 200.

[11] *Dunlop Pneumatic Tyre Co Ltd v Selfridge & Co Ltd* [1915] 1 AC 847 (HL).

[12] *Scruttons Ltd v Midland Silicones Ltd* (n 6).

[13] *New Zealand Shipping Co Ltd v A M Satterthwaite & Co Ltd* (The Eurymedon) [1975] 1 AC 154 (PC).

[14] See also *Beswick v Beswick* [1968] AC 5 (HL), and *Woodar Investment Development Ltd v Wimpey Construction UK Ltd* [1980] 1 WLR 277 (HL), 300 (Lord Scarman) indicating that, if Parliament failed to amend the law, the courts would be likely to do so.

[15] *New Zealand Shipping Co Ltd v A M Satterthwaite & Co Ltd* (n 13) at 169.

[16] In the summary of Lord Wilberforce's conclusion, suggesting implicit recognition that the preceding formal reasons, standing alone, were inadequate.

these words was highly influential. This was substantially the very same argument that had been made by Lord Denning, dissenting in *Scruttons Ltd v Midland Silicones Ltd*,[17] but summarily rejected by the majority there, only 13 years earlier, as heretical. The Supreme Court of Canada, in effect reversing a recent decision of its own, accepted that, in appropriate cases, the rule of privity should be relaxed.[18] Practical considerations were plainly influential: the Chief Justice of Nova Scotia pointedly remarked, in the intermediate court in the earlier Canadian case, that the (orthodox) result, permitting the personal liability of negligent employees (the employer being protected by an exemption clause), 'flies in the face of common sense, modern commercial practice, and labour relations.'[19] In England a similar (though not identical) conclusion was effected by statute at the end of the twentieth century.[20]

III. Vicarious Liability

Another illustration of the force of practical considerations is the expansion of vicarious liability in response to a perceived need to give a practical remedy for the sexual abuse of children. Fifty years ago it was confidently asserted that vicarious liability only applied where there was an employment relationship between the defendant and the wrongdoer, and where the wrongful act was committed in the course of the employment. A typical statement of the law was: 'The master is liable for any tort which the servant commits in the course of his employment.'[21] Two cases were decided together by the Supreme Court of Canada in 1999, both involving sexual assault on children. In the first case, the assault was committed by an employee of a residential home for children. Criminal assault was plainly outside the duties of the employee, and so the assault could not readily be said to meet the test of having occurred 'in the course of employment.' Nevertheless the court, quoting the Australian scholar John Fleming, unanimously held the employer to be liable:

> Fleming has identified similar policies lying at the heart of vicarious liability. In his view, two fundamental concerns underlie the imposition of vicarious liability: (1) provision of a

[17] *Scruttons Ltd v Midland Silicones Ltd* [1962] 1 AC 446, 467–68, (HL). The same point had also been made by Scrutton LJ, dissenting in the Court of Appeal, in *Patterson Zochonis & Co v Elder, Dempster Co Ltd* [1923] 1 KB 441–42, revd (but not overtly on the basis of Scrutton's argument) [1924] AC 522 (HL).

[18] *London Drugs Ltd v Kuehne & Nagel Int Ltd* [1992] 3 SCR 299, effectively reversing *Greenwood Shopping Plaza Ltd v Beatty* [1980] 2 SCR 228.

[19] *Greenwood Shopping Plaza v Neil J Buchanan Ltd* (1979) 99 DLR (3d) 289 (NSCA), at 295 (MacKeigan CJNS).

[20] Contracts (Rights of Third Parties) Act 1999.

[21] JA Jolowicz and TE Lewis (eds), *Winfield on Tort* 7th edn (Sweet & Maxwell, 1963) 732.

> just and practical remedy for the harm; and (2) deterrence of future harm. While different formulations of the policy interests at stake may be made (for example, loss internalization is a hybrid of the two), I believe that these two ideas usefully embrace the main policy considerations that have been advanced. First and foremost is the concern to provide a just and practical remedy to people who suffer as a consequence of wrongs perpetrated by an employee. This principle of fairness applies to the employment enterprise and hence to the issue of vicarious liability. While charitable enterprises may not employ people to advance their economic interests, other factors, discussed below, make it fair that they should bear the burden of providing a just and practical remedy for wrongs.[22]

The phrase 'just and practical remedy,' occurs three times in this short passage.

The second case, decided at the same time by the same panel of judges, also involved a sexual assault on a child, but in this case the employer was a young people's club and the assault occurred away from the club premises. In this case the court held, by a majority of four to three, that the club was not liable. McLachlin J, who had given the unanimous judgment of the court in the first case, dissented in the second case. Interestingly, the majority in the second case were also influenced by practical considerations, but these tended (in their opinion) to displace liability:

> If the Boys' and Girls' Club of Vernon were vicariously responsible for damages arising out of the criminal conduct of its employee Griffiths, which so far as this appeal is concerned must be taken to have been unknown, unauthorized and unforeseen, then it would be difficult to imagine many enterprises whose mandate includes mentoring or role models for children being able to escape vicarious liability to provide financial compensation for criminal sexual abuse by an employee. While on the positive side such an all-embracing attribution of no-fault liability would assist victims in the position of the appellants, it would also change the legal ground rules under which recreational organizations were thought to be governed under the existing case law. These organizations could be expected to respond rationally, if reluctantly, to a new harbinger of financial liability. They might vote with their feet. It is therefore important that here, as elsewhere, the test for vicarious liability... be applied with serious rigour.[23]

Both cases demonstrate the influence of practical considerations, but, in the minds of the majority in the second case, the crucial consideration was that people might be deterred from offering beneficial social services ('they might vote with their feet'). These two cases together demonstrate the strong influence of practical considerations, and demonstrate also some of their dangers if allowed free rein: practical considerations may cut in opposite directions, and judges are quite likely to be divided in their opinions. Related consequences are that the law is capable of rapid and radical change in the light of changing social conditions and changing judicial attitudes; from one point of view these are merits, but they come at the expense of predictability, stability and conceptual coherence.

[22] *Bazley v Curry* [1999] 2 SCR 534 at [29], followed in *Lister v Hesley Hall Ltd* [2002] 1 AC 215 (HL).
[23] *Jacobi v Griffiths* [1999] 2 SCR 570, at [30].

Practicalities include the consideration that a proposed legal rule must be capable of practical application without creating anomalies between fundamentally similar cases: a legal rule is not acceptable if it fails to ensure that like cases are decided alike, or if it is apt in practice to make important legal results turn on variations in facts that have no rational relationship to the justice of the result. Formerly, vicarious liability had been supposed to be part of the law relating to employment, but it was immediately clear from the reasoning in *Bazley v Curry* that the principle could not be confined to cases where there was an employment relationship between the defendant and the wrongdoer. The reasoning as to enterprise liability, the internalisation of costs and the desirability of strong incentives to take care in selecting staff applies with equal force to independent contractors and with even greater force to volunteers, and the Supreme Court mentioned 'agents' and 'volunteers'.[24] In 2012 a further important extension was made by the UK Supreme Court, which held that liability could be imposed on a religious brotherhood for sexual assaults by one of its members, even though there was no employment relationship between the brotherhood and the offender, and the brotherhood did not manage the institution in which the offences occurred. The reasons for this extension of liability again stressed the practical need to ensure an effective remedy (ie, a remedy against a solvent defendant) for the victim:

> Vicarious liability is a longstanding and vitally important part of the common law of tort. A glance at the Table of Cases in *Clerk & Lindsell on Torts*... shows that in the majority of modern cases the defendant is not an individual but a corporate entity. In most of them vicarious liability is likely to be the basis upon which the defendant was sued. The policy objective underlying vicarious liability is to ensure, insofar as it is fair, just and reasonable, that liability for tortious wrong is borne by the defendant with the means to compensate the victim. Such defendants can usually be expected to insure against the risk of such liability, so that this risk is more widely spread. It is for the court to identify the policy reasons why it is fair just and reasonable to impose vicarious liability and to lay down the criteria that must be shown to be satisfied... Sexual abuse of children is now recognized as a widespread evil... the courts have been tailoring this area of the law by emphasising the importance of criteria that are particularly relevant to this form of wrong. In this way the courts have succeeded in developing the law of vicarious liability so as to ensure that a remedy for the harm caused by abuse is provided by those that should fairly bear that liability.[25]

The reference to insurance in this passage is significant. Theoretically, and formally, the fact that a particular defendant is insured cannot be a reason for imposing liability. If it were, a vicious circle would arise: a prospective insurer could not

[24] (n 22) at 563–65.

[25] *The Catholic Child Welfare Society v Various Claimants* [2012] UKSC 56, [2013] 2 AC 1, at [34]. Vicarious liability has also been extended to a prison authority where a prisoner negligently caused injury in the course of an activity organised by the authority: *Cox v Ministry of Justice* [2016] UKSC 10, [2016] AC 660.

estimate the risk because the very existence of insurance would drastically increase it; and to excuse a defendant because of the absence of insurance would be to reward the improvident, and to reward those sufficiently wealthy to self-insure. Yet few would doubt that, as a matter of history, the practice of insurance has influenced the law of torts in the twentieth century, as Professor Steve Hedley shows in his chapter in the present volume, and the law of contracts. Insurance considerations have tended to the enlargement of tort liability for personal injuries, and, on the other hand, to the enforcement of contractual clauses excluding liability for business risks, such as property damage, that are readily insurable.

IV. Contractual Interpretation

A further illustration lies in the field of interpretation, or construction, of contracts. It is very difficult to adopt a single or simple approach to contractual interpretation, because almost every proposition on the subject can be, and has been, contradicted by a counter-proposition, or drastically modified by an open-ended exception. The reason for the difficulty, it is suggested, lies in the practical consequences of interpretation. A judge construing a contract is not engaged simply in determining the meaning of a text, because, having interpreted the text the judge will be called upon immediately to give assent to the application of the interpretation, and therefore to the practical consequences that the application will entail, backed by the coercive power of the state. It is this feature that distinguishes legal interpretation from literary, historical or philosophical interpretation. An employee may agree to work for a 'year'. On its face this means 12 months, but on proof that the parties used the word 'year' to mean a theatrical season of six months (or that the employee understood the word in that sense, and the other party had reason to know that), the word will be interpreted accordingly. A contractual document may include a numerical figure, but on proof that a decimal point was omitted by accident, the document will be rectified accordingly. The practical consequence of ignoring the parties' actual agreement, or the meaning they gave to the words used, would be a gross and unjust enrichment of the one party and a ruinous loss to the other, enforced by an officer of the state sworn to administer justice.

On the other hand, when judges have given effect to the face meaning of a contractual text (as in many cases they have rightly done), they have sometimes yielded to the temptation of making general assertions to some such effect as that the plain, literal and grammatical sense of the words must always prevail, or that extrinsic evidence is always as a matter of law inadmissible, or that prior negotiations cannot be referred to. These assertions also spring from a practical concern, namely that the stability, predictability and certainty of contracts will be undermined, and time and resources will be wasted if extrinsic evidence can too readily be introduced to vary the effect of contractual documents.[26] From the constant interaction of these two opposite sets of practical considerations spring the assertions of literalism, the dozens of exceptions to literalism, and the intractable difficulties of formulating any simple approach to contractual interpretation.

Implication of contractual terms is sometimes regarded as a process supplementary to, but separate from, interpretation,[27] and sometimes as an aspect of contractual interpretation.[28] The two approaches blend into each other: if interpretation cannot be made to yield a result that the court thinks practically necessary, the court has power to imply a term. As Lord Goff said, in interpreting a contract to avoid what he considered to be an unjust enrichment, '*if necessary*, a term will be implied into the contract to that effect.'[29] What would have made the implication *necessary* was the perceived practical need to avoid an unjust enrichment, by simple interpretation if possible, otherwise by implication of a term. From a conceptual point of view, interpretation of a text is distinct from the implication of a contractual term: by hypothesis, the implied term comes from a source other than the actual text. But when the court, in addressing the question of interpretation, is influenced by the thought that *if necessary* a term will be implied to secure the same practical effect as could be secured by interpreting the text in the way favoured by the court, a sharp distinction becomes impossible to maintain, because the court's interpretation of the text will necessarily be read in the light of the indication that the same practical result could, should and *would* have been attained by implying a term. In *Aberdeen City Council v Stewart Milne Group Ltd*[30] the UK Supreme Court had to decide whether a contractual clause entitling one of the parties to a bonus if land was sold for more than a certain price applied where a sale was made to an affiliated company for much less than the open-market price. Lord Hope held in favour of the pursuer on the basis of interpretation.[31] However, the words of the contractual text would have required a somewhat cumbersome gloss[32] to justify the result, and probably for this reason Lord Clarke preferred to reach the same result on the basis of an implied term: 'I would prefer to resolve this

[26] 'The law makes this distinction [between admissible background facts and inadmissible proof of subjective intentions] for reasons of practical policy'; Lord Hoffmann in *Investors Compensation Scheme Ltd v West Bromwich Building Society* [1998] 1 WLR 896 (HL), at 913.

[27] G Hall, *Canadian Contractual Interpretation Law* 2nd edn (LexisNexis, 2012) 150.

[28] *Attorney General of Belize v Belize Telecom Ltd* [2009] UKPC 11.

[29] *Pan Ocean Shipping Ltd v Creditcorp Ltd* [1994] 1 WLR 161 (HL) 164 (emphasis added).

[30] *Aberdeen City Council v Stewart Milne Group Ltd* [2011] UKSC 56, cited with approval in *Arnold v Britton* [2015] 2 WLR 1593 at [113–115], where, at [115], Lord Neuberger suggested that the result could also be explained 'as a case of correction by interpretation', suggesting a link with the concept of rectification, discussed below.

[31] ibid [20].

[32] Something would have to be read in to the effect that if a sale were to be made to a buyer dealing otherwise than at arms' length—which would have to be impliedly defined—the bonus would be calculated on the basis of the open-market value of the land—which would also require an implied definition.

appeal by holding that such a term should be implied rather than by a process of interpretation. *The result is of course the same.*'[33]

Since the three other judges agreed both with Lord Hope and with Lord Clarke, it may be concluded that they saw no sharp distinction between interpretation and implication, but they thought that by one means or the other, whichever was the more practically effective, the defender should be prevented from evading the obligation in question.[34]

The blurring of the distinction had important practical consequences, because its effect was to admit the full force of the pursuer's argument that the defender was seeking to evade the true spirit of the agreement, together with all surrounding facts tending to show what the true spirit of the agreement was. To the objection that extrinsic evidence is inadmissible, the answer would be that the parol evidence rule has not usually prevented proof of implied terms; to the objection that terms are only to be implied when strictly necessary to give efficacy to the agreement, the answer would be that the implied term is part of the interpretation of what the agreement is in the first place, and so conceptually prior to the question of giving efficacy to it.

On the power to imply terms, judicial assertions are to be found that are mutually irreconcilable: sometimes the courts have been very willing to imply terms, but, when an invitation to imply a term is refused courts have frequently issued very general and apparently uncompromising statements to the effect that the courts cannot make contracts for the parties, and that terms can only be implied in cases of the very strictest necessity, only to avoid an 'absurdity', or only when they are so obvious that both parties would certainly have conceded that the term in question 'went without saying'. There is no simple way of reconciling these contradictory statements. As Lord Wright wrote, three-quarters of a century ago, in discussing implied terms:

> The judge finds in himself the criterion of what is reasonable. The Court is in this sense making a contract for the parties—though it is almost blasphemy to say so. But the power of the Court to do this is most beneficial, and indeed even essential … Without this 'supplementing power' of the Court (as I choose to call it) it would often be practically impossible to make long forward contracts, because of the difficulty of seeing and providing for all possible contingencies.[35]

The reference to 'blasphemy' shows that Wright was conscious of the many judicial pronouncements apparently restricting the power of courts to imply terms; the

[33] ibid [33] (emphasis added).

[34] Another route to the same practical result might be through the concept of good faith, recently adopted by the Supreme Court of Canada as a 'general organizing principle': *Bhasin v Hrynew* 2014 SCC 71.

[35] Lord Wright of Durley, 'Some Developments of Commercial Law in the Present Century' reprinted in *Legal Essays and Addresses* (Cambridge University Press, 1939) 259.

words 'beneficial', 'essential' and 'practically impossible' indicate the reasons why he thought it necessary to risk incurring the charge of blasphemy by doubting those pronouncements.

A somewhat similar analysis may be made of the relation between interpretation and rectification (reformation). Historically, and conceptually, interpretation and rectification are quite separate concepts. By hypothesis, the process of rectification assumes the existence of a text that, as properly interpreted, mistakenly records the parties' true agreement: if it were not so, the court of equity would have had no reason and no power to intervene. But when the processes of interpretation and rectification are considered together by a single court, it becomes clear that they cannot be dissociated, especially in view of the modern relaxation of several of the restrictions formerly associated with rectification, and which had served to insulate rectification from the ordinary process of interpretation.[36] In *Chartbrook Ltd v Persimmon Homes Ltd*[37] the House of Lords dealt with the effect of a disputed contractual clause. The lower courts had interpreted the clause in favour of Chartbrook. The House of Lords took the opposite view. Lord Hoffmann said, after an extensive discussion of the law relating to rectification, 'on the assumption that the judge was right in his construction ... both parties were mistaken in thinking that it reflected their prior consensus and Persimmon was entitled to rectification.'[38] He then immediately added: 'Since, however, I think that the judge and the majority of the Court of Appeal were wrong on the question of construction, I would allow the appeal on that ground.'[39]

Evidently, the question of interpretation was here very closely linked with that of rectification. The reader cannot avoid the conclusion that the process of interpretation of the document in question was (to say the least) influenced by the knowledge that, if the interpretation argument failed, the rectification argument would—and *should*, for persuasive reasons of justice—succeed, with the same result. The combining of rectification arguments with questions of interpretation has the additional consequence of effectively eliminating any restraints (which may seem, as the law now stands, to vary in different common law jurisdictions) on admissibility of extrinsic evidence, because all relevant evidence of the parties' intentions is admissible in a claim for rectification, which will usually be pleaded as

[36] These relaxations include the recognition that rectification is appropriate where there was no mistake as to the actual text, but the parties mistakenly supposed it to have a particular meaning or legal effect; the abandonment of the need for proof of a completed agreement anterior to and separate from the writing; the recognition that rectification (perhaps with an option to rescind) may be appropriate where the parties in fact differed in their (subjective) intentions, but where the party favoured by the face meaning of the document had reason to know of the other's different intention; and the weakening or abandonment of the need for a specially onerous burden of proof.

[37] *Chartbrook Ltd v Persimmon Homes Ltd* [2009] 1 AC 1101.

[38] ibid [66].

[39] ibid [67].

an alternative,[40] and it is unrealistic to suppose that evidence of the parties' intentions and negotiations, admitted and considered by the judge in relation to the claim for rectification, can be excluded from the judicial mind on the question of interpretation if (as in *Chartbrook*) a result favouring one party on interpretation would be bound to be instantly reversed, in practical effect, by a result favouring the other party on rectification. The considerations of equity and justice that underlie a successful claim for rectification, especially the avoidance of unjust enrichment, cannot be excluded from the process of interpretation. In the earlier case of *Prenn v Simmonds*[41] where the literal meaning of the document tended to favour Prenn,[42] but where consideration of the overall purpose of the transaction, combined with general considerations of fairness and justice, tended to favour Simmonds, the trial judge decided for Prenn on interpretation, but ordered rectification in favour of Simmonds. The House of Lords also decided in favour of Simmonds, but based the result on interpretation. Lord Wilberforce concluded that:

> To sum up, Mr Prenn's construction does not fit in any way the aim of the agreement, or correspond with good sense, nor is it, even linguistically, acceptable. The converse of each of these propositions applies to Dr Simmonds's interpretation. I would accept it.
>
> *It follows, in consequence, that the alternative claim for rectification does not arise.* But I take this opportunity of stating, as it was drawn to the attention of the House by counsel at the bar, that the report of the judgment of Simonds J in *Crane v Hegeman-Harris Inc* which is contained in the All England Reports …—a judgment which has been much quoted and relied upon—appears to be incomplete, omitting several pages. A full transcript was made available to your lordships and should be consulted on future occasions.[43]

Lord Wilberforce stated that the claim for rectification 'does not arise.' If this means that the court's formal reasons did not depend on rectification, it is, of course, correct, but from the standpoint of an observer interested in judicial method, or of a historian interested in what actually occurred in the decision-making process, it is evident from the immediately following reference to the *Crane* case (a case on an important, and then disputed, aspect of rectification), that the question of rectification *had*, as a matter of fact, arisen, that it was extensively argued by counsel, and carefully considered even to the extent of tracking down the transcript of a misreported judgment. Evidently the possibility of a successful claim for rectification was in Lord Wilberforce's mind as he progressed towards his conclusion on the question of interpretation: indeed, the very same reasons that had induced the

[40] A former Lord Justice of Appeal has said that 'all but the most negligent of counsel will have pleaded rectification of the writing as well as the construction of the writing that best suits his client's interests'; R Buxton, '"Construction" and Rectification after Chartbrook' (2010) 69 *Cambridge Law Journal* 253.

[41] *Prenn v Simmonds* [1971] 1 WLR 1381 (HL).

[42] As held by the trial judge, and as Lord Diplock was inclined to hold; see (n 44) below.

[43] *Prenn v Simmonds* [1971] 1 WLR 1389 (emphasis added).

first-instance judge to decree rectification (giving effect to the true purpose of the agreement, and avoidance of unjust enrichment by mistake) offer a fair summary of Lord Wilberforce's reasons for his conclusion on interpretation. Once interpretation and rectification are perceived as alternative routes to the same destination, interpretation will often appear to be the easier way,[44] because, as is shown by Lord Wilberforce's reference to *Crane*, it avoids the need to grapple with contentious arguments, and to attempt to reconcile conflicting and sometimes badly reported cases about possible restrictions on the power of the court to rectify.[45] But it does not follow from the omission of the court expressly to base its conclusion on rectification that the possibility of rectification had, in fact, no influence on the result. It seems probable that the Law Lords adopted an interpretation favourable to Simmonds partly because they perceived the force of the evidence supporting the claim for rectification, and approved of the result, but were happy to avoid the difficult legal questions associated with rectification and its relation with interpretation.

V. Malicious Prosecution

A recent illustration of the force of practical considerations in considering a change in tort law is the case of *Crawford Adjusters v Sagicor General Insurance (Cayman) Ltd*[46] decided by the Judicial Committee of the Privy Council in 2013. This was a decision of a five-judge panel, sharply divided in their opinions. Lord Sumption, dissenting, went so far as to seek to limit the effect of the majority decision by saying that the decision would not affect English law, which could only be altered by a decision of the UK Supreme Court. Technically, no doubt, this is correct, since the Privy Council (hearing an appeal from the Cayman Islands) is not, strictly speaking, an English court. But the board of five judges were all members of the UK Supreme Court, and normally a decision of the Privy Council on a point of English law would be treated as an 'authority' by English courts, even though technically non-binding.

[44] The other members of the court agreed with Lord Wilberforce. Lord Diplock indicated that he was uneasy on the interpretation point, but added that 'such doubts as I have are not strong enough to justify my differing from the remainder of your Lordships' (ibid 1390). His reluctant acquiescence shows (by his reluctance) that he felt the force of the argument for a literal interpretation of the text, and (by his acquiescence) that he was not anxious to tackle the rectification point.

[45] *Crane v Hegeman-Harris Co Inc* [1939] 1 All ER 662. The omitted passage (see [1971] 3 All ER 245-8n, [1971] 1 WLR 1395–99) consists of a detailed analysis of the parties' negotiations, an approach that would have been difficult to integrate with Lord Wilberforce's confident assertion of a strict rule excluding evidence of negotiations, and 'a fortiori of Dr Simmonds's intentions,' (1385) on the question of interpretation.

[46] *Crawford Adjusters v Sagicor General Insurance (Cayman) Ltd* [2013] UKPC 17.

The issue was whether the tort of malicious prosecution applied to maliciously instituted civil proceedings. The majority (Lords Wilson and Kerr, and Lady Hale) held that it did. The facts were that an insurance company had brought a civil action against an insurance adjuster (Paterson) alleging that Paterson had fraudulently caused the insurance company to overpay a contractor for rebuilding work following hurricane damage. The allegations were published in a local newspaper and caused substantial damage. The main action was discontinued just before trial, and Paterson counter-claimed for abuse of process and malicious prosecution.

The claim based on abuse of process failed for lack of proof of a purpose outside the scope of the action, but the claim for malicious prosecution succeeded. Whether or not the decision is ultimately accepted in English law, or in other jurisdictions, the reasoning of both majority and dissenters raises issues highly relevant to the present enquiry.

Both majority and dissenters were influenced by whether other legal devices (notably, costs, defamation proceedings and undertakings) gave a sufficient remedy *in practice*. The majority thought that they did not. But the dissenters (Lords Neuberger and Sumption) thought that this argument was overridden by a different practical consideration, namely, the probable consequences of permitting the action: deterrence of meritorious litigation (the 'chilling effect' argument), and the possibility of successive litigation and counter-litigation (the 'loss of finality' argument). Lord Kerr said that 'conclusions on matters of policy in the legal context are not usually the product of empirical research. Customarily they are formed instinctually and constitute, at most, informed guesswork about the impact that the selection of a particular policy course will have.'[47] As is shown by the judicial difference of opinion in the *Crawford* case and also in *Jacobi v Griffiths* discussed above, 'guesswork' on such questions is apt to differ very sharply, suggesting that there must be some scope for empirical research, at least as an aid to judicial assessment of the accuracy of assumptions about the practical effect of proposed legal rules.

The approach of both majority and dissenters to earlier decisions invoked presumed practical considerations that were taken to have influenced those decisions. A quite recent House of Lords case[48] was distinguished by the majority on the basis that Lord Steyn in that case had (wrongly in Lord Wilson's opinion) thought that 'for essentially practical reasons' the extension of the tort to civil proceedings was not *necessary*. A different historical view of this practical question therefore justified the opposite legal conclusion in 2013. Lord Sumption, dissenting, considered that the whole basis of the tort of malicious prosecution was a response to the 'serious social evil' of abusive private prosecutions, and, these being, in his opinion, obsolete, the tort itself was of dubious value—or, at least, it was not to be extended. The dissenters stressed the practical dangers of extending the tort.

[47] ibid [94].
[48] *Gregory v Portsmouth City Council* [2000] 1 AC 419.

Lord Sumption explained the past distinction between civil and criminal proceedings as dependent on the fact that costs could be awarded to a successful defendant in civil proceedings (but not usually in criminal proceedings), giving the claimant a practical remedy, and so extension of the tort of malicious prosecution to civil proceedings was unnecessary. He thought that the practical effects of the rule proposed by the majority would be troublesome: 'even if the judges were Herculean, it would be pointless to cut off the head of the Lernaean Hydra merely to see it grow two more in its place'.[49] The word 'pointless' in this colourful classical allusion indicates Lord Sumption's concern with practicalities. Lord Neuberger, also dissenting, explained the anomalous group of cases where the action had admittedly been allowed in respect of certain kinds of civil proceedings as depending on the idea that in those kinds of case (bankruptcy petitions, etc) the claimant had no other practical remedy for the damage. Both dissenting judges stressed that the proposed new rule would complicate the law and require courts to determine difficult questions in the context of family proceedings, malicious defences and civil proceedings other than actions.

These pervasive practical considerations, manifest both in the majority and in the minority opinions, show why attention to the practical element in legal reasoning is necessary, and also why it has not always been welcomed. 'Informed guesswork' is not, at first glance, intellectually appealing, and it introduces a perpetual and radical instability, since perceptions of what is practically desirable vary from time to time, from place to place, and from judge to judge, as the *Crawford* case, with its extensive historical and comparative discussion of English and American law, well demonstrates. A commentator might regret this aspect of legal reasoning, but I doubt that any would deny that it has been, as a matter of history, and that it remains, a pervasive feature of the law.

VI. Constructive Trusts

There has been a sharp conflict of judicial and academic opinion on the question of the proprietary implications of constructive trusts. While some courts and commentators have welcomed the concept of the 'remedial' constructive trust as a useful and flexible tool of practical justice,[50] others have objected to a discretionary power to create retrospective property rights. Professor Birks wrote, in a vigorous book review:

> He [the author of the book under review] takes the view that proprietary rights are trivial constructs, constantly changing and therefore evidently malleable … Consequently he

[49] *Crawford Adjusters v Sagicor General Insurance* (n46) 144.

[50] *Pettkus v Becker* [1980] 2 SCR 834, *Peter v Beblow* [1993] 1 SCR 980, *Soulos v Korkontzillas* [1997] 2 SCR 217.

> sees no inherent difficulty in a discretionary, retrospective property right … This cavalier attitude to property must be rejected. Property rights cannot be deconstructed … [T]he discretion which the author favours would compel judges to do something for which they are no better qualified than any drinker propping up a bar … Put in plain language it is politically repulsive and intellectually disreputable.[51]

But four years later Birks wrote that whether or not a wrong or an unjust enrichment has a proprietary consequence 'is a matter of choice, not logic.'[52]

The question of the proprietary implications of the constructive trust arose in a series of cases concerning bribes, or secret commissions. In *Attorney General for Hong Kong v Reid*,[53] the Judicial Committee of the Privy Council, on appeal from New Zealand, held, departing from a case that had stood for more than a century,[54] that bribes received by a government official, and traceable proceeds of them, were held on a constructive trust for the government. The result was plainly influenced by practical considerations, the Judicial Committee saying that 'bribery is an evil practice which threatens the foundations of any civilized society … [and the court should prevent the property from being] sold and the proceeds whisked away to some Shangri La which hides bribes'.[55]

Subsequently the English Court of Appeal refused to follow the decision in *Reid*, the judgment of the court being given by Lord Neuberger MR,[56] but, three years later, the *Reid* case was effectively restored by the UK Supreme Court in *FHR European Ventures LLP v Cedar Capital Partners LLC*.[57] Lord Neuberger, by then the President of the Supreme Court, giving the judgment of a seven-member panel, in a change of opinion that he said extra-judicially might be thought to be a 'Damascene conversion',[58] introduced the question by saying that 'the decision as to which view is correct must be based on legal principle, decided cases, policy considerations, and *practicalities*.'[59] Though 'practicalities' occurs last in this list, the reasoning, the result and Lord Neuberger's change of opinion show that the concept of practicalities was highly influential. The court started by pointing out that the question was 'important in practical terms',[60] and, after grappling with

[51] P Birks, 'Book Review' (1999) 115 *LQR* 681, 685–86.

[52] P Birks, *Unjust Enrichment* (Oxford University Press, 2003) 31, referring, without disapproval, to *Attorney General for Hong Kong v Reid* [1994] 1 AC 324 and *Chase Manhattan Bank NA Ltd v Israel-British Bank (London) Ltd* [1981] Ch 105.

[53] ibid.

[54] *Lister v Stubbs* (1890) 45 Ch D 1 (CA).

[55] *Attorney General for Hong Kong v Reid* (n 51).

[56] *Sinclair Investments (UK) Ltd v Versailles Trade Finance Ltd* [2011] EWCA Civ 347, [2012] Ch 453.

[57] *FHR European Ventures LLP v Cedar Capital Partners LLC* (n 5).

[58] 'The Remedial Constructive Trust—Fact or Fiction?', Banking Services and Finance Law Association Conference, Queenstown, 10 August, 2014, para 2. It should be noted that the court in *Sinclair* considered itself bound by the 1890 Court of Appeal decision in *Lister*, but Lord Neuberger indicated then that he also favoured the result on principle.

[59] *FHR European Ventures LLP v Cedar Capital Partners LLC* (n 5) (emphasis added).

[60] ibid [1].

difficult and fine distinctions among the decided cases, gave as a principal reason for adopting a clear rule on the question (in favour of the proprietary claim) that 'it would be artificial, *impractical* and absurd if the issue whether a principal had a proprietary interest in a bribe to his agent depended on the mechanism agreed between the briber and the agent for payment of the bribe',[61] mentioning again, in conclusion, the influence of 'considerations of practicality and principle'.[62] Lord Neuberger was very anxious to reject the concept of 'remedial constructive trust';[63] the alternative, the 'institutional constructive trust' has commonly been supposed to depend on a pre-existing proprietary interest (or an analogous interest),[64] but it could not realistically be said, in many of the cases considered and approved by Lord Neuberger in *FHR*, that the principal had anything like a proprietary interest in the bribe or commission before it was paid to the agent; an agent's opportunity to take bribes is not an opportunity that in any real sense belongs to the principal, and to say that the payment, when made, became the principal's property is to assume the answer to the question in issue. Three weeks after the decision in *FHR* Lord Neuberger made an extra-judicial speech in which he said, after referring to the decision:

> There is much to be said for the [view that the] notion of a remedial constructive trust displays equity at its flexible flabby worst. I will seek to show, at least arguably, that it is unprincipled, incoherent and impractical, that it renders the law unpredictable, that it is an affront to the common law view of property rights and interests, that it involves the court usurping the role of the legislature, and, as if that were not enough, that the development of the remedial constructive trust is largely unnecessary. Apart from that, it's a pretty good concept.[65]

The thrust of this passage (at least for the sake of argument on the particular occasion)[66] is to reject the remedial constructive trust on formal grounds, but the inclusion of the words 'impractical' and 'unnecessary' shows that practical considerations were not absent from the speaker's mind. An alignment, or interdependence, as well as a tension, between formal and practical considerations is not uncommon. My suggestion is not that the decision in *FHR* was wrong, but that the reasoning of the court came closer to accepting the concept of remedial constructive trust than Lord Neuberger chose to admit. Although the court did not

[61] ibid [39] (emphasis added).

[62] ibid [46].

[63] ibid [47].

[64] Thus, Lord Neuberger in the *Sinclair* (n 56) case, at [88] had said that a constructive trust was not appropriate 'unless the asset or money is or has been beneficially the property of the beneficiary or the trustee acquired the asset or money by taking advantage of an opportunity or right which was properly that of the beneficiary'.

[65] 'The Remedial Constructive Trust—Fact or Fiction?' (n 57) para 6.

[66] The general tone of the speech (n 58) is rather light, and Lord Neuberger says in the final paragraph [42] that he may have exaggerated the case against the remedial constructive trust.

envisage the exercise of wide judicial discretion in particular cases that fell within the new rule, a limited discretion will be required (in the sense that all equitable remedies are 'discretionary') in order to assess the traditional equitable defences.[67] Moreover, the court in *FHR* plainly had a choice to make, and when a new case arises that does not fall precisely within the rule established there,[68] it will be open to a future court to make a similar choice on similar considerations, including practicalities, not very different from the considerations that would apply in a jurisdiction that accepted the concept of remedial constructive trust.

VII. The Importance of Historical Evidence

Instances demonstrating the influence of practical considerations on legal reasoning could readily be multiplied, but multiplication of instances beyond a certain point is unlikely to be fruitful, though, interestingly, for two opposite reasons: some will tend to say that it is unnecessary because the proposition that the law is practical is so obviously true that it needs no elaborate demonstration; others will say with Sir William Jones that 'if law be a *science*, and really deserve so sublime a name, it must be founded on principle, and claim an exalted rank in the empire of *reason*',[69] and, therefore, that merely practical considerations ought to be excluded from judicial reasoning (apparent exceptions being regrettable anomalies). Perhaps it might be more fruitful to think in terms of the two possible responses existing in mutual tension within the mind of each individual reader or listener, rather than dividing the audience into two separate groups, for many observers are pulled simultaneously in both directions. The line of thought that seeks a rational, consistent, stable and universal explanation of law will tend to see all apparent counter-examples, however many might be adduced, as anomalies. The appearance of a 'wild card' in the form of practical considerations tends to be unfriendly to any attempt to establish unchanging legal rules based exclusively on principle and reason. The rejection, for opposite reasons, of the significance of practical reasoning in law is itself a phenomenon worthy of consideration, for rejection of a proposition for opposite reasons usually points to an unresolved tension that warrants further attention.

It may seem elementary to say that assertions about the past should be tested by historical evidence, but, if this is to be done in the legal context, historical and non-historical assertions about the law must be disentangled, for different kinds of evidence are appropriate to each. Failure to recognise this can lead to strange

[67] As pointed out by W Gummow, 'Bribes and Constructive Trusts' (2015) 131 *LQR* 21, 26.
[68] An example might be a payment made to induce a breach of contract.
[69] W Jones, *An Essay on the Law of Bailment* (Printed for J Nichols for Charles Dilly, 1781) 123.

results. Consider the statement of the unanimous Supreme Court of Canada two years after the Canadian vicarious liability cases mentioned above:

> In general tort law attempts to hold persons accountable for their wrongful acts and omissions and the direct harm that flows from those wrongs. Vicarious liability, by contrast, is considered to be a species of strict liability because it requires no proof of personal wrongdoing on the part of the person who is subject to it. As such, it is still relatively uncommon in Canadian tort law.[70]

This last sentence is, to say the least, a strange statement. As the UK Supreme Court rightly pointed out in the quotation given above from the *Various Claimants* case, vicarious liability has not been 'relatively uncommon,' either in English or in Canadian tort law. On the contrary, it has been frequent throughout the twentieth and into the twenty-first century. The supposition that vicarious liability has been rare springs from a confusion of conceptual and historical propositions. If one starts with the premise that the only proper basis for civil liability is fault, of course it follows that liability without fault (including vicarious liability) may be described as anomalous. But there is a tendency to slide from the idea that vicarious liability is conceptually anomalous to the historical assertion that it has actually been rare in practice. Then the proposition that liability without fault has been rare in practice is in turn used to support the suggestion that the law 'properly understood' has always required proof of fault, and that exceptions ought to be rejected. This intellectual slippage runs the dangers of serious confusion of thought, of the distortion of history, and of the promotion of covert alteration in the law while avoiding the need to adduce persuasive reasons for change.

VIII. Implications for the Study of Law

These considerations have implications for the academic study of law. If, as suggested, practical considerations have, in the past, had an important influence on the law, it cannot be desirable, in seeking to understand the law from any point of view, to neglect them. Insofar as the law reflects practical considerations these must be taken into account by scholars, even, or perhaps one should say especially, from a purely academic point of view. It cannot be good scholarship to distort or to misrepresent the past. Since about the last third of the twentieth century there has been a tendency, manifest now in law schools in many common law jurisdictions, to disparage the practical aspects of the study of law, and to seek to reduce or eliminate the links between law schools and legal practice. In a study of English law schools, published in 2004, Fiona Cownie found that law was 'a discipline in transition … from doctrine to socio-legal studies,' concluding that

[70] *67122 Ontario Ltd v Sagaz Industries Canada Inc* [2001] 2 SCR 983, 204 DLR (4th) 542, 551.

> in embarking on the journey away from its purely doctrinal roots, academic law is cutting its closest ties with the legal profession, and bringing itself much nearer to the heart of the academy … it is moving away from the exclusive concern with doctrine and in doing so it is moving closer to the heart of the academy.[71]

These observations accurately describe familiar trends, but they suggest a linear scale, implying that the more distant academic law becomes from practice, associated here with 'doctrine', the more truly scholarly it must be, and vice versa.

This linear metaphor might, I suggest, be questioned. The operation of practical considerations has been part of the law itself, and, therefore, both from a historical and from a conceptual point of view the influence of such considerations is a proper and indeed a necessary part of the academic study of law, even from the most purely scholarly point of view, because practical considerations constitute an essential part of the phenomenon under study. This is an approach that can appeal to scholars of many different kinds. Socio-legal scholarship is often concerned with the practical effects of the law, and, if legal doctrine itself includes practical considerations, doctrine cannot be alien to that scholarship. Professor Ernest Weinrib, in *Corrective Justice*, has written that 'law is a phenomenon that exists only through a set of legal doctrines, institutions, and juristic activities. The university study of law can therefore be nothing other than the study of the practice of law.'[72] Though Professor Weinrib was not referring directly to the practical aspect of legal reasoning considered here, the point he makes is highly relevant. Particular legal doctrines are always open to criticism, and bad doctrinal analysis is always objectionable, but the suggestion that legal doctrine itself is somehow unworthy of academic attention cannot be supported either from a historical or from any scholarly perspective. Changes in legal doctrine, often prompted, as we have seen, by practical considerations, are an important part of the history of the law. The history of the law includes its recent history, and legal doctrine is an integral part of the law itself, and therefore of the subject matter of any scholarly legal study.

Links with the legal profession may be positively useful to legal scholarship insofar as they draw attention to the practical effect and operation of legal rules and procedures. Doctrine implies learning, and though the claim of the profession to be 'learned' is less commonly heard than formerly, academic lawyers cannot entirely avoid a special regard for judges (and, by extension, for practitioners), for it is the judges who have shaped, and continue to shape, the law itself, the phenomenon that is the subject of the academic's attention. Legal academic writing has often involved a kind of dialogue, with the judges treated as part of the audience, rather than merely as part of the data. A good law school must not only supply a variety of perspectives, but must also (variety of perspectives implying the independent existence of the phenomenon observed) impart to its students

[71] F Cownie, *Legal Academics: Culture and Identities* (Hart Publishing, 2004) 54, 198, 199.
[72] E Weinrib, *Corrective Justice* (Oxford University Press, 2012) 299.

as complete an understanding as possible of the law as it has actually worked in practice in the past, including the recent past. It is likely that such an understanding will be useful to students intending to enter professional practice, and will be valued for this very reason by the more thoughtful members (present and future) of the legal profession. But that is not the primary reason for including the practical element of legal reasoning, and it does not follow that service to the profession is, or should be, in itself a primary object of academic legal education, or that the law schools should involve themselves directly in seeking to train lawyers for practice. The practical aspects of law should be valued by academics, but valued primarily for academic reasons, insofar as they contribute to a better understanding of the law itself. To quote Professor Weinrib again:

> A disjunction between the practice of law and its university study would indeed be disquieting. This is not, however, because the disjunction would be a disservice to the legal profession (though it might be), but rather because it would be a disservice to the university itself.[73]

The law is a social phenomenon, but it is not, itself, a social science,[74] and efforts to make it conform to the patterns of thought of social sciences, or of other academic disciplines, are unlikely to be successful. Ironically, but perhaps not surprisingly, the law schools are also and at the same time under an apparently opposite pressure to cater to the immediate needs—or supposed needs—of practising lawyers. It might be thought that two opposite pressures would cancel each other, or would balance, but there is a danger that, instead, the law schools may drift towards separate solitudes, to the detriment both of practice and scholarship, and of the academic discipline of law.

IX. Conclusion

Perhaps some insight may be derived from Guido Calabresi's metaphor of the cathedral. He wrote, in a footnote to what has become one of the most widely-cited articles in the field of law and economics, that the article 'is meant to be only *one* of Monet's paintings of the Cathedral at Rouen. To understand the Cathedral one must see all of them.'[75] Monet's series of about 30 paintings, of the west front of the cathedral in changing lights, were all made from a single vantage point. It

[73] ibid.

[74] See G Samuel, 'Is Law Really a Social Science? A View from Comparative Law' (2008) 67 *Cambridge Law Journal* 288.

[75] G Calabresi and AD Melamed, 'Property Rules, Liability rules, and Inalienability: One View of the Cathedral' (1972) 85 *Harvard Law Review* 1089, 1090, fn 2. 'View' is the root meaning of the word 'theory.' (OED).

would be a mistake to press a metaphor too far,[76] but it is a fair implication that, in Calabresi's mind, the number of possible views of the building was very large—perhaps infinite. All the views have something in common, however, namely, the fabric of the building itself. Parts of it must be interconnected with other parts, and some parts must support others in ways that might not be apparent from a single perspective, or in certain lights. The artist need not be a builder, but when alterations or additions are proposed, it will be advisable to consult those who understand how the building was constructed and what actually holds it together. Neglect of the practical dimension of legal reasoning tends to distortion of the legal past, and therefore to a diminished understanding of the law from every point of view.

[76] Evidently the metaphor was not casually chosen, since Calabresi included in his footnote a reference to a published lecture by a Yale professor of art history (G Hamilton, *Claude Monet's Paintings of Rouen Cathedral* (Oxford University Press, 1960)) specifically on Monet's series of Rouen paintings.

16

Corrective Justice—An Idea Whose Time Has Gone?

STEVE HEDLEY*

Of all the subjects studied in the modern legal academy, tort and contract can probably claim to be the closest to their pre-twentieth century roots. Most legal subjects are much younger: labour law, administrative law, social security law were all twentieth century creations, and it is not really to the point that the courts were concerned with those topics long before. Constitutional Law, property, family law and criminal law have been in the academy longer, in some cases as long as tort and contract, but have changed utterly over that period—a trained nineteenth-century constitutionalist or family lawyer would be taken aback, perhaps even appalled, at what those subjects have become. Tort and contract lawyers, not so much. A nineteenth-century tort lawyer might be startled at how much the law had expanded its range today, but the general coverage of issues would not be much of a shock; and a nineteenth-century contract lawyer might be very pleasantly surprised at how little had changed, at how the basic approach is remarkably similar, and that statute had made so few inroads into basic common law principles.

Contract and tort, then, develop slowly when they develop at all, and this even though they are very active areas when it comes to litigation. One might wonder what there is left to discover about them, at least at the level of fundamental principle. This is why it is so surprising that in recent years there has been so much excitement around the theory of corrective justice that is now being proposed to explain them. It is not a new theory, to be sure—indeed, several of its proponents refer us back several centuries, to Immanuel Kant or even to Aristotle, to explain their approach. However, it is now being proposed as the proper explanation of basic private law institutions, in preference to what are seen as modern heresies such as that they serve the common good, or are economically efficient, or something of the sort. Indeed, the antiquity of the theory may even be seen as an advantage, allowing its proponents to hint that they are propounding not simply truths, but *timeless* truths.

* Email: s.hedley@ucc.ie, private-law-theory.org. All comments, criticisms and suggestions for improvement are very welcome. Many thanks to Shane Kilcommins for help with this chapter.

I. What Is Corrective Justice?

There is no canonical version of corrective justice theory as applied to private law, and much of the literature is taken up with debating different versions of it. Nonetheless, the main elements of the approach are clear enough. This article focuses on the theories of Coleman,[1] Weinrib[2] and Beever,[3] though it also makes reference to theorists influenced by them.[4] Naturally these writers do not have identical views on all issues, but the common ground between them is considerable, and the issue here is broad enough to encompass them all.

Suppose A deliberately and unjustifiably hits B, and B successfully sues A for compensation. What account can we give of why the law allows a remedy in such a case? One approach is to talk of the social purposes of the law, of how the law benefits us all in general. It is good that hitting people is discouraged—so it makes sense to allow a legal remedy that inconveniences A, and so perhaps deters A (and others) from hitting people so readily. B is perhaps injured and so deserves our sympathy and our help: an award of money might serve both purposes, providing recognition that B has suffered and covering some of the expenses incurred in consequence. So we *can* justify an award of damages—taking money from A and giving it to B—by reference to general aims pursued by the legal system, and placing the matter in a broader social context.

But, say the corrective justice theorists, to do so is to miss the point. It is not a coincidence that we want to take money from A *and* we also want the same sum to go to B: these things are related. And if we were really pursuing abstract social purposes, rather than something intrinsic to the relationship between A and B, those purposes would not coincide in this neat way. What is the best way to punish A for random violence might be a serious question with an uncertain answer; simply depriving A of a specific sum might not be the best way to do it. Equally, if we were really attentive to B's needs, this might not be the best way of fulfilling them. And it surely cannot be seen as a mere accident that the sum we wish to take from A is identical with the sum we wish to award to B. We are forced, therefore, by rational consideration of what the law provides, to the conclusion that it is not

[1] Especially as in J Coleman, *Risks and Wrongs* (Oxford University Press, 1992).

[2] Especially as in E Weinrib, *The Idea of Private Law* (Harvard University Press, 1995). See also the same author's *Corrective Justice* (Oxford University Press, 2012). Weinrib's examples in *The Idea of Private Law* tend to be drawn from tort, though he also sketches out how they apply to contract (at 50–53 and 136–40).

[3] Especially as in A Beever, 'The Law's Function and the Judicial Function' (2003) 20 *New Zealand Universities Law Review* 299, and *Rediscovering the Law of Negligence* (Hart Publishing, 2007).

[4] For other relevant work strongly influenced by corrective justice see S Smith, *Contract Theory* (Oxford University Press, 2004); R Stevens, *Tort and Rights* (Oxford University Press, 2007), and R Chambers, C Mitchell and J Penner (eds), *Philosophical Foundations of the Law of Unjust Enrichment* (Hart Publishing, 2009).

a matter of A alone or B alone, but a matter of what is just as between the two of them, excluding wider considerations.

> In corrective justice, then, the focus is on the *relationship between the parties* rather than on the parties as solitary individuals or as members of a wider community. We are interested in the wrongdoer only because he wronged the wrong-sufferer, and we are interested in the wrong-sufferer only because he was wronged by the wrongdoer. Hence, the reasons for holding the wrongdoer liable are the same reasons for finding that liability is owed to the wrong-sufferer. In corrective justice, the relationship between the parties forms a conceptual unity.[5]

It is this focus on the relationship between the parties—private law's *correlativity*, as it is termed—and its disdain for any broader social issues, that is the hallmark of corrective justice accounts. And when we look at the history of the law, this seems to point to something important—claimants under the forms of action were always under a burden not simply to explain why they deserved compensation, but why they deserved it *from the defendant they were now suing*, which chimes well with corrective justice. So far, so good.

But even seen through that historical lens, any exclusive theory of corrective justice reeks of overstatement. *Of course* the law was from the earliest days concerned with the relationship between claimant and defendant, but *why* was it so concerned? After all, the quarrel between A and B would certainly resolve itself one way or another even without the law's aid, perhaps going in favour of whoever had the larger cudgel, or the greater number of outraged relatives. While achieving justice between the parties was no doubt a consideration, the public interest was also served: providing a public forum for resolving grievances is one way of preventing other methods of dispute resolution, and so avoiding a threat to public order. Achieving corrective justice and maintaining public order are not opposed purposes, or at least not usually. So while it is legitimate to see corrective justice as playing a role in the law, it seems an error to conclude that this is *at the expense of* public purposes. Where corrective justice is part of the law, it is (at least in part) because it serves the public purpose that it should do so: and that part has been in steady decline from the middle of the nineteenth century to the present day. Private law has less and less to say on the personal relationship between the parties under consideration.

And it seems to sell modern *public* law short, to say that it is not really concerned with the relationship between A and B, or with fairness in that relationship. On the contrary, the public law response seems equally closely tied to it, perhaps more so than the private law response. A and B's relationship and previous dealings will be crucial in determining what defences are open to A, and how seriously the battery is viewed if there is no defence. A battery on a single occasion might demand a quite different response from a battery which was the culmination of a

[5] Beever, *Rediscovering Negligence* (n 3) 46 (footnote omitted).

series of harassing actions. And, of course, any close relationship between A and B changes the picture entirely—hitting your boss, hitting your drinking companion, hitting your child and hitting your spouse, are all serious matters, but serious matters likely to lead to quite different types of legal response. It is inaccurate, therefore, to say that public law is not concerned with the relationship between the parties. It is inaccuracy of a sort we are only likely to engage in if we accept the false distinction that corrective justice theorists try to force on us, that we have to *choose* between following broad public purposes and doing private justice between the parties. The two go hand in hand.

This raises in acute form the question of why corrective justice is *now* an issue, when it has always been one factor of importance in the law but never the whole truth. Why, suddenly, around the turn of the millennium, did we see an insistence that it is the key to the whole of private law, and that anyone who sees a significant role for public purposes within private law is making a mistake? This is very odd, especially since the overt role of the public within private law has been steadily growing for more than a century, and the situations where private law was traditionally thought relevant are now increasingly seen as public problems. (Issues over competing land uses are now part of planning law or environmental law; issues over preventable injuries are now matters of health and safety law; issues over unsatisfactory market transactions are now matters of consumer and trade regulation. In each case, the traditional common law approach is now simply one facet of a complex legal response to the problem.) We can speculate at various factors that might *now* make a corrective justice approach more attractive: the growth in status of public law, perhaps leading private lawyers to seek a similar status lest they simply be absorbed into public law; the growing sophistication of law-and-economics, which perhaps leads non-economists to feel they must develop a similarly sophisticated counter-theory. (Any serious account of relevant factors would have to distinguish, perhaps rather sharply, between different jurisdictions.) But whatever the reason, the emergence of a vocal corrective justice theory is clear enough, as is its influence in a wide variety of writing on tort and contract. And its leading feature has been the insistence on the *exclusivity* of corrective justice explanations—corrective justice is presented not as *part* of the explanation of private law, but as a *complete* explanation.

II. Assumptions

Current proponents of corrective justice take it to be a theory explaining private law, and to evaluate other, inconsistent, theories in the same spirit. The premise is that 'private law' calls for an explanation, and they seek to supply the best explanation. Unpacking this reveals two assumptions. Firstly, that their subject-matter is rigidly defined and requires some unitary explanation (though it need not explain *all* law). Secondly, a reluctance to commit themselves to a particular place and time (and so assuming that 'private law' has an essence which transcends particular legal jurisdictions). So a typical corrective justice theory of tort proposes that (say) tort is a coherent intellectual unity, but would be vague as to which jurisdiction it is describing, or at what date this description was being applied.

As to the first assumption, the usual approach is to propose a particular legal topic, and then to present corrective justice as the most convincing explanation of that topic—the alternative view is taken to consist of rival theories at a similar level of generality, and the existence of some such unitary explanation is taken for granted. What that topic is, depends on the writer. Weinrib's topic is private law: private law is wholly to be explained by corrective justice, and this includes both contract and tort.[6] Beever by contrast focuses on negligence, which he explains as an instantiation of corrective justice—he appears to concede (if only for the sake of argument) that other areas of tort may be based on other considerations.[7] Coleman's approach is more nuanced, contending that corrective justice does not explain all of tort law (indeed, he is rather vague about what his subject-matter is)[8] but the same binary opposition pervades his argument: the task he sets himself is to explain the 'core' of tort—a failure to provide a 'persuasive understanding' of this core would indicate that we 'simply [do] not understand tort law'—and his preferred explanation is corrective justice.[9]

It should be clear—though it is not very often remarked upon—that the controversial proposition here is one which corrective justice theorists assume, rather than one that they state. To say that areas of private law are somewhat influenced, or even *heavily* influenced, by considerations of interpersonal fairness would not be controversial, indeed it would seem to state the obvious. The controversial assertion is that these considerations of interpersonal fairness *wholly explain* particular areas of law, or constitute the *principal explanation* of it, claims which of course requires a strong definition of what those areas are. Because it is obvious that many factors appear in legal argument, any claim for the exclusivity or

[6] See especially Weinrib (n 2) ch 1, where he defines his task as being 'How are we to understand private law?' (1), which he takes to involve a choice between his own view and '[t]he usual view of legal scholars … that one understands law through its purposes' (3).

[7] Beever, *Rediscovering Negligence* (n 3) 70–71. Beever's reluctance to pronounce on other areas of tort is of course more about defining the scope of his book than about any broader doubts as to the relevance of corrective justice: 'I should perhaps confess that it is my belief that at least almost all of the law of tort, and the private law more generally, is based on corrective justice' (71). For another area of tort see the same author's *The Law of Private Nuisance* (Hart Publishing, 2013).

[8] Coleman (n 1) 198. Precisely what Coleman's subject-matter is is far from clear, not least because of his tendency to equate 'tort law' with 'accident law'—see (for example) 199, stating that his ch 18 concerns 'accident law', and ch 18 itself, which explicitly concerns tort law (361ff). Are those torts which do not involve accidents covered by Coleman's theory, or not? Or is Coleman's theory really a theory of negligence?

[9] Coleman (n 1) 199, which refers forward to his ch 19. By contrast, he argues that contract law has an economic explanation: chs 5–8.

primacy of one type of argument needs sharp fencing, to say which area is being so explained.[10]

The demonstration of the primacy of corrective justice usually takes the form of considering the merits of rival theories through this lens of the primary explanation—for example, the law-and-economics approach is considered and dismissed by Weinrib because if we sought to explain *all* of private law in that way, we would miss important features of it.[11] It is difficult, however, to find rival theories that can clearly be said to be engaged here. There are no multiple contenders to 'explain' the whole of private law: corrective justice theorists seem to be on their own here. The closest rival is indeed law-and-economics, but that discipline has long given up any attempt to explain why the legal system has the rules that it does.[12] If we are convinced that 'it takes a theory to beat a theory', then we can propose a 'pluralist' account of private law, which allows for many factors to influence it.[13] But such a theory is unlikely either to have a rigid view of what private law consists of, or to draw sharp contrasts between what private law does and what the rest of the law does. The fallacy is not that corrective justice has a major influence on the law, but that any one part of the legal system is truly distinct from any other part.

Where corrective justice theorists note this problem, they say it is a matter of coherence—if it were true that private law reflects a variety of concerns, perhaps mutually incompatible concerns, then it would be incoherent. Indeed, Weinrib seems to suggest that the law will be incoherent *whenever* it pursues several goals, because in some cases at least these goals will pull in different directions.[14] So, he says, it makes no sense to say that tort has the purpose *both* of compensating victims *and* of deterring wrongdoers: 'If compensation is justified at all, it is justified even for injuries that cannot be deterred. Similarly, if deterrence is justified, it is justified regardless of whether injury occurs ... The two goals do not coalesce into a single integrated justification'.[15] But if this is what we mean by incoherence, then incoherence is a fact of life. We ask many things of our legal system, and while

[10] As Dagan notes in the context of 'corrective justice' accounts of property, 'the integrity of private law does not require the neo-Kantians' more ambitious claims of an airtight distinction of private and public law and the exclusion of any collective or public value from our understanding of property. Quite the contrary': H Dagan, 'The Public Dimension of Private Property' (2012, ssrn.com/abstract=2045487) 1.

[11] Weinrib (n 2) 46–48. Coleman is less subject to this criticism, and indeed allows economic considerations considerable influence within tort (eg (n 1) 377–80); but this of course makes it very hard to discern precisely what his core contention actually is.

[12] 'This is a straw man. Of course, decades ago this was the project of Richard Posner. But the thought that efficiency analysis would provide a mechanism to predict the details of current doctrine is a serious misreading of the aims of modern scholarship': I Ayres, 'Valuing Modern Contract Scholarship' (2003) 112 *Yale Law Journal* 881, footnote omitted.

[13] eg H Dagan, 'Pluralism and Perfectionism in Private Law' (2011, ssrn.com/abstract=1868198).

[14] 'Understood from the standpoint of mutually independent goals, private law is a congeries of unharmonized and competing purposes' (Weinrib (n 2) 5).

[15] Weinrib (n 2) 38.

many of them are attainable, they are not *all completely* attainable because (as Weinrib notes) pushed to the absolute, they are not compatible with one another. Compromising between incompatible goals is not the same as abandoning those goals. The bar is being set too high—higher than corrective justice (or any other theory) can reach. As to this higher ideal of 'coherence', it is most unclear that it could ever be attained by any really-existing legal system; nor (given that it seems to require that we ignore most of the reasons why we want a legal system at all) is it obviously desirable. Humans are needy creatures, they want many things, and legal systems are one institution through which they get many of these things. Weinrib's 'coherence' seems more of a hindrance to this than a help; and a goal which is obviously unattainable needs careful justification.

As to the second assumption—the omnipresence and timelessness of corrective justice—it is often interesting to see how far you have to read a piece inspired by corrective justice concerns before you get any clue as to when or where it was written. Law differs from jurisdiction to jurisdiction; law changes from time to time. But for Weinrib and Beever at least, corrective justice is (apparently) timeless and omnipresent. Aristotle and Kant are cited on the assumption that they have something to tell us about 'the law'[16]—which, at least without further explanation, should be a deeply problematical claim for twenty-first century common lawyers. There is no sense of movement, of development, in these writings—legal change is barely acknowledged, and the only development deemed worthy of comment is over how explicitly the law commits itself to corrective justice. The whole panorama of legal development is before their eyes, but they do not see it.[17] Coleman is more aware of the complexities here, acknowledging that what a particular society makes of corrective justice will depend on what other moral practices that society accepts—an important insight, as it opens the way to a demonstration that the importance of corrective justice changes as the rest of society changes.[18] But this is still not quite the same thing as accepting that corrective justice itself changes. The same binary assumption remains: that at any one point, particular parts of the law will either test negative or test positive for corrective justice. These writers all assume that the essence of corrective justice is timeless, and that essence is either present or absent in particular legal systems at any one time.

[16] See eg Weinrib (n 2) ch 4.

[17] Beever (*Rediscovering Negligence* (n 3) 28–29) explicitly bases his understanding of negligence law on five 'great cases', which in historical order are *Palsgraf v Long Island Railroad Co* 162 NE 99 (NY CA 1928), *Donoghue v Stevenson* [1932] AC 562, *Bolton v Stone* [1951] AC 850, *The Wagon Mound (No 1)* [1961] AC 388 and *The Wagon Mound (No 2)* [1967] 1 AC 617. Beever is not much impressed by arguments stressing the historical context of decisions, even in relation to cases well outside the four decades his 'great cases' span—see for example his discussion (at 117) of *Winterbottom v Wright* (1842) 10 M&W 546, 152 ER 588.

[18] Coleman, *Risks and Wrongs* (n 1) 198–99 and ch 19.

It is important not to attack straw men here. When Beever and Weinrib attack modern case law developments by pointing out that they are departures from classic principles enunciated in famous old cases such as *Donoghue v Stevenson*,[19] it is tempting to accuse the corrective theorists of living in the past—much has happened over the last century that Lord Atkin could not have anticipated. Perhaps his vision for the law is in need of revision for a new century? But while there is truth in this, it misses a deeper point. All of us *live in the past* in the sense that our attitudes and our problem-solving techniques evolved to deal with problems that are now in the past and have been replaced by new, possibly quite different problems. In particular, it was perfectly natural that the courts of the late nineteenth century confronted the new problems they faced with old legal tools, focusing on the individual responsibility of the parties before them rather than looking wider. Only gradually was it appreciated that problems such as industrial injuries, pollution, road safety and properly regulated markets required collective solutions that the common law could not provide, and to which the common law could only contribute if adapted to be part of that collective provision. By the time 'classical' principles such as those in *Donoghue* were laid down, this process was well advanced: for example, as Lord Atkin would have known well, liability insurance was already very readily obtainable and was in some circumstances compulsory—and so the language of personal liability through tort which pervades his opinion was already to a great extent part of the past rather than the present. The truth is that tort law *never was* coherent, at least not in the sense that the corrective justice theorists use that word. Attempts to impose strict intellectual order on it have been rare, and never wholly successful. Indeed, it is hard to point to any area of common law that ever has been coherent, if 'coherence' is of the monomaniacal sort that corrective justice theorists demand. Attention to context has always been valued more than neatness of structure.

Yet it is by ignoring context that modern corrective justice theory flourishes, trying to argue from first principles about what form private law should take, while making no assumptions about what other institutions and resources are available to deal with the problems society has. The modern world has many features unknown to Aristotle and Kant and perhaps only dimly guessed at by Atkin, such as a massive governmental apparatus which consumes a large proportion of gross domestic product and from which, accordingly, a great deal is expected by the public, an all-pervasive health-and-safety culture, and an economy dominated not by individual traders but by huge multi-national corporations. *Of course* this affects how we view contract and tort principles. And if it is argued that the law's purposes have not really changed, the answer is that it is *people* who have purposes, and the context in which people are placed and decide what purposes are reasonable ones has changed a good deal. We cannot hope to explain the modern law of

[19] *Donoghue v Stevenson* [1932] AC 562.

obligations if we leave out the two most important things about it, namely that it is part of the legal system and that it is modern.

The assumption that private law forms a unit, not in the trivial sense that it can be discussed on its own, but in the fuller sense that we can explain it without looking to other areas of law and society, is naturally a hard one to sustain in argument. Contrary evidence is always showing up. In practice, corrective justice theorists usually seek to do it by narrowing the field of vision: leaving the explanation of something awkward to later researchers, or simply denying that the identified oddity is part of private law at all. Weinrib, whose *Idea of Private Law* concentrates on tort, identified four 'problematic doctrines' which seem to contradict his theory of corrective justice: liability under *respondeat superior*; abnormally dangerous activities; nuisance; and the *Vincent v Lake Erie* ruling on preservation of property.[20] Other writers have identified exemplary damages as problematical,[21] or any explicit resort to public policy in private law reasoning;[22] indeed, some corrective justice theorists decline to treat remedies in a corrective justice spirit at all, confining it to explaining what private law treats as wrongful without looking at what remedy a court might give in consequence of that wrong.[23]

Of course, each of these attempts to explain away matters inconvenient for corrective justice must be taken on their merits—and if I had found them largely convincing, I would perhaps not have written this paper. But it is the big picture that I am looking at here, and (as before) it is the gaps in the big picture that are interesting. When corrective justice theorists attempt to fill these gaps, they do so on the binary assumption that corrective justice, properly understood, either supplies the explanation for a particular liability (in which case 'rival' theories fall out of our contemplation) or it does not (in which case we are outside the realm of corrective justice altogether). The third possibility—that corrective justice has no exclusive realm and that some results can be made to seem reasonable from a number of perspectives—is neglected. So when a particular judicial opinion in a private law case seems wrong, by invoking 'public' or at any rate non-corrective reasons, a number of techniques are employed by corrective justice theorists to rationalise the result: asserting that the result is wrong and the opinion is wrongly reasoned, or claiming that the judge's reasons can be recast as corrective justice reasons, or saying that the case is not really about private law at all, as evidenced by the 'public' nature of the reasons the judge employed to solve it.[24] It is not that

[20] Weinrib (n 2) 184–96; *Vincent v Lake Erie Transportation Co* 124 NW 221 (Minn SC, 1910).

[21] A Beever, 'The Structure of Aggravated and Exemplary Damages' (2012) 23 *OJLS* 87.

[22] Beever, *Rediscovering Negligence* (n 3) ch 1, and see the same author's 'Policy in Private Law: An Admission of Failure' (2006) 25 *University of Queensland Law Journal* 287.

[23] G Keating, 'Is Tort a Remedial Institution?' (2010, ssrn.com/abstract=1633687).

[24] Examples of both the first and second can be found in Beever, *Rediscovering Negligence* (n 3) 357–64, discussing negligence liability in a context where insurance was clearly very much to the forefront of both the parties' and the judges minds, contrary to Beever's preferred view. The third argument pervades Beever's objections to exemplary damages, in (n 21) esp 102–04.

these arguments are wrong (though they often are), or that they are not illuminating (as an illustration of how corrective justice argument can be used, they are indeed instructive)—rather, they divert us from a proper consideration of the place of corrective justice in the law.

And arguments of this sort certainly involve their proponents in odd assertions. Why, for example, is it the case that if you negligently damage my stash of heroin, street value £10,000, I cannot recover anything from you through action in tort? A typical lawyerly response would be that allowing recovery for its value would conflict with important principles of public policy to do with the suppression of prohibited drugs. But Beever cannot countenance such a gross intrusion of public law principles into tort, so he explains it in a different way: rather, he says, because possession of heroin is illegal, in the eye of the law my goods were worthless, and so while in principle I can recover their value, the law's view of its value is zero.[25] Of course, if it were really true that the law thought illegal drugs were worthless, sentencing practice would be very different—judges handling such cases are very well aware of the monetary value of drugs seized, and act accordingly. The law does *not* treat illegal drugs as worthless, and indeed its treatment of drug trafficking would be nonsensical if it did.[26] The fact that some corrective justice theorists are driven to such desperate fictions is evidence of how unwilling they are to recognise public policy considerations even when they are glaring.

Most worrying in its implications is the argument that if a case cannot be reconciled with corrective justice then—right or wrong—it cannot be part of private law. This *is* pernicious, because it reduces corrective justice theory to an uninteresting tautology: that private law is based on corrective justice because any cases not based on corrective justice are not part of private law, and torts are based on corrective justice because if we see something that clearly is not so based, it cannot be a tort. What, then, do we do with elements of tort that do not fit with this vision? We eject them from the tort books and say that, right or wrong, these cases do not involve torts and should not be discussed when tort lawyers gather.

But why should we do this? What is the point of such a rigid definition of corrective justice, which is at best only an approximation to what was assumed in earlier centuries and is very far indeed from modern assumptions? One question worth asking is whether the theory is meant to be descriptive or normative. Yet neither hat really fits. It is not normative, because no reason is ever given why a corrective approach is a good one. Weinrib throughout disdains any normative argument, arguing purely about what the law *is*. Beever takes the same line, likening himself to an architect explaining the structure of the Eiffel tower—such an

[25] Beever, *Rediscovering Negligence* (n 3) 382.

[26] Indeed, the attention paid in modern drug control law to the value of any drugs involved in the case is a major factor in the erosion of the line between civil and criminal law in the area. See generally K Mann, 'Punitive Civil Sanctions: The Middleground Between Criminal and Civil Law' (1992) 101 *Yale Law Journal* 1795; A Ashworth, 'Is the Criminal Law a Lost Cause?' (2000) 116 *LQR* 225.

account should not be taken as an endorsement of the tower or even as a denial that it should be knocked down.[27] Coleman is more willing to tackle normative issues, but does not contend that the legal system *must* embody corrective justice: the claims of those unjustly injured can be met in other ways, such as by New Zealand's no-fault accident compensation scheme.[28] So there is no normative argument in favour of corrective justice. But is the corrective approach descriptive, either? Certainly it has no very adequate account of the many cases where the courts manifestly have *not* internalised a corrective justice approach. Some might say that corrective theorists want it both ways—when people point to normative defects in their argument they retreat into descriptivism (so if someone says the law should not be that way, their answer is that it is, in fact, that way), but then they deal with descriptive errors by retreating into normativity (so if a case is clearly incompatible with corrective justice, they say that it is wrong).

Some argue that corrective justice occupies a middle ground, an 'interpretive' ground, which might seem to have elements of description and prescription, but is in fact a distinct enterprise. I have argued elsewhere that this 'interpretivism' makes no coherent sense, at least not when used in the way corrective justice theorists use it. Interpretivism itself is respectable enough—there is clearly a case for saying that what tribunals do in divining the law *in individual cases* can be seen as seeking the best interpretation of the applicable law, though that is certainly not the only thing there is to say about it. But there are difficulties in scaling this process up, in looking not for the best legal explanation of *one case* to the best legal explanation of a *whole area of law*. Most of the 'interpretivism' currently on offer seems merely an attempt to smuggle in the very thing in issue (that we should be looking for a single explanation) as a methodological precept rather than as something that has to be demonstrated.[29]

III. Pedagogy is Not Philosophy

So where does this assumption, that private law (or tort, or contract, or whatever) forms a coherent unity, come from? Not from any recognised body of theory. It seems to have come from teaching practice. Legal culture is accepting of the idea that contract and tort form unities, because those who learn law systematically will have been taught this view early on and will very probably have internalised it—they will have difficulty thinking of law any other way. And of course those who teach those subjects have been through the same process—indeed, it may

27 Beever, *Rediscovering Negligence* (n 3) 515.
28 Coleman (n 1) 402.
29 See my 'The Shock of the Old: Interpretivism in Obligations' in C Rickett and R Grantham (eds), *Structure and Justification in Private Law* (Hart Publishing, 2008) 205.

be precisely because they find that way of thinking congenial that they end up spending large parts of their lives as contract or tort teachers. The result is a pervasive assumption that those subjects form coherent entities *even though* there is no point at which that unity was rationally demonstrated.

Many of the features which ground the corrective justice standpoint are simply the choices forced on generations of law teachers, who must somehow make their subject make sense to undergraduates relatively ignorant of the wider legal system. So for example:

1. Issues of responsibility are obscured. Tort teachers cannot also talk about corporate form, insurance or other means of social and legal control: the students do not have that kind of knowledge yet. So they talk as if we were all atomised individuals, corporate form has no significance here, and the rest of the legal system does not exist. Where the criminal law is mentioned, it is only to distinguish it from tort, not to note the various ways in which tort and crime operate in concert to force responsibility on individuals. A good teaching choice, and those other gaps in the students' knowledge will be filled soon enough.
2. The origin of contract terms is obscured. Contract teachers cannot talk of collective agreements and collective disagreements, government control of terms (of whatever sort), or the constantly shifting line society draws between what is hard-nosed bargaining and what is illegitimate bullying. Students do not have that kind of legal understanding yet. So the teachers talk as if potential contract terms just appear almost magically, as if the legal enforceability of terms was the only important issue around them, and the rest of the legal system does not exist. A good teaching choice, and those other gaps in the students' knowledge will be filled soon enough.
3. The operation of the law *as a system* is obscured. Law teachers talk as if the task were to examine each case individually and minutely, as if every case comes to court or even to the Supreme Court, where it can be anatomised and dissected. Indeed, judges who find neat solutions that do not involve complicated legal analysis tend to be criticised as slackers, and it is rarely that the mechanics of settlement are discussed. A good teaching choice, and those other gaps in the students' knowledge will be filled soon enough.

It is, I hope, clear that this chapter is not a critique of teaching practice. For current purposes I am neither for nor against the way in which tort and contract are taught in law schools. My point is that the compromises necessary to get through a term of teaching—the various simplifying assumptions we introduce so that tort and contract are teachable in the real world to real students—should not be confused with a defensible philosophy of either subject. I am quite happy to teach elementary tort principles to 18 year olds as if there were no such thing as liability insurance, in the knowledge that others from amongst my colleagues *will* teach them about it when the time is right. But when I see some of those colleagues claiming that a rigorous explanation or justification of modern tort principles should omit reference to insurance, I can see that something has gone wrong somewhere. It is like seeing discussions of childcare written as if babies are brought into the world by storks. No proper explanation or justification of tort can leave out how the law encourages or discourages such claims, how it provides a framework for tort disputes, or how it arranges for payment of awards.

The modern theory of corrective justice theory, then, has its origins in classroom practice, and indeed many of those who comment on it have noticed its origins in classroom disputes, particularly over whether particular cases or particular rules should be determined by what is fair between the parties affected, or whether the result should be the one that is best for society at a whole. And we have all been party to these arguments of individual fairness versus the common good (or, if the disputants are sophisticated enough to reach the higher levels of theory, corrective justice versus economic efficiency). These are good arguments to be having in the classroom—they emphasise that law matters, and that whatever the law does, it should do for a good reason. But the point should not be to produce an overall winner. Individualised fairness, on the one hand, and the collective good, on the other, can both put up a good fight, because the law gives a great deal of weight to both of them. One will win some rounds and the other will win others, but neither can deliver a knock-out blow to the other. And an individual scholar can, of course, focus on one rather than the other—but if they do so they are likely to omit features which all agree to be important.

The inward-looking focus of corrective justice, then, reflects the inward-looking focus of law teaching: we seek to explain particular concepts and institutions, and necessarily focus closely on them as we do so. But any overall justification worthy of the name must look more broadly. An obvious question about the development of corrective justice theory is whether its proponents have a serious interest in defending their values before a wider audience. For corrective justice in its purest form, the matter seems hopeless. It is several centuries too late to ask states to step back from defining their own laws, or from doing their best to define them in the way that suits the public interest. There will always be a few people that are horrified that law is instrumental—that it has a purpose, in other words[30]—but most people would be considerably more horrified if it *lacked* a purpose. The question is, whether the corrective justice theorists have a useful contribution to make, perhaps by indicating ways and means by which more attention to individualised justice would lead to better laws—or whether their work will simply degenerate into a litany of complaint against the reality of early twenty-first-century legal systems, a continual wail that they would have preferred to have been born in a different century.

So far, the signs are not good. The predominating voices from corrective justice theorists are not those urging compromise, but on the contrary those suggesting

[30] B Tamanaha, *Law As A Means To An End: Threat to The Rule of Law* (Cambridge University Press, 2006).

that a law of obligations not based on corrective justice is not really a law at all. Weinrib insists that an instrumental approach is politics rather than law,[31] and seems to think that one can no more be a little bit political than one can be a little bit pregnant. Beever similarly talks of the open recognition of policy as representing the 'disintegration' of law, and calls for a return to principles of 'justice', by which he means interpersonal justice.[32] (At one point, Beever seems to concede that morality and justice take many forms, of which the interpersonal is only one;[33] from which it seems to follow that much of what he rejects as 'instrumentalism' and 'policy' may in fact simply be a different sort of justice. But this insight then sinks from view.) The constant message is that a legal system which appeals to collective or instrumental concerns is not really a legal system at all.

Coleman comes rather closer to grasping the point, in his assertion that tort is not so much a body of doctrine as a *practice*, and that to understand tort law is to understand it from the point of view of those engaged in the practice.[34] Regrettably, he does not follow this line of thought very far. The majority of those engaged in the practice of tort law are legal practitioners, engaging in the practice in order to achieve the goals their clients want them to achieve. It therefore makes no sense at all to assert that 'instrumentalists'—those engaging in the practice as a way of achieving particular goals—are referring to criteria extrinsic to the practice. On the contrary: it is those who do *not* have instrumental reasons for engaging with the law that are the outliers. And understanding the practice involves a great deal—procedure, insurance, litigation funding and related areas of law—to which Coleman does not advert but which should be highly relevant to how we characterise the liabilities under consideration. Coleman's description of the practice, indeed, would make rather more sense as a description of the practice of *teaching tort law*, and this may in fact have been what he meant.[35] But law schools teach tort because it is an important part of the wider legal system, not the other way around. Academic discussion of tort can inform the legal system's development, but to treat such discussions as the core of the system is to pretend that the tail wags the dog.

All of this makes dialogue about the state of the law, and whether it can be improved, rather difficult. Nonetheless, I think there is a great deal of value in the corrective justice approach, once it is seen as a significant strand within modern thinking about obligations rather than as a purported 'explanation' of the whole. In what follows, I will seek to sketch out how this may be done. It is important to

[31] Weinrib (n 2) 6–8.

[32] Beever, *Rediscovering Negligence* (n 3) 515.

[33] ibid 42.

[34] Coleman (n 1) 200–03.

[35] Here as elsewhere, Coleman's language is opaque, but it seems that the interpretative community he is thinking of resides primarily in the law school: eg his appeal to what happens when 'one thinks about or teaches tort law' ((n 1) 198).

bear in mind, however, quite how path-dependent is the development of the modern law. We did not get to where we are by sudden decision, still less by rational design of the older system. Here as in other areas of enquiry, explaining where we are by reference to intelligent design contradicts the facts: both intelligence and design are frequently noticeable by their absence, or only apparent to a small degree. The evolution of the common law system is an elaborate process, involving much that is (by any definition) political.[36]

IV. Modern Obligations

There is considerable value in what corrective justice has to offer, both on the claimants' side of the equation and the defendants' side, though more on the former than the latter.

On the claimants' side, a leading feature of the corrective justice approach is its emphasis on rights.[37] This emphasis has proved a valuable one in terms of analysis. Yet presumably these rights do not stop dead at the boundaries of tort but also feature in the rest of the law. If we were to see a complete list of the rights protected by tort, might not that list seem very familiar to writers in other areas of the law? And how would it look when compared to supposedly foundational statements of the rights we all have, such as in national constitutions, Bills of Rights and Human Rights treaties? Here we see something extremely valuable (much of what makes sense in obligations does so because it seems to protect rights) combined with less valuable elements (rights should not be a tool to separate tort from the rest of the legal system, but on the contrary to show how it contributes to wider concerns). But the argument cannot proceed much further without answering the question: What are the rights?

Here Stevens at least is fairly forthcoming, providing a reasonably full list of the rights that tort protects.[38] Beever does not regard this as a sensible undertaking, and excuses himself from explaining what rights we have:

> This book is a theoretical examination of the law of negligence as it operates in terms of the categories of enquiry with which we are familiar ... Without becoming entirely unwieldy—and impossibly long—it cannot also become a philosophical investigation of personal and property rights.[39]

[36] For an interesting set of case-studies see TT Arvind and J Steele (eds), *Tort Law and the Legislature* (Hart Publishing, 2013).

[37] For discussion see D Nolan and A Robertson (eds), *Rights and Private Law* (Hart Publishing, 2012) especially ch 1 (D Nolan and A Robertson) and ch 2 (P Cane).

[38] Stevens (n 4) ch 2.

[39] Beever, *Rediscovering Negligence* (n 3) 62.

And throughout his account of negligence, he combines scepticism as to what rights people have (a matter for thorough examination and argument) with rigid insistence that this is the question we need to answer.[40] In the final analysis, Stevens seems to share this scepticism: he admits that there is much room for argument over which rights we have,[41] and even that a case can be made that rights-talk is empty;[42] nonetheless, he insists that questions of that sort are the right ones to be asking.[43]

It is this aspect of the theory that many will find its weakest. The most distinctive aspect of both accounts is the insistence on rights at the expense of policy: what academics and judges should be arguing over is not whether it would be *in the public interest* for the claimant to win the case but whether s/he has a *right* to win. But without a solid and principled account of the rights, this claim teeters on the edge of oblivion. If rights-talk is as vague as this, how is it superior to policy-talk? If it allows for as many different viewpoints as it seems to, then how is it any less 'political' than any other approach? Every criticism made of a policy-based approach—that it is vague, leads to endless argument and blurs the line between the political and the non-political—can be made with equal force of a rights-based approach.

It is far from clear how Beever's and Stevens's 'rights' relate to rights elsewhere in the law. Beever does not (so far as I can see) discuss this issue anywhere. Stevens takes a notably defensive position, observing that 'rights' have been defined in a number of ways, and then announcing that he is only engaging with one particular definition (the Hohfeldian claim right).[44] This he takes to excuse him from discussing rights more generally, as the expression is usually used more widely—he rejects any need to discuss human rights, as they are only 'rights' in a broader sense.[45] Again, Stevens rejects any similarity between 'rights' and the interests the law protects—this is simply a confusion, he thinks.[46] But again, the differences may simply be ones of emphasis. 'Interest' is a somewhat weaker word than right, but the strength of a right is always open to debate; rights are simply a sub-set of interests, with considerable scope for argument over how powerful an interest must be before it can claim recognition as a right. (Many people might have 'interests' in a house; which of those interests are powerful enough to be called

[40] A good example is in relation to nervous shock, where he discusses alternative views a corrective justice theorist might hold, concluding 'I do not argue here that either view necessarily captures the correct understanding of Kantian right nor that Kantian right necessarily provides the best understanding of interpersonal morality. My claim is that we need to decide whether people have a right to their psychological integrity or not. And if we decide that they do, we need to elucidate that right. When we have done so, the rest should fall into place': Beever, *Rediscovering Negligence* (n 3) 411.

[41] Stevens (n 4) 337–41.

[42] ibid 350.

[43] ibid, the concluding words of the book.

[44] ibid 4–5.

[45] ibid 5, 236–42.

[46] ibid 289–90.

'rights' might require argument.) And to look at tort's remedies through the lens of the interest protected opens the way to examining the maze of regulations that are also designed (amongst other things) to protect those interests. In corrective justice as currently practised there is a depressing reluctance to engage with public law, in the attempt to build up a 'common sense' picture of private law institutions without mentioning public law institutions, even traditional ones such as basic criminal law.

This is a pity, as a comparison between Stevens's list of rights and a human-rights-lawyer's list shows interesting differences of emphasis as well as some obvious similarities. Yet private law does not exist in a vacuum, and a theory which treats it as entirely self-sufficient can only have limited explanatory power. Of course, theories of private rights start from a very different place from theories of human rights. Private rights are thought of as primarily matters between individuals, with the state either absent or irrelevant (and of course for most of the history of obligations the King—the State—could Do No Wrong)[47] ; whereas human rights are primarily complaints that the state has fallen down on its obligations, with the notion that private individuals should respect each others' rights being a modern interloper of dubious status. It is indeed amazing, given that unpromising beginning, how much similarly there is between the content of the two sets of rights. This convergence, if it is a convergence, deserves further study.

In any serious study of what rights the law makes available, it is impossible to ignore the public and the political, no matter how 'private' the rights are said to be. Those tempted to bask in the obvious importance of tort and contract within the legal system, and the legal system's importance in the regulation of society, must surely realise that this importance reflects wider political judgements reflecting particular conceptions both of the public interest and of the role of tort and contract. The growth of negligence to its current status would have been impossible without certain key decisions—*political* decisions—about how claimants and defendants would be funded, and about what other avenues of complaint were to be made available. Or again, the law of defamation and of privacy is today strongly influenced by legal cases involving celebrities—some famous for particular abilities, some famous for being in the wrong place at the wrong time, some famous merely for being famous—and decisions made by those claimants, and the government's responses to them, have a serious influence on the development of the law. Very often, the key political question is simply, who has the ability to attract the state's attention. A theory of justice which is deliberately inward-looking, and sees politics as an aberration that rational people avoid, will miss much of what is going on.

Another focus of corrective justice is on the defendant's responsibility: the 'correlativity' which corrective justice theorists demand insists that it is vacuous to

[47] In the UK, the rule was in most situations abolished by the Crown Proceedings Act 1947, though see also Crown Proceedings (Armed Forces) Act 1987.

talk to rights unless those rights point to an effective remedy against the defendant who breaches the rights. Again, the insight is a valuable one, but very imperfectly realised in current theories of corrective justice. The law has not abandoned the personal responsibility of actual real people—how could it?—but tort and contract have little to say on it. Personal responsibility has largely moved elsewhere. Take any major category of tort litigation in the UK:

— *Car accidents:* The law goes to a great deal of trouble to establish personal responsibility, but does this through the criminal law, untrammelled by considerations of interpersonal rights or correlativity. The cost of the civil liability is met by compulsory insurance, and the personal civil defendant plays only a nominal part in any actual claim, which is indeed not much affected even if the defendant is untraceable, insolvent or uninsured.[48]
— *Accidents at work:* Personal liability here is, in the UK at least, maintained in form only, on condition that it is not allowed to affect anyone's rights. So we pretend that defendants personally responsible for accidents are liable for the result, but then invoke vicarious liability to ensure that someone else—the company, their insurers—picks up the bill, with a 'gentleman's agreement' that the employee's liability will remain theoretical only.[49]
— *Medical liability:* Again, it is taken for granted that individuals will not be held responsible, but rather will have taken out insurance.[50]

In relation to tort, it is no secret that liability is only rarely a matter of personal liability, almost invariably being borne by a company, perhaps an insurer, or perhaps the state.[51] The time for talk of corrective justice is well and truly gone. That this became so is partly a matter of governmental fiat—compulsory liability insurance is a major factor here—but also simply the economics of the matter, a claim against a single individual being far less of a good financial prospect. The law often makes that individual suffer for their misbehaviour, but it does not usually do so

[48] See generally P Cane, *Atiyah's Accidents, Compensation and the Law* 6th edn (Cambridge University Press, 2004) especially 175–77, 200–01, 208–12. Some argue that, while in theory the system depends on proof of fault (though we do not then insist that the award is met by the person at fault), in practice it operates on strict liability lines: see eg N Freeman Engstrom, 'Sunlight and Settlement Mills' (2011) 86 *New York University Law Review* 805.

[49] Cane, ibid especially 177–79. The 'gentleman's agreement' was discussed in *Morris v Ford Motor Co* [1973] QB 792. Some jurisdictions have preferred not to trust that insurers are 'gentlemen', explicitly enacting that insurers may not seek an indemnity from negligent employees, absent compelling circumstances such as employee fraud: see P Giliker, *Vicarious Liability in Tort* (Cambridge University Press, 2010) 32–34.

[50] Cane, ibid especially 179–81. For the effects of liability insurance on actual behaviour by medical professionals, see B CJ van Velthoven and PW van Wijck, 'Medical Liability: Do Doctors Care?' (2012) 33 *Recht der Werkelijkheid* 28. For those who suspect that I am cherry-picking my examples to minimise the importance of personal responsibility, I would point out that those three categories of claim together compromise over 85% of negligence personal injury claims: Cane, ibid 168.

[51] Some argue that mechanisms for enforcing tort judgments against individuals are today so feeble that personal tort liability is not a meaningful threat to most individuals: S Gilles, 'The Judgment-Proof Society' (2006) 83 *Washington and Lee Law Review* 603.

through the medium of tort; 'the claims which are brought closely match the areas where liability insurance is to be found'.[52]

We should not exaggerate, of course. There are occasionally cases where individual liability in tort actually matters. Damages claims are occasionally brought against individuals rich enough to satisfy tort claimants. But even in relation to those individuals—the Dominique Strauss-Kahns, the Jimmy Saviles—claimant lawyers will tend to look for other, corporate, deep-pocketed defendants rather than rely on the chancy business of suing a real person. In discussing the practical workings of defamation law, personal liability—or at least, the threat of personal liability—is a powerful force in a general sense, if not often actually used. And sometimes we see personal responsibility acting through tort but in a very indirect fashion, such as when liability insurers put pressure on potential defendants to act more responsibly.[53] It is not my case, therefore, that personal liability is *irrelevant* to tort, though it is much less significant than corrective justice theorists claim. Rather, its true significance and operation deserves investigation and is not elucidated by pretending that it is the standard way by which tort operates, ignoring the workings of insurance, corporate form and the state.

In contract too, the focus on individual agreement in contract is in many ways misleading, as it pretends that the detail of any contract derives from negotiation between the parties, rather than being provided for from outside—whether by one side's having prepared standard terms before the event, or by the state. 'Boilerplate' terms, which cannot be negotiated and can only with difficulty be rejected, are a major feature of the modern law, and where we have escaped from them it is usually by the state's substituting boilerplate of its own.[54] The fictions used to support the corrective justice approach appear to be enduring ones—generations of law students now have solemnly repeated that there is a 'duty to read' terms introduced by the other party, even though such a duty would not be acknowledged by other party and would in most cases be severely impracticable, if possible at all.[55] But again, it is important not to exaggerate. While in a large number of cases, contracts are not so much agreements as pre-manufactured items, agreement does sometimes play a role. The point is not that contract terms are never agreed—sometimes, if rarely, they are—as that the extent to which they are agreed demands careful investigation.

[52] R Lewis, 'How Important are Insurers in Compensating Claims for Personal Injury in the UK?' (2011, ssrn.com/abstract=1939971) 14. For discussion see R Merkin and S Dziobon, 'Tort Law and Compulsory Insurance' in Arvind and Steele (n 36) 303. Whether or to what extent the distribution of insurance reflects market forces, principled governmental action, or raw political power, is a discussion for another occasion.

[53] O Ben-Shahar and K Logue, 'Outsourcing Regulation: How Insurance Reduces Moral Hazard' (2012) 111 *Michigan Law Review* 197.

[54] For general discussion see M Radin, *Boilerplate—The Fine Print, Vanishing Rights, and the Rule of Law* (Princeton University Press, 2013) esp ch 4.

[55] For discussion see O Ben-Shahar, 'The Myth of the "Opportunity to Read" in Contract Law' (2008, ssrn.com/abstract=1162922).

So the notion of personal responsibility which corrective justice employs cannot work in the modern legal system, not because we have given up on the idea of personal responsibility, but because it plays a very different role in the modern legal system. As will be clear, the sticking points in the corrective justice account are mainly over the relevance of corporate form and the relevance of the welfare state. Corrective justice as currently expounded relies entirely on personal responsibility. It does its best to ignore or to minimise the importance of the ways in which we modify the law to make it applicable to corporate entities: by pretending that corporations are people, by extending vicarious liability so that corporations are guilty of whatever wrongdoings their employees commit. It also does its best to ignore the expanded role of the state, the modern idea that misfortunes which befall ordinary people are the state's responsibility, and that the injured are not merely objects of charity but have a right to expect the state to do something about their plight.

Seen in that light, it is obvious that the ideals of corrective justice cannot bear the weight that their supporters wish to place on them. We live in a world dominated by collectivities, where most serious economic activity, and most serious attempts to regulate it, must be dealt with at the collective level. The relatives of an employee killed at work would not regard it as acceptable to be told (as they would probably have been told a century-and-a-half ago) that they have a remedy only against an individual person who could be shown to have been at fault for the accident; the victim of a road accident would today not accept (as they would have had to accept in 1920) that whether they have a remedy must turn on the chance that the driver who ran them down has enough money to compensate. And corporate entities create problems which demand solutions: we might agree that people should be held to their bargains, yet regard it as unfair that one (large, corporate) party should be able to draft terms in advance and then secure 'agreement' from their customers simply by flourishing the document at them. The point is both political and moral: politically, the law is influenced by the existence of corporations, and morally, corporations lead to situations where a 'corrective justice' solution would actually be unjust. This does not imply that the law has abandoned the idea of personal responsibility, but it *does* imply that it will not take the simple form that corrective justice embodies.

Nor is this a recent state of affairs. In the same decade as *Donoghue v Stevenson*, liability insurance was made compulsory for car drivers, and employer liability insurance was by then already a standard feature of commercial law;[56] and the key decisions in contract law, establishing that a consumer's practical incapability of reading complex standard forms was no bar to treating them as having 'agreed' to those terms,[57] are around the same time. One might have thought that the last

[56] For an account of tort law's drift to collective concerns see S Hedley, 'Tort and Personal Injuries, 1850 to the Present' in Arvind and Steele (n 36) 235.

[57] Particularly *L'Estrange v Graucob* [1934] 2 KB 394.

gasp of the classical corrective justice theory was *Gowar v Hales* in 1927.[58] Here, in a case over a motor-cycle accident, the Court of Appeal were shocked to hear that the jury had been told that the defendant was insured—which, the court held, rendered a fair trial impossible, a fair trial being one where 'the real issue between the parties, the claimant and the defendant, should be decided upon the merits of that issue without a supervening and prejudicial circumstance not really material being introduced'.[59] Yet when we see much the same argument being made in the second decade of the twenty-first century, clearly something has gone wrong. Whatever may have been the right time for arguments based on the exclusivity of corrective justice, that time has long gone. It can still play its role, though, as one element in the legal system.

V. Conclusion

Common law process is a method for resolving disputes between individuals, relying on reasoned argument from those individual's lawyers as to the scope of their respective rights. It would therefore be surprising if it did not, to some degree at least, reflect concerns of a type that feature in corrective justice. It would, however, be equally surprising if it did not also reflect wider community concerns. Therefore, what we should expect to see—and, I suggest, we *do* see if we look—is a system which embodies both public and private concerns. There is much more to say on the balance between public and private, but an argument that seeks to exclude either completely cannot paint a faithful picture of the system as it is.

[58] *Gowar v Hales* [1928] 1 KB 191 (11 April 1927).
[59] Lord Hanworth MR at 194.

Afterword

17

How History Bears on Jurisprudence

BRIAN Z TAMANAHA

The relevance of history to jurisprudence is a burning topic of late, the focus of *Law in Theory and History* as well as of a recent symposium in the *Virginia Law Review*, 'Jurisprudence and (Its) History', both with contributions from eminent historians and theorists. That jurisprudence neglects history to its impoverishment is the thrust of these collections. The call for papers that resulted in this volume asserted: 'Apart from some notable exceptions, much of contemporary legal theory is uninformed by history, including legal history.'[1] The co-editors of the Virginia symposium, Charles Barzun and Dan Priel, write in their Introduction,

> there may be reason to think that turning to history could broaden the boundaries, and raise the ambitions, of a [jurisprudential] field that many lawyers, judges, and even legal scholars have written off as esoteric and dominated by concerns remote from their own.[2]

This chapter examines how history does and does not bear on jurisprudence, particularly on the subfield of legal philosophy. The presentation is organised around themes that emerge explicitly and implicitly from the essays in this volume. As we shall see, a strong case is made that legal philosophers will benefit from attention to history, but not that history is mandatory.

At the outset it is necessary to address a threshold question: Does legal theory ignore history? Though the editors and contributors to these collections appear to accept this proposition, I believe it is false. A great deal of contemporary legal theory is informed by history. Jeremy Waldron, Richard Posner, Duncan Kennedy, Neil MacCormick, Gerald Postema, Roberto Unger, William Twining and Roger Cotterrell, to name a few examples, are prominent jurists who construct theories

[1] 28th May 2012, UK IVR: UK. International Association for the Philosophy of Law and Social Philosophy.

[2] C Barzun and D Priel, 'Jurisprudence and (Its) History' 101 *Virginia Law Review* 849.

of law with substantial attention to history.[3] Many legal theorists draw on history to discuss the meaning and implications of early twentieth-century legal realism or pragmatism.[4] Critical legal theory, critical feminism and critical race theory use historical examples in their respective theories of legal domination (eg women's loss of legal personality upon marriage, exclusion from suffrage, slavery, Jim Crow and more).[5] Proponents of economic analysis who contend the common law reflects economic reasoning refer to the dominance of laissez faire thought among nineteenth-century judges to explain how this was originally implanted.[6] Theorists who write about international law or about legal globalisation discuss the historical spread of law via colonisation and the expansion over time of capitalism.[7] In addition, there are legal historians who employ and construct sophisticated theories of law in their work (like Christopher Tomlins in this volume).[8] Lots of contemporary legal theory makes use of history.[9]

What does appear to be true is the narrower assertion that much of contemporary *legal philosophy* or *analytical jurisprudence* ignores history. But it is a mistake to present legal philosophy as coextensive with jurisprudence or legal theory.[10] Jurisprudence and legal theory, broadly defined, are labels for work with a theoretical perspective on law. Legal philosophy today (though less so in the past) is narrowly philosophical in orientation, focusing on conceptual analysis, epistemological and metaphysical issues, universalistic assertions about law, and the like. Barzun and Priel repeatedly elide the difference between these contrasting orientations, for example, writing 'perhaps like other areas of philosophy, the subject matter of jurisprudence';[11] 'considering how jurisprudence can or should make

[3] For a partial list of examples, see eg J Waldron, *God, Locke, and Equality: Christian Foundations in Locke's Political Thought* (Cambridge University Press, 2003); J Waldron, *The Dignity of Legislation* (Cambridge University Press, 1999); RA Posner, *The Problems of Jurisprudence* (Harvard University Press, 1990); D Kennedy, "The Structure of Blackstone's Commentaries' (1979) 28 *Buffalo Law Review* 205; RM Unger, *Law in Modern Society* (Free Press, 1976); N MacCormick, *Institutions of Law* (Oxford University Press, 2007); GJ Postema, *Legal Philosophy in the Twentieth Century* (Springer, 2011); W Twining, *General Jurisprudence* (Cambridge University Press, 2009); R Cotterrell, *The Politics of Jurisprudence* 2nd edn (Oxford University Press, 2003). Several of my own legal theory books and articles also have significant historical elements, most recently BZ Tamanaha, *Beyond the Formalist-Realist Divide* (Princeton University Press, 2010).

[4] The literature on legal realism is vast and needs no citation, though examples are provided in Tamanaha, ibid. For a collection of legal theory works on pragmatism, see Symposium, 'On the Renaissance of Pragmatism in American Legal Thought' (1990) 63 *Southern California Law Review* 1569.

[5] See eg D Kairys (ed), *The Politics of Law: A Progressive Critique* 3rd edn (Basic Books, 1998).

[6] See Posner (n 3) 354–59.

[7] See eg A Anghie, Imperialism, Sovereignty and the Making of International Law (Cambridge University Press, 2007).

[8] See eg R W Gordon, 'Critical Legal Histories Revisited: A Response' (2012) 37 *Law & Social Inquiry* 200.

[9] Multiple examples are listed in N Lacey, 'Jurisprudence, History, and the Institutional Quality of Law' (2015) 101 *Virginia Law Review* 919, 931 fn 31.

[10] See BZ Tamanaha, 'The Third Pillar of Jurisprudence' (2015) 56 *William & Mary Law Review* 223; R Cotterrell, 'Why Jurisprudence is Not Legal Philosophy' (2014) 5 *Jurisprudence* 41.

[11] Barzun and Priel (n 2) 849.

use of history and why doing so might be philosophically profitable';[12] 'argument assumes particular philosophical or jurisprudential texts cannot transcend their times.'[13] By conflating jurisprudence and philosophy, these assertions paint a misleading image of the absence of history in theorising about law. Legal philosophy is not the whole of jurisprudence, but just one stream with unique concerns and self-imposed strictures.

In this chapter, I use jurisprudence and legal theory as broad terms that encompass various streams of theorising about law, and legal philosophy and analytical jurisprudence as narrower labels that refer to philosophically oriented legal theory. With this terminology in mind, let me describe a few salient themes that emerge from this volume, referring to the relevant chapters along the way.

I. Law is Historical or Temporal

The standard image of common law systems is a mix of precedents, statutes, maxims and principles that evolve through a continuous flow of legislative enactments and judicial interpretations in response to social, economic, political, technological and cultural influences. Law is like a constantly updated house in which new boards supplant worn ones, outdated internal and external structures are periodically remodelled, old wings are occasionally demolished and entirely new ones constructed. While law changes in connection with society, it remains stable and continuous through time, with the original structure and subsequent alterations influencing the shape and texture of present and future law. 'The Practical Dimension of Legal Reasoning', by Stephen Waddams, brings to life the evolving common law system by detailing changes in legal doctrine in multiple areas of law in response to policy preferences, practical considerations and expected social consequences. Stable yet dynamic, law moves gradually over time, comprised of a multitude of doctrinal threads that extend backward and project forward.

Law is historical by nature in a more fundamental sense not limited to common law systems. Legality involves binding prescriptions stated in general terms *in advance*.[14] Retroactive laws that penalise past behaviour are not genuine rules since they did not exist at the time of the original action and therefore could not be followed.[15] Legal rules help coordinate behaviour and enhance predictability about legal consequences because people know *beforehand* what will happen in situations addressed by the rules.[16] These commonplace observations presuppose

[12] ibid 852.

[13] ibid 859.

[14] See F Schauer, Playing by the Rules: A Philosophical Examination of Rule-Based Decision-Making in Law and in Life (Oxford University Press, 1991) 18.

[15] See L Fuller, *The Morality of Law* Revised edn (Yale University Press, 1964) 38–39.

[16] ibid ch 7.

the extended temporality of law. Law functions sequentially over time: laws are laid down (time 1), the legal rules govern subsequent behaviour by citizens (time 2), and legal actors enforce and apply pre-existing law to subsequent actions (time 3). There are temporal orderings in law other than this simplified scheme presents, but there is almost no sense in which law does not operate in the course of time (perhaps excepting natural law, taken up later).

Time is an inseverable aspect of law in other subtle respects as well, explored in Maks Del Mar's nuanced chapter, 'Modelling Law Diachronically: Temporal Variability in Legal Theory'. Del Mar conveys several temporal dimensions within law, including duration, direction, legal change and so forth. Thinking about temporality in law opens up avenues for further exploration, a number of which he articulates in this exploratory essay. In legal reasoning, for instance, consider how judges resort to past authorities and speculation about future consequences—temporally extended in opposite directions—sometimes as competing and sometimes as complementary justifications for legal rulings.

The fact that legal rules declared in the past are applied in the present raises another way in which history is part of legal practice. An understanding of legal doctrines sometimes can be facilitated by awareness of the surrounding social circumstances when the law was declared. What problems were legal officials addressing? What assumptions did they hold about the likely or desired social consequences of the law? These and other historical questions can bear on the meaning and import of the law, at least when the legal text is ambiguous or leaves unresolved questions. With laws of recent vintage, consideration of surrounding circumstances often occurs implicitly, when the underlying assumptions are subconsciously shared or understood. But for laws older than a generation, legal actors can and do draw on historical material—including legislative history, the history of legal doctrines, and social, economic, political or cultural history—to help discern the meaning of law. Even jurists who insist meaning depends solely on the legal text may look to history to discern the generally accepted meaning of its terms when originally enacted. Originalist constitutional theory in the United States is a high profile example of resort to history in this fashion to interpret law,[17] though it occurs in other contexts as well.

II. Law and Jurisprudence Interact Over Time

Another theme in this volume is how law and legal theory interact over time. Jurisprudential theories change to reflect changes in law, and sometimes law changes owing to theories of law. That they interact should not be surprising.

[17] See LB Solum, 'Intellectual History as Constitutional Theory' (2015) 101 *Virginia Law Review* 1111.

Jurisprudence involves theories *about* law, and many legal theorists in the course of history have been prominent practitioners and legal officials—like Oliver Wendell Holmes a century ago and Richard Posner today. What legal actors believe about law affects how they conduct their legal actions. When a novel theory of law wins over jurists, it can be internalised by legal actors and thereafter affect the operation of law. It is possible, for example, legal realist arguments that (in addition to rule application) judicial decisions involve matters of policy and contemplation of social consequences, which should be made explicitly, prompted greater consideration of policy by judges (thereby affecting how they decide cases) and greater acknowledgement of this in their written opinions (thereby affecting the style and content of judicial decisions).

Assertions about the interaction between history and jurisprudence over time are historical claims, which if true must be demonstrated through historical evidence. Joshua Getzler undertakes this effort in 'Law, Self-interest and the Smithian Conscience'. He discusses, on the one hand, how theorists like Thomas Hobbes and Adam Smith saw self-interest in law, and on the other, how courts treated self-interest, and Getzler inquires whether one set of ideas influenced the other. He found evidence of simultaneous reciprocal influence. Ian Williams's study, 'Legal Maxims in Early-modern Common Law Principle and Practice', found that legal theory and legal practice diverged in their respective treatments of maxims. This seems odd because the theoretical writers were themselves legal practitioners. Williams explains that these theoretical works were written for students and attempted to portray law as a science; accordingly, they were idealised accounts not meant to describe how maxims were actually treated by courts. Williams acknowledges his study does not answer the more difficult question whether treatment of maxims in legal education in turn affected legal practice.

Legal theory is part of the immediate context of law and law is part of the immediate context of legal theory. Whether one counts legal theory as internal to law broadly defined or as external to law in close interaction, law and legal theory appear to have a reflexive relationship, constituting a feedback loop with mutual influences operating across time.

III. Jurisprudence is Influenced by Social-historical Circumstances

The first theme above, law exists in history, is closely connected to another theme that emerges from the essays—jurisprudence exists in history.[18] Historicism is the

[18] Both positions are argued for in Lacey (n 9) 922–25.

general label for this position, which applies as much to jurisprudence as it does to law itself. As Christopher Tomlins explains in 'Historicism and Materiality in Legal Theory', it is now widely accepted that social practices and ideas—including law, jurisprudence, and just about everything—are products of their time and place. Two separable assertions are made in connection with this theme: 1) jurisprudential theories and debates reflect surrounding social, economic, political and cultural circumstances of the day; and, 2) to fully understand theories or debates one must attend to these circumstances.[19] One may accept the first proposition yet reject the second (as explained later), though they are often asserted together.

By relativising law and theory to the circumstances of their origins, historicism also carries a critical thrust. Though law and theories of law are often presented as fixed, historicism exposes them as contingent, contested and revisable, sending the message that nothing holds for all places and times (contra universalistic philosophical aspirations). Steve Hedley delivers a fulsome historicist critique in 'Corrective Justice—An Idea Whose Time Has Gone?'. Hedley challenges legal theorists who argue corrective justice wholly or principally explains private law. Modern social circumstances render such theories anachronistic, he argues. The pervasive view that law is an instrument to advance social policies means no single set of principles explains an entire area of private law. Furthermore, Hedley points out, the notion of personal responsibility at the core of corrective justice has a more limited scope of application in modern societies in which insurance is prevalent, many actions are taken by corporations, and social welfare systems have been constructed to socialise risk to individuals.

In 'Theory in History: Positivism, Natural Law and Conjectural History in Seventeenth- and Eighteenth-century English Legal Thought', Michael Lobban applies historicism to illuminate past understandings of natural law and legal positivism, uncovering many interesting insights along the way. For example, though natural law and legal positivism are now seen as antithetical, several centuries ago theorists applied the positivist account of law as the command of a superior to *both* natural law and municipal law: God was the superior in the former, the Sovereign in the latter. Unlike legal positivist philosophers today, furthermore, positivist theorists then were not focused on the separation of law from morality, and they utilised historical and sociological arguments in their accounts of law. In an unsettled age marked by pitched contests over the scope and exercise of political and legal power, the main objectives of positivists were to establish who had legal authority and to help rationalise the messy state of law. Lobban shows how legal positivist theories of law evolved in connection with issues and concerns of the day, with very different concerns and foci in the past compared to legal philosophers today.

Because it is useful for understanding past theories as well as for present critical purposes, historicism is common in jurisprudential work, as reflected in this

[19] ibid 924–25.

volume. To explain aspects of Vilhelm Lundstedt's legal theory that scholars have found incomprehensible or plainly wrong, Roger Cotterrell, in 'Reading Juristic Theories in and Beyond Historical Context: The Case of Lundstedt's Swedish Legal Realism', explains how Lundstedt's theory makes far greater sense when one considers his active role in Swedish politics and shared cultural commitments in Swedish society. In 'Legal Realism and Natural Law', Dan Priel and Charles Barzun convey the ideas of Karl Llewellyn and Jerome Frank on their own terms, pressing the argument that their views contained elements of natural law thought.

An implication of historicism is that *contemporary* jurisprudential theories are likewise influenced by surrounding political, economic, social and cultural circumstances. We too are in history's grasp, which affects current theories in ways opaque to us because we lack an external perspective on the contexts that influence our own ideas. Notwithstanding their universalistic ambitions and assertions, legal philosophers cannot escape history. As Jonathan Gorman put it in 'Legal Consciousness: A Metahistory,' 'no theorising, however analytically abstract and "unhistorical" or, contrastingly, substantive in its engagement with the past, takes place in a historical vacuum.'

IV. Historical Jurisprudence

Only a few passages are written in this volume about historical jurisprudence. 'Enormously popular in its day,' as Michael Lobban describes, historical jurisprudence, particularly Henry Maine's version, 'traced how law was influenced by "external" factors, including the changing nature of societies in which it applied'. In the standard jurisprudential account, repeated by Lobban, historical jurisprudence 'fell into decline in the twentieth century, as jurists turned away from looking to explanations of particular legal doctrines which rested on any kind of historical sociology.' This narrative consigns historical jurisprudence to the past, an interesting episode in the history of jurisprudence, but no longer alive.[20]

This volume and the Virginia symposium, however, should prompt us to reconsider the veracity of the conventional account. The core insight of historical jurisprudence—law is an aspect of society that develops over time in interaction with social, political, economic, cultural and technological changes—is reflected in most if not all the chapters in this volume. More pointedly, it would be difficult to identify more than a handful of legal theorists who would deny this core proposition.

I have argued elsewhere that, though the label fell into disuse, historical jurisprudence did not expire but rather its core insights carried on, morphing into sociological jurisprudence and legal realism, ultimately becoming a mainstream

[20] See B Bix, *Jurisprudence: Theory and Context* 6th edn (Carolina Academic Press, 2012) 275–76.

view of law.[21] Evidence of the continuing influence of historical jurisprudence is implicitly present in John Bell's chapter, 'Is Comparative Law Necessary for Legal Theory?' Bell persuasively argues legal theory benefits from attention to law in other societies, and it is essential to attend carefully to local social-legal contexts when attempting to understand law in other societies. These are historical jurisprudence insights. Henry Maine's successor, Frederick Pollock, characterised Maine as a founder of *comparative* jurisprudence.[22] As Roscoe Pound wrote, 'At first this wider historical jurisprudence was thought of as a comparative ethnological jurisprudence. But it was not long in assuming the name and something of the character of a sociological jurisprudence.'[23] Comparative jurisprudence, sociological jurisprudence and historical jurisprudence all revolve around the insight that law must be understood in social context, the latter stretching context out to include past, present and future.

To assert that the core insight of historical jurisprudence is widely accepted today is not to say everyone who holds this insight is a historical jurisprudent. Working within this jurisprudential tradition involves taking a developmental view of law tied to surrounding social changes. A chapter in this volume that squarely fits the historical jurisprudence framework—though it focuses more on legal change than on social factors—is 'Legal History and Legal Theory Shaking Hands: Towards a Gentleman's Agreement On the State', by Pierre Brunet and Jean-Louis Halperin. Brunet and Halperin depict the emergence of the legal state as a process involving the establishment of a hierarchical system of norms and institutions that coalesced in several stages over time. Lobban's tracing of the development of legal positivist theories in connection with social and legal circumstances is also an exercise in historical jurisprudence. The same can be said of the essays by Waddams and Hedley, which cover changes in law tied to social developments. A host of other theorists are developing accounts of law that comport with the historical jurisprudence tradition, including Nicola Lacey's focus on the institutional development of law,[24] and my work on the evolution of law.[25]

V. Must Legal Philosophy Be Historical? (No)

As we have seen, law exists in history, continuously changing over time in connection with society, law inherently has temporal elements, and legal actors use

[21] Tamanaha (n 10).

[22] F Pollock, 'The History of Comparative Jurisprudence' (1903) 5 *Journal of Society of Comparative Legislation* 74, 75–84.

[23] R Pound, 'The Scope and Purpose of Sociological Jurisprudence' (1911) 24 *Harvard Law Review* 591, 614. Although in this passage Pound is referring to the German wing, Pound states that a similar expansion had occurred in the English branch; 614–15 fn. 79.

[24] Lacey (n 9).

[25] BZ Tamanaha, 'Insights About the Nature of Law From History' (forthcoming 2016) *Archiv fur Rechts-und Sozialphilosophie*, available at http://papers.ssrn.com/sol3/papers.cfm?abstract_id=2441256.

history to understand and interpret law. Thus, Gerald Postema asserts, 'Time is not only among the conditions of the existence of law, but (if we are willing to put it this way) it is of its essence.'[26] The historicity of law, moreover, also holds for jurisprudence. 'Law and our [theoretical] understandings of it not only have a history, but that history is an intrinsic part of them', Postema declares. 'History, then, is an intrinsic part of the enterprise of jurisprudence.'[27]

But is that correct with respect to legal philosophy? Legal philosophy, to repeat, is focused on discerning the essential nature of law and on the analysis of legal concepts. History is intrinsic to historical jurisprudence and sociological jurisprudence, to be sure, and Postema's enlightening work in legal philosophy is deeply historically informed, but is it necessarily the case that history is an intrinsic part of legal philosophy? Taken up in turn below, the arguments for this proposition do not hold up.

Legal philosophers can account for and analyse temporal aspects of law without being concerned with history per se. If merely by recognising temporal aspects means they have in some sense incorporated history, then it is a hollow claim that empties history of much meaning. Virtually everything in known existence—all living things, all social institutions and practices, the very universe—is temporally extended. If that quality of law makes legal philosophy intrinsically historical, then it would seem all philosophy and science is necessarily historical as well. It is indeed true that science is contingent and develops in history tied to social contexts of theory construction and discovery, but scientific work and the philosophy of natural science can be done without consideration of natural history or the history of science.

Legal philosophers, moreover, can analyse the meanings and implications of the concept of law or property, etc, without concerning themselves with the various meanings attached to these concepts over time or the social circumstances in which these concepts arose. A philosopher can bracket historical and social context, analysing a synchronic slice of the concept of law in the here and now. This is the stance Joseph Raz adopts:

> Talk of *the* concept of law really means *our* concept of law. As has already been mentioned, the concept of law changes over time. Different cultures have different concepts of law. There is no one concept of law, and when we refer to the concept of law we just mean our concept of law.[28]

Raz thus explicitly recognises the social and historical contingency of concepts. Major doubts exist about whether he can ground universal truths claims on an

[26] GJ Postema, 'Jurisprudence, The Sociable Science' (2015) 101 *Virginia Law Review* 869, 885.
[27] ibid 888.
[28] J Raz, *Between Authority and Interpretation* (Oxford University Press, 2009) 32.

admittedly parochial concept of law,[29] but nothing prohibits Raz from limiting his focus to concepts in the here and now, and much can be learned from this focus.

Likewise, legal philosophers can discuss theories of historical figures—Hobbes, Locke, Bentham, Mill, Austin, Hart, Dworkin and so on—without attention to the social-historical circumstances that might have influenced them when setting forth their theories. What matters is the theory. It is not even necessary to understand what these historical figures actually meant or understood about their own theory, as Gorman points out in his essay. Theoretical positions identified with past theorists can be analytically reconstructed by critical interlocutors for the purposes of getting at crucial issues. This marks the difference between the history of philosophy and philosophy: the objective of the former is to correctly convey theories as constructed by their originators, which is enhanced by awareness of the social context of their creation, whereas the latter involves the analysis of theoretical positions.

Nor does the fact that legal philosophers live in history—a universal condition of our existence—entail that they are necessarily historical in a sense that affects their stance toward history in their work. Consider a distinction John Finnis draws 'between a theory, doctrine, or account and the subject matter of that theory, doctrine, or account. There can be a history of theories, doctrines, and accounts of matters that have no history.'[30] This distinction is analytically sound (though if all arguments for natural law fail, then there is nothing to it other than its social-historical manifestations). His point is the history of natural law theories has no bearing on whether a given account of natural law is true, which must be determined based on the soundness of the theory. (The point is essential to his argument because in the course of history many bad things have been done in the name of natural law.) This is a warning to avoid the genetic fallacy: the validity of a theory is not determined by its origins or historical uses and abuses, but on its merits. The upshot is that while legal philosophers live in history, the validity of theories they produce depends on whether they are illuminating or correct.

There appears to be no compelling argument that legal philosophy *must* be historical in other than a trivial sense.

VI. Should Legal Philosophy Be Historical? (Yes)

Philosopher Bernard Williams argued that philosophers *should* be more historical. Not only can a philosopher learn about a given concept by understanding its

[29] See BZ Tamanaha, 'Necessary and Universal Truths About Law?' (Ratio Juris, forthcoming 2016).
[30] J Finnis, *Natural Rights and Natural Law* (Clarendon Press, 1980) 24.

development over time, Williams observed, but historical awareness also helps philosophers obtain critical distance from their intuitions and assumptions, the better to see the possibility of alternatives.[31] He distinguished three levels of analysis:

> [T]here is no inherent conflict among three activities: first, the first-order activities of acting and arguing within the framework of our ideas; second, the philosophical activity of reflecting on those ideas at a more general level and trying to make better sense of them; and third, the historical activity of trying to understand where they come from. The activities are in various ways continuous with one another.[32]

The third level is not mandatory for philosophers, but it enriches their analysis.

> Philosophy has to learn the lesson that conceptual description (or, more specifically, analysis) is not self-sufficient; and that such projects as deriving our concepts *a priori* from universal conditions of human life, though they indeed have a place (a greater place in some areas of philosophy than others), are likely to leave unexplained many features that provoke philosophical inquiry.[33]

The essays in this volume present a host of insights that might be useful for legal philosophers engaged in analytical work, from Hedley's critique of corrective justice theory to Lobban's account of changing orientations of natural law and legal positivism over time. Historical awareness can help jar legal philosophers out of intellectual complacency of assuming the familiar.

For instance, legal philosophers today often write as if natural law and legal positivism are the only two possible types of theories of the nature of law. Legal philosopher Andrei Marmor declares:

> In the course of the last few centuries, two main rival philosophical traditions have emerged, providing different answers to these questions [the nature of law]. The older one, dating back to late mediaeval Christian scholarship, is called the natural law tradition. Since the early 19th century, natural law theories have been fiercely challenged by the legal positivism tradition promulgated by such scholars as Jeremy Bentham and John Austin.[34]

There is, however, a huge omission in Marmor's account. A century ago, jurists agreed there were *three* rival traditions. 'Jurisprudence, in its specific sense as the theory or philosophy of law', wrote John Salmond, 'is divisible into three branches, which may be distinguished as analytical, historical, and ethical.'[35] Roscoe Pound wrote in 1911:

> [I]t has been possible to divide jurists into three principle groups, according to their views of the nature of law and the standpoint from which the science of law should be

[31] B Williams, 'Philosophy as a Humanistic Discipline' (2000) 75 *Philosophy* 477, 491–94.
[32] ibid 491.
[33] ibid 489.
[34] A Marmor, 'The Nature of Law' *Stanford Encyclopedia of Philosophy*, at http://plato.stanford.edu/entries/lawphil-nature/.
[35] J Salmond, *Jurisprudence* 7th edn (Sweet & Maxwell, 1924) 4.

approached. We may call these groups the Philosophical School [natural law], the Historical School, and the Analytical School.[36]

One cannot say how or whether awareness of this third branch of jurisprudence might affect the theories of law constructed by contemporary legal philosophers, but it should at least prompt them to reconsider their narrow assumptions about what counts as theories of law. This is an example of what Bernard Williams alluded to when asserting that historical awareness opens up the possibility of alternatives.

Legal philosophers who ignore history stay at the first and second levels Williams identified. History is not required for legal philosophy, but nor is historical awareness prohibited by analytical strictures. Given the intellectual benefits of historical awareness spelled out by Williams, and illustrated in this volume, one might wonder why any legal philosopher would consider it prudent to abstain from attention to history. Since history is so interesting and useful, I suspect many legal philosophers do consult history when thinking about concepts, though it might not show up explicitly in their analytical work.

Yet, if legal philosophers wish to ignore history, that is their prerogative. Jurisprudence comes in different stripes, as I argued at the outset, and many contemporary jurisprudents attend to history. An optimist might even say it is becoming routine for many legal theorists to think historically.

[36] Pound (n 23) 591.

INDEX

www.ingramcontent.com/pod-product-compliance
Ingram Content Group UK Ltd.
Pitfield, Milton Keynes, MK11 3LW, UK
UKHW020133290926
15471UKWH00003B/451

9 781509 927975